NOTES ON THE GERMAN ARMY – WAR

DECEMBER, 1940

Prepared by the General Staff
THE WAR OFFICE

The Naval & Military Press Ltd

> **NOT TO BE PUBLISHED**
>
> The information given in this document is not to be communicated, either directly or indirectly, to the Press or to any person not holding an official position in His Majesty's Service.

M.I. 14, *December, 1940*

Published by

The Naval & Military Press Ltd
Unit 5 Riverside, Brambleside
Bellbrook Industrial Estate
Uckfield, East Sussex
TN22 1QQ England

Tel: +44 (0)1825 749494

www.naval-military-press.com
www.nmarchive.com

In reprinting in facsimile from the original, any imperfections are inevitably reproduced and the quality may fall short of modern type and cartographic standards.

INTRODUCTION

These *Notes on the German Army—War* are compiled from information available up to 31st December, 1940, and supersede *Notes on the German Army, 1938,* and *Periodical Notes on the German Army*, Nos. 12, 14, 16, 19–27 and 29.

They are intended to provide a compact review, for use in the field, of the organization and equipment of the German army at war, and may be used in conjunction with *The German Forces in the Field* and the *Order of Battle of the German Army*.

A duplicate set of the more important appendices is issued with the *Notes* in order to facilitate rapid reference on points of organization, strength and equipment.

In the *Notes* German compound words and designations have normally been printed as one word. Names beginning with "Armee-", "Divisions-", "Heeres-", or having as their second element "Abteilung", "Batterie", "Brigade", "Regiment", "Division" are, however, divided by a hyphen. This is in accordance with actual German military usage which, however, is frequently at variance with itself. The principle adopted in *The German Forces in the Field* and the *Order of Battle of the German Army* is similar.

Any corrections or suggestions for improving any of the above publications should be sent to the Director of Military Intelligence (M.I.14), War Office. Additions or corrections to these publications will be issued from time to time.

The War Office will also continue to issue *Periodical Notes on the German Army* in order that salient points regarding that army's development, organization and tactics may be brought to notice.

TABLE OF CONTENTS

CHAPTER I

ORGANIZATION AND STRENGTH OF FORMATIONS

Para.		Page
1.	The arms of the service	1
2.	Organization of the higher formations	1
3.	G.H.Q. troops	1
4.	Composition and strength of an army group	2
5.	Composition and strength of an army	2
6.	Composition and strength of a corps	2
7.	Composition, strength and fire power of an infantry division	3
8.	Composition, strength and fire power of a motorized infantry division	3
9.	Composition, strength and fire power of an armoured division	4
10.	Composition and strength of a mountain division	4
11.	Composition and strength of the cavalry division	5
12.	Composition and strength of an infantry regiment in an infantry division	5
13.	Composition and strength of a motorized infantry regiment in a motorized infantry division	5
14.	Composition and strength of a tank brigade in an armoured division	5
15.	Composition and strength of a lorried infantry brigade in an armoured division	5
16.	Miscellaneous units :—	
	(a) "Landwehr" units	6
	(b) Local defence (*Landesschützen*) units	6
	(c) Positional units (*Stellungseinheiten*)	6
	(d) Protective regiments (*Sicherungsregimenter*)	6
	(e) Instructional (*Lehr*) units	6
17.	Composition and strength of air defence troops	7
18.	Organization, composition and strength of coast defence troops	7

CHAPTER II

ADMINISTRATION, COMMANDS AND STAFFS

Para.		Page
1.	Organization of the High Command in war :—	
	(a) Supreme commander of the defence forces	10
	(b) War cabinet	10
	(c) Combined staff of the defence forces	10
	(d) War Ministry	10
2.	Administrative areas	11
3.	Chain of command in the field	11
4.	Staff of formations	11
5.	Chain of command for coastal defences	14
6.	Chain of command for air defences	14

CHAPTER III

INFANTRY

1.	General organization	15
2.	Organization, strength and armament of an infantry regiment (normal type) :—	
	(a) Organization :—	
	(i) Regiment	16
	(ii) Battalion	17
	(iii) Rifle company	17
	(iv) Machine-gun company	17
	(b) Strength	18
	(c) Armament	19
3.	Organization, strength and armament of a motorized infantry regiment :—	
	(a) Organization	20
	(b) Strength	20
	(c) Armament	20
4.	Organization, strength and armament of a lorried infantry regiment in an armoured division :—	
	(a) Organization :—	
	(i) Regiment	20
	(ii) Battalion	21
	(iii) Motor-cyclist company	21
	(iv) Rifle company	21
	(v) Machine-gun company	21
	(vi) Heavy company	21
	(b) Strength	22
	(c) Armament	23

Para.		Page
5.	Organization, strength and armament of a mountain rifle regiment :—	
	(a) Organization and strength	23
	(b) Armament	23
6.	Organization, strength and armament of a motor-cyclist battalion :—	
	(a) Organization :—	
	(i) Battalion	23
	(ii) Motor-cyclist rifle company	24
	(iii) Motor-cyclist machine-gun company	24
	(iv) Heavy company	24
	(b) Strength	25
	(c) Armament	26
7.	Organization, strength and armament of a motorized machine-gun battalion :—	
	(a) Organization :—	
	(i) Battalion	26
	(ii) Headquarters motor-cyclist platoon	26
	(iii) Machine-gun company	26
	(iv) Anti-tank company	26
	(b) Strength	27
	(c) Armament	27
8.	Frontier infantry regiment	27
9.	Organization of S.S. formations	27
10.	Parachute and air landing units	28
11.	Organization, strength and armament of a motorized anti-aircraft machine-gun battalion :—	
	(a) Organization :—	
	(i) Battalion	28
	(ii) Machine-gun company	28
	(b) Strength	28
	(c) Armament	28
	(d) Searchlight detachment	28
12.	Regimental specialists :—	
	(a) Assault detachments	29
	(i) Personnel	29
	(ii) Arms and equipment	29
	(b) Signallers	29
	(c) Pioneers	29
	(d) M.T. specialists	29
	(e) Other specialists	29
13.	Numbering of units	30
14.	Regimental transport	30
15.	Ammunition supply	30

Para.   *Page*

16. Equipment :—
    - (a) Personal 31
    - (b) Steel helmet 31
    - (c) Respirator 31
    - (d) Gas cape 31
    - (e) Signal equipment 31
    - (f) Tools 32
    - (g) Rangefinder 33
    - (h) Bivouacs 33
    - (i) Engineer equipment 33
    - (j) Anti-A.F.V. equipment 33

CHAPTER IV

CAVALRY AND RECONNAISSANCE UNITS

1. General organization and strength 40
2. Organization, strength and armament of a horsed cavalry regiment :—
    - (a) Organization 40
    - (b) Strength 41
    - (c) Armament 41
3. Organization, strength and armament of a mechanized reconnaissance unit :—
    - (a) Organization :—
        - (i) General 41
        - (ii) Mechanized reconnaissance unit .. 42
    - (b) Strength 42
    - (c) Armament 43
4. Organization, strength and armament of an infantry divisional reconnaissance unit :—
    - (a) Organization 43
    - (b) Strength 43
    - (c) Armament 44
5. Organization, strength and armament of a cyclist battalion :—
    - (a) Organization :—
        - (i) Battalion 44
        - (ii) Cyclist squadron 44
        - (iii) Motor-cyclist squadron 44
    - (b) Strength 45
    - (c) Armament 45
6. Numbering of units 46
7. Regimental specialists :—
    - (a) Signallers 46
    - (b) M.T. specialists 46
    - (c) Other specialists 46

Para.		Page
8.	Regimental transport	46
9.	Ammunition supply	46
10.	Equipment :—	
	(a) Personal	47
	(b) Saddlery	47
	(c) Steel helmet	47
	(d) Respirator	47
	(e) Gas cape	47
	(f) Signal equipment	47
	(g) Tools	47
	(h) Rangefinder	47
	(i) Bivouacs	48
	(j) Engineer equipment	48
	(k) Anti-A.F.V. equipment	48

CHAPTER V

SMALL ARMS, CLOSE SUPPORT AND ANTI-TANK WEAPONS

1.	Carbine, rifle and bayonet :—	
	(a) Carbine	51
	(b) Rifle	51
	(c) Bayonet	51
2.	Pistol and machine-pistols :—	
	(a) Pistol	51
	(b) Machine-pistols	51
3.	Light machine-guns :—	
	(a) Dreyse L.M.G. 13	51
	(b) L.M.G. 08/15	52
	(c) Knorr-Bremse	52
4.	Dual purpose machine-gun	52
5.	Heavy machine-gun	53
6.	Small arms ammunition	54
7.	Close support weapons :—	
	(a) 5-cm. (2-in.) light mortar	54
	(b) 7·5-cm. (2·95-in.) light close support infantry (cavalry) gun L.M.W..18	55
	(c) 7·5-cm. (2·95-in.) light close support infantry gun L..13	55
	(d) 7·5-cm. (2·95in.) assault gun	55
	(e) 8·1-cm. (3·16-in.) mortar L.15	55
	(f) 8·1-cm. (3·16-in.) mortar S. Gr.W.34	56
	(g) 10-cm. (3·94-in.) mortar	56
	(h) 15-cm. (5·9-in.) heavy infantry gun	56
	(i) 17-cm. (6·69-in.) medium trench mortar	56

Para.		Page
8.	Anti-tank weapons :—	
	(a) Anti-tank rifles	57
	(b) 3·7-cm. (1·45-in.) anti-tank gun	57
	(c) 4·7-cm. (1·85 in.) anti-tank gun	58
9.	Grenades	58
10.	Lance	59
11.	Sabre	59

CHAPTER VI

ARTILLERY

A—The Arm

		Page
1.	General organization	65
2.	General note on armament	66
3.	Artillery staffs :—	
	(a) Army	66
	(b) Corps	66
	(c) Division	66
	(d) Regiment	66
	(e) Field, medium or mountain artillery battery	66

B—Divisional Artillery

4.	Organization, strength and armament of the horse artillery battery in the cavalry division	67
5.	Organization, strength and armament of mountain artillery in a mountain division	68
6.	Organization, strength and armament of artillery in an infantry division	68
7.	Organization, strength and armament of artillery in a motorized infantry division	70
8.	Organization, strength and armament of artillery in an armoured division	70

C—Medium, Heavy and Super-Heavy Artillery

9.	Medium, heavy and super-heavy artillery	71

D—Regimental and other Specialists

10.	Regimental and other specialists :—	
	(a) Signallers	72
	(b) Survey specialists	72
	(c) Farriers	72
	(d) Mechanics	72
	(e) Anti-gas specialists	72
	(f) Artificers	72

Para.		Page

E—Artillery Survey Units

11.	Artillery survey units	72
	(a) Organization	73
	(b) Strength	73

F—Anti-Aircraft Artillery

12.	General organization	73
13.	Mobile and semi-mobile units	74
14.	Allotment of mobile and semi-mobile units to the field army	75
15.	Control of A.A. units operating with the army	75
16.	Static defences	75
17.	Armament	76

G—Coastal Defence and Fortress Artillery

18.	Organization and strength of coastal defence artillery	76
19.	Fortress artillery	77

H—Equipment

20.	Guns and howitzers	77
21.	Vehicles	77
22.	Signal equipment	78
23.	Technical equipment :—	
	(a) Command instruments	79
	(b) Observation instruments	79
	(c) Survey instruments	79
	(d) Predictor	79
	(e) Sound locator	80
	(f) Searchlights	80
24.	General system of ammunition supply in the field	80
25.	Types of ammunition :—	
	(a) Shells	81
	(b) Fuzes	81

CHAPTER VII

ARMOURED FIGHTING TROOPS

A—The Arm

1.	General :—	
	(a) Organization :—	
	(i) Armoured units	97
	(ii) Unarmoured units	97
	(b) Terminology	97
	(c) Strength :—	
	(i) Armoured units	97
	(ii) Unarmoured units	98

B—Armoured Units

Para.		Page
2.	Special types of A.F.Vs.	98
3.	Mixed tank regiment in an armoured division :—	
	(a) Organization :—	
	(i) Regiment	99
	(ii) Battalion	99
	(iii) Light squadron	99
	(iv) Medium squadron	100
	(b) Strength	101
	(c) Armament	102
	(d) Regimental specialists	102
	(e) Equipment	102
4.	Independent tank units	102
5.	Transport	102
6.	Regimental specialists :—	
	(a) Signallers	102
	(b) M.T. specialists	102
7.	Maintenance in the field	102
8.	Equipment	103

C—Unarmoured Units

Para.		Page
9.	Anti-tank battalion :—	
	(a) Organization :—	
	(i) Battalion	103
	(ii) Company	103
	(iii) Anti-aircraft company	104
	(b) Strength	104
	(c) Armament	104
	(d) Ammunition supply :—	
	(i) Light machine-gun	104
	(ii) Anti-tank gun	104
	(iii) Super-heavy machine-guns	104
	(e) Battalion specialists :—	
	(i) Signallers	104
	(ii) Mechanics	104
	(f) Maintenance in the field	105
	(g) Equipment :—	
	(i) Signal equipment	105
	(ii) Tools	105
	(iii) Equipment for the construction of road blocks	105

CHAPTER VIII

ENGINEERS AND ENGINEER EQUIPMENT

Para.		Page
1.	General organization	124
2.	Engineer battalion in an infantry division :—	
	(a) Organization :—	
	(i) Battalion	125
	(ii) Partially mechanized company	125
	(iii) Heavy mechanized company	125
	(iv) Bridging column	126
	(v) Electrical and mechanical tools park	126
	(vi) Reserve stores park	127
	(b) Strength	127
3.	Engineer battalion in a motorized infantry division :—	
	(a) Organization	127
	(b) Strength	127
4.	Engineer battalion in an armoured division :—	
	(a) Organization	128
	(b) Strength	128
5.	Engineer battalion in a mountain division :—	
	(a) Organization	128
	(b) Strength	128
6.	Engineer unit in the cavalry division	129
7.	G.H.Q. engineer battalion	129
8.	Training units and labour battalions :—	
	(a) Engineer training and experimental battalions	129
	(b) Labour battalions	129
	(c) Railway engineer units	132
	(d) Landwehr engineer units	132
9.	Armament	133
10.	Equipment :—	
	(a) Engineer tools and miscellaneous equipment	133
	(b) Carried by the man	134
	(c) In the vehicles of each engineer company	134
	(d) In the vehicles of the electrical and mechanical tools park	134
	(e) In the vehicles of the reserve stores park	134
11.	Explosives :—	
	(a) Demolition equipment	134
	(b) Anti-tank mines	135
	(c) Anti-personnel traps and mines	136

Para.		Page
12.	Pneumatic boats, pontoons, assault boats, motor boats and outboard motors :—	
	(a) Equipment carried by units :—	
	(i) Divisional engineer battalions	136
	(ii) G.H.Q. engineer battalions	136
	(b) Pneumatic boats	137
	(c) 3½/5-ton wooden pontoons	137
	(d) 9/18-ton pontoons and trestles	137
	(e) 24-ton Herbert pontoon bridge and trestles	138
	(f) Heavy tank rafts	139
	(g) Assault boats	139
	(h) Motor boats	139
	(i) Outboard motors	140
13.	Fixed bridges :—	
	(a) Small box girder bridge	140
	(b) Girder bridge	140
	(c) Improvised bridges	140
14.	Anti-tank obstacles :—	
	(a) Anti-tank mines	140
	(b) Wire obstacles	141
	(c) Other anti-tank obstacles	141
15.	Field searchlight projectors	141
16.	Special equipment for use in assault :—	
	(a) Flame-throwers	142
	(b) Bangalore torpedoes	142
	(c) Pole charges	142
	(d) Bell charges	142
	(e) Mine-exploding net	142
17.	Vehicles :—	
	(a) Three-ton lorry	143
	(b) Half-track tractor	143
	(c) Pontoon trailer	143
	(d) Trailer for motor-boat	143

CHAPTER IX

SIGNAL SERVICE

1.	General note on signal communications	146
2.	General organization	147
3.	Organization and strength of a signals unit in an infantry division	148
4.	Organization and strength of a signals unit in a motorized infantry division	148

Para.		Page
5.	Organization and strength of a signals unit in an armoured division	148
6.	Organization and strength of a signals unit in a corps	148
7.	Organization and strength of a signals unit in an armoured corps	148
8.	Organization and strength of a signals regiment in an army	148
9.	Organization and strength of a signals unit in a mountain division	149
10.	Organization and strength of the signals unit in the cavalry division	149
11.	Organization and strength of a signals section in a tank brigade	149
12.	Signals experimental and research establishments ..	150
13.	Cipher personnel	150
14.	Messenger dogs	150
15.	Carrier pigeons	150
16.	Despatch riders	150
17.	Armament of signal personnel	150
18.	Equipment :—	
	(a) Line telegraph :—	
	(i) General	151
	(ii) Exchanges	151
	(b) Line telephones :—	
	(i) Telephone No. 26	152
	(ii) Telephone No. 33	152
	(iii) Table telephone O.B.05	152
	(c) Teleprinters	152
	(d) Interception sets, W/T direction finders and ground listening sets	152
	(e) W/T jamming devices	153
	(f) W/T and R/T instruments	153
	(g) Cipher equipment	153
	(h) Visual equipment :—	
	(i) Signalling lamps	153
	(ii) Infra-red ray telephone	154
	(iii) Disc signalling equipment	154
	(i) Visual equipment for air co-operation ..	154
	(j) Light signals :—	
	(i) Verey light pistols	154
	(ii) Signal grenades	154
	(iii) Flares for communication with aircraft	154
	(k) Message throwers and projectors	154
	(l) Line construction :—	
	(i) Air line	154
	(ii) Types of cable	155
	(iii) Methods of laying	155
	(m) Vehicles :—	
	(i) Horse transport	156
	(ii) Motor transport	156

CHAPTER X

CHEMICAL WARFARE AND SMOKE

Para.		Page
1.	General policy	182
2.	General organization, administration and policy	182
3.	Defence :—	
	(a) Organization, administration and strength	183
	(b) Equipment :—	
	(i) Respirators	183
	(ii) Protective clothing	184
	(iii) Mobile laundries	184
	(iv) Decontamination materials	185
	(v) Anti-gas ointment	185
	(vi) Gas detectors	185
	(vii) Collective protection	185
4.	Offence :—	
	(a) Organization, administration and strength :—	
	(i) Special gas units	185
	(ii) Gas in smoke units	185
	(iii) Gas in tank units	186
	(iv) Gas in engineer battalions	186
	(b) Contemplated gases for offensive use :—	
	(i) General—all types	186
	(ii) Blister gas	186
	(iii) Choking gases	187
	(iv) Nose gases (toxic smokes)	187
	(v) Tear gases	187
	(c) Offensive weapons and equipment :—	
	(i) General	187
	(ii) Aerial spray	188
	(iii) Chemical aircraft bombs	188
	(iv) Projectors	188
	(v) Artillery shell	188
	(vi) Mortars	189
	(vii) Gas grenades	189
	(viii) Gas cylinders	189
	(ix) Gas mines	189
	(x) Bulk contamination	189
	(xi) Toxic generators	189
5.	Smoke :—	
	(a) Smoke units :—	
	(i) General	190
	(ii) Organization	190
	(iii) Strength	190
	(iv) Armament	190
	(b) Equipment :—	
	(i) Generator or " smoke candles "	190
	(ii) Pressure-type smoke apparatus	191

Para.		Page
	(c) Smoke units and apparatus in other arms of the Service :—	
	(i) Artillery	191
	(ii) Tank units	191
	(iii) Engineer units	191
	(iv) Aircraft	191
	(d) Other special smoke units	191
6.	Effect of weather conditions on the production of smoke or gas	191
7.	Bacteria	192

CHAPTER XI

THE ADMINISTRATIVE SERVICES

1.	General	194
2.	Supply and administrative services :—	
	(a) General	194
	(b) Supply services in a division :—	
	(i) Supply columns	195
	(ii) M.T. columns for petrol and oil	196
	(iii) Workshop companies	196
	(iv) Supply companies	197
	(c) Supply services in a corps	197
	(d) Supply services in an army :—	
	(i) Supply columns	197
	(ii) M.T. columns for petrol and oil	197
	(iii) Field workshops	197
	(iv) Supply battalions	197
	(v) Parks and depôts	198
3.	Medical service	198
4.	Veterinary service	199
5.	Provost service :—	
	(a) Military police	200
	(b) L. of C. guard battalions	201
	(c) Field security police	201
6.	Postal service	201

CHAPTER XII

POLICE, GENDARMERIE, SEMI-MILITARY FORCES AND LABOUR SERVICE

1.	General organization of the police	212
2.	The various branches of police :—	
	(a) Town constabulary	212
	(b) Barrack police	213
	(c) Rural constabulary	213

Para.		Page
	(d) Auxiliary police	213
	(e) Secret state police	213
	(f) Criminal police	213
	(g) Technical emergency corps	213
3.	Special bodyguard troops	214
4.	Semi-military and political organizations :—	
	(a) Schutz-Staffeln (S.S.)	214
	(b) Storm detachments (S.A.)	215
	(c) National Socialist Motor Corps	215
	(d) National Socialist Mounted Corps	216
	(e) National Socialist Flying Corps	217
5.	Hitler youth	217
6.	Railway, post and factory guards :—	
	(a) Railway guards and railway police	217
	(b) Post guards	217
	(c) Factory guards	217
7.	National labour service	217
8.	Ex-soldiers' organization	218
9.	Voluntary police corps	218
10.	Military farmers	218
11.	Czech police corps	218

CHAPTER XIII

UNIFORM

Para.		Page
1.	General notes on field service uniform :—	
	(a) Officers	220
	(b) Other ranks	220
	(c) Special types of uniform :—	
	(i) Armoured fighting troops	221
	(ii) Mountain troops and rifle battalions	221
	(iii) Raiding and reconnaissance parties	221
	(iv) Smoke units	221
2.	Distinguishing marks and badges of rank :—	
	(a) Distinguishing marks	221
	(b) Badges of rank	222
3.	National crests and badges :—	
	(a) National badge	222
	(b) National rosette	223
	(c) National colours	223
4.	Paramilitary formations :—	
	(a) Schutz-Staffeln (S.S.)	223
	(b) Storm detachments (S.A.)	223
	(c) National Socialist Motor Corps	223

Para.		Page
5.	Identity discs and means of identification	223
6.	Orders, decorations and medals	224
7.	Special badges	224
8.	Personal equipment	224
9.	Air Force uniform	224
10.	Uniform worn by parachute troops	224

CHAPTER XIV

AIR FORCE

1. General organization, distribution and strength :—
    - (a) General outline .. 232
    - (b) The air fleets (*Luftflotten*) .. 233
    - (c) The air corps (*Fliegerkorps*) .. 233
    - (d) The air divisions (*Fliegerdivisionen*) .. 233
    - (e) Territorial areas (*Luftgaue*) .. 233
    - (f) Formations and flying units :—
        - (i) *Geschwader* .. 235
        - (ii) *Gruppen* .. 235
        - (iii) *Staffeln* .. 235
    - (g) Types of aircraft in first line units .. 236
    - (h) Armament and bombs .. 237
2. Aircraft markings .. 237
3. The role of the German air force in co-operation with the army :—
    - (a) General .. 237
    - (b) Indirect support .. 237
    - (c) Direct support .. 238
    - (d) Liaison between army and air force .. 238
4. Tactics :—
    - (a) Indirect support .. 238
    - (b) Direct support .. 238
    - (c) Roles of different types of aircraft :—
        - (i) Bombers .. 239
        - (ii) Dive-bombers .. 239
        - (iii) Fighters .. 239
        - (iv) Ground attack .. 239
        - (v) Reconnaissance (including army co-operation) .. 239
    - (d) Army co-operation .. 239

CHAPTER XV

GERMAN PARACHUTE AND AIR-LANDING TROOPS

Para.		Page
1.	General	240
2.	Parachute troops :—	
	(a) General	240
	(b) Organization and armament	241
	(c) Maintenance	241
3.	Air-landing troops :—	
	(a) Organization and equipment	242
	(b) Maintenance	242
4.	Gliders	243
5.	Uniforms	243
6.	Landing grounds	243
7.	Method of landing :—	
	(a) Parachutists	244
	(b) Air-landing troops and troops transported by aircraft	245
8.	Objectives of parachute troops	256
9.	Objectives of air landing troops	246

CHAPTER XVI

TACTICS

		Page
1.	General	252
2.	The attack :—	
	(a) General	253
	(b) Forms of attack :—	
	(i) Frontal attack	253
	(ii) Envelopment	254
	(iii) Penetration	254
	(c) General conduct of the attack	254
3.	The defence :—	
	(a) Organisation of position	255
	(b) Advanced position	255
	(c) Battle outposts	256
	(d) The main line of resistance	256

Para.		Page
4.	Protection at rest	256
5.	Protection on the move	257
6.	Mechanized reconnaissance units	257
7.	A.F.Vs.	258
8.	Infantry	260
9.	Artillery	260
10.	Engineers	261
11.	Smoke	262
12.	Gas	262
13.	Irregular methods of warfare	263

LIST OF APPENDICES

	Appendix	Page
G.H.Q troops		
Specimen allotment of G.H.Q. troops to army and corps	I	8
Infantry		
Organization of an infantry division	II	34–35
Approximate strength in personnel and vehicles of an infantry division	III	36
Fire power of an infantry division	IV	37
Organization, strength and fire power of an infantry battalion	V	38–39
Cavalry and reconnaissance units		
Organization of a horsed cavalry regiment	VI	49
Organization of an infantry divisional reconnaissance unit	VII	50
Small arms		
Details of machine-pistols used by Germany	VIII	61–62
Note on captured small arms, close-support and anti-tank weapons likely to be used by Germany	IX	63
Artillery		
Organization of divisional artillery of an infantry division	X	82
Organization of a field artillery battery	XI	83
Organization of a medium artillery regiment	XII	84
Particulars of types of German guns	XIII	85
Particulars of types of captured guns likely to be used by Germany	XIV	92
Strength and equipment of anti-aircraft artillery	XV	93
Particulars of types of anti-aircraft guns used by Germany	XVI	95–96

	Appendix	Page
Armoured fighting troops		
Organization of an armoured division	XVII	107–108
Organization of a mechanized reconnaissance unit of an armoured division	XVIII	109–110
Organization of a tank brigade	XIX	111–112
Organization, tank strength and fire power of a mixed tank regiment	XX	113
Summary of A.F.Vs. and weapons in an armoured division	XXI	114
Particulars of types of tanks used by Germany	XXII	115–116
Distinguishing features of tanks used by Germany	XXIII	117
Particulars of types of armoured cars used by Germany	XXIV	120–121
Distinguishing features of German armoured cars	XXV	122
Engineers		
Organization of an engineer battalion in an infantry division	XXVI	144
Organization of a G.H.Q. engineer battalion	XXVII	145
Signals		
Organization, strength and transport equipment of a signals regiment in an army	XXVIII	158–159
Organization, strength and transport equipment of a signals unit in a corps	XXIX	160–161
Organization, strength and transport equipment of a signals unit in an armoured corps	XXX	162–163
Organization, strength and transport equipment of a signals unit in an infantry division	XXXI	164–165
Organization, strength and transport equipment of a signals unit in an armoured division	XXXII	166–167
German wireless transmitters	XXXIII	169
German wireless receivers	XXXIV	177
Comparative positions in the spectrum of German and British army wireless sets	XXXV	180
Administrative services		
Diagram showing the ration supply system in the German army	XXXVI	204–205
Diagram showing the supply of fuel for motor vehicles in the German army	XXXVII	206–207
Diagram showing the ammunition supply system in the German army	XXXVIII	208–209
Diagram showing the system of evacuation of prisoners in the German army	XXXIX	210–211
Uniform		
Orders, decorations and medals	XL	226
Assault and wound badges	XLI	230

	Appendix	Page.
Parachute and air-landing troops		
Organization of a parachute rifle regiment	XLII	248
Equipment of a group of parachutists	XLIII	249
Estimate of damage likely to be inflicted by a group of parachutists	XLIV	250
Organization, strength and armament of an infantry division for air-landing operations	XLV	251
Miscellaneous		
List of German abbreviations with English equivalents	XLVI	264
German coinage, weights and measures	XLVII	273
Conventional signs for military formations, units, etc.	XLVIII	275
Ground signs used by troops for communication with aircraft	XLIX	291
Road spaces	L	292

TABLE OF PLATES

	Plate
I.—Small arms, infantry support and anti-tank weapons	
Carbine (Karabiner 98 b)	1
Carbine (Karabiner 98 k)	2
Rifle (Gewehr 98)	3
Machine pistols :—	
Schmeisser M.P. 38	4
Neuhausen (short model)	5
Steyr-Solothurn S1–100 (long model)	6
Steyr-Solothurn S1–100 (short model)	7
Machine guns :—	
Dreyse L.M.G. 13	8
M.G. 34 (dual purpose) on heavy mounting	9
M.G. 34 (dual purpose) on A.A. mounting	10
Diagram of M.G. 34 on heavy mounting	11
08 hy. M.G. on tripod mounting	12
08 hy. M.G. on sledge mounting	13
Mortars :—	
5-cm. (2-in.) mortar	14
8·1-cm. (3·16-in.) mortar	15
10-cm. (3·94-in.) smoke mortar	16
17-cm. (6·69-in.) medium mortar	17
Infantry guns :—	
7·5-cm. (2·95-in.) infantry gun L.M.W. 18	18
7·5-cm. (2·95-in.) infantry gun L. 13	19
15-cm. (5·91-in.) heavy infantry gun	20

	Plate
Anti-tank weapons :—	
2-cm. (·79-in.) anti-tank rifle	21
3·7-cm. (1.45-in.) anti-tank gun	22 and 23

II.—Artillery

	Plate
10-cm. (3·93-in.) mountain howitzer	24
10·5-cm. (4·14-in.) gun-howitzer	25
10·5-cm. (4·14-in.) field gun K. 18	26
15-cm. (5·91-in.) howitzer S.F.H. 18	27 and 28
15-cm. (5·91-in.) field gun K.16	29
21-cm. (8·27-in.) howitzer	30
Railway guns :—	
21-cm. (8·27-in.) and 24-cm. (9·45-in.)	31
38-cm. (14·96-in.) "Theodor Kanone"	32
Long range gun on fixed mounting	33
Anti-aircraft guns :—	
2-cm. (·79-in.) A.A. and A.-Tk. gun	34 and 35
8·8-cm. (3·46-in.) A.A. gun	36 and 37

III.—Armoured fighting vehicles

	Plate
T.K.3 light tank (Polish)	38 and 39
Pz. Kw. I two-man light tank	40
Pz. Kw. I light commander's tank	41
Pz. Kw. I light tank converted to tractor or carrier	42
F.W.H.E. light amphibian tank	43 and 44
T.N.H.P. light tank (Czech)	45
Pz. Kw. II three-man light tank	46 and 47
Pz. Kw. II mounted on recovery vehicle	48 and 49
Pz. Kw. II mounted on tank carrier	50
7 T.P. light medium tank (Polish)	51
L.T. 35 light medium tank (Czech)	52
C.K.D. V.8. H. light medium tank (Czech)	53
Pz. Kw. III light medium tank	54, 55 and 56
Pz. Kw. IV medium tank	57
Pz. Kw. V heavy tank	58
Pz. Kw. VI heavy tank	59
Light reconnaissance car	60
Sd. Kfz. 223 light armoured car	61
A.S.P.6 medium armoured car	62
Heavy 8-wheeled armoured car	63
A.D.G.Z. 8-wheeled armoured car (ex-Austrian)	64
Armoured troop-carrier	65

	Plate
IV.—Pontoons, rafts and assault boats	
9/18-ton pontoon equipment made up as 18-ton bridge	66
Pneumatic boat raft	67
Assault boats	68, 69 and 70
V.—Uniform	
Field service uniform	71, 72 and 73
Uniform worn by armoured fighting troops	74 and 75
Distinguishing colours worn by various arms of the service	76
Army badges of rank	77
Army national badge	78
Air force—distinguishing colours worn by various arms of the service	79
Air Force—national badge and specialist badges	80
Air Force—badges of rank	81
Parachute troops	82, 83 and 84
National marking on German aircraft	85

	Page
Index	373

xxiv

CHAPTER I

ORGANIZATION AND STRENGTH OF FORMATIONS

1. The arms of the service

These are:—

Infantry (including infantry regiments of the normal type, some of which include rifle battalions, motorized infantry regiments in motorized infantry divisions, mountain rifle regiments, motorized machine-gun battalions, motorized anti-aircraft machine-gun battalions, fortress and frontier infantry regiments).

Mobile troops (including tank regiments, anti-tank units, lorried infantry brigades of armoured divisions, motor-cyclist battalions, horsed cavalry regiments, divisional reconnaissance units, mechanized reconnaissance units, and cyclist units).

Artillery.
Engineers.
Smoke troops.
Signals.
Services.

2. Organization of the higher formations

The arms of the Service are grouped together in *divisions* of the following types:—

Infantry.
Motorized infantry.
Armoured.
Mountain.
Cavalry.

Divisions are grouped into corps, corps into armies, armies into army groups.

3. G.H.Q. troops (*Heerestruppen*)

Army groups, armies, and corps have at present no combatant units on their permanent establishment. For particular operations these formations receive reinforcement from the troops in the G.H.Q. pool. This pool was formed on mobilization by withdrawing all the peace-time corps troops (with the exception of the corps signals unit).

The G.H.Q. pool includes the following units :—

Mobile troops	Tank units.
	Anti-tank and heavy anti-tank units.
Artillery	Medium, heavy and super-heavy artillery batteries.
	Artillery survey units.
Engineers	Engineer battalions.
	Bridge construction battalions.
	Bridging columns.
	Road construction battalions.
	Labour battalions.
Smoke detachments.	
Signals.	
Miscellaneous	Observation balloon, survey (mapping), and meteorological sections, and propaganda companies.*
Air Force units ..	Army co-operation units.
	Air signals units.

For a specimen allotment of G.H.Q. troops to army and corps *see* Appendix I.

4. Composition and strength of an army group (*Heeresgruppe*)

The composition of an army group is not fixed, but on the Western Front it consisted of 2–4 armies.

5. Composition and strength of an army (*Armee*)

The composition of an army is not fixed, but on the Western Front it consisted of 2–5 corps.

6. Composition and strength of a corps (*Armeekorps*)

The composition of a corps is not fixed, but on the Western Front it consisted of 2–5 divisions. Divisions may be transferred from one corps to another, whenever this is considered necessary for operational reasons.

---

* The propaganda companies consist of Press, film and camera sections, whose twofold functions are first, to provide propaganda material for the civil population at home and for neutral countries, by means of films, photographs, newspaper articles, and broadcast talks, and secondly, to maintain the morale of the fighting troops by the distribution of books, and specially printed newspapers, cinema performances, etc. The personnel of these companies are reservists, who in civil life were journalists, photographers, film-camera men, etc.

7. Composition, strength and fire power of an infantry division (*Infanterie-Division*). (*See* Appendices II, III, and IV)

The composition of a German infantry division is similar to that of a British division, although the former is weaker in artillery.

An infantry division consists of :—

Headquarters.

Divisional reconnaissance unit. (*See* Chapter IV, para. 4.)

Divisional signals. (*See* Chapter IX, para. 3.)

Divisional infantry headquarters.

Three infantry regiments. (*See* Chapter III, para. 2.)

Divisional artillery headquarters. (*See* Chapter VI, Sec. A, para. 3 (c).)

Divisional artillery (horsed). (*See* Chapter VI, Sec. B, para. 6.)

Divisional motorized A.A. M.G. battalion.* (*See* Chapter III, para. 11.)

Divisional anti-tank battalion. (*See* Chapter VII, Sec. C, para. 9.)

Divisional engineer battalion. (*See* Chapter VIII, para. 2.)

Services.† (*See* Chapter XI, para. 2 (b).)

The war establishment of an infantry division is about 17,000 men or 27,000 for a gross division (*i.e.*, including a proportion of G.H.Q. and L. of C. troops).

8. Composition, strength and fire power of a motorized infantry division (*motorisierte Infanterie-Division*). (*See* Appendix IV.)

The composition of a motorized infantry division is similar to that of an infantry division of normal type, but its units are motorized throughout.

The strength of a motorized infantry division is approximately the same as that of an infantry division of the normal type.

---

* It is not yet definitely established whether one of these units is to be included in each division, or whether they are to remain G.H.Q. troops.

† Each division also contains a number of ancillary units, such as a butcher unit and bakery company (*Schlächtereieinheit, Bäckereikompanie*).

Chapter I

9. **Composition, strength, and fire power of an armoured division** (*Panzer-Division*). (*See* Appendices XVII, XVIII, XIX, and XXI.)

   An armoured division consists of :—
   Headquarters.
   Divisional reconnaissance unit. (*See* Chapter IV, para. 3.)
   Divisional signals. (*See* Chapter IX, para. 5.)
   Tank brigade. (*See* para. 14 below.)
   Lorried infantry brigade. (*See* para. 15 of this chapter.)
   Divisional artillery regiment. (*See* Chapter VI, Section B, para. 8.)
   Divisional motorized A.A. M.G. battalion.* (*See* Chapter III, para. 11.)
   Divisional anti-tank battalion. (*See* Chapter VII, Section C, para. 9.)
   Divisional engineer battalion. (Chapter VIII, para. 4.)
   Divisional air force unit (12 close reconnaissance aircraft.)
   Mobile A.A. unit (Air Force) (attached).
   Services. (*See* Chapter XI, para. 2 (*b*).)

   All these units are mechanized throughout.

   The strength of an armoured division is approximately 12,000 men.

10. **Composition and strength of a mountain division**
    (*Gebirgs-Division*)

    A mountain division consists of :—
    Headquarters.
    Mountain divisional signals. (*See* Chapter IX, para. 5.)
    Three (or two) mountain rifle regiments. (*See* Chapter III, para. 5.)
    Mountain artillery regiment. (*See* Chapter VI, Section B, para. 5.)
    Mountain divisional artillery survey unit. (*See* Chapter VI, Section B, para. 5.)
    Mountain divisional anti-tank battalion. (*See* Chapter VII, Section C, para. 9.)
    Mountain divisional engineer battalion. (*See* Chapter VIII, para. 5.)
    Services. (*See* Chapter XI, para. 2 (*b*).)

    The strength of a mountain division is not at present known.

---

* It is not yet definitely established whether one of these units is to be included in each division, or whether they are to remain G.H.Q. troops.

11. Composition and strength of the cavalry division (*Kavallerie-Division*)

The cavalry division—only one is known to exist in the German army—contains four or more horsed cavalry regiments (*Reiter-Regimenter*). (*See* Chapter IV, para. 2.)

The strength of the cavalry division is not at present known.

12. Composition and strength of an infantry regiment (*Infanterie-Regiment*) in an infantry division

The German infantry regiment (*see* Chapter III, para. 2) is the equivalent of the British infantry brigade, but the fire power of the former is greater, as it includes close-support artillery in addition to mortars, machine-guns, and A.Tk. guns.

The strength of an infantry regiment is approximately 3,000 men.

13. Composition and strength of a motorized infantry regiment (*motorisiertes Infanterie-Regiment*) in a motorized infantry division

As above, but fully motorized. *Superseded NNor*

14. Composition and strength of a tank brigade (*Panzer-Brigade*) in an armoured division. (*See* Appendix XIX.)

A tank brigade in an armoured division consists of:—
Headquarters.
Brigade signal section. (*See* Chapter IX, para. 11.)
Two mixed tank regiments. (*See* Chapter VII, Section B, para. 3.) Each of two battalions.

A tank brigade contains 416 first-line tanks of various types. Its strength is approximately 4,600 men.

15. Composition and strength of a lorried infantry brigade (*Schützen-Brigade*) in an armoured division. (*See* Appendix XVII)

A lorried infantry brigade in an armoured division consists of:—
Headquarters.
Signal section.
Two lorried infantry regiments. (*See* Chapter III, para. 4.)
Or *One lorried infantry regiment and one motor-cyclist battalion.* (*See* Chapter III, para. 6.)

The strength of a lorried infantry brigade of two lorried infantry regiments is approximately 3,300, and that of a lorried infantry brigade, of one lorried infantry regiment and one motor-cyclist battalion, approximately 2,450.

16. Miscellaneous combatant units

(a) *"Landwehr" Units.*—" Landwehr " units are composed chiefly of men between the ages of 35 and 45. The men, a large proportion of whom are veterans of the last war, carried out a period of training in peace of either eight or sixteen weeks. " Landwehr " divisions are employed for the most part on guard duties at home and in the occupied territories, and their equipment is frequently inferior to that of active divisions.

(b) *Local defence (Landesschützen) units.*—Local defence (*Landesschützen*) units, corresponding approximately to the " Landsturm " of the last war, are composed mainly of men of 40 and upwards. Formed on mobilization, they were organized initially in battalions only, but many of the battalions have been grouped into regiments and the regiments into divisions. Details of the divisional and regimental organization are still lacking.

(c) *Positional units (Stellungseinheiten).*—The existence of such units is confirmed, but nothing is known about their organization and exact functions.

(d) *Protective regiments (Sicherungs-Regimenter).*—The organization and functions of these units are not known, but it has been established that they have no connection with the local defence (*Landesschützen*) units (*see* above) or the L. of C. guard (*Wach*) battalions (*see* Chapter XI, para. 5 (*b*)).

(e) *Instructional (Lehr) units.*—For each arm of the service there is one instructional unit (two in the case of engineers), normally stationed at the school of the arm and employed for training, demonstrations, and experiments.

Though their purpose is primarily instructional, these units may also be employed in whole or in part on active service. For example, one of the engineer instructional units was attached to the 6th Army during the campaign in Belgium, and portions of the artillery instructional unit were sent to Norway in April, 1940.

The non-divisional motorized infantry regiment " Grossdeutschland " is best assigned to this category. Its personnel is drawn from all over Germany from men who propose to make the army a career. After a period of service in it, other ranks normally obtain promotion. During the operations on the Western Front it was attached to an armoured division.

17. Organization, composition and strength of air defence troops

German anti-aircraft (*Flak*) units are organized as part of the Air Force. For details see Chapter VI, Sec. F.

18. Organization and composition of coast defence troops

The responsibility for coast defence is divided between the Navy and the Air Force.

Coastal batteries in Germany, sited with a view to repelling sea-borne or air attack, are manned by the Navy.

Torpedo-bomber and open-sea, fleet and coastal reconnaissance aircraft units are included in the Air Force.

APPENDIX I

SPECIMEN ALLOTMENT OF G.H.Q. TROOPS TO AN ARMY

1. Engineers
One engineer regimental H.Q.
Two engineer battalions.
One commander of construction units and staff.
Four bridge construction battalions.
Four bridging columns.

2. Artillery
One artillery regimental H.Q.
Two heavy artillery batteries (24-cm. (9·45-in.) guns).
One heavy artillery battery (15-cm. (5·91-in.) guns).
One observation balloon unit.
One meteorological section.

3. Other G.H.Q. troops
One survey (mapping) unit.
One meteorological section.

4. Army headquarter troops
One infantry company.
One infantry anti-tank platoon.
One armoured car troop.

5. Air Force
One army co-operation flight
One air signals unit.

SPECIMEN ALLOTMENT OF G.H.Q. TROOPS TO A CORPS

1. Engineers
Two bridging columns.
One bridging column (stores).

2. Artillery
Two artillery commanders and staffs.
Two artillery regimental H.Q.
Two medium artillery batteries (10·5-cm. (4·14-in.) guns).
Four medium artillery batteries (15-cm. (5·91-in.) hows.).
Two heavy artillery batteries (21-cm. (8·27-in.) hows.).

Two heavy artillery troops (21-cm. (8·27-in.) hows.).
One heavy artillery battery (24-cm. (9·45-in.) hows.).
One heavy artillery battery (30-cm. (11·97-in.) hows.).
Four heavy artillery troops (30-cm. (11·97-in.) hows.).
Two artillery survey units.

3. Other G.H.Q. troops

One infantry battalion for special employment.
One heavy anti-tank unit.
One anti-tank unit.
One " smoke " regimental H.Q.
One " smoke " unit.

4. Air Force

One army co-operation flight.
One mixed A.A. battery.

Note.—It is believed that all the above units are mechanised.

CHAPTER II

ADMINISTRATION, COMMANDS AND STAFF

1. Organization of the High Command in war

(a) *Supreme Commander of the Defence Forces.*—Hitler is the supreme commander of the defence forces and theoretically exercises this command in person.

(b) *War Cabinet.*—The War Cabinet is a small body with Hitler as president and six other members.

(c) *Combined Staff of the Defence Forces (Oberkommando der Wehrmacht).*—The Combined Staff of the Defence Forces is responsible for the formulation of policy in accordance with the directions of the supreme commander. The Chief of the Combined Staff, a senior general, acts as Hitler's chief adviser on matters concerning the defence forces, but has no executive command.

(d) *The War Ministry (R.K.M. or Reichskriegsministerium)* is under the immediate control of the Commander-in-Chief of the Army.

The General Staff at the War Ministry (*Generalstab des Heeres*) under the Chief of Staff of the Army is grouped in five main departments, each under a Deputy Chief of the General Staff (*Oberquartiermeister I–V*), (each department consisting of from one to five sections (*Abteilungen*). The organization is as follows:—

Oberquartiermeister I   Operations.
    Abt. 1.—Operations.
    Abt. 5.—Transport.
    Abt. 6.—Rear services.
    Abt. 9.—Topography.
    Abt. 10.—Manœuvres and operational planning.

Oberquartiermeister II   Training.
    Abt. 4.—Training.
    Abt. 11.—Military schools and officers' training.

Oberquartiermeister III ..   Organization.
    Abt. 2.—Organization.
    Abt. 8.—Technical services.

Oberquartiermeister IV ..   Intelligence.
    Abt. 3.—Eastern section.
    Abt. 12.—Western section.

Oberquartiermeister V   Historical.
    Abt. 7.—Historical.

Other R.K.M. departments co-ordinate with the general staff, include the following:—

Army Personnel Branch (*Heeres-Personalamt*).
General Army Branch (*Allgemeines Heeresamt*).
Army Administration Branch (*Heeres-Verwaltungsamt*).
Army Ordnance Branch (*Heeres-Waffenamt*).

In addition to the above departments special sections of the R.K.M. include the Inspectorates of Infantry, Artillery, Mobile Troops, Engineers and Fortifications, Signals, Medical Services, etc.

There is also the Attaché Branch (*Attaché-Gruppe*) which deals with foreign military attachés and visiting officers in Germany, and German military attachés abroad.

2. Administrative areas (*Wehrkreise*)

Germany is divided into a number of administrative areas (*Wehrkreise*), which in peace were each commanded by a senior officer, who also commanded the corps which bore the same number as the "Wehrkreis."

A list of "Wehrkreise" and particulars of their sub-divisions are given in "The German Forces in the Field" (4 (*d*) and 6 (*a*)).

3. Chain of command in the field

Under the Commander of Land Forces come—

Commanders of Groups of Armies.
Army Commanders.
Corps Commanders.
Divisional Commanders.

4. Staff of formations

The chief of staff of an army or corps is responsible to higher authority as well as the army or corps commander. The system in force is that, if the chief of staff does not agree with the proposals of his commander, he must point out the fact. If, however, the commander is not convinced by the arguments put forward by his chief of staff, the latter must comply with the wishes of the commander, at the same time recording in writing his objection to the commander's proposals. By this action he covers himself if called upon by a higher authority to account for what occurred. It is reported that this system very seldom causes friction. The chief of staff of a division is not responsible to higher authority for the decisions of his commander.

The staffs of an army, corps or division are all organized in the same way and consist of the following sections :—

Section I (*Generalstab*). This section is staffed exclusively by General Staff officers and is divided into four parts*—

I(*a*) Operations.
I(*b*) Material.
I(*c*) Intelligence.
I(*d*) Training.

It does not concern itself with any routine matters.

Section II (*Adjutantur*). This corresponds approximately to the "A" and "Q" branches in a formation of the British army. It is headed by a General Staff officer and deals with all routine matters.

Section III (*Feldjustizamt*). A legal branch which is staffed by officials.

Section IV (*Intendantur*). This includes representatives of all the various services.

Section V. Chaplains' Service.

For organization of work, the sections of the staff of formations are divided into three groups—

(i) *Tactical group*.—(*Führungs-Abteilung*) comprising I(*a*) and I(*c*) of Section I.

(ii) *Supply group*.—(*Quartiermeister-Abteilung*) comprising I(*b*) of Section I and the whole of Section IV.

(iii) Personnel, etc., group (*Adjutantur*) comprising Sections II, III and V. The postal section, pay section, divisional services and divisional H.Q. troops are attached to this section.

The following officers are attached to the various staffs :—*

(*a*) *Army*.—With the headquarters of each army is a senior officer of each of the following arms of the service :—

Cavalry.
Artillery.
Engineers.
Anti-tank.
Signals.

These officers act as technical advisers to the army commander and keep him in touch with all matters relating to their arm. They are known as "Höherer Kavallerieoffizier 1," etc., the number corresponding to that of the army.

---

* For the composition of air force staffs ("Koluft" officers) attached to various army formations, *see* Chapter XIV, para. 3 (*d*).

(b) *Corps.*—At each corps headquarters there is a senior officer of each of the following arms of the service :—

    Engineers.
    Signals.
    Anti-tank units.

These officers come directly under the Chief of Staff of the corps. They command the units of their own arm of the service within the corps, and are responsible for their technical and tactical training. They are also available to give advice to the corps and divisional commanders. They are known as " Kommandeur der Pioniere 2," etc., the number corresponding to that of the corps.

There may also be an artillery officer who carries out duties similar to those of the C.C.R.A. and C.C.M.A. in the British army.

(c) *Division.*—An artillery officer, known as "Artillerie-Kommandeur 3 " (or whatever the number of the division may be) commands all the artillery in a division and acts as adviser to the divisional commander. For details of his staff, *see* Chapter VI, Sec. A, para. 3 (c).

Before the war there was also an " Infanterie-Kommandeur " of equivalent status who was responsible for advising the divisional commander in matters of infantry training. At present, owing to lack of officers, this appointment is often vacant, but is likely to be filled when sufficient officers are available.

The following officers are believed to be attached to groups of the divisional staff as under :—

Tactical group
    C.R.A. of the division.
    C.R.E. of the division.
    C. Signals of the division.
    A.Tk. battalion cmdr.
    Officer in technical charge of the divisional M.T.
    Where applicable, the air liaison officer.

Supply group
    Cmdr. of the light columns and the divisional train.
    Divisional provost marshal.
    Divisional postal section commander.
    C.R.E.
    C. Signals. } For questions of supply of material.

5. Chain of-command for coastal defences

The coastal defences, which are the responsibility of the Commander-in-Chief of the Navy, are divided into the North Sea and Baltic stations.

    (a) *North Sea Station* (*Wilhelmshaven*).—This is sub-divided into the following fortress commands:—

        (i) Wilhelmshaven.

        (ii) Elbe and Weser Estuaries (Cuxhaven).

        (iii) Ems Estuary (Emden).

    (b) *Baltic Station* (*Kiel*).—This is sub-divided into the following fortress commands:—

        (i) Kiel.

        (ii) Pomeranian Coast (Swinemünde).

        (iii) Pillau.

Each of the fortress commands enumerated in sub-paras. (*a*) and (*b*) above contains a coast artillery unit and certain coastal anti-aircraft artillery units (*see* Chapter VI, Sec. G, para. 18 (*b*)).

6. Chain of command of air defences

All air defences are the responsibility of the Air Force. For details *see* Chapter VI, Sec. F, and Chapter XIV.

CHAPTER III

INFANTRY

1. General organization

The infantry arm is controlled by the Inspectorate of Infantry in the War Ministry. It consists of :—

(i) Infantry regiments (normal type) (*Infanterie-Regimenter*), some of which include rifle (*Jäger*) battalions.

(ii) Motorised infantry regiments (*motorisierte Infanterie-Regimenter*) in motorised infantry divisions.

(iii) Mountain rifle regiments (*Gebirgsjäger-Regimenter*).

(iv) Motorised machine-gun battalions (*motorisierte Maschinengewehr-Bataillone*).

(v) Motorised anti-aircraft machine-gun battalions (*Flugabwehr-Bataillone motorisiert*).

(vi) Fortress (*Festungs*) and frontier (*Grenz*) infantry regiments.

(vii) Certain S.S. and police regiments (*S.S. "Totenkopf"* and *"Verfügungs" Standarten* and *S.S. Polizei-Schützen-Regimenter*).

(viii) Positional units (*Stellungseinheiten*). (See Chapter I, para. 16 (c).)

(ix) Protective regiments (*Sicherungs-Regimenter*). (See Chapter I, para. 16 (d).)

The following units, which are under the Inspector of Mobile Troops (*Inspekteur der schnellen Truppen*) are included in this chapter for convenience :—

(i) Lorried infantry regiments in armoured divisions (*Schützen-Regimenter*).

(ii) Motor cyclist battalions (*Kradschützen-Bataillone*).

Parachute and air landing units (*Fallschirm- und Luftlandungseinheiten*) are described in Chapter XV.

Chapter III

2. Organization, strength and armament of an infantry regiment (normal type) (*Infanterie-Regiment*)

(a) *Organization*

(i) *Regiment.*—An infantry regiment consists of :—
   Headquarters.
   A signal section.
   A motor-cyclist despatch rider section.
   A mounted infantry platoon, consisting of headquarters and three sections.
   A pioneer platoon. This has recently been added, and no details of its strength and organization are as yet known.
   An infantry gun (13th) company (horse-drawn) of headquarters, signal section, three platoons each of two sections, each of the latter being armed with one 7·5-cm. (2·95-in.) light infantry gun; and one platoon of two sections, each of the latter being armed with one 15-cm. (5·91-in.) heavy infantry gun.*
   †An anti-tank (14th) company. This unit, which is fully mechanized, consists of headquarters and four platoons. Each of the latter consists of three sections each armed with one 3·7-cm. (1·45-in.) anti-tank gun; and one light machine-gun section; it is thought that the company no longer possesses a signal section.
   A light infantry column (*see* para. 14 below).
   Three battalions‡ (described in sub-para. (ii) below).
   (*See also* Appendices II and V.)

---

* It is believed that the Germans intend to give further support to their infantry by means of 7·5-cm. (2·95-in.) guns, mounted on converted light medium (Pz. Kw. III) tanks. These weapons are described as "assault guns" (*Sturmgeschütze*), and their role as that of highly mobile, close support artillery. It is claimed that the guns were successfully used on the Western Front, in the summer of 1940, but the scale of issue to units is not yet known.

† It is believed that the anti-tank company of an infantry regiment may be in process of reorganization into three anti-tank platoons each of four anti-tank guns. One anti-aircraft platoon of four 2-cm. (·79-in.) super-heavy anti-aircraft machine-guns may also be added, but it is not yet established whether these machine-guns have, in fact, been issued.

‡ A limited number of the normal infantry regiments contain a rifle (*Jäger*) battalion in the place of one of their normal battalions. These special rifle battalions are trained in ski-ing and mountain warfare. They contain a mountain gun company armed with four 7·5-cm. (2·95-in.) mountain guns. This company is an integral part of the battalion which is otherwise organized as a normal infantry battalion, but its transport is on a pack basis.

(ii) *Battalion*.—A battalion consists of headquarters, signal section, three rifle companies and one machine-gun company. These companies are numbered consecutively from 1 to 12 throughout the regiment, Nos. 4, 8 and 12 companies being machine-gun companies. (*See* Appendix V.)

(iii) *Rifle company*.—A rifle company consists of headquarters, an anti-tank rifle section armed with three anti-tank rifles, and three platoons. Each of the latter is divided into one light mortar section and four rifle sections; each rifle section includes one light machine-gun and one machine pistol. Platoon and company commanders also carry a machine pistol.

(iv) *Machine-gun company*.—A machine-gun company consists of headquarters, three machine-gun platoons and one mortar platoon. Each machine-gun platoon is divided into two machine-gun sections, each armed with two machine-guns. The mortar platoon consists of three mortar sections, each of two mortar sub-sections, each of one 8·1-cm. (3·16-in.) mortar.

(*See over for strength and armament.*)

Chapter III

(b) *Approximate Strengths.*

	Officers	Other ranks	H.T. 1 or 2-horsed wagons	H.T. 4-horsed wagons	2-horsed field kitchens	M.T. Solo motor-cycles	M.T. M.C. combinations	M.T. 2-seater cars	M.T. 4-seater cross-country cars	M.T. Motor limbers	M.T. Field cookers on lorries	M.T. Lorry workshop	M.T. Lorries (light or medium)
Regt.	95	2,993	1	—	1	4	2	—	—	—	—	—	2
Regtl. H.Q.	6	28	3	—	—	—	—	—	—	—	—	—	1
Reg'tl Sig. Sec.	1	48	—	—	—	—	—	—	—	—	—	—	—
M.C.D.R. Sec.	—	—	—	—	—	—	—	—	—	—	—	—	—
M.I. Pl.	1	31	1	—	1	—	—	—	—	—	—	—	1
Pioneer Platoon	—	—	—	—	—	—	—	—	—	—	—	—	—
Inf. Gun Coy.	5	185	3	11*	—	—	—	—	—	—	—	—	5
Sig. Sec. in Inf. Gun Coy.	—	23	1	2	—	—	—	—	—	—	—	—	—
Lt. Pl. in Inf. Gun Coy.	1	32	—	2	—	—	—	—	—	—	—	—	1
Hy. Pl. in Inf. Gun Coy.	1	34	—	—	—	—	—	—	—	—	—	—	—
A.Tk. Coy.	5	165	—	—	—	16	6	—	11	25	1	1	6
A.Tk. Coy. Sig. Sec.†	—	22	—	—	—	4	2	—	6	—	—	—	—
H.Q. Pl.	1	11	—	—	—	3	1	—	1	—	—	—	—
A.Tk. Pl.	1	34	—	—	—	1	1	—	1	6	—	—	—
Lt. Inf. Col.	2	97	—	—	—	4	—	—	—	—	—	—	3
Bn.	25	813	39	—	5	4	1	—	2	—	—	—	1
Bn. H.Q.	6	15	40	—	—	—	—	—	—	—	—	—	—
Bn. Tpt.	1	28	5	—	1	—	—	—	—	—	—	—	—
Bn. Sig. Sec.	1	38	1	—	—	—	—	—	—	—	—	—	—
Rifle Coy.	4	183	5	—	1	—	—	—	—	—	—	—	—
Rifle Pl.	1	48	1	—	—	—	—	—	—	—	—	—	—
A.Tk. Rifle Sec. in Rifle Coy.	—	7	2	—	—	—	—	—	—	—	—	—	—
M.G. Coy.	5	185	19	—	1	—	—	—	—	—	—	—	—
M.G. Pl.	1	31	—	—	—	—	—	—	—	—	—	—	—
Mortar Pl.	1	64	—	—	—	—	—	—	—	—	—	—	—
M.G. Coy. H.Q.	1	12	—	—	—	—	—	—	—	—	—	—	—
M.G. Coy. Tpt.	—	16	—	—	—	—	—	—	—	—	—	—	—

* This figure does not include six four-horsed and two six-horsed gun limbers.
† It is possible that the A.Tk. company no longer has a signal section.

(In cases where the strength of personnel and/or vehicles is not known, columns have been left blank.)

(c) *Armament.*

	L.M.Gs.†	Hy. M.Gs.†	2-cm. (·79-in.) A. Tk. rifles.	3·7-cm. (1·45-in.) A. Tk. guns.	5-cm. (2-in.) mortars.	8·1-cm. (3·16-in.) mortars.	7·5-cm. (2·95-in.) light infantry guns.	15-cm. (5·91-in.) heavy infantry guns.	Machine pistols.
Regt.	112	36	27	12	27	18	6*	2*	144
Inf. Gun Coy.	—	—	—	—	—	—	6	2	—
Lt. Inf. Gun Pl.	—	—	—	—	—	—	2	—	—
Hy.Inf.Gun.Pl.	—	—	—	—	—	—	—	2	—
A. Tk. Coy.	4	—	—	12	—	—	—	—	—
A. Tk. Pl.	1	—	—	3	—	—	—	—	—
Bn.	36	12	9	—	9	6	—	—	48
Rifle Coy.	12	—	3	—	3	—	—	—	16
Rifle Pl.	4	—	—	—	1	—	—	—	5
A. Tk. Rifle Sec. in Rifle Coy.	—	—	3	—	—	—	—	—	—
M.G. Coy.	—	12	—	—	—	6	—	—	—
M.G. Pl.	—	4	—	—	—	—	—	—	—
Mortar Pl. in M.G. Coy.	—	—	—	—	—	6	—	—	—

* It is believed that the number of light infantry guns in a regiment is to be reduced to four and it is possible that the number of heavy infantry guns will be increased to four.

† Eventually both the light and the heavy machine-gun will be replaced by the dual purpose weapon (M.G. 34) and it is believed that the change has already been made in all active units and in the majority of units formed on and since mobilisation.

3. Organization, strength and armament of a motorized infantry regiment (*motorisiertes Infanterie-Regiment*) in a motorized infantry division

(*a*) *Organization.*—The motorization of eighteen infantry regiments is now complete. Their organization is thought to be similar in general to that of a normal infantry regiment with the following differences:—

(i) The mounted infantry platoon is replaced by a 15th company for purposes of reconnaissance. This company has—

Six* light armoured cars.

Three motor-cyclist platoons.

(ii) The 13th (infantry gun) company is mechanised, the guns being drawn by semi-track tractors.

(*b*) *Strength.*—It is probable that the strength of a motorized infantry regiment will be approximately the same as that of an infantry regiment of the normal type (*see* para. 2 (*b*)). The number of vehicles in this unit is believed to be 334. Semi-track vehicles may eventually be introduced for transport of personnel.

(*c*) *Armament.*—This is the same as for an infantry regiment of normal type (*see* para. 2 (*c*)), with the additions mentioned in (*a*) (i) above.

4. Organization, strength and armament of a lorried infantry regiment (*Schützen-Regiment*) in an armoured division

(*a*) *Organization.*

(i) *Regiment.*—A lorried infantry regiment forms part of the lorried infantry brigade (*Schützen-Brigade*) in an armoured division.

It consists of headquarters (one platoon of four light and two heavy armoured cars and one motorized signal platoon), and two battalions.

---

* It is believed that this number may be increased.

(ii) *Battalion.*—Each battalion consists of headquarters, signal section and five companies, the latter being numbered consecutively from 1 to 10 throughout the regiment.

The five companies of the battalion are :—
- One motor-cyclist company (No. 1).
- Two rifle companies (Nos. 2 and 3). ⎫
- One machine-gun company (No. 4). ⎬ Carried in lorries.
- One " heavy " company (No. 5). ⎭

(iii) *Motor-cyclist company.*—The motor-cyclist company consists of headquarters, three platoons, each of three sections (each of the latter being armed with a machine-gun on a light mounting) ; and one platoon of two sections, each armed with two machine-guns on heavy mountings.

(iv) *Rifle company.*—Each rifle company consists of headquarters and three platoons, each of three sections. Each of the latter is divided into a rifle sub-section and a sub-section armed with a machine-gun on a light mounting. Each section is carried in a Krupp six-wheeled lorry. The machine-guns are in some cases mounted on a narrow platform behind the driving seat.

(v) *Machine-gun company.*—The machine-gun company consists of headquarters, signal section and three platoons. Each platoon is divided into two machine-gun sections, each of two sub-sections, each armed with one machine-gun on heavy mounting.

(vi) *Heavy company.*—The heavy company consists of :—

An anti-tank platoon organized in the same way as the equivalent unit in the anti-tank company of an infantry regiment of the normal type (*see* para. 2 (*a*) (i)).

A close support platoon which is believed to consist of four sections each armed with one 7·5-cm. (2·95-in.) infantry gun. These guns have pneumatic-tyred carriages and are towed behind six-wheeled lorries, as are also the ammunition trailers.

An engineer platoon of three sections, each armed with one machine-gun on a light mounting.

(b) *Approximate Strengths.**

	Officers.	Other ranks.	Motor-cycles.	M.C. combinations.	2-seater cars.	4-seater cars.	6-wheeled lorries or motor limbers.	Vans.	Field cookers on lorries.	Light lorries for repairs, supplies, etc.	Heavy lorries for repairs.	3-ton bridging lorries.	Pontoon trailers.	Ammunition trailers.
Regt.	1	—	—	—	—	—	—	—	—	—	—	6	6	4
Regt. Sig. Sec.	—	—	—	—	—	—	—	—	—	—	—	—	—	—
Bn.	1	—	—	—	—	—	—	—	5	—	1	3	3	2
Bn. Sig. Sec.	—	—	—	—	—	—	—	—	—	—	—	—	—	—
M.C. Coy.	4	152	8	41	—	5	—	—	1	10	—	—	—	—
M.C. Pl. with L.M.Gs.	1	34*	2	9	—	1	—	—	—	1	—	—	—	—
M.C. Pl. with Hy. M.Gs.	—	18	—	10	—	—	—	—	—	—	—	—	—	—
Rifle Coy.	4	174	1	1	—	1	6	—	1	5	—	—	—	—
Rifle Pl.	1	45	—	—	—	—	—	—	—	—	—	—	—	—
M.G. Coy.	4	121	—	—	—	—	—	—	1	5	—	—	—	—
M.G. Pl.	1	31	—	—	—	—	—	—	—	—	—	—	—	—
Hy. Coy.	4	—	3	1	—	1	3	—	1	6	—	—	—	2
A.Tk. Pl.	1	30	1	1	—	1	4	—	—	1	—	—	—	—
Cl. Sup. Pl.	1	32	—	—	—	—	—	—	—	—	—	—	—	2
Eng. Pl.	1	—	—	—	—	—	—	—	—	—	—	3	3	—

* In cases where the strength of personnel and/or vehicles is not known, columns have been left blank.

(c) *Armament.*

	Dual purpose M.Gs. on light mounting.	Dual purpose M.Gs. on heavy mounting.	3·7-cm. (1·45-in.) A.Tk. guns.	7·5-cm. (2·95-in.) Inf. guns.	2-cm. (·79-in.) Super-heavy M.Gs.
Regt. ..	68	32	6	8	2
,, H.Q.	6	—	—	—	2
Bn. ..	31	16	3	4	—
M.C. Coy.	9	4	—	—	—
Rifle Coy.	9	—	—	—	—
M.G. Coy.	—	12	—	—	—
Hy. Coy.	4	—	3	4	—

5. Organization, strength and armament of a mountain rifle regiment (*Gebirgsjäger-Regiment*)

(a) *Organization and strength.*—Mountain rifle regiments are primarily regarded as Alpine troops and are equipped as such. Full details regarding their organization and strength are not available, but they are believed to be organized in the same way as normal infantry regiments (*see* para. 2), except that their transport is almost entirely on a pack basis.

(b) *Armament.*—The only difference in armament between a mountain rifle regiment and an infantry regiment of the normal type (*see* para. 2 (*c*)) lies in the equipment of the 13th Company, which in the case of the former unit is believed to consist of eight 7·5-cm. (2·95-in.) mountain guns.

6. Organization, strength and armament of a motor-cyclist battalion (*Kradschützen-Bataillon*)

(a) *Organization.*

(i) *Battalion.*—A motor-cyclist battalion forms part of the lorried infantry brigade in an armoured division. It consists of headquarters (one platoon of four light and two heavy armoured cars, and one motorized signal platoon), three motor-cyclist rifle companies, one motor-cyclist machine-gun company and one heavy company.

(ii) *Motor-cyclist rifle company.*—A motor-cyclist rifle company is organized in three platoons, each of three sections, each of the latter having one machine-gun on a light mounting; and one machine-gun platoon with two machine-guns on heavy mountings.

(iii) *Motor-cyclist machine-gun company.*—A motor-cyclist machine-gun company consists of headquarters and three platoons, each of two machine-gun sections. Each of the latter is provided with two machine-guns on heavy mountings.

(iv) *Heavy company.*—The heavy company is organized in the same way as the equivalent unit in a lorried infantry regiment in an armoured division (*see* para. 4 (*a*) (vi)).

(See opposite for strength and armament.)

Chapter III

(b) Strength.*

	Officers.	Other ranks.	Motor-cycles.	M.C. combinations.	2-seater cars.	4-seater cars.	6-wheeled lorries or motor limbers for drawing guns.	Field cooker on light lorry.	Light lorries for supplies, repairs, etc.	Heavy lorries for repairs.	3-ton bridging lorries.	Pontoon trailers.	Ammunition trailers.
M.C. Bn.	1	174	8	41	—	5	—	—	10	1	3	3	2
Sig. Sec.	4	45	2	9	—	1	—	1	1	—	—	—	2
M.C. Rifle Coy.	1	—	—	—	—	—	—	—	—	—	—	—	—
Rifle Pl. in Rifle Coy.	—	7	—	—	—	—	—	—	—	—	—	—	—
A.Tk. Rifle Sec. in.	—	—	—	—	1	—	—	1	—	—	—	—	—
Rifle Coy.	4	—	—	—	—	—	—	—	—	—	—	—	—
M.C. M.G. Coy.	1	—	—	—	—	—	—	—	—	—	—	—	—
M.C. M.G. Pl.	4	—	—	—	—	—	—	—	—	—	—	—	—
Hy. Coy.	1	30	3	1	—	1	7	1	6	—	3	3	2
A.Tk. Pl.	1	32	1	1	—	1	3	—	1	—	—	—	—
Cl. Sup. Pl.	1	—	—	—	—	—	—	—	—	—	—	—	2
Eng. Pl.	1	—	—	—	—	—	4	—	—	—	3	3	—

* In cases where the strength of personnel and/or vehicles is not known, columns have been left blank.

(c) *Armament.*

	Dual purpose M.Gs. on light mounting.	Dual purpose M.Gs. on heavy mounting.	3·7-cm. (1·45-in.) A.Tk. guns.	7·5-cm. (2·95-in.) Inf. guns.	2-cm. (·79-in.) Super heavy M.Gs.
M.C. Bn.	37	18	3	4	2
Bn. H.Q.	6	—	—	—	2
M.C. Rifle Coy.	9	2	—	—	—
M.C.M.G. Coy.	—	12	—	—	—
Hy. Coy.	4	—	3	4	—

7. Organization, strength and armament of a motorized machine-gun battalion (*motorisiertes Maschinengewehr-Bataillon*).

(a) *Organization.*

(i) *Battalion.*—A motorized machine-gun battalion consists at present of headquarters, headquarters motor-cyclist platoon, signal section, three machine-gun companies and one anti-tank company. This organization cannot, however, be regarded as being permanent, and the unit may eventually include engineers, armoured cars and infantry guns.

(ii) *Headquarters motor-cyclist platoon.*—Details of this unit, which is used for reconnaissance and inter-communication, are not known. It is armed with three or four machine-guns on light mountings.

(iii) *Machine-gun company.*—A machine-gun company consists of four platoons each armed with four machine-guns. Three of these platoons, armed with dual purpose machine-guns on heavy mountings, are carried in light six-wheeled lorries, and the fourth, armed with dual purpose machine-guns on light mountings, on motor-cycles and sidecars.

(iv) *Anti-tank company.*—The anti-tank company is, it is believed, organized in the same way as the equivalent unit in an infantry regiment of normal type (*see* para. 2 (*a*)).

(b) *Strength.**

	Officers.	Other ranks.	Motor-cycles, medium, solo.	Motor-cycles, heavy, with sidecars.	Passenger cars.
M.G. Bn.	26	964	87	70	181
H.Q. incl. M.G. Pl.	6	104	7	10	33
M.G. Coy.	5	234	22	18	38
A.Tk. Coy.	5	158	14	6	34

(c) *Armament.*

	Dual purpose machine-guns on light mounting.	Dual purpose machine-guns on heavy mounting.	3·7-cm. (1·45-in.) A.Tk. guns.
Bn.	? 20	36	12
H.Q. M.C. Pl.	? 4	—	—
M.G. Coy.	4	12	—
A.Tk. Coy.	4	—	12

8. Frontier infantry regiment (*Grenz-Infanterie-Regiment*)

The organization, strength and armament of a frontier infantry regiment are the same as those of ordinary infantry regiments.

9. Organization of S.S. formations (*see also* Chapter XII, para. 4)

Certain S.S. formations are permanently embodied, and fully trained for military service. They may be divided into two categories :—

(a) The S.S. (*Verfügungstruppen*) of which there are the following regiments—" Leibstandarte Adolf Hitler," " Standarte Germania," " Standarte Deutschland " and " Standarte Der Führer." The last three have been combined into the " S.S. Verfügungsdivision," which is organized, armed and equipped as an ordinary motorized division.

---

* First and second line transport *not* included.

(b) S.S. (*Totenkopf*) units. An "S.S. Totenkopf-Division" is known to have been formed. It is organized, armed and equipped as an ordinary motorized division.

10. Parachute and air-landing units

The Air Force has now taken over all responsibility for the provision and training of men employed in parachute units, and they are now exclusively Air Force personnel.

For further details of parachute and air-landing troops *see* Chapter XV.

11. Organization, strength and armament of a motorized anti-aircraft machine-gun battalion. (*Flugabwehr-Bataillon motorisiert*)*

(a) *Organization*.

(i) *Battalion*.—A motorized anti-aircraft machine-gun battalion consists of headquarters and three machine-gun companies.

(ii) *Machine gun company*.—Each company has three platoons, each of two sections. Each section is armed with two 2-cm. (·79-in.) super-heavy machine-guns (*überschwere M.G.*).

(b) *Strength*.—No details are yet known.

(c) *Armament*.—The battalion has thirty-six 2-cm. (·79-in.) super-heavy M.Gs. (*überschwere M.G.*). These weapons can be used against tanks as well as in their primary role against aircraft.

(d) *Searchlight detachment*.—The battalion is believed to have a searchlight detachment with searchlights of the light 60-cm. (1 ft. 11¼ in.) type.

---

* This was previously known as "Maschinengewehr-Bataillon schwer motorisiert."

To date a number of anti-aircraft machine-gun battalions have been identified and it is believed that they will be provided on the scale of one per division, though it is possible that the present allotment per division may be only one company. Their primary role is A.A. defence, with A.Tk. defence as their secondary role.

12. Regimental specialists

(a) *Assault detachments (Stosstrupps).*

(i) *Personnel.*—These detachments of infantry, specially trained as raiding parties for a particular operation, are composed of carefully selected volunteers from within their company. A typical party consists of one officer, four N.C.Os. and approximately forty other ranks.

(ii) *Arms and equipment.*—All personnel carry respirators if gas is anticipated and each man carries, in addition to his rifle and bayonet, four hand grenades, two in his belt and two in his boots. Each of the four N.C.Os. is armed with a machine pistol. It is believed that three heavy machine guns are placed at the disposal of the detachment by the battalion and two light machine guns are made available by the company. The officer has under his charge two messenger dogs on lead. He carries a Verey pistol, whistle and pocket torch. Other equipment includes wire cutters, gloves, daggers, spades and tent canvas for the removal of dead and wounded men and captured material.

Where the operation demands the destruction of a particular objective, engineers, to the number of about sixteen, may be added to the detachment. They carry pole charges, smoke grenades and flame throwers. All personnel wear a distinctive sign which can be easily seen. (*See also* Chapter VIII, para. 16.)

(b) *Signallers.*—All signallers are trained regimentally. The strengths of the various signal sections, so far as these are known, are given in the paragraphs dealing with the various types of infantry units. Their equipment is shown in para. 16 (*e*).

(c) *Pioneers.*—Approximately one section of each company in an infantry regiment is trained in pioneer duties n the field. Sections can be formed into a battalion pioneer platoon as required, but they do not handle mines or explosives.

(d) *M.T. specialists.*—All drivers of motor transport in infantry units are trained as mechanics and can carry out minor repairs. Mechanics with more specialized knowledge are carried on the repair lorries which accompany the headquarters of companies, battalions and regiments.

(e) *Other specialists.*—All infantry units down to companies include armourers and anti-gas specialists, and battalions include tailors and cobblers.

13. Numbering of units

All infantry regiments (including motorized and frontier infantry, and mountain rifle regiments) are numbered in one continuous series. Except for the mountain rifle (*Gebirgsjäger*) regiments and the rifle battalions included in certain normal infantry regiments they wear white numerals. These mountain rifle units wear green numerals.

Lorried infantry (*Schützen*) regiments and motor-cyclist (*Kradschützen*) battalions are numbered in two different series. When part of an armoured division, both wear pink numerals.

14. Regimental transport

Details, so far as these are known regarding the types and numbers of vehicles in regimental first line transport, are included in the paragraphs dealing with the strength of the various types of infantry units.

First line transport is divided into actual vehicles required for fighting (*Kampffahrzeuge*), battle transport (*Gefechtstross*) which includes unit cookers, baggage transport (*Gepäcktross*) and supply transport (*Verpflegungstross*). The horse portion of the latter carries the current day's rations; the mechanized portion carries the rations for the next day which it has collected from the divisional refilling point.

The second line transport of infantry regiments consists of a light infantry column (*leichte Infanteriekolonne*). It consists of thirty-nine two-horsed wagons with a total capacity of 19 tons. It is organized in a headquarters, an ammunition section and a stores section, and carries ammunition and all stores, except rations, from the divisional refilling point to units.

15. Ammunition supply

The system of ammunition supply is the same as that in the British army, *i.e.*, systematic replacement of ammunition as it is expended. Ammunition comes up from the M.T. echelons in rear to the light infantry column and thence by way of battalion and company reserves to the individual rifleman or machine-gunner.

The following table shows the scale of issue of ammunition:—

Weapon.	On the man or with the gun.	Company and battalion reserve.	Remarks.
Rifle	90 rounds per man in rifle coys. 45 rounds per man in other coys.	40 rounds per man.	
Machine pistol	6 magazines each holding 32 rounds, in ammunition pouches.		
Light machine-gun.	3,100 rounds per gun divided between the gun team and the company and battalion reserve.		The L.M.Gs. in the A.Tk. coy. each have 1,000 rounds.
Heavy machine-gun.	5,250 rounds per gun divided between the company limbers and the battalion reserve.		
Revolver	32 rounds per man.	Not known.	
Grenade	Not known.	Not known.	

16. Equipment

(a) *Personal.*—The weight carried by the infantryman has been considerably reduced as his pack is now carried on a limber.

(b) *Steel Helmet.* (*See* Chapter XIII, para 1 (a).)

(c) *Respirator.* (*See* Chapter X, para. 3 (b) (i).)

(d) *Gas Cape.* (*See* Chapter X, para. 3 (b) (ii).)

(e) *Signal Equipment.*—The telephone and wireless equipment carried by an infantry regiment of normal type is given below. It is probable that approximately the same amount

Chapter III

is carried by a motorized infantry regiment and a mountain rifle regiment.

	Medium cable (miles).	Light cable (miles).	Exchanges.	Field Telephones.	Pack Wireless Sets.	Medium Lamps.	Small Lamps.	Messenger Dogs.
Regt. Sig. Sec.	9	5	4	12	4	2	—	
Inf. Gun Coy.		8		12				
A.Tk. Coy...	—	2½	—	4	5	—	—	—
Rifle Bn. Sig. Sec.	—	5	4	6	4	4	—	3
Rifle Coy.	—	—	—	—	—	—	2	—
M.G. Coy.	—	8	4	6	—	—	2	—
M.C. Bn.	5	5	1?	5	2			

Details of the above equipment are given in Chapter IX.

It is not at present known what telephone and wireless equipment is carried by a lorried infantry regiment in an armoured division, a motor-cyclist battalion, a motorized machine-gun battalion, a frontier battalion, or a fortress battalion.

In addition to telephone and wireless equipment, the following signal equipment is also provided :—

   (i) White strips for communication with aircraft, with a red back for use on snow. (*See* Appendix XLIX.)

   (ii) Flares to show the positions of the leading infantry.

   (iii) Verey pistols with red, white, green, yellow and other coloured lights.

   (iv) Red and white signalling discs.

All the above are used in accordance with recognized codes. (i) and (ii) are issued down to and including headquarters of companies; (iii) and (iv) down to and including headquarters of platoons.

(*f*) *Tools.*—Every infantryman carries an entrenching tool of some kind. Details regarding the reserves of tools carried on the company, battalion and regimental vehicles are not at present known.

(g) *Rangefinder*.—This is of the "inverted image" type and is similar to that in use in machine-gun battalions in the British army.

(h) *Bivouacs*.—Each infantryman has a camouflaged coloured waterproof sheet complete with poles, pegs and cords. A number of these sheets can be fastened together to make improvised shelters or tents.

(i) *Engineer Equipment*.—Six large and six small pneumatic boats are carried in the vehicles of the engineer platoon of a motor-cyclist battalion and of each battalion of a lorried infantry regiment in an armoured division.

Pneumatic boats are also carried by other infantry units, but the number and types are not at present known.

(j) *Anti-A.F.V. Equipment*.—Each anti-tank platoon carries twelve rolls of concertina wire for road blocks.

Chapter III

APPENDIX II

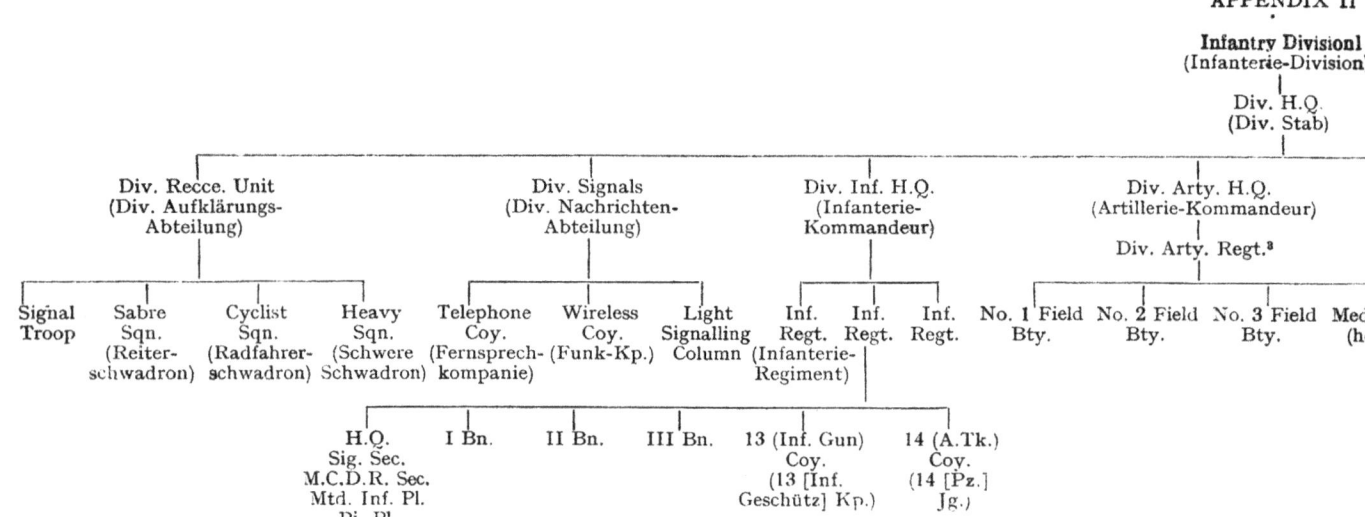

Infantry Division1
(Infanterie-Division)

Div. H.Q.
(Div. Stab)

- Div. Recce. Unit (Div. Aufklärungs-Abteilung)
  - Signal Troop
  - Sabre Sqn. (Reiterschwadron)
  - Cyclist Sqn. (Radfahrerschwadron)
  - Heavy Sqn. (Schwere Schwadron)
- Div. Signals (Div. Nachrichten-Abteilung)
  - Telephone Coy. (Fernsprechkompanie)
  - Wireless Coy. (Funk-Kp.)
  - Light Signalling Column
- Div. Inf. H.Q. (Infanterie-Kommandeur)
  - Inf. Regt. (Infanterie-Regiment)
    - H.Q.
      Sig. Sec.
      M.C.D.R. Sec.
      Mtd. Inf. Pl.
      Pi. Pl.
    - I Bn.
    - II Bn.
    - III Bn.
    - 13 (Inf. Gun) Coy. (13 [Inf. Geschütz] Kp.)
    - 14 (A.Tk.) Coy. (14 [Pz.] Jg.)
  - Inf. Regt.
  - Inf. Regt.
- Div. Arty. H.Q. (Artillerie-Kommandeur)
  - Div. Arty. Regt.[3]
    - No. 1 Field Bty.
    - No. 2 Field Bty.
    - No. 3 Field Bty.
    - Med

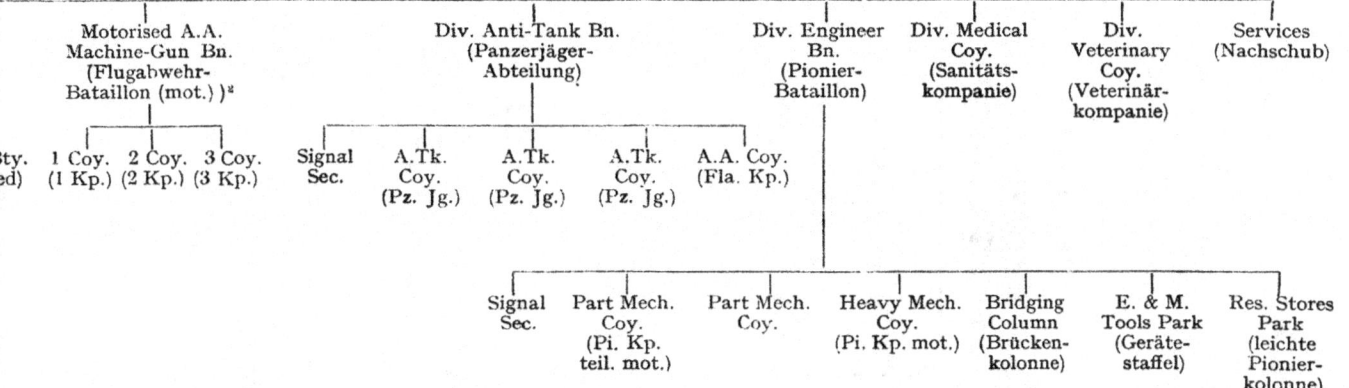

Notes:—

[1] This diagram shows what is considered to be the theoretical organization of an infantry division at the present time. New formation divisions may not all be organized on this basis, but it is believed to be the intention that all divisions will be organized and equipped on this basis.

[2] It has not yet been definitely established whether it is intended to include one of these units in each division, or whether they are to remain G.H.Q. troops.

[3] In some divisions the peace-time organization of one field regiment of three horsed batteries and one medium regiment of one horsed and one mechanized battery, may have been retained

APPENDIX III

APPROXIMATE STRENGTH IN PERSONNEL AND VEHICLES (H.T. AND M.T.) OF AN INFANTRY DIVISION

	Officers.	O.Rs.	Motor Cycles.	Motor Vehicles.	Horsed Transport.	Horses.
Divisional H.Q.	12	140	12	26	—	20
Divisional Recce. Unit	15	560	30	30	3	213
Divisional Signals	15	456	28	102	7	56
Divisional Inf. H.Q.	4					
Divisional Infantry	285	8,997	135	210	612	1,440
Divisional Artillery H.Q.						
Divisional Artillery	89	2,156	12	23	178	1,785
Divisional Anti-Tank Bn.	20	770	80	170	—	—
Divisional Engineer Bn.	20	667	26	53	19	52
Divisional Medical Coy.	15	463	17	86		50
Divisional Veterinary Coy.	6	228	—	—		188
Services (units of which strength known)	16	515	16	340		—
Total	497	14,952	356	1,040	819	3,804
*Motorized A.A.M.G. Bn.	21	800	137	147	—	—

* It has not yet been definitely established whether it is intended to include one of these units in each division, or whether they are to remain G.H.Q. troops.

APPENDIX IV

FIRE POWER OF AN INFANTRY DIVISION

	Div. Recce. Unit.	Div. Inf.	Div. Arty.	Mot. M.G. Bn. (A.A.).[1]	Div. A.Tk. Bn.	Div. Eng. Bn.	Total.
Machine pistols (excl. those in armoured cars)	—	432	—	—	—	—	432
Machine guns, light mounting	24	336	24	—	18	28	430
Machine guns, heavy mounting	8	108	—	—	—	—	116
2-cm. (·79-in.) A.Tk. rifles	—	81	—	—	—	—	81
2-cm. (·79-in.) A.A. and A.Tk. guns	—	12 [a]	24	36	12	—	84
3·7-cm. (1·45-in.) A.Tk. guns	3	36	—	—	36	—	75
5-cm. (2-in.) mortars	3	81	—	—	—	—	84
8·1-cm. (3·16-in.) mortars (see note [3])	3 [3]	54	—	—	—	—	57
7·5-cm. (2·95-in.) infantry guns	2	18	—	—	—	—	20
15-cm. (5·91-in.) infantry guns	—	6	—	—	—	—	6
10·5-cm. (4·14-in.) gun-howitzers	—	—	36	—	—	—	36
10·5-cm. (4·14-in.) guns	—	—	4	—	—	—	4
15-cm. (5·91-in.) howitzers	—	—	8	—	—	—	8

Notes.—[1] It has not yet been definitely established whether it is intended to include one of these units per division, or whether they are to remain G.H.Q. troops. The 2-cm. (·79-in.) super-heavy A.A.M.G.s can also be used for an anti-tank role.

[2] The existence of three 8·1-cm. (3·16-in.) mortars in the div. recce. unit is not confirmed.

[3] The issue of four 2 cm. (·79-in.) A.A. and A.Tk. guns to the A.Tk. coy. of the infantry regiment has not yet been confirmed.

Chapter III

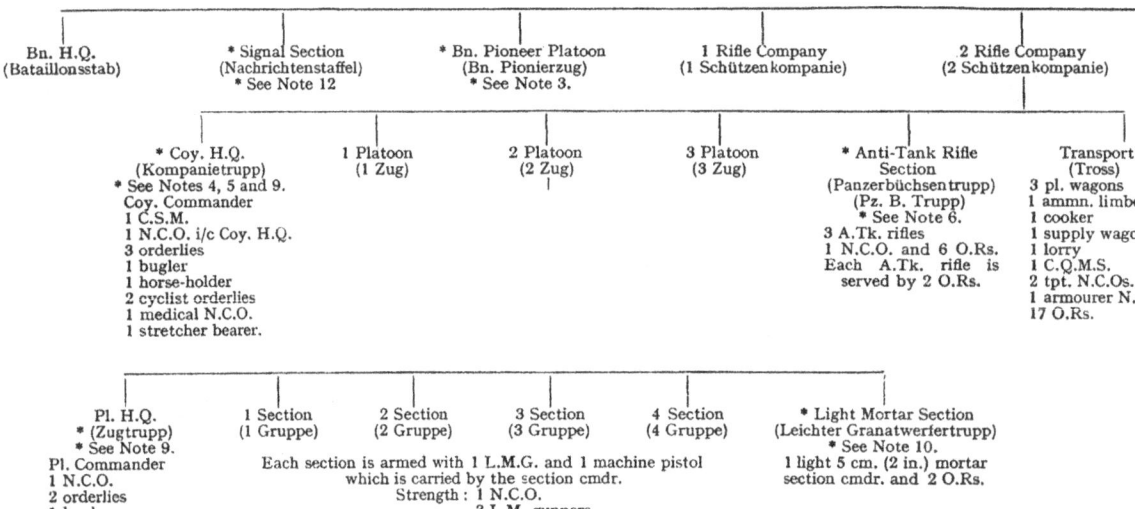

| Bn. H.Q. (Bataillonsstab) | * Signal Section (Nachrichtenstaffel) * See Note 12 | * Bn. Pioneer Platoon (Bn. Pionierzug) * See Note 3. | 1 Rifle Company (1 Schützenkompanie) | 2 Rifle Company (2 Schützenkompanie) |

Under 1 Rifle Company:

- * Coy. H.Q. (Kompanietrupp) * See Notes 4, 5 and 9.
  - Coy. Commander
  - 1 C.S.M.
  - 1 N.C.O. i/c Coy. H.Q.
  - 3 orderlies
  - 1 bugler
  - 1 horse-holder
  - 2 cyclist orderlies
  - 1 medical N.C.O.
  - 1 stretcher bearer.
- 1 Platoon (1 Zug)
- 2 Platoon (2 Zug)
- 3 Platoon (3 Zug)
- * Anti-Tank Rifle Section (Panzerbüchsentrupp) (Pz. B. Trupp) * See Note 6.
  - 3 A.Tk. rifles
  - 1 N.C.O. and 6 O.Rs.
  - Each A.Tk. rifle is served by 2 O.Rs.
- Transport (Tross)
  - 3 pl. wagons
  - 1 ammn. limber
  - 1 cooker
  - 1 supply wagon
  - 1 lorry
  - 1 C.Q.M.S.
  - 2 tpt. N.C.Os.
  - 1 armourer N.C.
  - 17 O.Rs.

Under 1 Platoon:

- Pl. H.Q. * (Zugtrupp) * See Note 9.
  - Pl. Commander
  - 1 N.C.O.
  - 2 orderlies
  - 1 bugler
  - 1 stretcher bearer
- 1 Section (1 Gruppe)
- 2 Section (2 Gruppe)
- 3 Section (3 Gruppe)
- 4 Section (4 Gruppe)

Each section is armed with 1 L.M.G. and 1 machine pistol which is carried by the section cmdr.
Strength: 1 N.C.O.
3 L.M. gunners.
6 riflemen.

- * Light Mortar Section (Leichter Granatwerfertrupp) * See Note 10.
  - 1 light 5 cm. (2 in.) mortar section cmdr. and 2 O.Rs.

Strength (approx.).
Rifle Coy. = 4 officers, 183 O.Rs.
M.G. Coy. = 5 officers, 185 O.Rs.
Bn. H.Q. = 6 officers, 15 O.Rs.
Bn. Signal Section = 1 officer, 38 O.Rs.
Bn. Tpt. = 1 officer (M.O.), 26 O.Rs.

Battalion = 25 officers, 813 O.Rs.

Vehicles (approx.).
(a) *Horsed*—
One or two-horsed wagons 40
Field kitchens 5
(b) *Mechanised*—
Motor-cycles, solo 4
Motor-cycle, side-car 1
Cars 2
Light lorries 6

Fire Power.
Machine pistols 48
M.Gs. on light mountings 36
M.Gs. on heavy mounting 12
Anti-tank rifles 9
Light mortars, 5 cm. (2 in.) 9
Mortars, 8·1 cm. (3·16 in.) 6

APPENDIX V

Infantry Battalion
(Infanterie-Bataillon)

See Notes 1 and 2

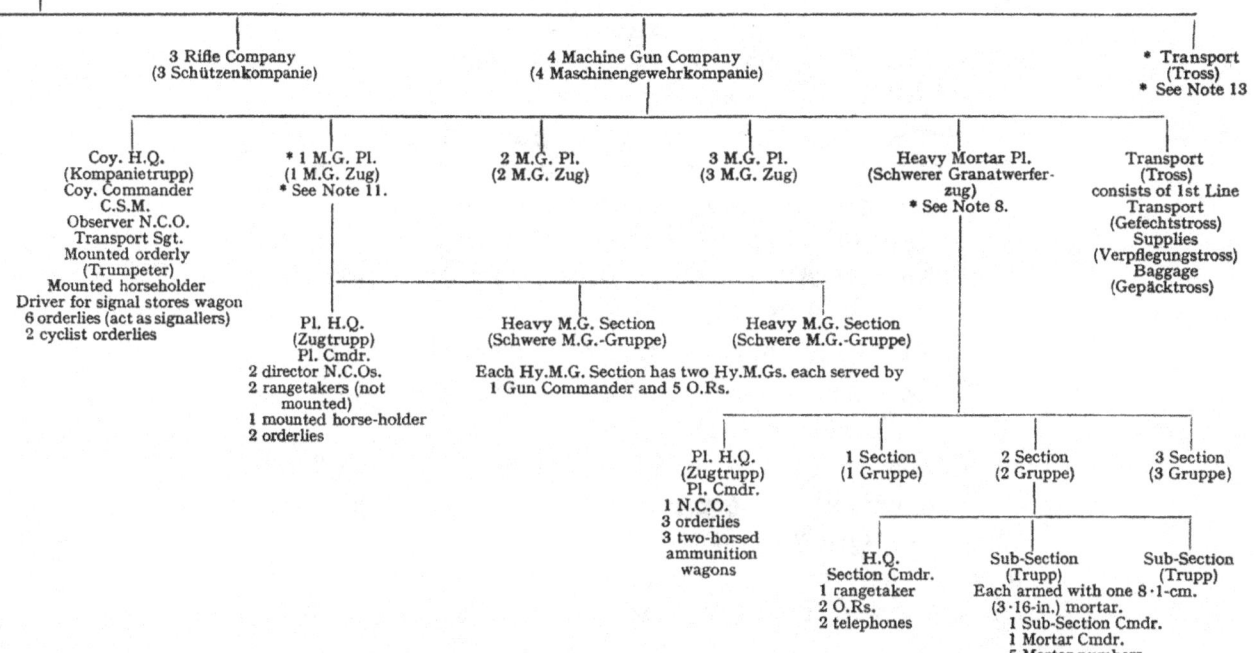

Notes:—

1. This diagram incorporates the changes that have taken place in the organization of the rifle company (*Schützenkompanie*) and of the machine-gun company (*M.G.-Kompanie*) as laid down in the addenda, dated 13 Oct., 1939, to H. Dv. 130/2b and H. Dv. 130/3a (German Army Manuals).
2. The companies are numbered consecutively throughout the regiment, 4, 8 and 12 being the machine-gun companies.
3. The pioneer platoon is formed as and when required from personnel within the battalion who are trained in pioneer duties; each coy. usually provides one section; the pioneer platoon normally carries no mines or explosives.
4. As bn. H.Q. have six cyclists the coy. H.Qs. will therefore not provide cyclist service to bn. H.Q.
5. There is no signal personnel included in a rifle coy. H.Q., signallers being allotted to companies from the bn. signal section as required.
6. The A.Tk. rifles are only used at ranges up to 300 yards; they may be placed under the command of the platoons in action.
7. Each rifle company has three heavy mountings for the light M.Gs. in the company; these are taken out only when specially ordered and are distributed among the platoons considered most suitable.
8. The mortars of the mortar platoon of the M.G. coy. are usually placed under the command of the forward rifle coys. in action; each mortar together with 48 rounds carried in a one-horse two-wheeled cart.
9. Company and platoon commanders and section commanders in rifle coys. are armed with a machine pistol, which is carried by the bugler until action takes place.
10. On the march the 5-cm. light mortar is carried on the platoon wagon together with 20 rounds.
11. The four Hy.M.Gs. of the M.G. platoon are carried on two 2-horsed M.G. limbers fitted with twin A.A. mountings; the ammunition is carried in a 2-horsed wagon.
12. The bn. signal section includes: two small telephone sub-sections (*kl. Fernsprechtrupps " a "*), four pack wireless sub-sections (*Tornisterfunktrupps " d "*), two small lamp sub-sections (*kl. Blinktrupps*), one messenger dog sub-section (*Meldehundtrupp*).
13. Consists of 1st line transport "A" echelon (*Gefechtstross*), 1st line transport "B" échelon (*Verpflegungstross I*), supply transport (*Verpflegungstross II*), baggage transport (*Gepäcktross*). Strength about 26 O.Rs.; an assistant M.O. is stated to be on strength of transport.

CHAPTER IV

CAVALRY AND RECONNAISSANCE UNITS

1. General organization and strength

Shortly after the outbreak of war, all armoured and cavalry units were given the official designation of " mobile troops " (*schnelle Truppen*). These include the following :—

    Tank regiments (*Panzer-Regimenter*). (See Chapter VII, Sec. B, paras. 3 and 4.)

    Anti-tank units (*Panzerjäger-Abteilungen*). (See Chapter VII, Sec. C, para. 9.)

    Lorried infantry regiments and lorried infantry brigades of armoured divisions (*motorisierte Schützen-Regimenter* and *Schützen-Brigaden*). (See Chapter III, para. 4.)

    Motor-cyclist battalions (*Kradschützen-Bataillone*). (See Chapter III, para. 6.)

    Cyclist units (*Radfahrer-Abteilungen*).*

    Divisional reconnaissance units (*Divisions-Aufklärungs-Abteilungen*).

    Horsed cavalry regiments† (*Reiter-Regimenter*).

    Mechanized reconnaissance units (*motorisierte Aufklärungs-Abteilungen*).

Only the last four are dealt with in this chapter, other " mobile troops " being included in the chapters shown.

2. Organization, strength and armament of a horsed cavalry regiment (*Reiter-Regiment*)

(*a*) *Organization*—A horsed cavalry regiment consists of headquarters, a mechanized headquarters squadron, four horsed sabre squadrons and one horsed machine-gun squadron.

Details of the regiment's organization are shown in Appendix VI.

---

  * Excluding cyclist home defence battalions (*Radfahrer-Wachbataillone*) and cyclist battalions in mountain divisions.

  † The mounted infantry platoons (*Reiterzüge*) of infantry regiments do not form part of the cavalry arm.

(b) *Strength**—

	Officers.	Other ranks.	Horses.	4-horsed limbers.	H.T. 4-horsed field kitchens.	4-horsed field smithies.	Ammunition trailers.	4-seater cars.	Signal lorries.	Motor limbers.	M.T. Armoured cars.	2-seater cars.*	Solo M.C.	M.C. combinations.	Light lorries.
Regt.															
H.Q. Sqn.				–	–	–					6	3			
Sig. Tp.				–	–	–					–	3			
Eng. Tp.	1	56	–	–	–	–	–	4	–	–	–	–	3	1	5
Recce. Tp.				–	–	–				3					
A.Tk. Tp.	1	30	–	–	–	–	–	1	–	3	–	–	3	1	1
Cav. Gun Tp.	1	32	–	–	–	–	–	–	–	3	–	–	1	1	2
Sabre Sqn.	4	201	213	1	1	1	–	–	–	–	–	–	–	–	–
Sabre Tp.	1	51	52	–	–	–	–	–	–	–	–	–	–	–	–
M.G. Tp. in Sabre Sqn.	–	27	37	–	–	–	–	–	–	–	–	–	–	–	–
M.G. Sqn.					1	1	–	–	–	–	–	–	–	–	–
M.G. Tp.					–	–									

(c) *Armament*—

	Dual purpose M.Gs. on light mountings.	Dual purpose M.Gs. on heavy mountings.	3·7-cm. (1·45-in.) A.Tk. guns.	7·5-cm. (2·95-in.) Cav. guns.
Regt.	40	20	3	2
H.Q. Sqn.	4	—	3	2
Sabre Sqn.	9	2	—	—
M.G. Sqn.	—	12	—	—

* In cases where the strength of personnel and/or vehicles is not known, columns have been left blank.

3. Organization, strength and armament of a mechanized reconnaissance unit (*motorisierte Aufklärungs-Abteilung*)

(a) *Organization.*—

(i) *General.*—These units form part of the cavalry division, armoured divisions, and motorized infantry divisions, and are also employed as G.H.Q. troops.

(ii) *Mechanized reconnaissance unit.*—In an armoured division each unit consists of :—
>Headquarters.
>Signal troop.
>Two armoured car squadrons.
>One motor-cycle rifle squadron.
>One heavy squadron.
>Light ammunition column.

For details of organization, *see* Appendix XVIII.

In a motorized division, the composition is the same, except that there is only one armoured car squadron and no heavy squadron. It is thought, however, that this organization is only temporary, and the composition may, therefore, have been increased. Alternatively, mechanized reconnaissance units of motorized divisions may be temporarily reinforced for particular operations.*

(b) *Strength*†—

	Officers.	Other ranks.	Heavy armoured cars.	Light and super-light armoured cars.	Motor-cycles.	M.C. combinations.	2-seater cars.	4-seater cars.	Signal lorries.	Motor limbers.	Field kitchens on lorries.	Light lorries (for supplies, repairs, etc.).	Heavy lorries.	Light lorries (for personnel).	Ammunition trailers.
Mech. Recce. Unit	30	701	12	42									6		2
Sig. Tp.	1		–	–		4		6	–	–		4	–	–	–
Armd. C. Sqn.	5		6	21				1	–	–	1	–	–	2	–
Mixed Tp.	1		2	3				–	–	–	–	–	–	–	–
Lt. Tp.	1		–	9				–	–	–	–	–	–	–	–
M.C. Sqn.	4	152	–	–	8	41	–	5	–	–	1	10	–	–	–
M.C. Tp. with L.M.Gs.	1	34	–		2	9	–	1	–	–	–	1	–	–	–
M.C. Half-Tp. with hy.M.Gs,	–	18	–	–	–	10	–	–	–	–	–	–	–	–	–
Hy. Sqn.	4		–	–					–	6	1				2
A.Tk. Tp.	1	30	–	–	3	1	–	1	–	3	–	1	–	–	–
Cav. Gun Tp.	1	32	–	–	1	1	–	–	–	3	–	–	–	2	1
Eng. Tp.	1	56	–	–	3	1	–	4	–	–	–	–	–	5	–
Mortar Tp.															

* The term "armoured reconnaissance unit" (*Panzer-Aufklärungs-Abteilung*) also occurs. It is thought to be an alternative term for the mechanized reconnaissance unit of an armoured division.

† In cases where the strength of personnel and/or vehicles is not known, columns have been left blank.

(c) *Armament—*

	Dual purpose M.Gs. on light mountings.	Dual purpose M.Gs. on heavy mountings.	2-cm. (·79-in.) super-heavy machine guns.	3·7-cm. (1·45-in.) A.Tk. guns.	7·5-cm. (2·95-in.) cav. guns.	8·1-cm. (3·16-in.) mortars.	5-cm. (2-in.) light mortars.
Mech. Recce. Unit	63	6	12	3	2	3	3
Armd. C. Sqn. ...	24	1	6	—	—	—	—
M.C. Sqn.	9	4	—	—	—	—	3
Hy. Sqn.	6	—	—	3	2	3	—

4. Organization, strength and armament of an infantry divisional reconnaissance unit (*Divisions-Aufklärungs-Abteilung*)*

(a) *Organization.*—A unit consists of :—
  Headquarters.
  Signal troop.
  Sabre squadron.
  Cyclist squadron.
  Heavy squadron.

Details of the unit's organization are given in Appendix VII.

(b) *Strength†—*

	Officers.	O.Rs.	Horses.	H.T. 4-horsed limbers.	H.T. 4-horsed field kitchens.	H.T. 4-horsed field smithies.	M.T. Bicycles.	M.T. Motor limbers.	M.T. 4-seater cars.	M.T. 2-seater cars.	M.T. Armd. cars.	M.T. Solo M.C.s.	M.T. M.C. combinations.	M.T. Light lorries.	M.T. Field kitchens on lorries.
Inf. div. recce. unit.															
H.Q. and Sig. Tp.															
Sabre Sqn.	4	201	213	1	1	1									
Cyclist Sqn. ...	4	177					126	1				2	20	5	1
Heavy Sqn. ...															

* These units were formed on mobilization from the corps cavalry regiment (*Kavallerie-Regiment*).

† In cases where the strength of personnel and/or vehicles is not known, columns have been left blank.

(c) *Armament*—

	Dual purpose M.Gs. on light mountings.	Dual purpose M.Gs. on heavy mountings.	3·7-cm. (1·45-in.) A.Tk. guns.	5-cm. (2-in.) mortars.	8·1-cm. (3·16-in.) mortars.	7·5-cm. (2·95-in.) cavalry guns.
Inf. div. recce. unit	24	8	3	3	3	2
H.Q. and Sig. Tp. ...	—	—	—	—	—	—
Sabre Sqn. ...	9	2	—	—	—	—
Cyclist Sqn.	9	2	—	3	—	—
Heavy Sqn.	6	4	3	—	3	2
M.G. Tp. ..	—	4	—	—	—	—
Cavalry Gun Tp.	2	—	—	—	—	2
A.Tk. Tp.	1	—	3	—	—	—
Armd. Car Tp. ..	3	—	—	—	—	—
Mortar Tp. ...	—	—	—	—	3	—

5. Organization, strength and armament of a cyclist battalion (*Radfahrer-Bataillon*)

(a) *Organization*—

(i) *Battalion.*—The cyclist battalion forms part of the cavalry division (*see* Chapter I, para. 11), and consists of headquarters, signal troop, three cyclist squadrons and one motor-cycle squadron.

(ii) *Cyclist squadron.*—The organization of this unit is the same as its equivalent in an infantry divisional reconnaissance unit (*see* para. 4 (*a*) and Appendix VII).

(iii) *Motor-cyclist squadron.*—The organization of this unit is the same as its equivalent in a mechanized reconnaissance unit (*see* para. 3 (*a*) (ii) and Appendix XVIII).

(b) *Strength**—

	Officers.	Other ranks.	Bicycles.	Motor-cycles.	M.C. combinations.	4-seater cars.	Field kitchens on lorries.	Light lorries (for supplies, repairs, etc.)
Cyclist Bn.								
Sig. Tp.	1	24	—	—	—	—	—	—
Cyclist Sqn.	4	177	126	2	20	1	1	5
Cyclist Tp. ..	1	50	42	—	4	—	—	1
M.G. Tp. in Cyclist Sqn.	—	19	—	—	8	—	—	1
M.C. Sqn.	4	152	—	8	41	5	1	10
M.C. Tp. with L.M.G.s ..	1	34	—	2	9	1	—	1
M.C. Half-Tp. with Hy.M.Gs.	—	18	—	—	10	—	—	—

* In cases where the strength of personnel and/or vehicles is not known, columns have been left blank.

(c) *Armament*—

	Dual purpose M.Gs. on light mountings.	Dual purpose M.Gs. on heavy mountings.	5-cm. (2-in.) mortars.
Cyclist Bn. ..	36	8	9
Cyclist Sqn.	9	2	3
M.C. Sqn.	9	2	—

Chapter IV

6. Numbering of units

Horsed cavalry regiments, cyclist units, divisional reconnaissance units and mechanised reconnaissance units are numbered in separate series.

The horsed cavalry regiments and cyclist units wear yellow numerals. Reconnaissance units wear pink numerals with the letter "K" or "S."

7. Regimental specialists

(a) *Signallers.*—All signallers are trained regimentally. The strengths of the signal sections, so far as is known, are given in the paragraphs dealing with the various types of cavalry units. Such details of their equipment as are available are given in para. 10 (f).

(b) *M.T. Specialists.*—All men in mechanized cavalry units are trained as mechanics and can carry out minor repairs. Mechanics with more specialized knowledge are carried on the repair lorries which accompany the squadron and regimental headquarters of mechanized units.

(c) *Other Specialists.*—All cavalry units, down to and including squadrons, include armourers and anti-gas specialists. Horsed squadrons are also provided with farriers.

8. Regimental transport

Details, as far as these are known, regarding the types and numbers of vehicles in regimental first-line transport, are included in the paragraphs dealing with the strength of the various types of cavalry units.

First line transport is divided into actual vehicles required for fighting (*Kampffahrzeuge*), battle transport (*Gefechtstross*), which includes unit cookers, baggage transport (*Gepäcktross*) and supply transport (*Verpflegungstross*). The horsed portion of the latter carries the current day's rations, the mechanized portion carries the rations for the next day which it has collected from the divisional refilling point.

The second-line transport of cavalry regiments in war consists of a light cavalry column. This column, which is fully mechanized, carries ammunition and stores of all kinds, except rations, from the divisional refilling point to units.

9. Ammunition supply

It is believed that men armed with the carbine each carry seventy-five rounds of ammunition in their pouches and saddle wallet.

10. Equipment

(a) *Personal.*—See Chapter XIII, para. 1.

(b) *Saddlery.*—The cavalry saddle is similar to the British universal pattern type. It weighs twenty-one pounds stripped and is used with a saddle blanket. Appointments include nosebag, wallets and a bucket taking the butt of the carbine. The weight of the saddle complete is thirty-two pounds.

(c) *Steel helmet.*—See Chapter XIII, para. 1 (a). The badges worn are shown in Plate 78.

(d) *Respirator.*—See Chapter X, para. 3 b (i).

(e) *Gas cape.*—See Chapter X, para. 3 (b) (ii).

(f) *Signal equipment.*—Cavalry signal units are equipped as follows:—

	Pack wireless sets.	Long range wireless sets.
Sig. tp. in horsed cav. regt.	4	—
Sig. tp. in div. recce. unit	4	—
Sig. tp. in cyclist bn.	4	—
Sig. sec. in mech. recce. unit	4	4

Details of the types of W/T sets used are given in Chapter IX, Appendices XXXIII and XXXIV.

The following signal equipment is also provided for cavalry units:—

(i) Red and white strips for communication with aircraft (*see* Appendix XLIX).

(ii) Flares to show positions of leading troops.

(iii) Verey pistols with red, green, white and other coloured lights.

(iv) Red and white signalling discs.

All these means of communication are used in accordance with recognized codes. (i) and (ii) are issued down to and including headquarters of squadrons, (iii) and (iv) down to headquarters of troops.

(g) *Tools.*—No information is at present available regarding the number and distribution of tools in cavalry units.

(h) *Rangefinder.*—See Chapter III, para. 16 (g).

(*i*) *Bivouacs.*—For description of the bivouac sheet in use, *see* Chapter III, para. 16 (*h*). This sheet is carried on the saddle.

(*j*) *Engineer equipment.*—Six large and six small pneumatic boats of the type described in Chapter VIII are carried in the vehicles of the engineer platoon of the heavy company of a mechanized reconnaissance unit.

Pneumatic boats are also carried by engineer troops in other cavalry units, but no details as to number and types are at present known.

(*k*) *Anti-A.F.V. equipment.*—It is believed that each cavalry anti-tank platoon carries twelve rolls of concertina wire for road blocks.

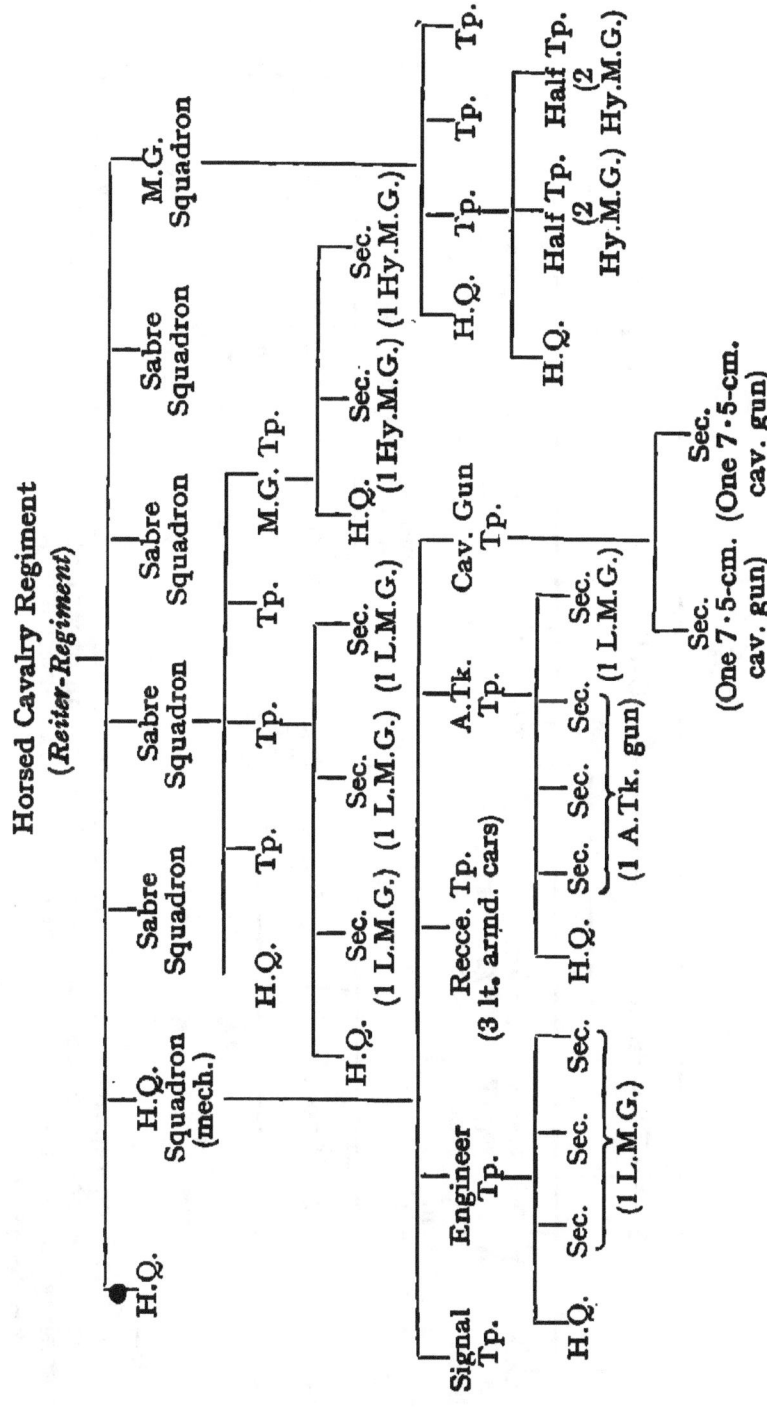

Chapter IV

APPENDIX VII

Infantry Divisional Reconnaissance Unit

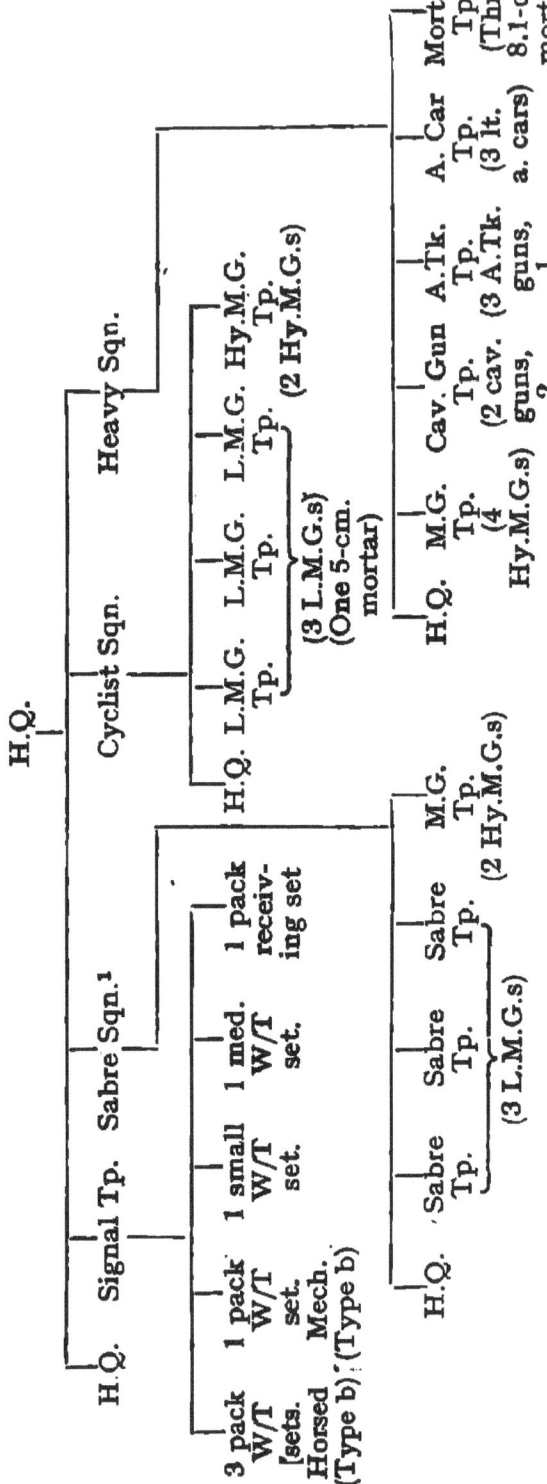

Notes :—

[1] It has been reported that the sabre squadron has been in some cases replaced by an additional cyclist squadron. It is not yet known whether this change in organization is general or whether it is an isolated case, due possibly to a shortage of horses or of trained horsemen.

[2] Existence not confirmed.

CHAPTER V

SMALL ARMS, CLOSE SUPPORT AND ANTI-TANK WEAPONS

1. Carbine, rifle and bayonet

(a) *Carbine.*—There are two types of carbine, known as "Karabiner 98b" and "Karabiner 98k" respectively. Both of these have a calibre of ·79-cm. (·31-in.) and are sighted up to 2,200 yards. The former type is 4 ft. 1¼ in. long and weighs 9 lb. and the latter 3 ft. 7¼ in. long and weighs 8·58 lb. (*see* Plates 1 and 2).

(b) *Rifle.*—The rifle is known as "Gewehr 98." It has a calibre of ·79-cm. (·31-in.) and is sighted up to 2,200 yards. Its weight is 9 lb., and it is 4 ft. 1¼ in. long (*see* Plate 3).

A new rifle is now in production. It is 4 inches shorter than the "Gewehr 98," is lighter and has a shorter bayonet. It is sighted up to 2,750 yards.

(c) *Bayonet.*—The bayonet is the sword pattern known as "Seitengewehr 84/98." It is 1 ft. 3 in. long and weighs 1 lb. 4 oz.

2. Pistol and machine-pistols

(a) *Pistol.*—The pistol is the 1908 pattern, known as "Pistole 08." Its calibre is ·9-cm. (·35-in.) and its weight 1 lb. 14½ oz. It is semi-automatic and its magazine holds eight cartridges.

(b) *Machine-pistols.*—The types in most general use are the "Schmeisser" machine-pistol 28/11 and the "Steyer Solothurn S.1–100." Other types in less general use are the "Neuhausen," the "Erma" and the "Bergmann." Details of these weapons are given in Appendix VIII. (*See also* Plates 4, 5, 6 and 7.)

3. Light machine-guns

(a) *Dreyse L.M.G.* 13. (*See* Plate 8.)—Until recently the machine-gun in universal use in the German Army. It may still be found in some units and in reserve and "Landwehr" formations. Its calibre is ·79-cm. (·31-in.) and its weight with mounting 26 lb. The feed is by magazines holding twenty-five rounds. It operates by recoil action and is air-cooled. The barrel has to be changed after 150 to 200 rounds have been fired at a rapid rate. The normal rate of fire of this weapon is 150 rounds per minute, but it can be made to fire single shots by pressing the top part of the trigger. Only direct fire is possible. It is normally mounted on a light adjustable bipod, but can be mounted on a tripod for anti-aircraft use. It is believed to have been replaced by the dual purpose machine-gun described in para. 4 below.

(b) *L.M.G. 08/15.*—Some units are still armed with an obsolescent water-cooled machine-gun, known as L.M.G. 08/15. This weapon is believed to have been replaced by the dual purpose machine-gun described in para. 4 below.

(c) *Knorr-Bremse.*—This light machine-gun is also presumed to be in service with the German Army. It is of ·79-cm. (·31-in.) calibre, weight with mounting 22 lb., overall length 4 ft. 2 in. The capacity of the magazine is 25 rounds and its weight when full 2·3 lb. A rate of fire of from 500 to 2,000 rounds is claimed, but the practical rate of fire is considerably lower, as the barrel has to be changed after 200 rounds continuous fire, 250 rounds intermittent fire, or after 300 rounds firing in bursts with long pauses.

4. Dual purpose machine-gun. (*See* Plates 9, 10 and 11)

A new dual purpose machine-gun, known as M.G. 34, has been introduced and is replacing, throughout the whole army, both the light machine-guns described in para. 3 and the heavy machine-gun described in para. 5.

This weapon can be mounted on a bipod for use as a light machine-gun or on a tripod for use as a heavy machine-gun. This tripod can be adjusted so that the gun can be employed as an anti-aircraft weapon.

This weapon, which has a calibre of ·79-cm. (·31-in.) resembles the light machine-gun, but is more strongly made and has a different method of loading. It has a metal belt consisting of ten strips each holding twenty-five cartridges. The strips are joined by means of a cartridge which, when removed, is sufficient to disconnect them. These belts are extremely flexible. For anti-aircraft fire special bands on a drum are used. The weight of this machine-gun, without mounting, is 15½ lb. It is provided with a telescopic sight.

The maximum range of this machine-gun on the bipod mounting is 2,200 yards ;. on the tripod mounting, using the telescopic sight, its maximum range is 3,800 yards.

The gun fires at a rate of 900 rounds per minute, but in practice the maximum rate of fire on a bipod is 110-120 rounds per minute and on a tripod 300-350 rounds per minute. It is air-cooled and the barrel has to be changed after 250 rounds have been fired continuously.

5. Heavy machine-gun. (*See* Plates 12 and 13)

The heavy machine-gun, which is known as *M.G.* '08 and is of the Maxim type, has a calibre of ·79-cm. (·31-in.), and weighs 57 lb. It is operated by recoil action assisted by a muzzle attachment, and is water-cooled. Its average sustained rate of fire is 250 rounds per minute. The feed is by belts each holding 250 rounds. The weapon is mounted on either a tripod or sledge mounting, both of which are adaptable for anti-aircraft use. The weight of the tripod is 67·2 lb., and that of the sledge mounting 85·1 lb. The direction dial and clinometer are included in one instrument which can be attached to the gun. A small detachable bullet-proof shield weighing $1\frac{1}{4}$ lb. is provided with each gun.

In all active and reserve units of the army this weapon will eventually be replaced by the dual purpose machine-gun described in para. 4.*

---

* For details of the 2-cm. (·79-in.) A.A. and A.Tk. gun (super-heavy M.G.) *see* Appendix XVI.

6. Small arms ammunition

The weapons mentioned in paras. 1 (a), 1 (b), 3, 4 and 5 fire the following types of ammunition :—

Type.	Description.	Colour of distinguishing ring on base of cartridge case.
"sS"	Ordinary type of streamlined ammunition.	Green.
"SmK"	Armour piercing ammunition.*	Red.
"SmK L'spur."	Armour piercing ammunition with tracer.	Red (Black tip to bullet).
"S.pr"	Phosphorus-filled tracer and incendiary * bullet for attack upon lighter-than-air aircraft.	Black (bullet is blue).
"SmKH"	Armour piercing incendiary	Yellow.

* This ammunition (when fired from a rifle, see para. 1 (b)) will at 90°, at a range of 440 yards, penetrate steel plates ·33-in. thick, and at a range of 110 yards, steel plates ·39-in. thick.

7. Close support weapons

(a) *5-cm. (2-in.) light trench mortar (see* Plate 14).—One of these 5-cm. mortars is issued to each rifle platoon in all infantry units. The barrel is mounted on a base plate about 18 in. square. The projectile weighs 1¾ lb. and both H.E. and smoke are used. It is inserted at the muzzle and fired by means of a trigger. Range from 50 to 500 yards is obtained by elevation and depression of the barrel and not by altering the charge. Both elevation and traverse (16½° right and left) are by screw. The 100 per cent. zone at 350 yards range is about 24 yards. The mortar is generally laid direct on the target, but small aiming posts are used if necessary, or an ordinary prismatic compass. The sight is detachable. The weapon weighs 31 lb. and the detachment is three men. It is carried on the march in the platoon wagon. In action it is carried in two loads, though over short distances the No. 1 carries the whole mortar assembled.

Five small " suitcases " each containing nine rounds are carried by the detachment.

Personnel are trained to be able to fire for effect after three ranging rounds; fire is generally put down in bursts of ten rounds. Rate of fire six rounds in eight–nine seconds. Both H.E. and Smoke are available.

(b) *7·5-cm. (2·95-in.) light close support infantry (cavalry) gun L.M.W. 18.* (*See* Plate 18.)—This weapon, which is a close support howitzer on a low mounting, is known either as the " Infanteriegeschütz " (infantry gun) or " Kavalleriegeschütz " (cavalry gun). Its maximum range is 3,900 yards. A special type of breech mechanism facilitates the maintenance of a rapid rate of fire of from 15 to 20 rounds per minute. This weapon has a box trail with a traverse of 12 degrees. It fires a high explosive shell which weighs $14\frac{1}{4}$ lb. and has a good splintering effect up to a radius of 20 yards. It is normally horse-drawn or towed by a motor vehicle, but can, if necessary, be carried on pack in six loads.

(c) *7·5-cm. (2·95-in.) light close support infantry gun L. 13.* (*See* Plate 19.)—This new weapon is replacing the *L.M.W.* 18. It is mounted on a tubular split trail carriage, can be drawn by motor vehicle or horses, or carried on pack animals in seven loads. It fires two types of shell, the lighter of which weighs 10 lb. and has a range of 5,600 yards, the heavier shell weighing 14 lb. and having a range of 4,200 yards. Ricochet fire can be employed at all ranges up to 2,400 yards. Rate of fire is 20 rounds per minute. A dial sight is fitted.

(d) 7·5-cm. (2·95-in.) assault gun (*Sturmgeschütz*). This weapon, which made its appearance during operations on the Western Front in the summer of 1940, is a 7·5-cm. gun, possibly an adaptation of the piece used for the 7·5-cm. close support infantry gun, mounted on a special type of light medium (Pz. Kw. III) tank with a squat turret. This gun fires from the stationary position and its role is that of highly mobile, close support artillery, and not that of an A.F.V.

(e) *8·1-cm. (3·16-in.) mortar.* (*See* Plate 15.)—This mortar is of the Stokes-Brandt type and is known as *L.* 15; it is being replaced by a lighter model *S. Gr. W.* 34. It is the standard weapon in Smoke units and of the heavy mortar platoon of the machine-gun companies of rifle battalions. Its rate of fire is from 20 to 25 rounds per minute. Its weight in action is 187 lb., made up as follows :—

Mortar	68·2 lb.
Mounting	61·6 lb.
Base plate	55·0 lb.
Sighting apparatus	2·2 lb.

The weapon is muzzle-loaded and is fired either by means of a device applied to the breech or by percussion after the shell has dropped down the barrel. There are two types of shell, H.E. and smoke, the former weighs 9·6 lb. and has five charges giving a maximum range of 5,000 yards. No details are available concerning the smoke shell which is fired by this weapon. Shells are packed in fours in a metal box which can be carried on the back like a pack. In motorized units the mortar is trailed behind a M.T. vehicle which takes the personnel. It is mounted on heavy rubber tyres and can be drawn by the team across any type of country. It can, if necessary, be carried by three men or on one pack animal.

(f) 8·1-*cm.* (3·16-*in.*) *mortar* (*S. Gr. W.* 34).—This is a lighter model of the mortar described in (e) above. Its weight in action is 125 lb., range 65 yards to 2,070 yards. Range is adjusted by alteration of elevation and addition of secondary charges. The mortar is normally carried on a one-horsed, two-wheeled cart, together with 48 rounds of ammunition carried in "suitcases," each holding four rounds. The weight of each round is believed to be 14·3 lb. When off-loaded the mortar detachment of three carry 21 rounds.

(g) 10-*cm.* (3·94-*in.*) *mortar* (10-*cm. Nebelwerfer*). (*See* Plate 16.)—This weapon forms part of the equipment of smoke units. The equipment consists of the tube, base plate, bipod, sight bracket and sights. The weight without sights is 23 lb. The weapon is carried on a special mortar cart. There is every likelihood that this mortar is intended for the projection of chemical warfare agents as well as smoke.

(h) 15-*cm.* (5·91-*in.*) *heavy infantry gun* (*S. Inf. G.* 33). (*See* Plate 20.)—This weapon is now replacing the 17-cm. mortar (*see* para. (i) below) in the infantry gun company of the infantry regiment. It is noticeably more powerful than a mortar, being a well-developed howitzer. It is believed to have a maximum range of 6,000 yards with an 80 lb. shell, a rate of fire of four rounds per minute with maximum traverse of 6° and elevation of + 80° and to have a weight in action of 3,300 lb. The gun has a box trail, is fitted with a dial sight, and five charges are available.

(i) 17-*cm.* (6·69-*in.*) *medium trench mortar*. (*See* Plate 17.) —This weapon is believed to be obsolete but may appear in "Landwehr" units. It throws a 100 lb. shell 1,200 yards.

It has to be removed with its bed (from which it can be fired in an emergency) from a wheeled travelling carriage and mounted on a bed-plate; it takes 35 minutes to assemble and lay.

8. Anti-tank weapons

(a) *Anti-tank rifles.*—Anti-tank rifles are being issued on the scale of one per platoon or equivalent unit.

There are at least three types of anti-tank rifles in use with the German army : the Polish anti-tank rifle re-named the " Tankbüchse " (*see* Appendix IX), a new weapon of German manufacture, based on the Polish model, and the model 38 with barrel No. 318.

Only approximate details are available of the new German pattern (*see* Plate 21), but its calibre is ·79-cm. (·31-in.), weight 22 lb., and overall length about 6 ft. 6 in. The weapon fires single rounds and is fed by magazines containing ten cartridges.

The model 38 anti-tank rifle, which was of ·79-cm. (·31-in.) calibre, has a new barrel No. 318 of 1·3 cm. (·51-in.) calibre, firing armour piercing, tracer and armour piercing incendiary ammunition. Penetration is not known.

It is possible that the Germans may also make use of the Czech ·79-cm. (·31-in.) anti-tank rifle, model *Z.B.* 26, the Czech 1·2-cm (·47-in.) anti-tank rifle model *Z.K.* 395 and the Besa 1·5-cm. machine-gun. The 1·5-cm. (·58-in.) Besa anti-tank weapon has an overall length of 4 ft. 9 in. and weighs 95 lb. without mounting and 195 lb. with mounting. It is claimed to have a rate of fire of 450 rounds a minute and an effective range of up to 1,000 yards against light tanks. Penetration claimed is 20 mm. (·78-in.) of armour at 550 yards and 32 mm. (1·26-in.) at 200 yards.

It is believed that the 2-cm. (·79-in.) anti-tank rifle has proved unsatisfactory and is being withdrawn from service.*

(b) *3·7-cm. (1·45-in.) anti-tank gun.* (*See* Plates 22 and 23.)—This is at present the main anti-tank weapon. It has a maximum range of 4,400 yards and its weight in action is 880 lb. Its best range is about 400 yards. At normal, steel plates 33 mm. (1·3 in.) thick are penetrated at 650 yards, plates 43 mm. (1·69 in.) at 330 yards. Its rate of fire is 12 rounds per minute. It has a split trail. When the trails

---

* For details of the 2-cm. (·79-in.) A.A. and A.Tk. gun (super-heavy M.G.) *see* Appendix XVI.

are closed, the gun has a traverse of four degrees, and when open, a traverse of fifty-eight degrees. The gun has two shields fitted one above the other; the upper shield moves with the gun in traverse. There are four types of shell—armour-piercing with and without tracer and high explosive with and without tracer. The weight of the armour-piercing shell is 1·68 lb. and that of the high explosive 1·37 lb. The gun is mounted on a well-sprung carriage and is fitted with low pressure pneumatic tyres for transportation as a trailer behind an M.T. vehicle. It can be drawn by the detachment across country.

(c) 4·7-*cm.* (1·85-*in.*) *anti-tank gun.*—The 3·7-cm (1·45-in.) anti-tank gun has not proved effective against modern A.F.Vs.; there is evidence that a 4·7-cm. (1·85-in.) anti-tank gun has been brought into service.

The 4·7-cm. gun adopted is believed to be the Skoda dual purpose anti-aircraft and anti-tank gun, with a muzzle velocity of 2,520 feet per second, firing a 3·63 lb. armour piercing shell. The maximum range of this weapon is 11,700 yards, but the penetration performance is not known.

9. Grenades

Two models of hand grenade are in use with the German Army, the old "Stielhandgranate" Model 24 and the improved Model P.H. 39. The main characteristics of the two grenades are as follows:—

	Model P.H. 39	*Model 24*
Length	41-cm. (16-in.)	35·5-cm. (14-in.)
Weight	610 grammes (1 lb. 5 oz.)	600 grammes (1 lb. 4 oz.)
Delay action of time fuze	4½ sec.	5½ sec.

On the Model 24 grenade there is a screwed cap at the end of the handle. When the cap is removed it exposes a button attached to a friction wire, and this is pulled out to ignite the fuze. Model P.H. 39 is primed by removing a safety cap at the end of the handle. When the cap is pulled off the fuze is ignited and the grenade is thrown immediately. The effect of Model P.H. 39 is said to be six to eight times greater than that of Model 24 and it is principally designed for use against blockhouses, concrete pill boxes and light medium tanks.

In the case of Model 24, the heads may be disconnected from the handles and tied in a bunch of six round the head of a seventh grenade for throwing against tanks, or tied on to a board as a kind of Bangalore torpedo for blowing up obstacles.

10. Lance

The cavalryman is no longer equipped with a lance.

11. Sabre

This is a single-edged cut-and-thrust weapon with a basket hilt.

Chapter V

Chapter V

APPENDIX VII

GERMAN MACHINE PISTOL

Type.	Calibre.	Weight.	Length of weapon.	Length of barrel.	Magazine capacity.
Bergmann Machine Pistol (1)	·9-cm. (·35-in.)	8·8 lb.			32 rounds in box magazine.
Erma Machine Pistol	·9-cm. (·35-in.)	9 lb. (without magazine).			32 rounds.
Neuhausen Machine Pistol— Short barrel model Long barrel model	·76-cm. (·29-in.) ·9-cm. (·35-in.)	8 lb. 14 oz. 9 lb. 2 oz.			30 rounds. 40 rounds.
Schmeisser Machine Pistol (2)	·89-cm. (·34-in.)	9·7 lb. with empty 50-round magazine. 11 lb. with full magazine.	31·5 in.	7·8 in.	20, 25 or 50 round box magazines.
Steyr-Solothurn Machine Pistol S 1–100 (3)	·9-cm. (·35-in.)	9·2 lb. without bayonet. 9·9 lb. with bayonet.	31·5 in. without bayonet. 39 in. with bayonet.	8·1 in.	30 rounds box magazine.
Machine Pistol 38	·9-cm. (·35-in.)	9 lb. 4 oz. without magazine.	32 in. with butt extended. 24 in. with butt folded.	8·5 in	32 rounds box magazine.

(1) The Bergmann is also made in ·76-cm. (·29-in.) and ·77-cm. (·3-in.) calibres.
(2) The Belgian model is of ·9-cm. (·35 in.) calibre.
(3) There is also a short model (*see* Plate 7), of which full details are not available.

Maximum rate of fire.	Sights.	Effective range.	Ammunition.	Weight of cartridge.	Velocity.	Bayonet.
500 R.P.M. Practical 120 R.P.M.		218 yards.	Parabellum.	192 grains.		Yes.
520 R.P.M.						
800 R.P.M.			Mauser.			
800 R.P.M.						
500 R.P.M. 250/320 R.P.M. sustained fire.	Graduated from 100 to 1,000 metres in 100-metre stages (109 yards to 1,093 yards.)		Parabellum.	185 grains.	370 metres/sec. (1,209 f/s.)	Yes.
			Mauser.	200 grains.	420 metres/sec. (1,371 f/s.)	Yes.
	Double V backsights for 100 and 200 metres (109 yards and 218 yards). Ring foresight.	109 yards ?	Parabellum			No.

APPENDIX IX

NOTE ON CAPTURED SMALL ARMS, CLOSE SUPPORT AND ANTI-TANK WEAPONS LIKELY TO BE USED BY GERMANY

1. Machine-guns

(a) *Polish.*—It is probable that the German army has taken into service the light and heavy machine-guns of the Polish army, namely the ·79-cm. (·31-in.) Browning light machine-gun M.28, weight 22 lb., magazine capacity 20 rounds and maximum rate of fire 600 rounds per minute, and also the ·79-cm. (·31-in.) Browning machine-gun M.30, total weight of gun with mounting 103½ lb., water-cooled, belt fed, with a maximum rate of fire of 600 rounds per minute.

2. Mortars

(a) *Polish.*—The Polish mortars now possibly in service with the German army are the 4·6-cm. (1·82-in.) M.30 mortars weighing 15·4 lb., firing a 1½-lb. bomb with an effective range of 765 yards and the 8·1-cm. (3·16-in.) Stokes-Brandt mortar weighing 129 lb. in the firing position, firing a bomb weighing 7 lb. 2 oz., with an effective range of 3,200 yards.

(b) *French.*—It is very probable that the Germans have taken into service all the captured French 8·1-cm. (3·16-in.) mortars, in view of their similarity in design and performance to the standard German 8·1-cm. (3·16-in.) mortar.

3. Anti-tank guns and rifles

(a) *Polish.*—The Polish anti-tank rifle has been taken into service in the German army and re-named the "Tankbüchse." It is of ·79-cm. (·31-in.) calibre, weight 19·8 lb., overall length 6 ft. 6 in. It is fired from the shoulder like an ordinary rifle, having a special recoil brake, and is hand-operated, firing single rounds. Penetration claimed is 20-mm. (·78-in.) armour plate of hardness 500 Brinell at 90° at 327 yards.

(b) *French.*—The following anti-tank guns have most probably been taken into service :—

  (i) 2·5-cm. (·97-in.) Hotchkiss, which has a muzzle velocity of 3,000 ft. per second, fires a ·7-lb. armour piercing shell, with penetration of 60 mm. (2·36 in.) at normal at 100 yards, and rate of fire 20–25 rounds per minute.

  (ii) 2·5-cm. (·97-in.) Puteaux, the performance of which is similar to that of the 2·5-cm. Hotchkiss.

  (iii) 4·7-cm. (1·85-in.) anti-tank gun M.39, which has a muzzle velocity of 2,800 ft. per second, fires a 3·8 lb. armour piercing shell, with penetration of 80 mm. (3·14-in.) at 220 yards at 15°. Its rate of fire is 20 rounds per minute.

  (iv) 7·5-cm. (2·95-in.) anti-tank gun (new model), which has a muzzle velocity of 2,100 ft. per second and fires a 14-lb. armour piercing shell. Penetration is not known, but its rate of fire is thought to be about 12 rounds per minute.

Chapter V

CHAPTER VI

ARTILLERY

Note.—German calibres and their English equivalents (to two places of decimals) are given below :—

cm.	in.	cm.	in.
2	0·79	28	.11
3·7	1·45	30·5	11·99
4·7	1·85	35	13·75
7·5	2·95	36	14·15
7·7	3·03	38	14·93
8·8	3·46	40·6	15·96
10	3·93	42	16·5
10·5	4·14	45	17·69
12·7	4·99	47	18·47
15	5·91	52	20·44
17	6·69	55	21·62
19·4	7·62	60	23·58
21	8·26	65·5	25·74
24	9·43	80	31·44

A.—The Arm

Note.—For particulars of types of artillery weapons *see* Appendices XIII and XIV.

The main types of artillery weapons are shown in Plates 24 to 37.

1. General organization

(a) The Inspector of Artillery in the War Ministry is responsible for the tactical and technical development of the artillery arm and ensures that the training of artillery units is carried out on uniform lines.

(b) Anti-aircraft and coastal artillery units come under the control of the Air Ministry and Admiralty respectively.

(c) The basic units and sub-units of the German artillery together with their approximate British equivalents are as follows :—

German.	*British.*
Regiment	Regiment.
Abteilung	Battery.
Batterie	Troop.
Zug ..	Section.

The " four-gun troop " organization is adopted throughout the German artillery, and there is no indication at present of any projected change.

2. General note on armament

A notable point in the German artillery organization is the weakness in field artillery. Although reinforced to some extent by the inclusion of six light and two heavy infantry guns for close support tasks in each of the three infantry regiments of a division, and probably assault guns, the number of artillery weapons available in the infantry division (48 gun-hows., guns and howitzers) does not correspond to theoretical requirements for the effective support of a divisional attack. It should be remembered, however, that the Germans make much use of dive bombers (Stukas) to carry out tasks normally allotted in other armies to artillery.

3. Artillery staffs

(a) *Army.*
> There is a senior artillery officer on army staff (*see* Chapter II, para. 4).

(b) *Corps.*
> It is believed that there is an officer on each corps staff who carries out duties similar to those of the C.C.R.A. and of the C.C.M.A. in the British army.

(c) *Division.*
> Artillery commander.*
> Lieutenant-colonel or colonel (mainly for technical gunnery work).
> General staff officer.
> Adjutant.
> Orderly officer.
> Signal officer (from divisional signals).

(d) *Regiment.*
> Commander.
> Adjutant.
> Orderly officer.
> Signal officer (an artillery officer).

(e) *Field, medium or mountain artillery battery.*
> Commander.
> Adjutant.
> Orderly officer.
> Signal officer (artillery officer).
> Survey officer.

---

* The divisional artillery commander also commands any additional artillery which may be temporarily allotted to the division.

Chapter VI

B.—Divisional Artillery

4. Organization, strength and armament of the horse artillery battery* in the cavalry division

(a) Organization.

(i) *Battery.*—The horse artillery battery consists of headquarters, signal section, survey section, meteor section, and three troops. For composition of battery staff *see* Section A, para. 3 (*e*).

(ii) *Troop.*—A horse artillery troop consists of headquarters, two sections each armed with two 7·5-cm. (2·95-in.) field guns and one light machine gun for A.A. and local defence, and two ammunition echelons. It is probable that each troop also includes two 2-cm. (·79-in.) A.A. and A.Tk. guns.

(b) Strength.—

	Officers.	Other ranks.	Horses.	Gun limbers.	Ammunition wagons.	6-horsed store wagons.	6-horsed observation wagons.	2-horsed field kitchens.	2-horsed G.S. wagons.	4-horsed telephone wagons.	4-horsed wireless wagons.	Wireless lorries.	M.C. combinations.	M.C.s.	4-seater cars.	Medium lorries (for baggage).
Bty.	21	535	580	12	24	6	4	3	4	4	1	1	2	2	2	4
Headquarters	4	26	23	–	–	–	–	–	–	–	–	–	2	2	2	1
Bty. Sig. Sec.	1	39	26	–	–	–	1	–	–	1	1	1	–	–	–	–
Bty. Svy. Sec.	1	8	–	–	–	–	–	–	1	–	–	–	–	–	–	–
Tp.	5	154	177	4	8	2	1	1	1	1	–	–	–	–	–	–

(c) Armament.—

	†7·5-cm. (2·95-in.) field guns.	Light machine guns.	2-cm. (·79-in.) A.A. and A.Tk. guns.
Bty.	12	6	6
Tp.	4	2	2

* This battery may have been expanded to a regiment since mobilization.

† It is believed that this equipment is replaced by the 10·5-cm. (4·14-in.) gun-howitzer when the theatre of war is more suited to the latter weapon.

5. Organization, strength and armament of mountain artillery in a mountain division*

(a) Organization.

(i) *Regiment.*—The mountain artillery regiment consists of headquarters, signal section and two batteries. For composition of regimental staff *see* Section A, para. 3 (*d*).

(ii) *Battery.*—A mountain artillery battery consists of headquarters, signal section and three troops. For composition of battery staff *see* Section A, para. 3 (*e*).

(iii) *Troop.*—A mountain artillery troop consists of headquarters and two sections, each armed with two 7·5-cm. (2·95-in.) mountain guns and two ammunition echelons. Its transport consists largely of pack animals.

(b) Strength†—

	Officers.	Other ranks.	Horses and mules.	Mountain carts.
Regt. .. .. Regt. Sig. Sec. Bty. .. Bty Sig. Sec. Tp.	1 1	73 63	25 23	1 1

(c) Armament.—

	7·5-cm. (2·95-in.) mountain guns.
Regt.	24
Bty.	12
Tp.	4

6. Organization, strength and armament of artillery in an infantry division. (*See* Appendix X)

In peace time each division had one field regiment of three batteries and one medium regiment of one horsed and one mechanized battery. On mobilization the mechanized battery of the medium regiment was in most cases withdrawn to the G.H.Q. pool, and the horsed battery was incorporated in the field regiment. In some divisions, however, the peace-time organization of one field and one medium regiment may have been retained.

---

* The mountain division also has a divisional survey unit. Details of this unit are not known, but its organization probably resembles that of the G.H.Q. survey unit described in Section E

† In cases where the strength of personnel and/or vehicles is not known, columns have been left blank.

Chapter VI

(a) *Organization.*

(i) *Regiment.*—The field artillery regiment consists of headquarters, signal section (provided by divisional signals), three field batteries and one medium battery. For composition of regimental staff *see* Section A, para. 3 (d).

(ii) *Field battery.*—A field battery consists of headquarters, signal section, survey section, and three troops. All batteries have a mechanized ammunition column. (*See* Appendix XI.)

(iii) *Field troop.*—A field artillery troop consists of headquarters, signal section, transport and ammunition echelons, and two sections each of two 10·5-cm. (4·14-in.) gun-howitzers* and one L.M.G. for A.A. and local defence. It is also probable that a section of two 2-cm. (·79-in.) A.A. and A.Tk. guns has been added. (*See* Appendix XI.)

(iv) *Medium battery.*—The medium battery consists of headquarters, signal section, survey section, and three troops. (*See* Appendix X.)

(v) *Medium troop.*—Two troops are equipped with four 15-cm. (5·91-in.) howitzers each, and the third troop with four 10·5-cm. (4·14-in.) guns. In addition, each troop has two L.M.Gs. for A.A. and local defence and probably also two 2-cm. (·79-in.) A.A. and A.Tk. guns. Medium troops also have mechanized light ammunition columns, which can, if necessary, be concentrated under battery control. (*See* Appendix X.)

(b) *Strength.*—

	Officers.	Other ranks.	Horses.	Gun limbers.	Ammunition wagons.	6-horsed store wagons.	6-horsed observation wagons.	2-horsed field kitchens.	2-horsed G.S. wagons.	4-horsed telephone wagons.	4-horsed wireless wagons.	6-horsed telephone wagons.	Wireless cars.	Motor-cycles.	M.C. combinations.	4-seater cross-country cars.	Medium lorries.
Regt.	89	2,156	1,785	48	96	12	16	12	16	19	5	2	4	6	6	6	13
Regt. Sig. Sec...	1	46	39	–	–	–	–	–	–	3	1	1	–	–	–	–	–
Field Arty. Bty...	21	520	430	12	24	3	4	3	4	4	1	–	1	1	1	1	3
Bty. Sig. Sec.	1	40	36	–	–	1	–	–	1	1	–	1	–	–	–	–	–
Bty. Svy. Sec.	1	8	–	–	–	–	1	–	1	–	–	–	–	–	–	–	–
Tp.	5	149	127	4	8	1	1	1	1	1	–	–	1	1	1	–	1
Medium Bty.	21	536	435	12	24	3	4	3	4	4	1	1	1	1	1	1	4
Bty. Sig. Sec.	1	40	36	–	–	1	–	–	–	1	1	1	1	–	–	–	–
Bty. Svy. Sec.	1	8	–	–	–	–	1	–	1	–	–	–	–	–	–	–	–
10·5-cm. Gun Tp.	5	149	127	4	8	1	1	1	1	1	–	–	–	–	–	–	1
15-cm. How. Tp.	5	157	127	4	8	1	1	1	1	1	–	–	–	–	–	–	1

* In certain "Landwehr" divisions the field artillery batteries are reported to consist of one troop of 7·7-cm. (3·03-in.) guns and two troops of 10·5-cm. (4·14-in.) field hows. (1916 pattern).

(c) *Armament.*—

Weapon.	Field Battery.	Medium Battery.	Total.
10·5-cm. gun-hows.	12	—	36
10·5-cm. guns	—	4	4
15-cm. hows.	—	8	8
L.M.Gs.	6	6	24
2-cm. A.A. and A.Tk. guns.	6	6	24

7. Organization, strength and armament of artillery in a motorized infantry division

A motorized infantry division contains the same number and types of guns as a normal infantry division, and the organization and strength of its artillery regiment, battery and troop are the same. All are, however, fully mechanized.

8. Organization, strength and armament of artillery in an armoured division

Each armoured division has at present one field regiment of two mechanized batteries, although recent information suggests that a third battery of heavier weapons is being added as equipment becomes available.

(a) *Organization.*—The field artillery regiment consists of headquarters, signal section, meteor section, map-printing section, and two batteries. The organization of a field artillery battery and a troop is the same as that of the equivalent units in an infantry division. (*See* Appendix XI.) All are, however, fully mechanized.

(b) *Strength.*—

	Officers.	Other ranks.	Motor-cycles.	M.C. combinations.	2-seater cars.	4-seater cross-country cars.	Light lorries.	Medium lorries.	Medium tractors.	Observation lorries.	Signal lorries.	Telephone lorries.	Light tracked lorries.	Wireless cars.	Light telephone cars.
Regt.	47	1065	67	33	12	28	9	36	78	15	14	5	3	10	12
Regt. Sig. Sec.	1	51	1	1	—	—	1	—	—	1	4	3	1	2	—
Bty.	21	500	32	15	6	13	4	17	39	7	5	1	1	4	6
Bty. Sig. Sec.	1	49	3	1	—	—	—	—	—	1	5	1	1	4	—
Bty. Svy. Sec.	1	8	—	1	—	—	1	—	—	—	—	—	—	—	—
Tp.	5	142	9	4	2	4	1	5	13	2	—	—	—	—	2

(c) *Armament*.—

	10·5-cm. gun-howitzers.	Light machine-guns.	2-cm. (·79-in.) A.A. and A.Tk. guns.
Regt.	24	12	12
Bty.	12	6	6
Tp.	4	2	2

C.—Medium, Heavy, and Super-heavy Artillery

9. Medium, heavy, and super-heavy artillery

Corps and army artillery as such do not exist in the German army. For operations an *ad hoc* allotment of artillery is made to corps and armies from the artillery in the G.H.Q. pool. To this artillery the Germans apply the terms " medium " (*schwere* (s)), " heavy " (*schwerste* (ss)), and " super-heavy " (*überschwere*).

Medium (*schwere* or *s*) *artillery* includes :—

10·5-cm. (4·14-in.) guns.
15-cm. (5·91-in.) howitzers.

Heavy (*schwerste* or *ss.*) *artillery* includes :—

15-cm. (5·91-in.) guns.
21-cm. (8·26-in.) guns.
24-cm. (9·43-in.) guns.
21-cm. (8·26-in.) howitzers.
24-cm. (9·43-in.) howitzers.
30-cm. (11·79-in.) howitzers.

Super-heavy (*überschwere*) *artillery* includes :—

30·5-cm. (11·98-in.) howitzers—and probably some howitzers up to 42-cm. (16·5-in.) calibre.
28-cm. (11-in.) guns.
30·5-cm. (11·98-in.) guns.
38-cm. (14·93-in.) guns.

At present the organization and strengths of the heavy and super-heavy artillery regiments and batteries are not known. For a specimen allotment of these units to army and corps *see* Appendix I.

The mechanized medium artillery batteries, which were withdrawn to the G.H.Q. pool, on mobilization, from the medium artillery regiments of infantry divisions, were organized and equipped in the same way as the horsed medium batteries, which have been retained as part of the divisional artillery of infantry divisions. (*See* Appendix XII.) Recent information suggests, however, that the mechanized medium batteries in the G.H.Q. pool have been reorganized into homogeneous batteries of guns and howitzers. Mechanized medium batteries have, in addition to mechanized ammunition columns, petrol columns which carry sufficient petrol to move the batteries 280 miles.

D.—Regimental and other Specialists

10. Regimental and other specialists

(*a*) *Signallers.*—Regimental, battery and troop signal sections are composed entirely of artillery personnel, who are trained within the unit.

(*b*) *Survey specialists.*—

(i) *Higher formations.*—Artillery survey units are G.H.Q. troops and are allotted to corps and divisions as required. (*See* Section E.)

(ii) *Field artillery regiment.*—None.

(iii) *Battery.*—Survey party of one officer and eight other ranks.

(iv) *Troop.*—Two computors.

(*c*) *Farriers.*—All horsed artillery units include farriers in their establishments.

(*d*) *Mechanics.*—Certain personnel in all mechanized artillery units are trained as mechanics.

(*e*) *Anti-gas specialists.*—All artillery units down to and including troops have anti-gas specialists in their establishments.

(*f*) *Artificers.*—Each artillery battery includes artificers.

E.—Artillery Survey Units

11. Artillery survey units

In peace time the artillery survey units formed part of the divisional artillery of the infantry division. On mobilization they were withdrawn to the G.H.Q. pool and are now allotted to armies and corps as required.

(a) *Organization.*—An artillery survey unit consists of :—
> Headquarters.
>> Signal section (with sufficient cable to lay lines to two troops).
>> Meteorological section (organized in two detachments to permit of " leap-frogging ").
>> Map-printing section (capable of producing about a hundred copies of a photostat map each hour).
>> Survey troop (including a meteorological section).
>> Sound ranging troop (provided with sufficient instruments to establish four sound ranging posts on the divisional front).
>> Flash spotting troop (provided with personnel and instruments capable of manning five observation posts, each with a pack wireless set and connected by telephone with the troop decoding centre).
>> Observation balloon troop (of three observation balloons).

(b) *Strength.*—

	Officers.	Other Ranks.	Motor-cycles.	M.C. combinations.	Medium lorries.	Observation lorries.	Signal lorries.	Telephone lorries.	Light-tracked lorries.	Wireless cars.	Field kitchens on lorries.
Arty. Survey Unit	1	37	1	1	1	1	3	1	1	2	3
Sig. Sec.						1	3			2	—
Map Printing Sec.											
Meteorological Sec.											
Svy. Tp.											1
Sound-ranging Tp.											1
Flash-spotting Tp.											1

F.—Anti-Aircraft Artillery

12. General organization

In Germany anti-aircraft artillery forms part of the Air Force and is under control of the Air Ministry.* Its principal tasks are defence of the home country and defence

---

* With the exception of a few coastal units manned by the Navy, and Army mot. A.A. M.G. Bns. (*see* Chapter III, para. 11). A.A. artillery is known to the Germans as " Flak " (from " FLug-AbwehrKanone ").

of the zone of the armies. To fulfil these functions it is divided into mobile and semi-mobile units, and static defences. Mobile and semi-mobile units are mainly employed in the zone of the armies, but may also be used according to the needs of the situation to reinforce the static defences.

13. Mobile and semi-mobile units

The basic mobile or semi-mobile unit is the gun battery, supported by searchlight, balloon and transport units.

For active operations batteries are generally grouped into regiments. The peace-time establishment of an active regiment is two mixed gun-batteries and a heavy searchlight unit. There is no definite establishment for a regiment in war, two or more batteries of various types being allotted to a regiment according to circumstances. Regiments, in turn, may be grouped into brigades and brigades into corps, for which formations there is no definite establishment.

Batteries are organized as follows :—

(a) *Mixed battery* (mechanized).
 (i) Three heavy troops, each composed of :—
  Four 8·8-cm.* (3·46-in.) guns.
  Two 2-cm. (·79-in.) guns.
 (ii) Two light troops, each composed of :—
  Twelve 2-cm. (·79-in.) guns.
  Four 60-cm. (23·58-in.) searchlights.

(b) *Mixed battery* (reserve).
 Organized as (a) above, but not all are mechanized; non-mechanized batteries are moved as required by a transport unit.

(c) *Light battery* (mechanized).
 (i) Three light troops, each composed of :—
  Twelve 2-cm. (·79-in.) guns.
   Or
 (i) Two light troops, each composed of :—
  Twelve 2-cm. (·79-in.) guns ; and
 One troop, composed of :—
  Nine 3·7-cm. (1·45-in.) guns.
 (ii) One searchlight troop, composed of :—
  Sixteen 60-cm. (23·58-in.) searchlights.

---

* 10·5-cm. (4·14-in.) guns may in some cases replace 8·8-cm. (3·46-in.) guns.

(d) *Heavy searchlight unit* (mechanized).
    Three troops, each composed of :—
        Nine 150-cm. (60-in.) searchlights.
        9 sound-locators.

(e) *Balloon barrage unit* (mechanized).
    Three troops, each composed of :—
        16 balloons.
        48 kites (for use in high winds).

(f) *Transport unit* (mechanized).
    Details are not known as reorganization is taking place.

14. Allotment of mobile and semi-mobile units to the field army

The allotment of mobile or semi-mobile units to the field army varies according to needs. An A.A. corps works with an army group, and it is believed that each army and army corps is usually allotted two or more A.A. batteries grouped under a regimental H.Q. It is also probable that each armoured division is allotted a light or a mixed battery.

Nothing is known of the allotment or organization of A.A. M.G. units of the Air Force, which are armed with heavy M.G.s, but their role is probably similar to that of light A.A. batteries.

15. Control of A.A. units operating with the army

A general officer of A.A. artillery at army group H.Q. controls the allocation of regimental staffs and units within the A.A. corps.

Commanders of A.A. units and formations are directly under the orders of the army commander under whom they are operating, and are responsible for advising him upon all A.A. matters. Under his direction A.A. units are sometimes employed against special targets such as concrete works or ships ; they are also provided with armour-piercing ammunition for anti-tank operations, for which their mobility and rate of fire make them very suitable.

16. Static defences

It is probable that there is no general fixed organization of static defences, but that they vary according to the size and importance of the area which they are designed to protect. It is believed that they are equipped with 10·5-cm. (4·14-in.), 12·7-cm. (4·99-in.) and possibly 15-cm. (5·91-in.)

guns, in addition to guns of smaller calibre. They appear to be organized on a territorial basis into groups (*Gruppen*) under regimental staffs, sub-divided into sub-groups (*Untergruppen*) under battery staffs, controlling a selection of troops of various types in accordance with local needs.

In addition to mobile and semi-mobile units, the static defences contain :—

(*a*) Special units for the defence of vulnerable points in the rear of the zone of the armies and in the home country, such as important bridges or factories.

(*b*) Fortress A.A. artillery (*Festungsflak*) which, as its name implies, was intended primarily for the protection of fortified areas such as the Siegfried Line. Certain units of this fortress artillery have been moved into France.

17. Armament

For particulars of types of A.A. artillery weapons *see* Appendix XVI.

For particulars of strengths and armaments of—

(*a*) A typical active A.A. artillery regiment,

(*b*) An active light A.A. artillery battery,

see Appendix XV.

G.—Coastal Defence and Fortress Artillery

18. Organisation and strength of coastal defence artillery

Coastal defence is the responsibility of the Navy.

(*a*) *Coast artillery units.*—There are six coast artillery units (*Abteilungen*), manned by the Naval Artillery Corps. The headquarters of these units are situated as follows :—

Marine Artillerie Abteilung	I	Kiel.
	II	Wilhelmshaven.
	III	Swinemünde.
	IV	Cuxhaven.
	V	Pillau.
	VI	Emden.

Each of these units consists of one heavy coast artillery company, two anti-aircraft artillery companies and one air observer's section. Nothing further is known regarding the organization of these units.

(*b*) *Anti-aircraft coast defence units.*—Anti-aircraft coastal artillery consists of eight units, known as *Marine-Flak-artillerie-Abteilungen*, which are organized into a number of troops, varying between two and five.

19. Fortress artillery

Under the terms of the Treaty of Versailles all land fortresses except that at Königsberg were dismantled. Little is known about the armament of this fortress, but since 1933 twelve 17-cm. (6·69-in.) guns and six 15-cm. (5·91-in.) guns have been provided.

On the Siegfried Line field guns, howitzers and anti-tank guns are mounted in concrete works. Many of the field guns are believed to be obsolescent German field guns and ex-Czech equipment. It is thought, however, that there are some fixed gun defences with 17-cm. (6·69-in.) and 28-cm. (11-in.) weapons.

H.—Equipment

20. Guns and howitzers

The efficiency of the 10·5 cm. (4·14-in.) gun-howitzer, and its marked advantage over the field gun as regards fire effect, moral effect and suitability for almost any type of gun position, have led to the almost complete abolition of the latter weapon. The only regular unit still equipped with the field gun is the horse artillery battery. It is possible, however, that some of the artillery of "Landwehr" formations still includes field guns and howitzers of an obsolescent type.

The Germans have adopted very marked standardization. The same principles of design and manufacture appear to have been adopted throughout the range from the 10·5-cm. (4·14-in.) gun-howitzer to the 24-cm. (9·45-in.) howitzer.

21. Vehicles

The numbers and types of vehicles in any particular unit are given under the section of these "Notes" dealing with the type of artillery in question.

The guns in mechanized troops are drawn by half-tracked vehicles. These travel fast on the roads and the sprung carriages do not appear to suffer thereby. The rate of movement of mechanized medium artillery on roads is normally up to thirty miles an hour.

22. Signal equipment

The following equipment is carried by signal sections, in artillery units:—

	Heavy cable (miles).	Light cable (miles)	Telephones.	Exchanges.	Pack Wireless sets.
(a) *Horse Arty.*					
Bty.	6¼	2½*	16	3	6
(b) *Mtn. Arty.*					
Regt.	16¼	5*	10	1	7
Bty.	16¼	5*	10	1	5
(c) *Horsed Fd. Arty.*					
Regt.	20	7½*	21	4	5
Bty.	15‡	5*	15	2	5†
d) *Mech. Fd. Arty.*					
Regt. (Mot. Inf. Div. or Armd. Div.)	39	—	28	3	5
Bty. (Mot. Inf. Div.)	27½	—	20	1	5
Bty. (Armd. Div.)	16	—	10	1	7
(e) *Horsed Med. Arty.*					
Regt.	20	7½*	21	4	5
Bty.	15	5*	15	2	5
(f) *Mech. Med. and. Hy. Arty.*					
Regt.	31	4*	22	3	5
Bty.	14	1*	10	1	5
Arty. Survey Unit	14	1*	10	1	6
(g) *A.A. Arty.* Regt. / Hy. Bty. / Lt. Bty.	Not known.				
(h) *C.D. Arty.* Bty.	Not known.				

* Although confirmation is not available it appears to be the policy to reduce the amount of light cable and increase the heavy cable in all artillery units.

† Two of the R/T sets are carried on pack, and three in a light limbered G.S. wagon.

‡ Ten portable cable carriers, carried in one light limbered telephone wagon, and one pack horse with a cable carrier are included in the cable telephone detachments of the battery signal section.

Details of the above equipment are given in Chapter IX.

Artillery units are also provided with—

    (i) White ground strips for communication with aircraft, with a red back for use on snow.

    (ii) Red and white discs for semaphore.

    (iii) Verey pistols with red, white, green, yellow and other coloured lights.

All the above are used in accordance with recognized codes.

23. Technical equipment

(a) *Command instruments.*—Each troop has a light portable mechanical meteorological reckoner. The principle of this instrument is the same as the reckoner used at the British Coast Artillery School.

Every artillery battery headquarters has a meteorological reckoner which works mechanically with a battery fire control board. The latter has a jointed range and line arm which enables the troop positions and the battery zero line to be accurately marked on the board. For any target for which co-ordinates are known it is possible to read off the range, angle of sight and switch from the battery zero point, corrected for the conditions of the moment.

Each troop has one, and each battery headquarters three computing tents in which the instruments described above are set up.

(b) *Observation instruments*—

    (i) "*Scissors*" *stereotelescope.*—In addition to the normal scale of directors, each troop has two and each battery headquarters three stereotelescopes mounted on directors. They are very effective for picking out objects at long range in bad light.

    (ii) *Rangefinder.*—No details are known of types and scale of rangefinders issued to field and medium artillery units.

(c) *Survey instruments.*—Battery survey detachments have a vertical surveyor's pole, and survey troops in artillery survey units have a horizontal surveyor's bar mounted on a stand. Both can be illuminated with electric bulbs at night.

(d) *Predictor.*—The predictor (known as *Zeiss* 27 (a)) is a heavy and complicated instrument, which is mounted on a pair of quickly detachable trailer axles and towed behind a six-wheeled lorry. Power is supplied by a portable accumulator system. The instrument includes a rangefinder 13 or 16 ft. long. Its maximum range is twenty-five miles, but for practical purposes this can be reduced to ten miles. At the latter distance the error is about a hundred yards.

Thirty seconds are required between the first sight of an aircraft and the transmission of the data to the guns.

(e) *Sound locator.*—The Kieler Ringtrichter sound locator is used.

(f) *Searchlights.*—

	60-cm. (1-ft. 11½-in.).	150-cm. (4-ft. 11½-in.).
Diameter of mirror	60-cm. (1-ft. 11½-in.).	150-cm. (4-ft. 11½-in.).
Candle power (in million Heffner candles).	80	1,100
Effective range under good atmospheric conditions.	3,800 yards	14,000 yards
Weight in action	370 lb.	4,950 lb.

24. General system of ammunition supply in the field

The normal chain of ammunition supply is from railhead or army ammunition park to ammunition delivery point by lorries of the ammunition section of the divisional supply column, thence in light lorries of field battery or medium troop ammunition columns to wagon lines or troop positions. If the distance from railhead is too great for the above system to be possible, ammunition sections from the army supply columns are interposed and work from railhead to a point half-way between railhead and the ammunition delivery point, where the ammunition is taken over by the divisional supply columns. Corps have no ammunition columns working with divisions, the corps columns all being required to maintain the corps artillery. (*See* also diagram at Appendix XXXVIII.)

The amount of ammunition carried in front of railhead by field and medium artillery is believed to be as under :—

Weapon.	Where carried.	R.p.G.
10·5-cm. (4·14-in.) gun-how.	With Tp. and in Bty. Amn. Coln.	102
10·5-cm. (4·14-in.) gun-how.	In Amn. Sec. of Div. Sup. Coln.	148
10·5-cm. (4·14-in.) gun	With Tp. and in Tp. Amn. Coln.	78
10·5-cm. (4·14-in.) gun	In Amn. Sec. of Div. Sup. Coln.	72
15-cm. (5·91-in.) how.	With Tp. and in Tp. Amn. Coln.	60
15-cm. (5·91-in.) how.	In Amn. Sec. of Div. Sup. Coln.	90

In the case of mobile anti-aircraft artillery units the scale is believed to be :—

Weapon.	With the Tp.	In light A.A. Amn. Coln.
2-cm. (·79 in.) super-heavy M.G.	900 r.p.g.	Nil
3·7-cm. (1·45 in.) A.A. gun ..	600 r.p.g.	204 r.p.g.
8·8-cm. (3·46-in.) A.A. gun ..	192 r.p.g.	183 r.p.g.

25. Types of ammunition

(*a*) *Shells.*—H.E. is the standard ammunition for all types of artillery weapon. The allotment of smoke shell to field artillery units is very low and this type of ammunition is only carried in the divisional supply column.

(*b*) *Fuzes.*—The normal fuzes (*Aufschlagzünder*), which are known as "Az. 23 (0·25)," "Az. 23 umg, M.2.V," and "Az. 23 (0·8) umg," can be set either for delay or instantaneous action. A clockwork time and percussion fuze (*Doppelzünder* S/60) is used almost entirely for registration with high air bursts, a procedure on which the Germans lay stress. It is, however, expensive and the proportion carried is therefore low.

APPENDIX X

DIVISIONAL ARTILLERY—INFANTRY DIVISION

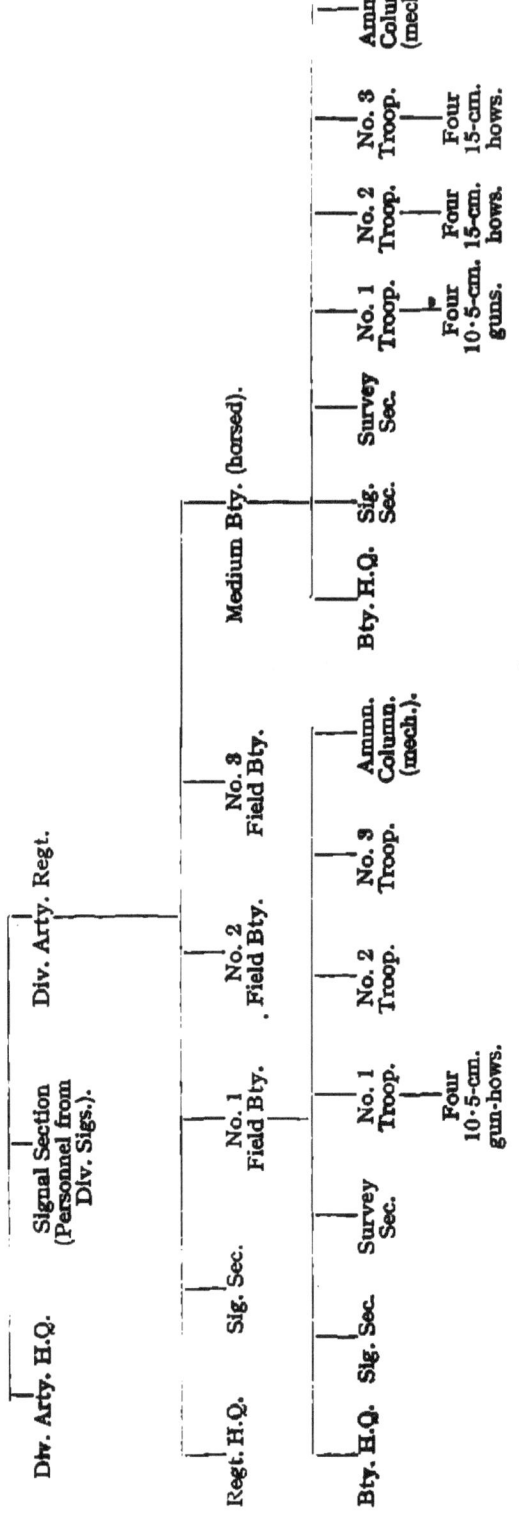

Note.—In some divisions the mechanized medium battery may have been retained. For its organization and armament, *see* Appendix XII.

APPENDIX XI
FIELD ARTILLERY BATTERY.

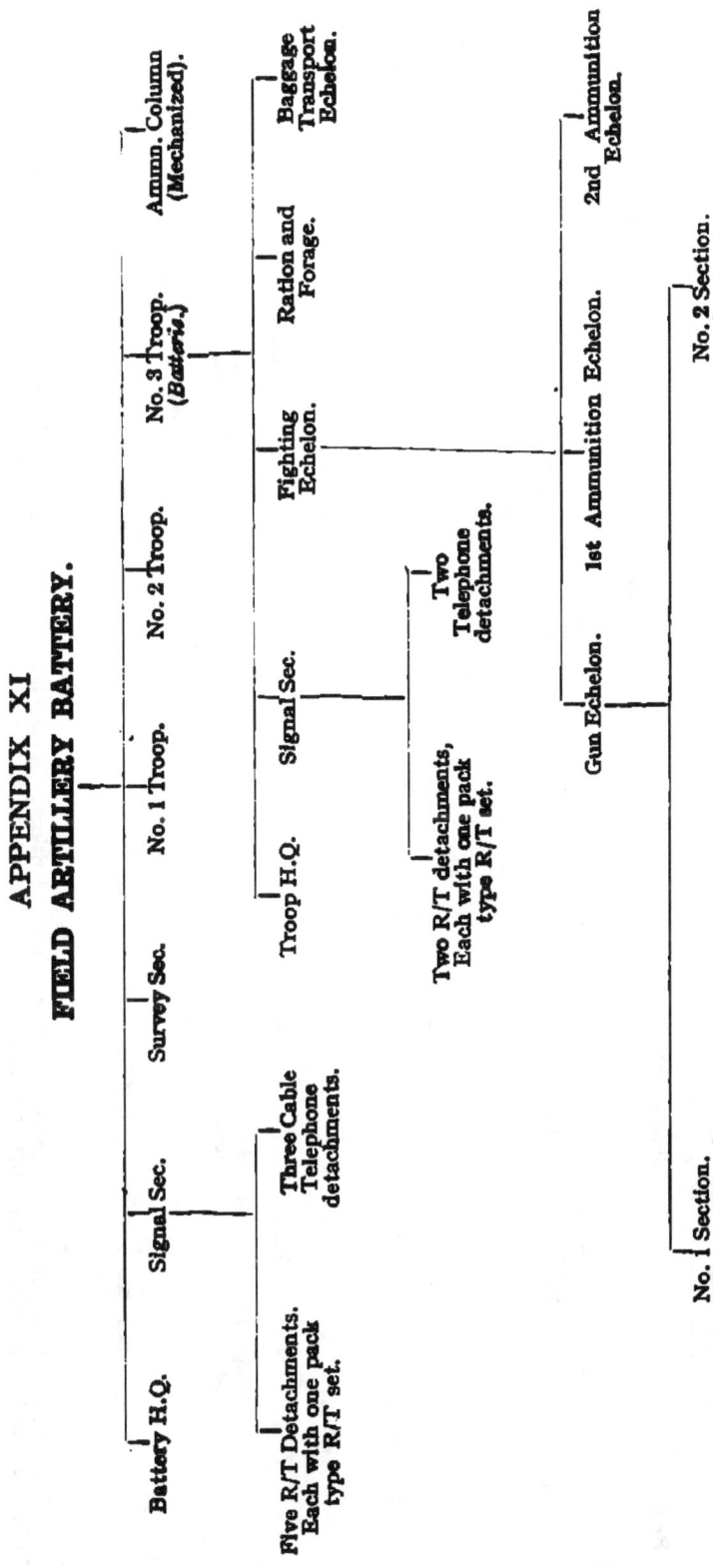

Each troop has two L.M.Gs. and probably two 2-cm. A.A. and A.Tk. guns for local and A.A. defence.

APPENDIX XII

MEDIUM ARTILLERY REGIMENT.

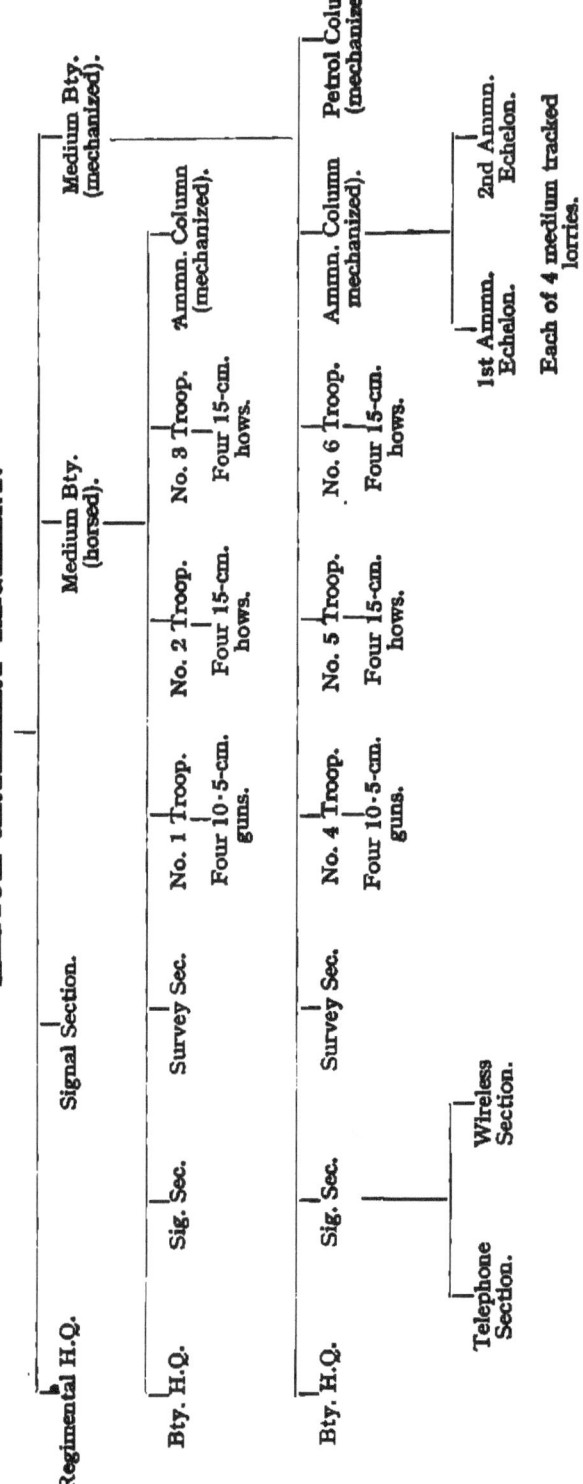

Note.—This organization may still be found in some infantry divisions. In most cases, however, the horsed medium battery has been incorporated in the divisional field regiment (*see* Appendix X) and the mechanized medium battery withdrawn to the G.H.Q. pool.

APPENDIX XIII.

PARTICULARS OF TYPES OF GERMAN GUNS.

Serial.	Calibre.	Type.	Length of bore.	M.V.	Weight of shell.	Maximum range.	Elevation.	Depression.	Traverse.	Weight in action.	Method of Transport.	Remarks.
1	7·5-cm.	Mountain gun (Geb. K.15).	Cal. 10·7	f.s. Normal third charge 1,000. Super fourth 1,250	lb. 12	yds. 7,650	° 50	° 9	° 7	Tons. ·62	7 loads of which heaviest 340 lbs.	
2	7·5-cm.	Mountain gun (new model).	22	1,600	13	10,900	60	30	70	·89	2 loads or 6 pack loads.	
3	7·5-cm.	Field gun (F.K.L./25).	25	1,470	14·3	10,000	45	7	60	·92	H.T.	
4	7·5-cm.	Field gun (F.K.16, n/A.).	35·9	2,170	12·9	13,000	40	9	4	1·3		This is a 7·5-cm. piece mounted on the F.K.16, 7·7-cm. carriage.
5	7·5-cm.	Long range field gun	42	2,300	14·5	15,300	40	7	60	1·62	H.T. or M.T.	Same carriage as 10·5-cm. L.F.H.18.
6	7·7-cm.	Field gun (F.K.16).	35	1,975	13·4	11,700	40	10	4	1·875	H.T.	Carriage and cradle as for L.F.H.16 10·5-cm. how. with strengthened recuperator springs.

PARTICULARS OF TYPES OF GERMAN GUNS—continued.

Serial.	Calibre.	Type.	Length of bore.	M.V.	Weight of shell.	Maximum range.	Elevation.	Depression.	Traverse.	Weight in action.	Method of Transport.	Remarks.
				f.s.	lb.	yds.	°	°	°	Tons		
7	8-cm.	Gun (M.18) (Skoda).	Cal. 25		17·5	13,000	45	10	7	1·3		
8	8-cm.	Gun (M.30) (Skoda).				14,100				1·6		
9	8·35-cm.	Gun (M.1930) (Skoda).	33	1,760	22	27,000	85			2·4	H.T. or M.T.	May be gun referred to as 8·5-cm. on armoured carriers as A.Tk. gun.
10	8·8-cm.	A.A. gun	56	2,750	19·8	16,000	85	0	360	5·15		Now definitely in use as A.Tk. gun.
11	10-cm. (Plate 24)	Mountain howitzer (M.16/19) (Skoda).				10,800	75			2·25		
12	10-cm.	Howitzer (M.14/19) (Skoda).		1,450	35	11,800 (1933 model 14,800)				1·49		Improved in 1933, lengthening gun.
13	10-cm.	Howitzer (M.30) (Skoda).				13,000				1·75		
14	10·5-cm.	Howitzer (L.F.H.18).	22	1,280	33·1	10,500	40	10	4	1·45		Carriage same as 7·7-cm. F.K.16 and 7·5-cm. F.K.16. n/A.

Chapter VI

	Calibre	Type	Weight	Muzzle velocity	Length (cal.)	Range	Elevation			Shell weight	H.T. or M.T.	Replaces
15	10·5-cm. (Plate 25)	Gun howitzer (L.F.H.18).	22·8	Normal charge 1,290. Super charge 1,540.	31·79	12,000	40	5	56	1·915		Replaces L.F.H.16
16	10·5-cm.	Gun howitzer	30	1,650	36	13,000	17	8	58	2		
17	10·5-cm.	Gun (K.17 or K.17/04).	45	2,130	40·7	15,400	45	2	6	3·3		
18	10·5-cm. (Plate 26)	Gun (K.18).	40	2,650 or 2,800	35	19,700	50	3	60	5·5	H.T. or M.T. for which there are 2 loads on solid rubber tyres.	
19	10·5-cm.	Gun (M.35) (Skoda).				21,500						
20	12-cm.	Gun (M.1937) (Skoda).				25,000						
21	15-cm.	Infantry howitzer (14. L.6) (Skoda).	6			8,800						
22	15-cm.	Howitzer (M.14/16) (Skoda).	14		91	8,900				2·5		
23	15-cm.	Howitzer (S.F.H.13 or 13/02).	17	1,250	92·6	9,296	45	10	5	2·25		
24	15-cm.	Howitzer (M.25) (Skoda).	18	1,480	91	13,000	71		7	3·68		
25	15-cm.	Howitzer (M.15) (Skoda).	20	1,640		13,000	65	5		3·74		
26	15-cm. (Plates 27 and 28).	Howitzer (S.F.H.18).	22	1,970	95·7	16,400	50	3	60	4·5	M.T. with piece pulled back or in 2 loads.	Standard medium how. It is possible that a how. of same type but 29·5 cal. is in service.

PARTICULARS OF TYPES OF GERMAN GUNS—continued.

Serial.	Calibre.	Type.	Length of bore.	M.V.	Weight of shell.	Maximum range.	Elevation.	Depression.	Traverse.	Weight in action.	Method of Transport.	Remarks.
27	15-cm.	Howitzer (L/32).	Cal. 32	f.s. 2,000	lb. 94·25	yds. 16,700	° 45	° 1	° 57	Tons 8·25		In service as well as S.F.H.18. Carriage modern and probably interchangeable with 10·5-cm. L/52 gun.
28	15-cm.	Howitzer (M.97) (Skoda).	40	2,300	120	22,000	45	6	6	16·2		
29	15-cm.	Gun (M.15/16) (Skoda).	42	2,480	113·5	25,000	42	3	8	10·7	H.T. or semi-tracked vehicles, 2 loads.	Improved 15-cm. K.P. of last war. Carriage probably interchangeable with 21-cm. how. 1916/32.
30	15-cm. (Plate 29)	Gun (K.16).										
31	15-cm.	Gun	42	2,480	113·5	25,000	42	3	60	12	2 loads drawn by semi-tracked vehicles.	Piece, probably the same as K.16.
32	15-cm.	Gun (M.15/20) (Skoda).	55	2,920	112	27,500	45	6	5	14	2 loads	
33	15-cm.	Gun (K.18).	49		100	27,200	45	4	60	12·6		Unconfirmed and range doubtful.
34	15·4-cm.	Long range gun				50 miles.						
35	19·4-cm.	Gun		2,620		32,800						
36	21-cm.	Howitzer (M.18) (Skoda).	10	1,380	277	11,000	71		360	8·9		Existence not confirmed.

Chapter VI

No.	Calibre	Type									Remarks
37	21-cm.	Howitzer (M.1916/92).	14·5	1,850	265	16,400				In 2 loads	Carriage interchangeable with 15-cm. gun, K.16.
38	21-cm.	Howitzer									New design with longer piece. Photographs received but no particulars.
39	21-cm. (Plate 30)	Howitzer (Lg. 21-cm. Mrs.).	14·6	1,450	264	11,100	70	6	4	9	3 loads	Great War model fitted with new carriage, also used for 15-cm. gun K.16.
40	21-cm.	Gun (Skoda).	40?	2,620		32,400	45	7	360		3 loads	It is known that 12 of these guns are in production.
41	21-cm.	"Fernkanone"				40 to 47 miles.						A number of these guns are said to exist. Unconfirmed.
42	21-cm.	Super long range gun.	160			81 miles.						Vertex of trajectory 132,000 ft. Particulars of this gun follow fairly closely those of the original Paris gun.
43	21-cm. (Plate 31)	Railway gun				20,800						A number of reports have been received about this gun but it may have been the 24-cm. railway gun which is known to exist.
44	22-cm.	Gun				57,000						Unconfirmed.
45	24-cm.	Gun (M.16). (Skoda)	·30	2,620	470?	33,000				79·1		Same carriage as 30·8-cm. howitzer.

PARTICULARS OF TYPES OF GERMAN GUNS—continued.

Serial.	Calibre.	Type.	Length of bore. Cal.	M.V. f.s.	Weight of shell. lb.	Maximum range. yds.	Elevation. °	Depression. °	Traverse. °	Weight in action. Tons	Method of Transport.	Remarks.
46	24-cm.	Howitzer				21,800					3 loads. Speed 25 m.p.h.	12 of these howitzers were ordered by Turkey from Skoda but only 2 delivered. Remainder taken over by Germany. Said to be best gun produced by Skoda.
47	24-cm.	Gun (Krupp, 1897).	46	2,780	396	35,000	45	4	360		3 heavy cross country vehicles.	Same gun as 24-cm. Krupp, 1897. Life with full charge 250 rounds.
48	24-cm. (Plate 31)	Railway gun	46	2,780	396	44,000						Carriage believed to be interchangeable with 21-cm. gun.
49	24-cm.	Railway gun	50	3,040	396	44,500	45		360	184		
50	28-cm.	Howitzer				21,000						Known to exist but details not confirmed.
51	28-cm.	Gun	53			41,000					5 loads	Probably 11-in. Naval gun.
52 53	28-cm. 28-cm.	Railway gun Super long range gun	125 to 130	5,900	660	45,000 130 to 158 miles.						Unconfirmed. Vertex of trajectory 198,000 ft. A range of 130 miles is possible.
54	30·5-cm.	Howitzer	14		838	14,000				24	6 loads	Last war model. There is possibly a new Skoda model with a range of 20,000 yds.

Chapter VI

55	30·5-cm.	Howitzer (M.16).	12	1,080	630	13,500	75	360	23	
56	30·5 or 38-cm. (Plate 32)	Railway gun (Theodor Kanone).	42?							This heavy railway gun with high M.V. is known to exist but there are no particulars available. Unconfirmed.
57	36-cm.	Gun	17			62 miles.				
58	38-cm.	Howitzer (Skoda).			1,840	18,500			61	24 or 32 of these guns are known to have been under construction for the new battleships and some may have been devoted to Army use.
59	38-cm.	Gun				50,000 (?)				Not confirmed.
60	38-cm.	Gun	50	2,790	2,100	79 miles. 49,000	40	30		12 of these guns are known to exist.
61	40·6-cm.	Railway gun			2,200	16,400	65			At least one of these Howitzers known to exist.
62	42-cm.	Howitzer (Skoda).								
63	47-cm.	Howitzer (Skoda).				35,000			4 loads 4 m.p.h. Very noisy in movement.	Unconfirmed but fairly reliably reported.
64	52-cm.	Howitzer		4,500	4,480	33,000				Unconfirmed.
65	80-cm.	Howitzer				86 miles.				Unconfirmed. Life stated to be 550 rounds which is unlikely.
66	80-cm.	Gun								
67	80-cm.	Howitzer	40	2,460	16,700	46,000		1,000		Unconfirmed but possible.

APPENDIX XIV

PARTICULARS OF TYPES OF CAPTURED GUNS LIKELY TO BE USED BY GERMANY

Serial.	Calibre.	Type.	Country from which captured.	Length of bore, in calibres.	M.V.	Weight of shell in lbs.	Maximum Range in yards.	Elevation.	Depression.	Traverse.	Weight in action in tons.	Method of Transport.	Remarks.
1	7·5-cm.	Mountain gun (Schneider M.19).	Poland	13·35	1,310	14	9,600	40	10	10	1,540 lbs.	7 pack loads	
2	7·5-cm.	Mountain gun	France	13·35	1,310	14	9,600	40	10	10	1,540 lbs.	7 pack loads	
3	7·5-cm.	Field gun	France	30·5	2,050	12·5	14,000	18	11	6	1¼ tons.		
4	10-cm.	Field gun (Skoda, 1914)	Poland		1,800	35	11,000	48	8	5	2·25		
5	10·5-cm.	Field gun (French, 1913 model).	Poland	22		35	13,400	37	0	6	2·3		
6	10·5-cm.	Howitzer (Bofors).	Holland	22	1,560	30·8	11,400	45	5	8	1·65		
7	10·5-cm.	Gun (Bofors)	Holland	40	2,460	35	18,500	45	3	60	3·5	M.T. or H.D.	
8	10·5-cm.	Gun (Schneider)	France	37·5	2,410	35	18,900	43	0	50	3·4	M.T. or H.D.	
9	10·5-cm.	Howitzer	France	17	1,450	34¼	11,200	50	6	53	1·8	H.D.	
10	15·5-cm.	Howitzer	France	11·2	1,480	94·5	12,500	42	0	6	3·3	M.T.	
11	15·5-cm.	G.P.F. gun	France	29·8	2,380	95	21,400	35	0	60	11·2	M.T.	
12	22-cm.	Gun	France	27·8	2,500	226	25,000	37	0	21	22	M.T., 4 loads	
13	22-cm.	Howitzer (M.31)	Poland				14,700				12·5		
14	24-cm.	Railway gun	France	30·83	2,760	357	26,000	35	0	360	140		
15	28-cm.	Railway gun	Belgium			287	35,000	45	0	2·15	150		
16	30·5-cm.	Railway gun	France	30	2,820	693	37,000	38			182		
17	34-cm.	Railway gun	France	43	2,860	980	36,400	37			270		
18	37-cm.	Railway gun	France	28·5	1,885	1,560	24,600	40		12	250		Can be used without change to wheel tracks in any country in Europe, except Spain.
19	40-cm.	Railway gun	France	22	1,740	1,980	17,500	65			187	M.T.	

APPENDIX XV

STRENGTH AND EQUIPMENT OF ANTI-AIRCRAFT ARTILLERY

(1) *Active Anti-Aircraft Regiment.*

	Officers.	O.Rs.	2-cm. (·79-in.) A.A. guns.*	8·8-cm. (3·46-in.) A.A. guns.	60-cm. (23·58-in.) searchlights.	150-cm. (60-in.) searchlights.	Sound Locators.	Motor Vehicles.	Trailers.	Motor cycles.
Regiment			60	24	16	27	27			
Regimental Staff	6	6	-	-	-	-	-			
Signal Section	-	9	-	-	-	-	-			
Baggage Section	-	14	-	-	-	-	-			
Ammn. Column	2	88	-	-	-	-	-	24	-	5
Mixed Battery			30	12	8	-	-	179	44	72
H.Q. Staff	7	46	-	-	-	-	-	11	-	12
Signal Section	1	31	-	-	-	-	-	8	-	-
Heavy Troop	5	167	2	4	-	-	-	28	6	13
Light Troop	5	186	12	-	4	-	-	38	13	15
Searchlight Battery.						27	27			
Signal Section	1	31	-	-	-	-	-	8	-	
Searchlight Troop				-	-	9	9			

(2) *Active Light Anti-Aircraft Battery.*

	Officers.	O.Rs.	2-cm. (·79-in.) A.A. guns.*	60-cm. (23-in.) searchlights.	Motor vehicles.	Trailers.	Motor cycles.
Battery			36	16			
H.Q. Staff	6	36	-	-	11	-	12
Signal Section	1	31	-	-	8	-	-
Light Troop	5	186	12	-	38	13	15
Searchlight Troop			-	16			

* This weapon is identical with the Army's 2-cm (·79-in) A.A. and A.Tk. gun.

Chapter VI

Chapter VI

APPENDIX XV

PARTICULARS OF TYPES OF ANTI-AIRCRAF

Serial.	Calibre.	Type.	Country of origin if not German.	Length of bore (cals.).	M.V. (f/s).	Weight of shell (lb.).	Maximum horizontal range (yds.).	Maximum vertical range (ft.).
1	2-cm. (·79-in.)	2-cm. A.A. & A. Tk. gun (super-heavy M.G.) Plates 34–35.	—	65	2,950	308	6,124	12,468
2	3·7-cm. (1·45-in.)	3·7-cm. A.A. gun ..	—	50	2,800	1·4	8,744	15,600
3	3·9-cm. (1·5-in.)	3·9-cm. A.A. gun ..	—	65	3,117	1·98	10,940	18,045
4	4-cm.	4-cm. A.A. gun, M/36	Polish	60	2,950	2·2	12,400	16,300
5	4·7-cm. (1·85-in.)	4·7-cm. A.A. gun ..	Czech.		2,620	3·3	11,695	24,000
6	5·5-cm. (2·2-in.).	5·5-cm. A.A. gun ..	Polish					
7	7·5-cm. (2·95-in.)	7·5-cm. A.A. gun, M/31	Danish	46	2,800	14·7	17,500	36,000
8	7·5-cm. (2·95-in.)	7·5-cm. A.A. gun, L/59	Czech.	59	2,665	14·3	17,000	34,500
9	7·5-cm. (2·95-in.)	7·5-cm. A.A. gun, L/60		60	2,775	14·3	17,815	37,000
10	7·65-cm. (3-in.)	7·65-cm. A.A. gun ..	Czech.	55	2,620	17·6	18,800	37,500
11	8-cm. (3·1-in.)	8-cm. A.A. gun, L/50	Czech.	50	2,460	17·6	16,600	29,520
12	8·3-cm. (3·3-in.).	8·3-cm. A.A. gun, L/55	Czech.	55	2,625	22·4	20,710	39,500
13	8·8-cm. (3·46-in.)	8·8-cm. A.A. gun, L/56 (Plates 36 and 32).	—	56	2,750	19·8	16,000	37,000
14	9-cm. (3·54-in.)	9-cm. A.A. gun ..	Czech.	50	2,540	22·4	13,700	30,000
15	10·5-cm. (4·14-in.)	10·5-cm. A.A. gun ..	—	60	2,950	32·2	19,100	42,640
16	12·7-cm. (4·99-in.)	12·7-cm. A.A. gun ..	—	50	2,500	55	19,500	42,000
17	15-cm. (5·91-in.)	15-cm. A.A. gun ..	—		3,450	89		66,000

Note :—Blank spaces denote no information available

UNS USED BY GERMANY

Rate of fire (r.p.m.)		Elevation.	Depression.	Traverse.	Weight in action.	Method of transport.	Remarks.
heoretical.	Practical.						
280		90°	0°	360°	1,012 lb.	Towed by light tractor.	Fires self-destroying tracer ammunition.
150		85°	−10°	360°	1·7 tons	Towed by 6-wheeled Herschell on Krupp lorries.	Fires self-destroying tracer ammunition.
120	80					Towed by Krupp Diesel lorry.	Fires self-destroying tracer ammunition.
140	80	90°	− 5°	360°	1·9 tons	Lorry drawn.	Fires self-destroying tracer ammunition.
25	15	85°	−10°	360°	1·7 tons		
				360°			
		90°	0°	360°	2·8 tons	Lorry drawn.	
20	20	85°	− 3°	360°	2·9 tons	Lorry drawn.	
20	20	85°	− 3°	360°	2·9 tons	Tractor drawn.	
20	20	85°	− 1°	360°	3·9 tons	Lorry drawn.	
20	20	80°	− 3°	360°	3·8 tons	Tractor drawn.	
15	9	90°	0°	360°	7,480 lb.	Railway or tractor drawn.	
25	15	85°	− 3°	360°	5·2 tons	Tractor drawn.	
15	8	80°	0°	360°	6·4 tons		
15	15	80°	10°	360°	11·7 tons	Tractor drawn.	
20	12	90°	0°	360°		Tractor drawn.	
15	10						

CHAPTER VII

ARMOURED FIGHTING TROOPS
(Panzertruppen)

A.—The Arm

1. General

(a) *Organization.*—This arm of the Service is controlled by the Inspectorate of Mobile Troops in the War Ministry. It includes:—

    (i) Armoured units (i.e., tank regiments and tank battalions in armoured divisions or organized as independent units).

    (ii) Unarmoured units (i.e., anti-tank battalions).

These two types of units are described respectively in Sections B and C.

(b) *Terminology.*

(i) *Armoured units.*—The basic units and sub-units are the "Regiment," "Abteilung," "Kompanie," and "Zug," which, to correspond with British nomenclature, have been translated as "regiment," "battalion," "squadron," and "troop."

Tanks classified in the German army as "medium" and "light medium" correspond to cruiser and light cruiser tanks in the British army.

(ii) *Unarmoured units.*—The basic units and sub-units are the "Abteilung," "Kompanie," and "Zug," which have been translated as "battalion," "company," and "platoon."

(c) *Strength.*

(i) *Armoured units.*—The Germans are believed to have a minimum of thirteen armoured divisions. Each armoured division is thought to include one tank brigade of two tank regiments, each of two mixed tank battalions, each of approximately 100 tanks. (*See* Appendices XVII and XIX.)

In addition, a number of independent tank units is known to exist.

(ii) *Unarmoured units.*—(a) Heavy anti-tank battalions (*schwere Panzerjäger-Abteilungen*). These are G.H.Q. troops and are allotted to armies and corps as required.*

(b) Anti-tank units (*Panzerjäger-Abteilungen*).—One in each armoured, motorized, infantry and mountain division.

(c) Infantry anti-tank companies (*Panzerjägerkompanien*). One in each infantry regiment.

B.—Armoured Units

Note.—Details of the various known types of tanks and armoured cars are given in Appendices XXII and XXIV. Distinguishing features of German tanks and armoured cars are set out in Appendices XXIII and XXV.

2. Special types of A.F.Vs.

(a) *Super-heavy tanks.*—These probably exist in small numbers but, so far as is known, they have not yet been issued to units. (*See* Appendix XXII, Note 1.)

(b) *Flame-throwing tanks* (*Flata*).—There are reliable reports of the existence of flame-throwing tanks. They are probably light tanks of German or ex-Polish type, which are said to be suitable for conversion.

(c) *Armoured troop-carrying vehicles.*—These are half-tracked vehicles, lightly armoured all round. The front closely resembles that of a medium six-wheeled armoured car, the rear portion of the vehicle being armoured at the back and at the sides to a level some 4 ft. above the top of the tracks and open at the top. The armour slopes outwards at rear and sides to a point about 18 in. above the rear mudguard over the tracks. (*See* Plate 65.) Numbers of these vehicles were used on the Western Front by lorried infantry of armoured divisions.

(d) *Armoured commanders' cars* (*Befehlspanzer*).—These vehicles, which are similar in appearance to the armoured troop-carrying vehicles described above, are equipped with wireless and are used by divisional commanders and by commanders of armoured corps or groups.

---

* Details of the organization of these units are lacking, but they are armed with 8·8-cm. (3·46-in.) A.A. guns and 4·7-cm. (1·85-in.) and 3·7-cm. (1·45-in.) A.Tk. guns.

3. Mixed tank regiment (*Panzer-Regiment*) in an armoured division

(a) *Organization*—(*see* Appendix XIX).

(i) *Regiment.*—At present there are two mixed tank regiments in the tank brigade of an armoured division. Each of these regiments consists of :—

    H.Q. and H.Q. light tank troop with two light tanks, each armed with one 2-cm. (·79-in.) machine-gun and one light machine-gun, two light tanks each armed with two light machine-guns, and one commander model light tank.

    Signal section containing two wireless and two 'telephone sections ; the wireless sections are carried in medium tanks.

    Regimental workshop company. (*See* para. 7.)

    Two mixed tank battalions.

(ii) *Battalion.*—A mixed tank battalion consists of :—

    H.Q. and H.Q. light tank troop, similar to that at regimental headquarters.

    Headquarters sqn., consisting of reserve tank crews.

    Signal section, consisting of two light telephone sub-sections, one W/T transmitter carried in a Pz. Kw. II tank and four W/T transmitters mounted on two Pz. Kw. IV tanks.

    Three light tank squadrons.

    One medium tank squadron.

    Light tank column for fuel, ammunition and spare parts.

(iii) *Light squadron.*—A light tank squadron consists of :—

    Headquarters containing one commander model light medium tank.

    H.Q. troop containing one light tank armed with one 2-cm. (·79-in.) machine-gun and light machine-gun, and two light tanks each armed with two light machine-guns.

    Liaison section, with one cross-country motor car and eight M.Cs., for communication when W/T is not used, and reconnaissance of routes, assembly places, etc.

    Three troops each containing three light tanks each armed with one 2-cm. (·79-in.) machine-gun and one light machine-gun and two light tanks each armed with two light machine-guns.

    One troop of five light-medium tanks each armed with one 3·7-cm. (1·45-in.) gun and two light machine-guns.

(iv) *Medium squadron.*—A medium tank squadron consists of :—

Headquarters containing one medium tank armed with one 7·5-cm. (2·95-in.) gun and one light machine-gun.

H.Q. troop containing three light tanks each armed with one 2-cm. (·79-in.) machine-gun and one light machine-gun and two light tanks each armed with two light machine-guns.

Liaison section, similar to that in light squadron.

Four troops each containing three medium tanks each armed with one 7·5-cm. (2·95-in.) gun, and two light machine-gun.

(b) *Strength.*

(b) Strength

	Officers	Other Ranks	Medium Tank Pz. Kw. IV	Light Medium Tank Pz. Kw. III	3-man Light Tank Pz. Kw. II	2-man Light Tank Pz. Kw. I	Total First Line Tanks	Reserve Tanks	Motor cycles	Motor cars	Lorries for men	Lorries	Trailers
Regiment—													
Regt. H.Q. Staff	6	7	—	—	—	—	—	—	—	3	—	—	—
H.Q. Lt. Tank Tp.	2	29	—	—	3	2	5	—	1	1	1	—	—
Reg. Sig. Sec.	1	32	2	—	1	—	3	—	1	1	—	3	—
H.Q.M.C.D.R.Sec.	—	6	—	—	—	—	—	—	6	—	—	—	—
Regt. Transport	2	18	—	—	—	—	—	—	—	1	—	5	—
Regt. Workshop Co.	5	134	—	—	—	—	—	—	7	4	—	28	12
Battalion—													
Bn. H.Q. Staff	6	21	—	—	—	—	—	—	—	5	—	—	—
H.Q. Lt. Tank Tp.	2	29	—	—	3	2	5	—	1	1	1	—	—
Bn. Sig. Sec.	1	32	2	—	1	—	3	—	1	1	1	3	—
Bn. H.Q.M.C.D.R.Sec.	—	11	—	—	—	—	—	—	11	—	—	—	—
H.Q. Bn. H.Q. Sqn.	1	7	—	—	—	—	—	—	1	4	—	—	—
Bn. Transport	1	17	—	—	—	—	—	—	2	1	—	5	—
Lt. Tank Column	1	48	—	—	—	—	—	—	7	—	—	—	—
Lt. Tank Sqn.	5	208	—	6	10	8	24	2–4	15	4	5	10	1
Med. Tank Sqn.	5	210	13	—	3	2	18	2–4	15	4	5	18	1
Total of Battalion	32	999	15	18	37	28	98	8–16	82	28	23	66	4
Total of Regiment	80	2,224	32	36	78	58	204	16–32	179	66	47	168	20

(c) Armament.—*See* Appendices XX and XXI.
(d) Regimental specialists.—*See* para. 6.
(e) Equipment.—*See* para. 8.

4. Independent tank units

There are a number of unallotted tank regiments and battalions (which are believed to be organized in the same way as tank regiments and battalions in an armoured division) which may be allotted to infantry corps or divisions.

So far as is known, no units have yet been equipped with infantry tanks.

5. Transport

Details of estimated numbers of vehicles in first line transport of a tank unit are given in para. 3 (b) above.

Each tank battalion has a light tank column which carries fuel, ammunition and spare parts.

6. Regimental specialists

(a) *Signallers.*—Signal personnel are trained within the unit. One man in each tank acts as a wireless operator. Such details of signal equipment as are known are given in para. 8.

(b) *M.T. specialists.*—All tank personnel are trained as mechanics and can carry out minor repairs. Mechanics with more specialised knowledge are included in the establishments of squadron, battalion and regimental headquarters. (*See* para. 7.)

7. Maintenance in the field

Each tank squadron and the headquarters troop of each battalion has a light aid section which carries spare parts on a generous scale and is organized to carry out running repairs with the utmost despatch. It consists of mechanics, wireless instrument mechanics and motor drivers. Its transport includes light lorries for spare parts and tools and a converted tank for transporting spare parts and mechanics across country to stranded tanks. At battalion headquarters there is a light aid section under an officer who can when necessary arrange for all the light aid sections to proceed to any part of the front where their services are urgently required.

Each regiment has a workshop company which is equipped with machine tools and can carry out all but the heaviest repairs. It produces its own power and is therefore quite independent of stationary workshops. The workshop company consists of two identical platoons which may each be attached to a battalion or may "leap-frog" behind the regiment, so as to ensure continuity in repair work. The workshop company, in addition, has a breakdown platoon for bringing in stranded tanks, and an armoury and a signals repair shop.

Spare parts are also carried in the light tank column in each battalion.

8. Equipment

Signal equipment.—Each commander's tank is equipped with wireless apparatus capable of sending and receiving, and each of the other tanks with receiving apparatus only.

A system of flag signals is also used.

C.—Unarmoured Units

9. Anti-tank Battalion (Panzerjäger-Abteilung)*

(a) Organization

(i) *Battalion.*—An anti-tank battalion, which is fully mechanized, forms part of each infantry, motorized infantry, armoured and mountain division. It consists of headquarters, signal section, three anti-tank companies and probably one anti-aircraft company.

(ii) *Company.*—An anti-tank company consists of headquarters, signal section and three platoons. Each platoon consists of four sections, each armed with one 3·7 cm. (1·45-in.) A.Tk. gun, and one section armed with two light machine-guns.

(iii) *Anti-aircraft company.*—This is believed to consist of twelve 2-cm. super-heavy (·79-in.) A.A. and A.Tk. machine-guns.

---

* *Note.*—To emphasise the offensive character of anti-tank units these are now officially described as "tank hunter" (*Panzerjäger*) instead of "anti-tank defence" (*Panzerabwehr*) units.

(b) *Strength**

Details of organization are not yet confirmed, but are believed to be as follows :—

—	Officers.	Other ranks.	Motor-cycles.	M.C. combinations.	4-seater cars.	Motor limbers.	Field kitchen on lorry.	Lorries for repairs, petrol, supplies, baggage.	Wireless cars.	Telephone car.
A.Tk. Bn. Sig. Sec.	1	36	2	1	1	—	—	—	8	1
A.Tk. Coy.	4	152	6	12	32	12	1	4	—	—
A.Tk. Pl.	1	42	1	3	10	4	—	—	—	—
A.A. Coy.										
A.A. Pl.										

* In cases where the strength of personnel and/or vehicles is not known, columns have been left blank.

(c) *Armament*—See Appendix XXI.

(d) *Ammunition supply*

   (i) *Light machine-gun.*—About 1,000 rounds are carried on the vehicle with the weapon. A reserve is carried in the company and battalion ammunition vehicles.

   (ii) *Anti-tank gun.*—330 rounds per gun are carried by the company and a further 25 rounds per gun in the battalion ammunition vehicles.

   (iii) *Super-heavy machine-guns.*— No information is available.

(e) *Battalion specialists*

   (i) *Signallers.*—Signal personnel are trained within the unit. The strength of the signal section is given in sub-para. (b) above and the signal equipment provided, in sub-para. (g) (i) below.

   (ii) *Mechanics.*—All drivers of M.T. vehicles in this unit are given a thorough mechanical training. Mechanics with more specialised knowledge are carried in the lorry workshop attached to each company.

(f) *Maintenance in the field*

Each anti-tank company has one lorry workshop and four other lorries carrying petrol and oil, ammunition, baggage and supplies.

(g) *Equipment*

(i) *Signal equipment.—*

	Pack Wireless Sets.	Medium cable (miles).	Light cable (miles).
A.Tk. Bn. Sig. Sec.	2 Type d 6 ,, b	4	4
A.Tk. Coy. Sig. Sec.	5		

(ii) *Tools.—*No details are available regarding the tools carried in anti-tank battalions.

(iii) *Equipment for the construction of road blocks.—* Each platoon carries twelve rolls of concertina wire.

Chapter VII

Chapter VII

APPENDIX XVII

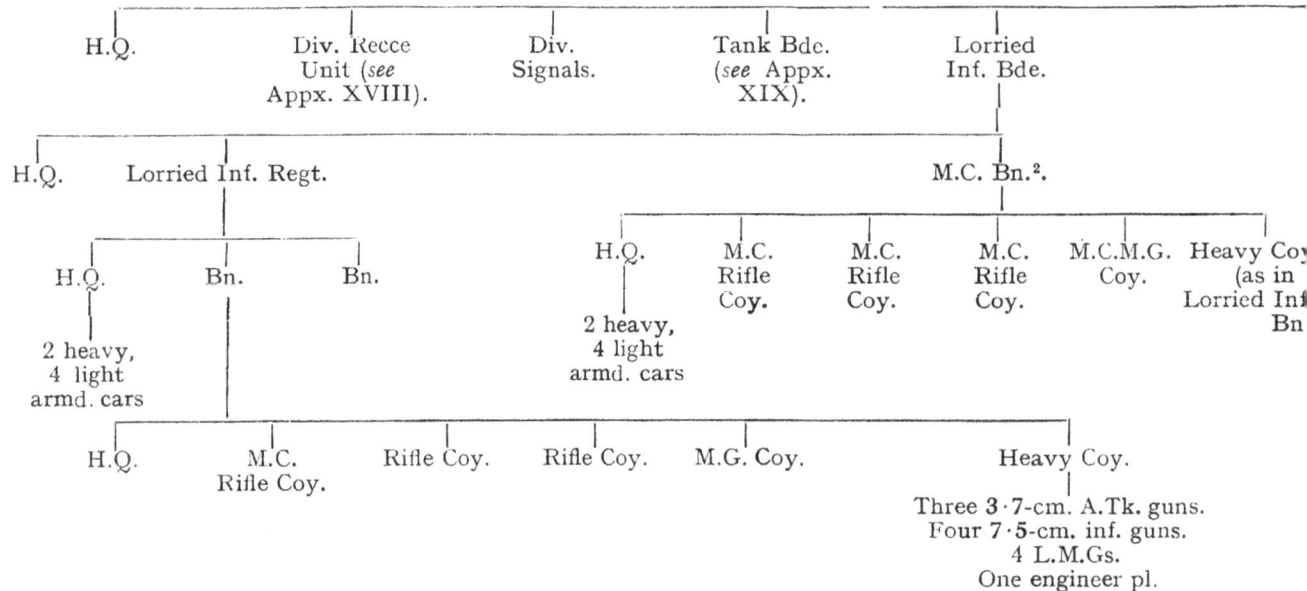

NOTES:—

[1] It has not yet been definitely established whether it is intended to include one of these units in each division, or whether they are to remain G.H.Q. troops.

[2] This may have been expanded to form a regiment or replaced by a second lorried infantry regiment.

ARMOURED DIVISION ON

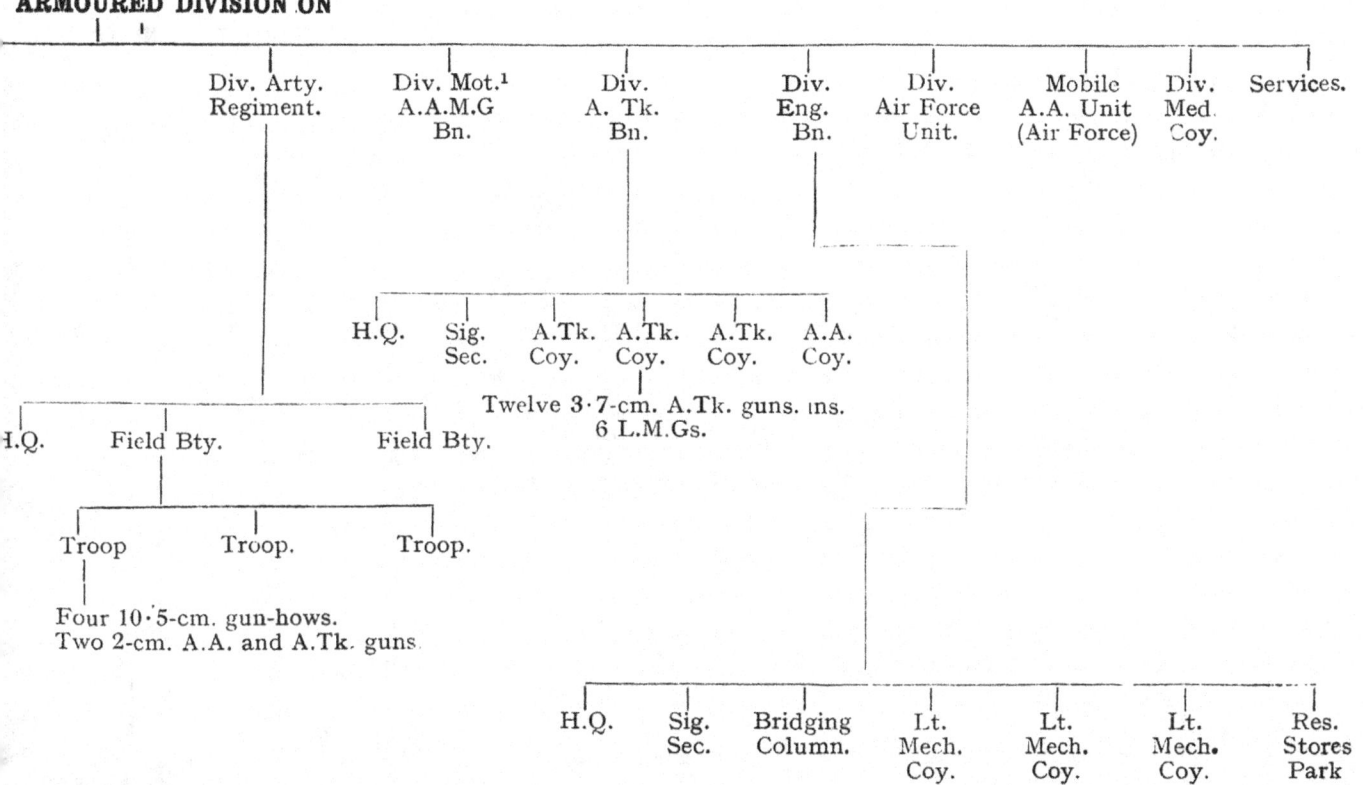

Chapter VII

APPENDIX XVIII

MECHANISED RECONNAISSANCE

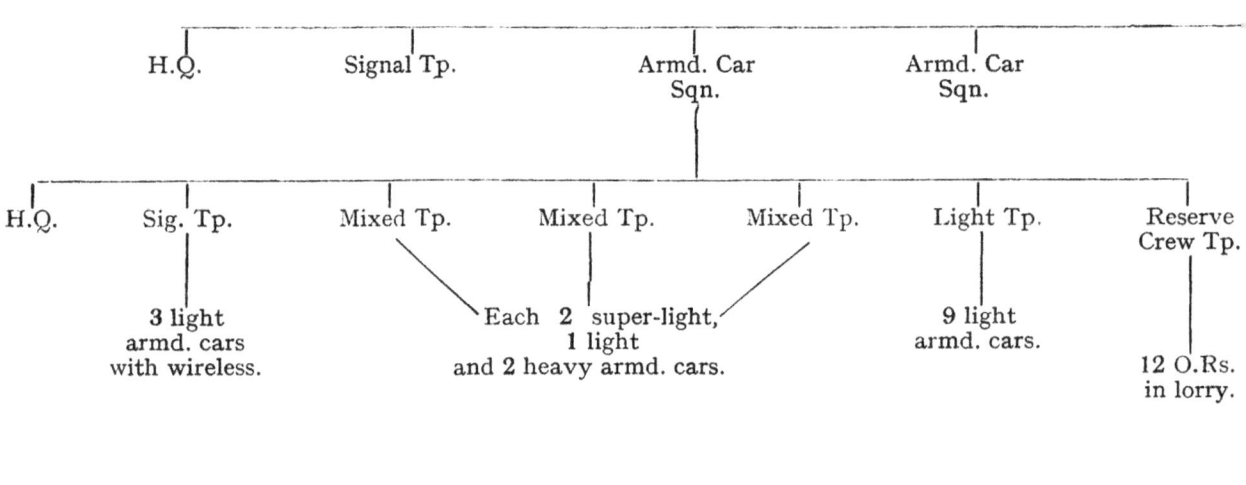

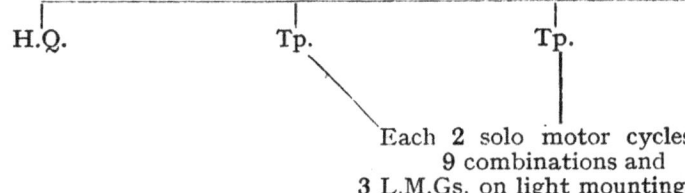

Note.—Armour of above armoured cars is as follows :—
1. Super-light armoured cars : 10 mm. in front, less at sides. Proof against A.P. S.A.A. in front but onl[y]
2. Light armoured cars : 10 mm. in front, 8 mm. at sides. Proof against A.P. S.A.A. all round.
3. Heavy armoured cars : 30 mm. on turret, 5–20 mm. elsewhere. All plates inclined from normal.

Types of German armoured cars are shown in Plates 60 to 64.

NIT OF AN ARMOURED DIVISION.

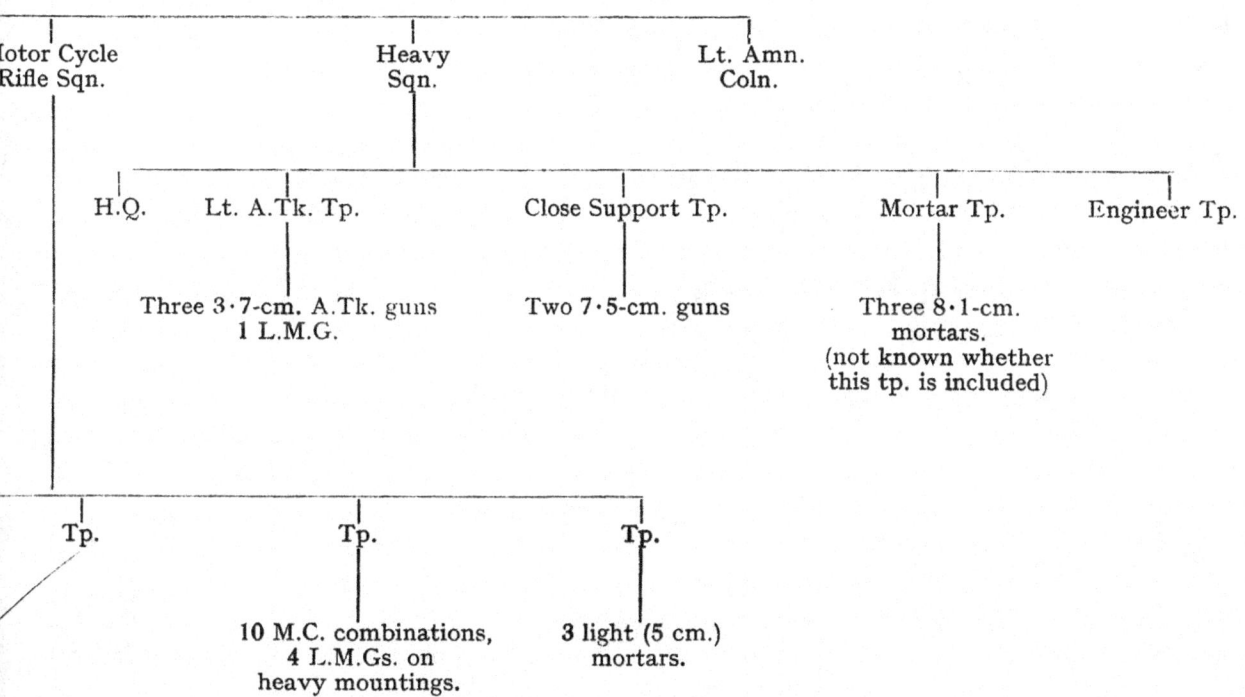

gainst S.A.A. at sides, as plates are vertical.

Chapter VII

APPENDIX XI

TANK BRIGADE

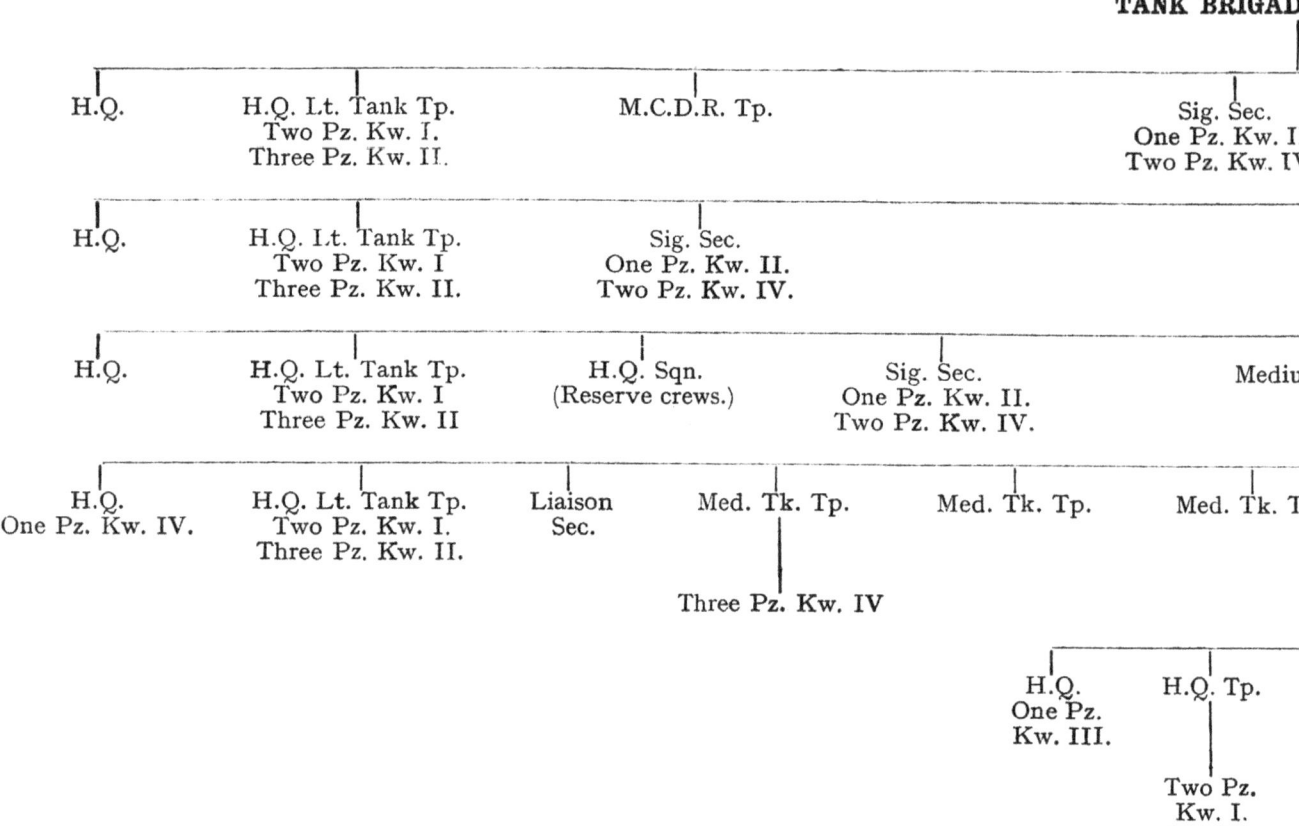

Note.—The above is the organization of a tank brigade, equipped entirely with German tanks. It is to be expected, however, that certain tank brigades, whether independent or in armoured divisions, will be equipped with Czech, Polish or other captured tanks, and in such cases there may be variations from the above organization. Pz. Kw. V/VI tanks may also have been issued to units.

Types of tanks used by Germany are shown in Plates 38 to 59.

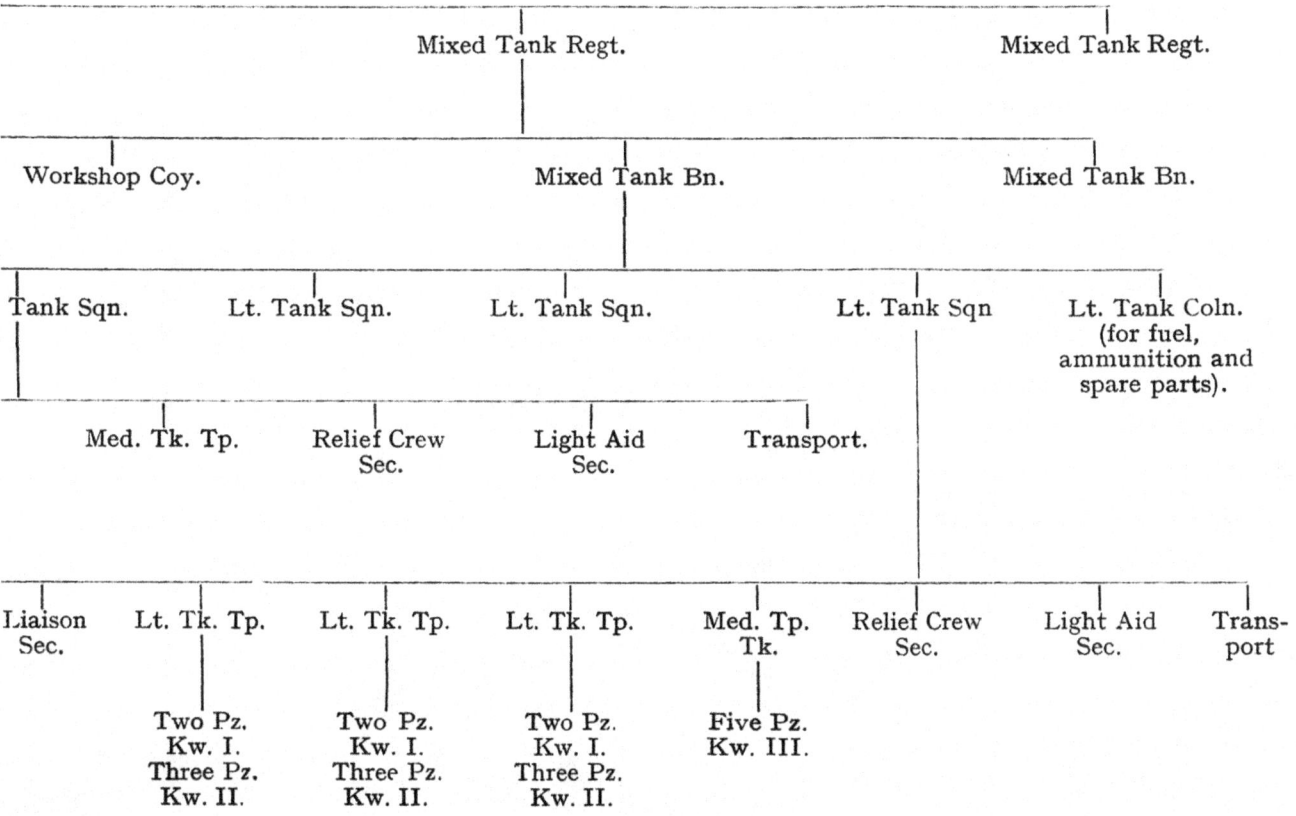

Chapter VII

APPENDIX XX

MIXED TANK REGIMENT

(i) *Organization.*—See Appendix XIX.

(ii) *Tank Strength*

Unit.	Pz. Kw. I.	Pz. Kw. II.	Pz. Kw. III.	Pz. Kw. IV.	
Regtl. H.Q.	2	4	—	2	
Bn. H.Q.	2	4	—	2	
Light Squadron	8	10	6	—	
Med. Squadron	2	3	—	13	
Total Regt. (excluding reserve tanks).	58	78	36	32	204

Note.—The figures given above are for a regiment equipped with German tanks throughout. It is to be expected, however, that certain tank regiments will be equipped with Czech, Polish, and other captured tanks. Pz. Kw. V/VI tanks may also have been issued to units.

(iii) *Fire Power*

Unit.	L.M.G.s	2-cm. (·79-in.).	3·7-cm. (1·45-in.).	7·5-cm. (2·95-in.).
Regtl. H.Q.	10	2	—	2
Bn. H.Q.	10	2	—	2
Light Squadron	37	10	5	—
Med. Squadron	32	3	—	13
Total Regt. (excluding Reserve Tanks),	316	72	30	32

Note.—(1) It is believed that each tank in the regiment is also equipped with two machine pistols, a total of 408 machine pistols.

(2) A proportion of tanks at regimental, battalion and squadron H.Q. are commanders' models with reduced armament.

APPENDIX XXI

ARMOURED DIVISION—SUMMARY OF A.F.Vs. AND WEAPONS
(excluding Div. H.Q. and reserve tanks).

Unit	Pz. Kw. V or VI (see Plates 58 and 59)	Pz. Kw. IV (see Plate 57)	Pz. Kw. III (see Plates 54, 55 and 56)	Pz. Kw. II (see Plates 46 and 47)	Pz. Kw. I (see Plate 40)	Heavy Armd. Cars (see Plates 60 to 64)	Light Armd. Cars (see Plates 60 to 64)	L.M.G.s	Heavy M.G.s	2-cm. Super-heavy M.G.s	3·7-cm. Gun	7·5-cm. Gun	10·5-cm. Gun-How.	5-cm. Light Mortar	8·1-cm. Mortar
Recce. Unit	—	—	—	—	—	12	42	63	6	12	3	2	—	3	3
Tank Bde.	—	66	72	160	118	—	—	642	—	146	60	66	—	—	—
A.Tk. Bn.	—	—	—	—	—	—	—	18	—	12	36	12	—	—	—
Lorried Inf. Bde.	—	—	—	—	—	4	8	105	50	4	9	—	—	—	—
Motorized A.A. M.G. Bn.	—	—	—	—	—	—	—	—	—	36	—	—	—	—	—
Div. Artillery	—	—	—	—	—	—	—	12	—	12	—	—	24	—	—
Engineer Bn.	—	—	—	—	—	—	—	29	—	—	—	—	—	—	—
Total	—	66	72	160	118	16	50	869	56	222	108	80	24	3	3
	Tanks					Armd. Cars		Fire Power							

Chapter VII

APPENDIX XXI

PARTICULARS OF TYPES O[F]

Serial No.	Type.	Name.	Country of Origin.	Weight.	Crew.	Dimensions. 1. Length. 2. Width. 3. Height. 4. Belly clearance.	Armour Basis (thickest plate known).	Armament.	Ammunition Carried.
1	Light	T.K. T.K.F. T.K.S.	Poland	2·5 tons	2. Dvr. and gnr.	1. 8 ft. 6 in. 2. 6 ft. 0 in. 3. 4 ft. 6 in. 4. 1 ft. 0 in.	10 mm.	2 ·79-cm. Hotchkiss or 1 2-cm. A.Tk. gun.	2,300 rds.
2	Light	Pz. Kw. I	Germany	5·7 tons	2. Dvr. and gnr.	1. 13 ft. 0 in. 2. 6 ft. 5 in. 3. 5 ft. 8 in. 4. 1 ft. 0 in.	14 mm.	2 L.M.Gs.	1,625 A.P., S.A.
3	Light	Light Cmdrs. Tank Pz. Kw. I	Germany	5·7 tons	3. Dvr., gnr. and cmdr.	1. 13 ft. 0 in. 2. 6 ft. 5 in. 3. 5 ft. 8 in. 4. 1 ft. 0 in.	14 mm.	1 L.M.G.	
4	Light amphibian.	F.IV. H.E.	Czecho-slovakia.	6·2 tons	3. Dvr., gnr. and cmdr.	1. 16 ft. 9 in. 2. 8 ft. 2 in. 3. 6 ft. 11 in. 4. 1 ft. 0 in.	14 mm.	1 Hy. M.G.	4,000 rds.
5	Light	T.N. H.P.	Czecho-slovakia.	8·5 tons, now raised to 10 tons.	3–4. 2 gnrs., cmdr., wireless operator, dvr.	1. 15 ft. 2 in. 2. 6 ft. 9 in. 3. 7 ft. 4 in. 4. 1 ft. 4 in.	25 mm. (may be increased by 50%)	1 3·7-cm. gun 2 Hy. M.Gs.	90 rds. for gun 2,700 rds. for M.Gs.
6	Light medium.	A.H. IV Sv.	Czecho-slovakia.	10 tons	3. Dvr., gnr., and cmdr.-gnr.	1. 16 ft. 6 in. 2. 6 ft. 7 in. 3. 7 ft. 3 in. 4. 1 ft. 2 in.	24 mm.	1 3·7-cm. gun. 1 M.G. in hull.	120 rds. for gun 3,000 rds. for M.G.
7	Light	Pz.Kw. II	Germany	9 tons	3. Dvr., gnr. and wireless operator.	1. 14 ft. 8 in. 2. 6 ft. 0 in. 3. 5 ft. 6 in. 4.	15 mm.	1 2-cm. Hy. M.G. 1 L.M.G.	
8	Light medium.	7 T.P.	Poland	9·5 tons	2. Dvr., gnr., cmdr. - wireless operator.	1. 15 ft. 0 in. 2. 7 ft. 11 in. 3. 7 ft. 2 in. 4. 1 ft. 3 in.	25 mm.	1 3·7-cm. Bofors. 1 L.M.G. coaxially mounted.	80 rds. for gun 4,000 rds. for L.M.G.
9	Light medium.	L.T. 35	Czecho-slovakia.	11·5 tons	3. Dvr., cmdr., gnr.-wireless operator.	1. 16 ft. 2 in. 2. 7 ft. 6 in. 3. 7 ft. 10 in. 4.	25 mm.	1 3·7-cm. gun. 1 L.M.G. coaxially mounted. 1 L.M.G. on ball mounting forward in hull.	90 rds. for gun. 3,000 rds. for L.M.G.
10	Light medium	C.K.D. V.8.H.	Czecho-slovakia.	16·5 tons	4. Dvr., cmdr., 2 gnrs.	1. 17 ft. 6 in. 2. 7 ft. 6 in. 3. 7 ft. 8 in. 4. 1 ft. 6 in.	36 mm.	1 4·7-cm. gun. 1 Hy. M.G. coaxially mounted. 1 Hy. M.G. to left of driver.	90 rds. for 4·7-cm. gun. 3,000 for Hy. M.Gs.
11	Light medium.	Pz. Kw.III	Germany	18–20 tons	3–4. Dvr., 2 gnrs. (and hull gnr.-wireless operator).	1. 16 ft. 5 in. 2. 7 ft. 6 in. 3. 7 ft. 6 in. 4.	30 mm.	1 3·7-cm. gun. 1 L.M.G. coaxially mounted. 1 L.M.G. in hull.	
12	Medium	Pz. Kw.IV	Germany	22 tons	5. Dvr., hull gnr., wireless operator, cmdr., gnr. and ldr.	1. 17 ft. 0 in. approx. 2. 7 ft. 3 in. 3. 8 ft. 6 in.	43 mm.	1 7·5-cm. gun. 1 L.M.G. coaxially mounted. 1 L.M.G. on ball mounting to right of driver.	
13	Heavy.	Pz. Kw. V	Germany	32–35 tons	7–8. 1 dvr., cmdr., wireless operator, 3 gnrs., 1–2 ldrs.	1. 25–26 ft. 2. 9 ft. 3. 10–11 ft. 4.	50 mm.	1 7·5-cm. and 1 3·7-cm. gun mounted coaxially horizontally. 3 L.M.Gs. (1 in main turret, 1 in each subsidiary M.G. turret fore and aft).	
14	Heavy	Pz. Kw. VI	Germany	35 tons	7–8. 1 dvr., cmdr., wireless operator, 3 gnrs., 1–2 ldrs.	1. 25–26 ft. 2. 9 ft. 3. 10–11 ft. 4.	50 mm.	1 10·5-cm. and 1 3·7-cm. gun mounted coaxially vertically. 3 L.M.Gs. (1 in main turret, 1 in each subsidiary M.G. turret fore and aft).	

Note 1. *Super-heavy Tanks.*—It is reported that experiments are being carried out with several types of super-heavy tanks with weights between 60 and 120 tons 15 cm. and the armour basis 70 mm. and over. Details are not at present known. None of these tanks has, as far as is known, been issued to units.

Note 2. *Amphibian Tanks.*—Reports have been received of experimental amphibian tanks of varying types ranging up to super-heavy.

Note 3. Numbers of Czech T.N.H.P. amphibian tanks have made their appearance in occupied France (*see* Plate 45).

TANKS USED BY GERMANY

Engine.	Drive.	Maximum Speed on roads.	Radius of Action.	Suspension.	Performance. 1. Trench crossing. 2. Step. 3. Wtr. forded. 4. Max. gradient.	Inter-communication.	Remarks.
4 h.p., 4-cyl. Ford. 5 h.p., 6-cyl. Fiat.	Front sprocket.	28 m.p.h.	85 miles	2 prs. of bogies. Carden-Lloyd system.	1. 5 ft. 0 in. 2. 1 ft. 4 in. 3. 1 ft 8 in. 4. 45°	Flag	May be equipped with 2-cm. M.Gs. and used as A.Tk. M.G. carriers. Carden-Lloyd design. Poland had 750.
0/100 h.p. V.8. Air cooled.	Front sprocket.	32 m.p.h.	95 miles	5 bogies, 1 independently sprung; 4 connected by girder.	1. 4 ft. 7 in. 2. 3. 2 ft. 0 in. 4. 45°	W/T receiver	A large number of these tanks is in existence, and may be converted to M.G. carriers. Standard German A.F.V.
0/100 h.p. V.8. Air cooled.	Front sprocket.	32 m.p.h.	95 miles	5 bogies, 1 independently sprung; 4 connected by girder.	1. 4 ft. 7 in. 2. 3. 2 ft. 0 in. 4. 45°	W/T and R/T	Armoured office with fixed square turret.
20 h.p., 4-cyl. Water cooled.	Rear sprocket.	28 m.p.h. 3½ m.p.h. in water.	90 miles	4 large wheels	1. 7 ft. 1 in. 2. 2 ft. 8 in. 3. 4. 35°–45°	W/T, flag and lamp.	100 of these are known to exist. An improved model may have been produced.
25 h.p.,6-cyl. Water cooled.	Front sprocket.	53 m.p.h.	125 miles	2 prs. of large wheels. Leaf springing.	1. 6 ft. 5 in. 2. 2 ft. 8 in. 3. 1 ft. 4 in. 4. 40°–45°	R/T, flag and lamp.	A large number of these has been delivered to Germany, and may be replacing Pz. Kw. I. The model with increased armour may be used as an "I" tank.
20 h.p., 4-cyl Praga. Water cooled.	Front sprocket.	53 m.p.h.	93 miles	4 large wheels.	1. 6 ft. 7 in. 2. 2 ft. 0 in. 3. 2 ft. 7 in. 4. 40°–45°	R/T and coloured lights.	Combination of Skoda-Praga known to the Czechs as the S.P.2. Very good on trials and had been approved for large-scale production.
25 h.p. V.S. Air cooled.	Front sprocket.	28 m.p.h.	125 miles	5 wheels, Christie type. Older type has 6 small bogies, 4 connected by girder.	1. 4 ft. 11 in. 2. 1 ft. 11 in. 3. 2 ft. 6 in. 4. 45°	W/T receiver	May be converted to flame thrower. A large number in existence. Standard German A.F.V.
40 h.p., 6-cyl. Diesel. Water cooled.	Front sprocket.	22 m.p.h.	90 miles	8 bogie wheels. 2 prs. of twin bogies on rocker with leaf springing.	1. 6 ft. 0 in. 2. 2 ft. 6 in. 3. 3 ft. 0 in. 4. 40°	W/T	This vehicle is probably being manufactured for Germany with an increased armour basis.
10 h.p., 6-cyl.	Front sprocket.	22 m.p.h.	70 miles	9 small bogie wheels, 1 independent; 2 bogies with twin bogie wheels on rocker with leaf springing.	1. 6 ft. 6 in. 2. 2 ft 7 in. 3. 2 ft. 7 in. 4. 40°	R/T and W/T, lamp and flag	Considered to be the best tank in the Czech army.
45 h.p. V.8	Rear sprocket.	27 m.p.h.	77 miles	9 bogie wheels, 1 independent bogie; 4 prs. of bogies each with semi-elliptic leaf springing connected by outside bearer girder.	1. 7 ft. 6 in. 2. 3 ft. 3 in. 3. 3 ft. 3 in. 4. 41°	W/T and R/T, lamp.	Latest design of Czech tank. Will probably be extensively used by the Germans.
300 h.p.	Front sprocket.	28 m.p.h.		(a) Latest type with 6 small rubber bogies independently sprung. (b) 5 wheels, Christie system. (c) 8 small bogies in 4 prs. with leaf springing.	1. 2. 3. 2 ft. 11 in. approx 4.	W/T	Standard German A.F.V. Commander or communication tank, has a fixed turret with dummy guns. Good observation.
350 h.p.	Front sprocket.	31 m.p.h.		8 small bogie wheels. 4 prs. with leaf springing.	1. 2. 3. 3 ft. 6 in. 4.	W/T and R/T	The armour plating on this tank has recently been increased considerably which will probably impair its efficiency and performance. Standard German A.F.V.
650 h.p. (?)	Rear sprocket.	20 m.p.h. (?)	75–85 miles	11 small bogies. 1 fixed independent bogie; 5 prs. of bogies, each pr. sprung on knee action system. Suspension protected by armoured skirting.	1. 11 ft. 6 in. 2. 4 ft. 7 in. 3. 3 ft. 4 in. 4.	W/T and R/T	These particulars require confirmation.
650 h.p. (?)	Rear sprocket.	20 m.p.h. (?)	75–85 miles	11 small bogies. 1 fixed independent bogie; 5 prs. of bogies, each pr. sprung on knee action system. Suspension protected by armoured skirting.	1. 11 ft. 6 in. 2. 4 ft. 7 in. 3. 3 ft. 4 in. 4.	W/T and R/T	These particulars require confirmation.

These tanks are reported to be armed with machine guns, A.Tk. weapons, guns, and possibly flame throwers. The guns are of calibre varying between 4·7 cm. and

APPENDIX XXIII

DISTINGUISHING FEATURES OF TANKS USED BY GERMANY

1. T.K., T.K.F. and T.K.S.

Suspension.—Normal Carden Lloyd light tankette with outside girder bearer on the suspension. Three jockey wheels connected by girder.

May either have twin cupolas or built-up box-shaped hull.

2. Pz. Kw. I

Suspension.—Five bogie wheels with spokes, the last four being connected by an outside girder bearer. Rear idler wheel almost on the ground. Four jockey wheels.

Turret.—Two L.M.Gs. mounted coaxially on roller type mounting. The turret has a rounded back and is on the right-hand side of the tank, and very squat.

General appearance.—Wide track base; squat, streamlined turret. Two bulges in front plate of hull house driving and steering mechanism.

3. Light Commander's Tank

Suspension.—Same suspension as Pz. Kw. I.

The hull is built up to form a square fixed turret, which has a L.M.G. mounted on the right-hand side in a ball mounting. A square cupola is mounted on the top of the turret.

4. F.IV. H.E. (Amphibian)

Suspension.—Four large bogie wheels. High front idler wheel. Float which comes down as far as the top of the bogie wheels.

The vehicle has twin screws at the rear, and a small round turret with Hy.M.G. on ball mounting. On the top of the turret is a round lookout cupola approximately a quarter of the size of the main turret.

5. T.N. H.P.

Suspension.—Four large bogie wheels studded with rivets. Low rear idler wheel. Three jockey wheels.

Turret.—Round turret surmounted by round observation cupola on the right-hand side. 3·7-cm. gun and Hy. M.G. mounted coaxially in turret, and one Hy.M.G. mounted in the hull to left of driver.

6. A.H. IV Sv.

Suspension.—Four large bogie wheels, Christie type. One jockey wheel.

Turret.—Round turret on left-hand side surmounted by round observation cupola. One 3·7-cm. gun, one M.G. mounted in turret.

7. Pz. Kw. II

Suspension.—Five large bogie wheels, Christie type, four jockey wheels.

Turret.—Similar to Pz. Kw. I. Has one Hy.M.G. (with very long barrel) and one L.M.G. in roller type mounting. The back of the turret is flat.

General appearance.—Wide track base; very squat and streamlined.

8. 7 T.P.

Suspension.—Eight small bogie wheels. Two bogies. High front driving sprocket. Spoked rear idler wheel. Four jockey wheels.

Turret.—High turret with long barrelled gun in round mounting. Square bulge at back of turret to take W/T set.

General appearance.—Similar to Vickers 6-ton light tank.

9. L.T. 35

Suspension.—Eight small bogie wheels. Four bogies. One independent bogie below front sprocket. Four jockey wheels. Both idler wheel and driving sprocket have large outside rim which overlaps the edge of the track.

Hull.—High, built-up hull, particularly noticeable from the rear. Round turret surmounted by observation cupola situated on the left-hand side. The 3·7-cm. gun and L.M.G. are mounted side by side on oblong face of turret. A large buffer and recuperator above and extending halfway along the gun barrel.

10. C.K.D. V. 8. H.

Suspension.—Eight bogie wheels. Four bogies connected by an outside girder bearer. One independent bogie below high front idler wheel. Four jockey wheels.

Turret.—Streamlined, tapering towards the rear, surmounted by cupola on right-hand side. 4·7-cm. gun and Hy. M.G. mounted coaxially in oblong turret face. Entrance to turret in hull to the left, behind turret.

11. Pz. Kw. III

Suspension.—(1) Six small independent bogie wheels with heavy rubber tyres.

(2) Eight small bogie wheels.

(3) Five large bogie wheels. Christie type. Three jockey wheels.

Turret.—Similar to Pz. Kw. II, but has large door on each side. 3·7-cm. gun and L.M.G. mounted in bulge-shaped mounting. Built into the rear of the turret and situated centrally is a small lookout conning tower which is round.

12. Pz. Kw. IV

Suspension.—Eight small bogie wheels. Four bogies. Four jockey wheels.

Turret.—Identical to that of Pz. Kw. III but with 7·5-cm. gun. Horizontal engine air louvres at rear on each side of built-up hull.

13. Pz. Kw. V/VI

Suspension.—Almost covered by armoured skirting. Ten small bogie wheels. One independent bogie wheel. Four jockey wheels.

Turret.—Turret round at rear, surmounted by observation cupola to the rear. Massive gun mounting with either a 10·5-cm. gun mounted below a 3·7-cm. gun, or a 7·5-cm. gun mounted at the side of a 3·7-cm. gun. Two small auxiliary turrets with one L.M.G. each, one forward to right of driver, one behind main turret on the left.

Chapter VII

APPENDIX XXIV

PARTICULARS OF TYPES OF ARMOURED

Serial.	Type.	Name.	Weight.	Crew.	Dimensions. 1. Length. 2. Width 3. Height. 4. Belly clearance.	Armour Basis (thickest plate known).	Armament.
1	Light	Leichter Panzer-spähwagen (Light Recce. car).	1·7 tons	2 (3 when wireless carried). Driver. Gunner.	1. 10 ft. 2. 5 ft. 6 in. 3. 5 ft. 3 in. 4. 1 ft. 6 in.(?)	10 mm.	1 L.M.G. (convertible to A.A.).
2	Light	Tatra 30	2·5 tons	3 1 Driver. 1 Gunner and 1 Commander.	1. 13 ft. 2. 4 ft. 10 in. 3. 6 ft. 6 in. 4. 1 ft. 11 in.	14 mm. ?	2 L.M.Gs.
3	Light	Horch 36 or Sd. Kfz. 221–2–3 (three types).	4–4·1 tons	2–3 Driver and Gunner (when wireless carried W/T Operator).	1. 10 ft. 2. 7 ft. 6 in. 3. 5 ft. 4 in. 4. 1 ft. 2 in.(?)	10 mm.	1 2-cm. Hy. M.G and 1 L.M.G. or models with W/T. 1 1·3-cm. Hy. M.G., or 1 L.M.G.
4	Medium	A.S.P.6	6·4 tons	4 1 Driver. 2 Gunners. 1 W/T Operator.	1. 16 ft. 5½ in. 2. 7 ft. 6 in.–9 ft. 3. 8 ft. (or 9 ft. with grid aerial).	14 mm.	1 2-cm. Hy. M.G. 1 L.M.G.
5	Medium	A.D.K.Z., Mk. 1 and Mk. II.	7 tons	3		14·5 mm.	1 A.Tk. gun and 1 M.G. in turret
6	Medium	PA II or PA/XXIV	8 tons	5 2 Drivers. 2 Gunners. 1 Commander.	1. 20 ft. 2. 7 ft. 2 in. 3. 8 ft. 1 in. 4. 12 in.	All plates are curved. Thickness unknown.	4 M.G.s, 1 L.M.G. (for A.A.?).
7	Medium	PA IV	8·7 tons	5 2 Drivers. 2 Gunners. 1 Commander.	1. 19 ft. 7 in. 2. 6 ft. 9 in. 3. 8 ft. 10 in. 4. 1 ft. 8 in.(?)	14 mm.	1 2-cm. Hy M.G (for A.Tk. and A.A. purposes). 2 L.M.Gs.
8	Heavy	(Heavy 8-wheel Armd. C.)	9–10 tons	4–5 2 Drivers. 1 or 2 Gunners. 1 Commander.	1. 17 ft. 6 in. 2. 8 ft. 3. 9 ft. 4. 1 ft. 8 in.(?)	30 mm.	1 2-cm. Hy. M.G 1 L.M.G.
9	Heavy	A.D.G.Z.	11·5–12 tons	7 (can carry 12).	1. 19 ft. 6 in. 2. 7 ft. 1 in. 3. 9 ft. 1 in. 4. 12 in.	18 mm.	2 Hy. M.Gs., 2 L.M.Gs., 3 Light automatic (not mounted).

Note.—All crews of armoured cars are armed with machine-pistol

ARS USED BY GERMANY

Number of Wheels.	System of Steering.	Engine.	Drive.	Maximum Speed on Roads.	Radius of Action.	Inter-communication.	Remarks.
4	Front two wheels.	Horch 6 cyl. (?). (Front engine.)	Rear two wheels.	40–50 m.p.h.	175 miles.	Flag (or sometimes W/T).	Standard scout car, vulnerable and unlikely to operate without support. No turret (open fighting cab).
6	Front two wheels.	24 h.p. Tatra. (Front engine.)	Four rear wheels.	37 m.p.h.	155 miles.	Flag and probably W/T.	Used in the Czech army.
4	All four wheels	75 h.p. 8-cyl. Horch. (Rear engine.)	All four wheels.	56 m.p.h. (20 m.p.h. across country.)	175 miles.	Flag; only Sd. Kfz. 223, has W/T with grid aerial.	Good cross country performance. Has open top, protected by wire-net grids.
6	Dual control fore and aft.	100 h.p. 6-cyl., or 90 h.p. Diesel. (Front engine.)	Four rear wheels.	50 m.p.h.	200–240 miles.	W/T and flag	Standard German armoured car. May be seen in large numbers.
	Either direction at speed.	100 h.p. air-cooled.		40 m.p.h.		W/T	Very quiet, owing to hydraulic drive.
4	Dual control fore and aft. All four wheels can steer.	75 h.p. Skoda 4-cyl. water-cooled.	All four wheels.			Flag and probably W/T.	Used in the Czech army.
4	Dual control fore and aft. All four wheels can steer.	100 h.p. (Rear engine.)	All four wheels.	35 m.p.h.		W/T and flag	Used in the Czech army—replacing PA II.
8	Dual control fore and aft.	90–100 h.p. (Rear engine.)	All eight wheels.	53 m.p.h.	250 miles ?	W/T	Standard German armoured car. May be seen in large numbers.
8	Dual control fore and aft.	150 h.p. Steyr. (Front engine.)	All eight wheels.	50 m.p.h.	186 miles.	Flag and probably W/T.	Used in the Austrian army.

probably on a scale of 2 machine-pistols per vehicle.

APPENDIX XXV

DISTINGUISHING FEATURES OF GERMAN ARMOURED CARS

1. Light recce. car

Four wheels. Standard shaped mudguards. Square grilled radiator.

The vehicle has no turret, and the machine-gun is mounted behind a shield. The fighting compartment is octagonal in shape.

A spare wheel is fixed on to the rear of the body.

2. Tatra 30

Six wheels, with very wide flat front mudguards; the rear mudguard covers both back wheels.

The radiator in front is very narrow, and the hull is built up to the shape of an ordinary van and is surmounted by a round turret. One machine-gun is mounted in the hull to the left of the driver, and the other machine-gun which is mounted in the turret on a ball mounting can be elevated to a high angle.

3. Sd. Kfz. 221, 222 and 223

Four wheels with angular mudguards.

Short square nose, tapering towards the front. The hull is built up to form an eight-sided cab, which is surmounted by a small open turret protected from hand grenades by wire netting grids. The sides of the hull are built up to form an angle of approximately 120° with the top plate.

When wireless is fitted, a frame aerial is raised approximately 2 ft. above the top of the vehicle.

4. A.S.P.6

Six wheels. Large angular mudguards; rear mudguard covers the two back wheels.

Very long sloping front plate (or bonnet), with grilled front radiator. The sides of the body are built up to form an angle with the top plates. A streamlined turret, similar to that of the Pz. Kw. II light tank, is fitted but the gun mounting is not the roller type.

A large grid aerial which forms a frame, with five bars running lengthways, is fitted over the top of the vehicle.

5. A.D.K.Z., Mk. I and Mk. II

Has an A.Tk. gun as well as a M.G. in turret.

Good air-cooled engine and steering in either direction at speed. May be found incorporated in M.T. columns. Very quiet owing to hydraulic drive.

6. P.A.II or P.A.XXIV

Four wheels inlet into the body.

The vehicle is symmetrical in shape, squat and all the plates are curved. The centre of the vehicle is built up into a round dome in which four machine-guns in ball mountings are diagonally placed. The vehicle is known, from its appearance, as "The Tortoise."

7. P.A.IV

The vehicle has a similar appearance to P.A.II, though not quite so streamlined. It is symmetrical, and the hull is boat-shaped, rising in the middle to a tall dome-shaped turret with one heavy machine-gun on ball mounting. Below the turret is mounted fore and aft a L.M.G. in a square machine-gun compartment.

8. Heavy 8-wheeled armoured car

Eight wheels which are partly protected by large angular mudguards, one mudguard covering two wheels.

The front of the vehicle is built out to house the driving cab. A streamlined turret, similar to that of the A.S.P.6 and Pz. Kw. II light tank, is mounted well forward on the vehicle. The rear of the vehicle houses the engine protected by long sloping back plates.

9. A.D.G.Z.

Eight wheels; the two centre wheels are twin wheels and are placed close together; the front and rear wheels are single, and all are let into the hull of the vehicle.

The sloping front plates have seven large horizontal radiator air louvres. On the extreme left of the hull a L.M.G. is mounted fore and aft. There is a large round turret with the top sloping towards the front and a flat face in which two machine-guns are fixed on ball mountings.

CHAPTER VIII

ENGINEERS AND ENGINEER EQUIPMENT

1. General organization

The German engineers may be divided into two separate categories :—

Field engineers,
Fortress engineers.

(a) *Field engineers.*—All field engineer units are controlled by the Inspector of Engineers in the War Ministry.

The duties of field engineers include bridging, ferrying, demolitions, construction of obstacles and laying and removal of mine fields. Apart from the " Baubataillone " (construction battalions—*see* para. 8 (b)) engineers are not normally engaged in road improvement or construction.

Field engineers are trained and armed as infantry and are frequently employed to defend zones of obstacles which they have created. Selected engineers known as " Stosstrupps-pioniere "* are trained to take part with the infantry in raiding parties and as assault troops in attacking fortified positions. The equipment which engineers are trained to use when attacking pillboxes without the support of tanks includes flame-throwers, Bangalore torpedoes (*gestreckte Ladungen*) and pole charges (*geballte Ladungen*).† The flame-throwers are directed at the loopholes in the pillbox. On reaching the wire, gaps are made with Bangalore torpedoes. Pole charges are placed against the outside walls of pillboxes. Their detonation has a shattering effect on the guns and their crews, resulting sometimes in putting the whole pillbox out of action. (For description *see* para. 16 (a), (b) and (c).

---

* The formation of " Pionier-Sturmbataillone " (engineer assault battalions) has recently been reported.

† Two forms of pole charges are in use, one consisting of one or more standard slabs of T.N.T. affixed to a pole and the other consisting of six grenades bound round a seventh (stick) grenade.

It is to be noted that in several instances field engineers were employed during the Polish campaign in clearing villages and in storming barricades.

(b) *Fortress engineers.*—Fortress engineers come under the jurisdiction of the Inspectorate of Fortresses in the War Ministry. The Inspector acts as the head of the Fortress Engineer Corps, and is responsible for the lay-out, construction and upkeep of fortresses, and for the preparation of obstacles and demolitions in frontier areas.

2. Engineer battalion in an infantry division. (*See* Appendix XXVI)

(a) *Organization*

(i) *Battalion.*—Each infantry division includes an engineer battalion which consists of headquarters, signal section,* two partially mechanized companies, a heavy mechanized company, a bridging column,† an electrical and mechanical tools park and a reserve stores park. The battalion commander may employ his three companies on the construction of bridges, which is believed to be their most important role. Whether a partially mechanized or the heavy mechanized company is used, depends on the tactical situation.

(ii) *Partially mechanized company.*—A partially mechanized company consists of headquarters, a reserve stores troop and three platoons each of three sections. It is armed with nine light machine-guns, and carries a few large and small pneumatic boats.

In this unit the men march and the equipment is carried in H.T. and M.T. vehicles.

(iii) *Heavy mechanized company.*—A heavy mechanized company is organized in the same way as a partially mechanized company. The company is transported in 9 lorries each carrying 1 N.C.O. and 16 men, 24 anti-tank

---

* The signal section contains one telephone and one wireless sub-section, each divided into two detachments; the telephone detachment contains six telephone operators and two drivers, the wireless detachment consisting of four W/T operators and two drivers.

† On mobilization the bridging column was, in most cases, detached from the divisional engineer battalion and withdrawn to the G.H.Q. pool (*see* Chapter I, para. 3).

mines, 1 light machine-gun, 1 mechanical saw, picks and shovels, and in 3 lorries, each carrying 12 men, explosives, ammunition, picks and shovels.

(iv) *Bridging column.*—A bridging column is a fully mechanized unit, consisting of three platoons, two of which are equipped with pontoon bridging material and the third with motor-boats, outboard motors and pneumatic boat equipment.

Exact information on the total amount of equipment is not available, but it may be assumed that enough is carried to build either a medium or a heavy standard bridge and also either a light or a medium special bridge. Details of these bridges are as follows :—

Type "B" equipment.	Carrying capacity in metric tons.	Length in yards.	Remarks.
Standard bridge :			
Medium..	9	84–90	Connected rafts. Of this the trestle and ramp sections account for 26–35 yards.
Heavy	18	55–59	
Special bridge :			
Light	4	134–144	Half-pontoons spaced out.
Medium..	8	78–88	Whole pontoons spaced out.

The bridging column transports and maintains the bridging equipment. The erection of the bridges is however the duty of the companies described in sub-paras. (ii) and (iii) above.

The transport laid down in the 1939 edition of the German training manual (*Ausbildungsvorschrift*) for the bridging column of an engineer battalion in an infantry division is as follows :—

Vehicles.—5 motor-cycles, 2 M.C. combinations, 3 four-seater cars, 2 light lorries, 19 medium cross-country lorries, 8 five-ton medium tractors.

Trailers.—16 pontoon, 4 shore transom, 4 trestle, 2 ramp, 1 cable and 2 motor boat (*M-Boot*).

(v) *Electrical and mechanical tools park.*—This is a fully mechanized unit which carries the battalion commander's reserve of tools.

(vi) *Reserve stores park.*—This is a fully mechanized unit which carries the battalion commander's reserve of explosives, ammunition, light tools, wire and all smaller engineer stores.

(b) *Strength.*—

Approximate strength and equipment of an Engineer Bn. in a German Inf. Div.	Strength.			Bridging Equipment.				Armament.			Horses		M.T.						H.T.	
	Officers.	N.C.Os.	Other ranks.	Pontoons.	Pneumatic boats (large).	Pneumatic boats (small).	Outboard motors.	L.M.Gs.	Rifles.	Pistols.	Draft.	Rider.	Bicycles.	Motor cycles.	4-seater cars.	Lorries.	Trailers.	Field kitchens.	Field kitchens.	Tool carts.
H.Q. & Signal Section.	5	7	28	–	–	–	–	–	30	10	6	4	4	7	1	1	–	1	1	2
Part.Mech.Coy. (2).	4	31	155	–	4	6	–	9	155	35	16	5	4	5	–	6	2	1	1	7
Heavy Mech. Coy.	4	30	153	–	4	6	–	9	153	35	–	–	–	5	4	17	2	1	–	–
Br. Coln.	6	30	154	20	*24	*22	8	–	174	16	–	–	–	7	3	29	29	1	–	–
E. & M. Tools Park.	2	12	36	–	–	–	–	1	36	14	–	–	–	2	1	12	–	1	–	–
Res.Stores Park	1	5	24	–	–	–	–	–	24	6	–	–	–	2	–	4	1	–	–	–
Total ..	26	146	705	20	36	40	8	28	727	151	38	14	12	33	7	75	36	4	3	16
		851																		

* These figures are unconfirmed and it is possible that the total number of pneumatic boats in a bridging column may amount to 64 instead of only 46 given in the above table.

3. Engineer battalion in a motorized infantry division

(a) *Organization.*—Each motorized infantry division includes an engineer battalion which is organized in the same way as the equivalent unit in an infantry division except that it has three heavy and no partially mechanized companies.

(b) *Strength.*—The strength of the unit is approximately the same as that of an engineer battalion in an infantry division (*see* para. 2 (b) above).

4. Engineer battalion in an armoured division

(a) *Organization.*—Each armoured division includes an engineer battalion. It consists of three* light mechanized companies, one mechanized bridging column and one reserve stores park.

(b) *Strength.*—

Approximate strength and equipment of the Engineer Bn. in a German Armoured Division.	Strength.				Armament.			Motor Transport.					Rate of march.		Length of Col. in yards when marching at	
	Officers.	Officials.	N.C.Os.	Other Ranks.	L.M.Gs.	Rifles.	Pistols.	4-seater cars.	Lorries.	Tractor trailers.	Motor cycles.	Length of column (halted) in yds.	km. (miles) per hour.		25 km. (15½ mile per hour.	15 km. (9¼ miles) per hour.
H.Q.	6	4	35	29	–	29	45	5	2	–	5	87	Day	Night	262	174
Light Mechanized Coy.(3)	4	–	30	153	9	153	34	4	17	–	5	387			1161	774
Br. Column	6	–	30	154	1	154	36	3	43	27	11	311			952	621
Reserve Stores Park.	2	–	12	36	1	36	14	1	12	–	2	218			654	436
Total	26	4	167	678	29	678	197	21	108	27	33	1777	25 (15½)	15 (9¼)	5331	3553

5. Engineer battalion in a mountain division

(a) *Organization.*—The engineer battalion in a mountain division consists of headquarters, signal section and three companies. Details regarding the composition of the latter are not known. This unit carries trestle bridging equipment, but no pontoons.

(b) *Strength.*—It is believed that the strength of the mountain brigade engineer battalion is approximately 15 officers and 420 other ranks. It is known that pack animals and motor vehicles are included in the transport of this unit, but no figures can be given at present.

---

* In some cases possibly only two.

6. Engineer unit in the cavalry division

It is believed that the cavalry division includes an engineer unit, but its composition and strength are not at present known. It may consist of one or more light mechanized companies.

7. G.H.Q. engineer battalion. (*See* Appendix XXVII)

(*a*) *Organization.*—A G.H.Q. engineer battalion is organized as follows: Headquarters, signal section, three heavy mechanized companies, three bridging columns (*Brückenkolonnen*), reserve stores park (*leichte Pionierkolonne*), electrical and mechanical tools park (*Gerätestaffel*).

(*b*) *Strength.*—The strengths of the various units which make up a G.H.Q. engineer battalion are the same as their equivalents in an infantry division (*see* para. 2 (*b*)).

The total war strength of a G.H.Q. engineer battalion is 38 officers and 1,249 other ranks.

8. Training units and labour battalions

(*a*) *Engineer training and experimental battalions.*—Two of these units are in existence. One trains in military construction and the building of semi-permanent bridges and the other carries out experiments with the normal types of engineer equipment.

(*b*) *Labour battalions.*—The following were formed on mobilization:—" Baubataillone " (construction battalions), " Strassenbaubataillone " (road construction battalions) and " leichte Strassenbaubataillone " (mobile road construction battalions). These units were employed in Poland for the removal of obstacles in the path of the German armoured divisions as well as in assisting first line engineer units in bridge construction. On the Western Front they were employed in road building, wiring, the mining of shelters in rock, etc. Their rank and file is reported to consist of war veterans and young men who had completed their compulsory labour service (*Arbeitsdienst*) at the commencement of the war. Their equipment includes picks, shovels and pneumatic drills and hammers.

There are also "Festungsbautruppen" (fortress construction units), which are employed under the direction of the fortress engineers on the maintenance and improvement of permanently fortified zones.

There is also a "Baulehrbataillon" (construction training battalion) which apart from providing normal infantry training such as all German engineer units undergo, gives special training in demolitions. In the particular instance reported instruction was given to selected men in scouting, quick firing and the removal of explosives from mined bridges. Organized into sections, 15 strong, armed with one light machine-gun, five machine-pistols, and hand grenades, these men were subsequently employed in an attempt to seize bridges over canals in the German attack on Holland. They were clad in various uniforms.

The mobilization strength of a construction company (*Baukompanie*) is as follows:—

	Strength.			Horses.			Armament.		Transport.			
	Officers.	N.C.Os.	Other Ranks.	Heavy Draft.	Light Draft.	Rider.	Carbines.	Pistols or Machine-Pistols.	Vehicles (horse-drawn).	Motor Cycles.	M.C. Combinations.	Bicycles.
Company H.Q.												
Commander	1	–	–	–	–	1	–	1	–	–	–	–
Sergeant major	–	1	–	–	–	–	–	1	–	–	–	–
Technical N.C.O. (also gas N.C.O.)	–	1	–	–	–	–	–	–	–	–	–	–
Surveyor N.C.O. (topographer)	–	1	–	–	–	–	–	–	–	–	–	–
Medical N.C.Os.	–	2	–	–	–	–	–	–	–	1	1	–
Technicians	–	–	2	–	–	–	–	–	–	–	–	–
Assistant surveyors	–	–	2	–	–	–	–	–	–	–	–	–
Runner	–	–	1	–	–	–	–	–	–	–	–	–
Cyclist	–	–	1	–	–	–	–	–	–	–	–	1
Clerk	–	–	1	–	–	–	–	–	–	–	–	–
Groom	–	–	1	–	–	–	–	–	–	–	–	–
Total—Coy. H.Q.	1	5	8	–	–	1	–	2	–	1	1	1

Chapter VIII

	Strength.			Horses.			Armament.		Transport.			
	Officers.	N.C.Os.	Other Ranks.	Heavy Draft.	Light Draft.	Rider.	Carbines.	Pistols or Machine-Pistols.	Vehicles (horse-drawn).	Motor Cycles.	M.C. Combinations.	Bicycles.
(b) *No. 1 Platoon.*												
Platoon commander	1	–	–	–	–	–	–	1	–	–	–	–
N.C.O. for special duties.	–	1	–	–	–	–	–	1	–	–	–	–
Section leaders ..	–	7	–	–	–	–	–	–	–	–	–	–
Other ranks (including cyclist).	–	–	115	–	–	–	–	–	–	–	–	1
Total—No. 1 Platoon	1	8	115	–	–	–	–	2	–	–	–	1
(c) No. 2 Platoon as for No. 1 Platoon.	1	8	115	–	–	–	–	2	–	–	–	1
(d) No. 3 Platoon as for No. 1 Platoon.	1	8	115	–	–	–	–	2	–	–	–	1
(e) *Transport.*												
Supply N.C.O.	–	1	–	–	–	–	–	–	–	–	–	–
Storekeeper	–	–	1	–	–	–	–	–	–	–	–	–
Drivers (seated)	–	–	4	–	–	–	–	–	–	–	–	–
Shoemakers ...	–	–	2	–	–	–	–	–	–	–	–	–
Tailors	–	–	2	–	–	–	–	–	–	–	–	–
Cooks	–	–	4	–	–	–	–	–	–	–	–	–
Large 2-horsed field kitchens.	–	–	–	4	–	–	–	–	2	–	–	–
2-horsed supply or baggage carts.	–	–	–	–	4	–	–	–	2	–	–	–
Total—Transport..	–	1	13	4	4	–	–	–	4	–	–	–
Summary.												
(a) Company H.Q.	1	5	8	–	–	1	–	2	–	1	1	1
(b) No. 1 Platoon	1	8	115	–	–	–	–	2	–	–	–	1
(c) No. 2 Platoon	1	8	115	–	–	–	–	2	–	–	–	1
(d) No. 3 Platoon	1	8	115	–	–	–	–	2	–	–	–	1
(e) Transport..	–	1	13	4	4	–	–	–	4	–	–	–
Total strength of Construction Coy.	4	30	366	4	4	1	–	8	4	1	1	4
When mobilized as a construction coy. for concrete work the following modification is applicable—												
(a) Company H.Q. has attached to it for special duties officer with motor cycle.	1	–	–	–	–	–	–	1	–	1	–	–
(b) The organization of the platoon remaining—												
Platoon commander	1	–	–	–	–	–	–	1	–	–	–	–
N.C.O for special duties.	–	1	–	–	–	–	–	1	–	–	–	–
Section leaders ..	–	7	–	–	–	–	–	–	–	–	–	–
Other ranks (including cyclist).	–	–	115	–	–	–	–	–	–	–	–	1
Total—No. 1 Platoon	2	8	115	–	–	–	–	3	–	1	–	1

(c) *Railway engineer units.*—Details of the organization and the functions of railway engineer units and railway construction units in the German army are at present lacking; but it may be assumed that they are composed in the main of German State Railway personnel mobilized for the purpose of repairing and maintaining railway equipment in any theatre of war or in German-occupied territory outside Germany itself.

(d) *Landwehr engineer units.*—The strength of a Landwehr engineer company in a Landwehr divisional engineer battalion is as follows :—

Landwehr Engineer (Pioneer) Company. (*Landwehr- Pionierkompanie*).	Strength.			Horses.			Armament.			Vehicles (horse-drawn).	Bicycles.
	Officers.	N.C.Os.	Other Ranks.	Heavy Draft.	Light Draft.	Rider.	Rifles or Carbines.	Pistols or Machine-Pistols.	L.M.Gs.		
(a) *Company H.Q.*											
Company commander	1	–	–	–	–	2	–	1	–	–	–
Sergeant-major	–	1	–	–	–	–	–	1	–	–	–
Gas N.C.O. ..	–	1	–	–	–	–	–	1	–	–	–
Orderly	–	–	1	–	–	–	1	–	–	–	–
Cyclists	–	–	2	–	–	–	2	–	–	–	2
Groom	–	–	1	–	–	–	1	–	–	–	–
Total—Company H.Q.	1	2	4	–	–	2	4	3	–	–	2
(b) *No. 1 Platoon.* *Platoon H.Q.*											
Platoon commander	1	–	–	–	–	1	–	1	–	–	–
N.C.O.	–	1	–	–	–	–	–	1	–	–	–
Surveyor (on bicycle)	–	–	1	–	–	–	1	–	–	–	1
Cyclist	–	–	1	–	–	–	1	–	–	–	1
Orderlies (including bugler).	–	–	2	–	–	–	2	–	–	–	–
Platoon.											
N.C.Os. (section leaders).	–	3	–	–	–	–	3	–	–	–	–
L.M.G. section leaders	–	3	–	–	–	–	3	–	–	–	–
Sappers ..	–	–	27	–	–	–	27	–	–	–	–
L.M.G. team..	–	–	9	–	–	–	–	9	–	–	–
Driver ..	–	–	1	–	–	–	1	–	–	–	–
Groom	–	–	1	–	–	–	1	–	–	–	–
L.M.Gs. ..	–	–	–	–	–	–	–	–	3	–	–
2-horse tool carts	–	–	–	–	2	–	–	–	–	1	–
Total—No. 1 Platoon	1	7	42	–	2	1	39	11	3	1	2
(c) No. 2 Platoon as for No. 1 Platoon.	1	7	42	–	2	1	39	11	3	1	2
(d) No. 3 Platoon as for No. 1 Platoon.	1	7	42	–	2	1	39	11	3	1	2

	Strength.			Horses.			Armament.			Vehicles (horse-drawn).	Bicycles.
Landwehr Engineer (Pioneer) Company. (*Landwehr-Pionierkompanie*).	Officers.	N.C.Os.	Other Ranks.	Heavy Draft.	Light Draft.	Rider.	Rifles or Carbines	Pistols or Machine-Pistols.	L.M.Gs.		
(e) Fighting Transport.											
Tools N.C.O. (on bicycle).	–	1	–	–	–	–	1	–	–	–	1
Medical N.C.O. (on bicycle).	–	1	–	–	–	–	–	1	–	–	1
Shoeing smith	–	–	1	–	–	–	–	1	–	–	–
Tailor	–	–	1	–	–	–	1	–	–	–	–
Shoemaker	–	–	1	–	–	–	1	–	–	–	–
Armourer's assistant	–	–	1	–	–	–	–	1	–	–	–
Drivers (mounted)	–	–	6	–	–	–	6	–	–	–	–
Driver	–	–	1	–	–	–	1	–	–	–	–
Cooks ..	–	–	2	–	–	–	2	–	–	–	–
4-horsed tool carts ..	–	–	–	–	12	–	–	–	–	3	–
2-horsed field kitchen	–	–	–	2	–	–	–	–	–	1	–
Total—Fighting transpt.	–	2	13	2	12	–	12	3	–	4	2
(f) Supply Transport (1st echelon).											
Ration orderly ..	–	–	1	–	–	–	1	–	–	–	1
Storekeeper ..	–	–	1	–	–	–	1	–	–	–	–
Driver (seated) ..	–	–	1	–	–	–	1	–	–	–	–
2-horsed supply cart	–	–	–	–	2	–	–	–	–	1	–
Total—Supply transpt.	–	–	3	–	2	–	3	–	–	1	1
Summary.											
(a) Company H.Q.	1	2	4	–	–	2	4	3	–	–	2
(b) No. 1 Platoon	1	7	42	–	2	1	39	11	3	1	2
(c) No. 2 Platoon ..	1	7	42	–	2	1	39	11	3	1	2
(d) No. 3 Platoon	1	7	42	–	2	1	39	11	3	1	2
(e) Fighting transport	–	2	13	2	12	–	12	3	–	4	2
(f) Supply transport	–	–	3	–	2	–	3	–	–	1	1
Total strength of Landwehr Engineer (Pioneer) Coy.	4	25	146	2	20	5	136	39	9	8	11

9. Armament

See paragraphs 2 (*b*), 4 (*b*) and 8 (*d*) above.

10. Equipment

(*a*) *Engineer tools and miscellaneous equipment.* (For pontoon and portable bridging equipment and searchlights carried *see* paragraphs 12 and 15 respectively.)

(b) *Carried by the man.*—The men in each section (6 to 8 men) in each engineer company carry between them three shovels, two felling axes, one hand axe, two picks and four entrenching tools.

(c) *In the vehicles of each engineer company* :—

Field forge.
Equipment for measuring the width of rivers.
Earth augers.
9 mechanical saws (each of which has a two-stroke engine and can fell a tree 20 in. in diameter in one minute).
3 steel " monkeys " for driving piles.
3 wire-rope ladders.
Steel wire-rope and blocks.
About 4,000 yards of barbed wire.
Rolls of concertina wire for tank obstacles.
Smoke candles.
Carpenter's tools.
Reserve of shovels, picks, felling axes and hand axes.

(d) *In the vehicles of the electrical and mechanical tools park* :—

Piledriver.
Oxyacetylene plant.
2 small electric generating sets.
4 electric lighting sets.
4 electric hand drills.
Power drill.
2 well-boring sets.
Possibly a few differential tackles.

(e) *In the vehicles of the reserve stores park.*—This unit carries the battalion commander's reserve of tools, wire and all other small engineer stores, details of which are not known.

11. Explosives

(a) *Demolition equipment.*—Each engineer company is believed to carry :—

(i) Three compressors, each equipped with hose and a drill. These are primarily employed in the demolition of concrete.

(ii) Three electric exploders. Each of these will fire charges through a total resistance of 200 ohms. They are spring-operated, compact and light.

(iii) The amount of standard explosive carried is believed to be as follows :—

> Partially mechanized company—1,750 lbs.
> Heavy mechanized company—2,200 lbs.
> Reserve stores park—4,400 lbs.
> Total divisional engineer battalion—10,100 lbs.
> Divisional supply column—5,500 lbs.
> Total carried in division—15,600 lbs.

The standard explosive is T.N.T. and is normally supplied in slabs of four different sizes, from 100 gr. (3·5 ozs.) up to 3 kg. (6·6 lbs.). The two smaller sizes are wrapped in waxed paper, the larger sizes being in zinc containers. All sizes of slabs are provided with one or more threaded holes for taking a detonator ; no intermediate primer is necessary. The safety fuze is similar in appearance and operation to our own, whilst the instantaneous fuze has a green gutta-percha covering, but in other respects is similar and can be handled in the same manner.

(b) *Anti-tank mines.*—The scale of issue of anti-tank mines in general is believed to be as follows :—

Partially mechanized company	200
Heavy mechanized company	300
Reserve stores park	800
Total divisional engineer battalion	1,500
Divisional supply column	800
Total carried in division	2,300

Two types were met with on the Western Front, viz. :—

(i) *"Teller" mine.*—This mine weighs 19 lbs., and contains 11 lbs. of T.N.T. ; it is 12 ins. in diameter and 4 ins. high, with a convex top and flat bottom ; a handle is provided on one side for easy carriage. The mine is primarily pressure detonated, but holes are also provided for the insertion of additional detonators and igniters ; these can be used for connection by means of instantaneous fuze to other mines or for detonating the mine by means of trip wire, etc., or when it is moved.

The mines are generally laid on or near roads and buried about 2 in. below the surface.

(ii) *Heavy or box mine.*—The mine consists of a rectangular cast-iron box about 17 in. × 16 in. × 10½ in., and contains 37 lbs. of explosive made up of 84 standard 200 gr. (7 ozs.) T.N.T. slabs. This mine is pressure operated, but is also provided with holes for the insertion of pull igniters; it is also arranged to explode if tampered with and should therefore be neutralised only by trained engineers.

(c) *Anti-personnel traps and mines.*—These can be divided into two main types :—

(i) *Elementary booby traps.*—These consist of one or more small T.N.T. slabs or cartridges and a push or pull igniter, actuated by the usual trip devices (doors, cupboards, light switches, etc.).

(ii) *The anti-personnel shrapnel mine ("S-mine").*—This mine is cylindrical in shape, about 4 in. in diameter by 6 in. high, and weighs about 9 lbs. It contains 1 lb. of explosive and 250 steel bullets packed round the explosive. The mine is detonated by a push or pull igniter operated by contact-boards, trip wires, etc. It is of the "bounding" type, that is to say, it is projected into the air by a secondary charge before the mine proper explodes, scattering the bullets. Dummy mines are freely used and require careful examination, as they may have booby traps attached.

12. Pneumatic boats, pontoons, assault boats, motor boats and outboard motors

(a) *Equipment carried by units* :—

(i) *Divisional Engineer Battalions.*

2/4-ton pneumatic boats.
3½/5-ton wooden pontoon and (steel) trestles.
9/18-ton steel pontoons and trestles.
Assault boats.
Motor boats.
Out-board motors.

(ii) *G.H.Q. engineer battalions.*

9/18-ton steel pontoons and trestles.
24-ton Herbert light alloy pontoons.

(*b*) *Pneumatic boats.*—These boats correspond to the folding boat equipment in the British Army. They are made of rubberized fabric in the form of a ring which is bulkheaded off into several air chambers so that the boat cannot easily be sunk. They are in two sizes, the larger of which takes about 10 minutes to inflate.

The larger size is 18 ft. long and 6 ft. wide and has an available buoyancy of about $2\frac{1}{2}$ tons. Rolled and packed for transport the boat occupies a cylindrical space 7 ft. long by 3 ft. in diameter and weighs approximately 350 lbs.

The smaller boat is 10 ft. long and 4 ft. wide, has a crew of 2 men and an available buoyancy of about 600 lbs. This boat weighs 115 lbs.

These boats are light for their load capacity and when inflated can be carried easily at the double, 8 men for the large and 2 for the small boat. Although stable they are somewhat cumbersome and slow in the water, being particularly difficult to control in a wind. Some form of rowlocks or loops is provided to assist in rowing or steering the boats when used singly or as rafts.

Boats are provided with rings for lashing on superstructure for making rafts and bridges. No details of the superstructure used are available, and, in fact, it is not known whether any special superstructure exists; it is possible that only improvised decking or decking borrowed from other equipment is used. (*See* Plate 67.)

(*c*) $3\frac{1}{2}/5$-*ton wooden pontoons.*—The pontoons are 12 ft. long by 5 ft. beam and weigh about 300 lbs. They are gunwale-loaded and open and can be used singly for the $3\frac{1}{2}$-ton bridge or joined (like our own equipment) to form 24 ft. long pontoons for the 5-ton bridge. The pontoons, being open and splayed, can be nested for transport.

To form the superstructure roadbearers and chesses are in effect joined together and form complete units of roadway about 20 ft. long by 2 ft. wide. Any number of such units can be used side by side, 5 being used to form a 10 ft. roadway.

(*d*) 9/18-*ton pontoons and trestles* (*see* Plate 66).—The pontoon is similar to our own but not decked over. The inner measurements are 24 ft. 6 in. by 5 ft. beam by 3 ft. 3 in. and the weight is about 1,600 lbs. In addition to a crew of 4 it has a carrying capacity of 15 men in marching order or 10,000 lbs. with 9-in. free-board. Being undecked it is more suitable for ferrying than the British pontoons but has the disadvantage of a definite minimum of free-board which must be strictly observed. When used in bridge or raft the pontoons are gunwale loaded.

The superstructure consists of steel joists 7 in. × 3 in. × 21 ft. weighing 350 lbs. and chesses 10 in. × 2 in. × 12 ft. 3 in. weighing 50 lbs. The load is also shared by heavy riband joists which are racked down at two places to intermediate transoms passing under the roadbearers. Eight roadbearers are used for the medium bridge and 14 for the heavy bridge. The equipment includes steel trestles; piers consist of single trestles for either the medium or heavy bridge whilst floating piers are of one or two pontoons respectively.

(e) *24-ton Herbert pontoon bridge and trestles.*—The pontoons or boats are upwards of 60 ft. in length and divided laterally into eight or nine sections. They are of steel or light alloy, gunwale loaded and are used to a minimum free-board of 12 in.; the bow is provided with a raised bulwark to assist in the rough water experienced on large rivers. The pontoon sections are decked and provided with hatches and it is possible for the maintenance crew to rest and sleep inside. The pontoon weighs approximately 10 tons and displacement with the free-board mentioned is nearly 60 tons.

The equipment also includes trestle piers, either of steel or piled timber construction. The latter are used for shore bays at river crossings or shallow dry gaps, whilst the steel trestles built up of standard parts can be contructed to a height of over 60 ft. above foundation level and still carry the full load for which the bridge is designed.

The main girders carrying the roadway are composed of sections in the form of pyramids 6 ft. 6 in. high with bases 8 ft. 3 in. long by 4 ft. 6 in. wide. Transoms are hung in special stirrups from the apex of each pyramid and the transoms in turn carry the road bearers. A standard bay is 82 ft. 6 ins., *i.e.*, 10 pyramid sections, pin connected.

From the information available it is calculated that in 82 ft. 6 in. bays the bridge would take British class 18 loads, that is to say medium tanks and artillery. However, with closer spacing of pontoons thus reducing the length of a bay, the load capacity could probably be increased to take a 35-ton tank.

The pontoons are too large to be used conveniently on any but the largest rivers, and the construction and launching takes too long to be considered in any way as an assault operation. The Herbert equipment may therefore be classified as " a semi-permanent " bridge, and its use is probably confined to back areas.

(f) *Heavy tank rafts.*—If the Herbert bridge is excluded, it will be noted that none of the bridges mentioned above are capable of taking the 22-ton or 35-ton tanks which are known to have been used on the Western Front.

There is evidence that a special heavy raft was used, which was probably designed for the purpose. This consisted of a small box girder section (similar to the " K-Brückengerät " described below) 60 ft. long and supported at each end by a pair of double pontoon piers. The exact load capacity of this raft is not known, but the available buoyancy of the complete raft as described would be over 45 tons, and the strength of the superstructure is, no doubt, proportionate. Loading of the raft is by means of special 8-ft. shore bays made of lattice girders.

With regard to the 22-ton tanks, there is no evidence either of the existence of a new pontoon equipment to take these loads or that the old equipment has been strengthened. It is probable, therefore, that the same heavy raft is used in principle, though in emergency the 18-ton pontoon equipment could probably be overloaded to this extent.

(g) *Assault boats* (*see* Plates 68, 69 and 70).—These are of new design and consist of light wooden keel-less boats designed for speed and capable of taking 16 men in addition to the crew of two. The out-board motor is a completely separate unit—a 12 h.p. 4-cylinder engine with the screw at the end of a 6-ft. shaft casing which also takes the exhaust under water. The boat when loaded is capable of 15 to 20 knots. Four men are required to carry the engine and eight for the boats, which can be nested for transport.

(h) *Motor boats.*—These boats are used only for assisting pontoon bridging operations and not for the transport of troops. Only about six men can be carried, but they are provided with 100 h.p. 6-cylinder water-cooled petrol engines. The equipment includes a grapple hook, a long length of steel wire rope for towing rafts, also a searchlight. The boats are capable of towing a treble 18-ton raft at six knots. The boats will be invaluable in the construction of bridges with the new Herbert equipment.

Chapter VIII 140

(i) *Out-board motors.*—There are three types of outboard motors in use. The latest of these is a model with a 33 h.p. 4-cylinder petrol engine used for towing in bridging operations or for ferrying. (*See also* (g) *above.*)

13. Fixed bridges

(a) *Small box girder bridge.* (*K-Brückengerät*) This is almost certainly a copy of our present standard "Small box girder bridge, Mark II." The principal members are similar, and the launching nose used is identical. The tracked load carrying capacities and corresponding spans are probably equal to or greater than the following :—

4 girder 48 ft. span	25 tons.
4 girder 64 ft. span	} 21 tons.
2 girder 32 ft. span	
2 girder 64 ft. span	10 tons.

(b) *Girder bridge.*—There is also a larger through type sectional girder bridge capable of spanning gaps of at least 140 ft., and probably capable of taking heavy loads. No definite details are available.

(c) *Improvised bridges.*—All engineering companies carry a small supply of timber of various sizes for the construction of improvised bridges, etc. It is intended that this should be supplemented out of local resources, for which purpose various power tools are also carried (*see* para. 10 above).

14. Anti-tank obstacles

(a) *Anti-tank mines.*—These have been described in para. 11 of this chapter, and are used as follows :—

(i) *Minefields.*—These are sited in accordance with principles similar to those adopted in the British Army, the mines being spaced at regular intervals. The number of rows is not fixed, but the whole minefield is designed to give a density of at least one mine to every 14 in. of front. Frequent use is made of minefields consisting of mixed anti-personnel and anti-tank mines with the object of impeding the rapid neutralization of the minefield by engineer troops.

(ii) *Road and passage blocks.*—These may consist of a number of mines disposed at intervals as in the case of a minefield, or isolated mines may be used, a board being placed across the top of the mine to increase the contact area.

(iii) *In conjunction with other obstacles.*—Anti-tank and anti-personnel mines are frequently concealed in all types of road blocks and arranged to operate either under pressure or by the pull of a wire when a portion of the obstacle is removed.

(iv) *Suspended mines.*—Various devices are used whereby a vehicle running into a wire stretched between trees across a road may cause a mine to explode either underneath the tank or vehicle or when released from above or pulled from the side.

(b) *Wire obstacles.*—Concertina wire disposed in depth across the road is occasionally used. The spacing between concertinas decreases from front to rear of the obstacle. Anti-tank and anti-personnel mines, concealed within the obstacle, are used to increase its effectiveness.

(c) *Other anti-tank obstacles.*—These include :—

(i) *Dragon's teeth.*—These comprise anything from four to eight rows of reinforced concrete blocks of varying heights up to 6 ft.; the blocks are broader at the base than at the top, and are cast in rows from front to rear with substantial reinforced connecting sills or foundations. Dragon's teeth are designed to stop a tank through bellying. Continuous rows of these obstacles are constructed in front of prepared positions, usually with the addition, on the enemy side, of a ditch 10 ft. wide and a bank.

(ii) *Felled trees*, in forest roads tied together, and containing concealed anti-personnel mines.

(iii) *Rails and steel sections*, are employed to form barriers and road blocks. They are usually of varying heights and spaced at about 4-ft. centres. Barriers are also formed of special angle iron frameworks 6 ft. 6 in. in height, and designed to stop a tank by providing an unscalable slope.

15. Field searchlight projectors

Small searchlights are carried in engineer units on the following scale :—
- (a) In each engineer company—2.
- (b) In the electrical and mechanical tools park—10.
- (c) On the motor boat in a bridging column—1.

Chapter VIII 142

These searchlights are of 12-in. diameter.

The engineers do not provide the personnel in searchlight units for anti-aircraft defence. These units are part of the Air Force. (*See* Chapter VI, Section F.)

16. Special equipment for use in assault

(*a*) *Flame-throwers.*—It is believed that two types of portable flame-thrower similar to those developed in the last war are still used. These are the " Kleif " and the " Grof." The former is operated by a team of two men, and projects burning oil or cresote a distance of about 25 yards. Short jets of flame are normally used, but in one continuous jet the duration is about 10 seconds. The container is carried by one man who also directs the flame.

The " Grof " is carried by two men, one carrying the fue and the other the compressed nitrogen cylinder, whilst a third operates the valves and directs the flame. Additional men may be included in the party for additional supplies of fuel and nitrogen. The flame is projected 35 yards and in one continuous jet will last about a minute.

(*b*) *Bangalore torpedoes* (*Gestreckte Ladungen*).—These are used for blowing a gap in barbed wire fencing. They can be made in various ways out of standard slabs or grenades arranged for detonation by fuze and secured to a long plank, which is slid under the fence. The " torpedo " may be anything up to 10 ft. long and, if necessary, two such units may be joined together. Under favourable circumstances a gap up to 6 yards in width can be blown in the barbed wire entanglement.

(*c*) *Pole charges* (*Geballte Ladungen*).—For use against pillboxes. These charges consist of a number of 1 kg. (2·2 lbs.) or 3 kg. (6·6 lbs.) slabs or grenades tied together and fixed to the end of a pole. After a heavy bombardment and under cover of close supporting fire and (if possible) smoke, engineers run up carrying the charge, place it on the sill of the embrasure, light the fuze and retire.

(*d*) *Bell charges.*—Special charges are made up in shaped disc containers curved to fit the top of a steel cupola and intended to destroy the latter. Each charge contains about 55 lbs. of explosive and, if necessary, two can be used one on top of the other.

(*e*) *Mine exploding net* (*Knallennetz*).—This is a net made of instantaneous fuze, and used for clearing a passage for tanks through a mine-field by detonating the mines. The net is in units 50 ft. long by 8 ft. broad, with a 6 in. mesh, and weighs about 20 lbs. Two nets rolled up can be carried by one man, and are considered sufficient for clearing a passage through most mine-fields. The detonation of the net is initiated by means of a safety fuze.

17. Vehicles

(a) *Three-ton lorry.*—The normal type of heavy six-wheeled lorry as made by Henschel. Both the sides and the ends let down. When tools are carried, a long wooden cupboard, L-shaped in section, is placed along each side of the lorry. The men sit on these facing inwards. When the sides of the lorry are let down, the shelves of the cupboards are exposed.

(b) *Half-track tractor.*—This is the normal type of Krauss-Maffei tractor and draws the trailers described in sub-para. (c) and (d) below.

(c) *Pontoon trailer.*—This is a large vehicle with four double wheels.

(d) *Trailer for motor boat.*—This vehicle has a single axle and two double wheels. It includes telescopic launching-ways, so that the motor boat can slide off direct into the water.

APPENDIX XXVI

COMPOSITION OF AN ENGINEER BATTALION IN AN INFANTRY DIVISION[1]

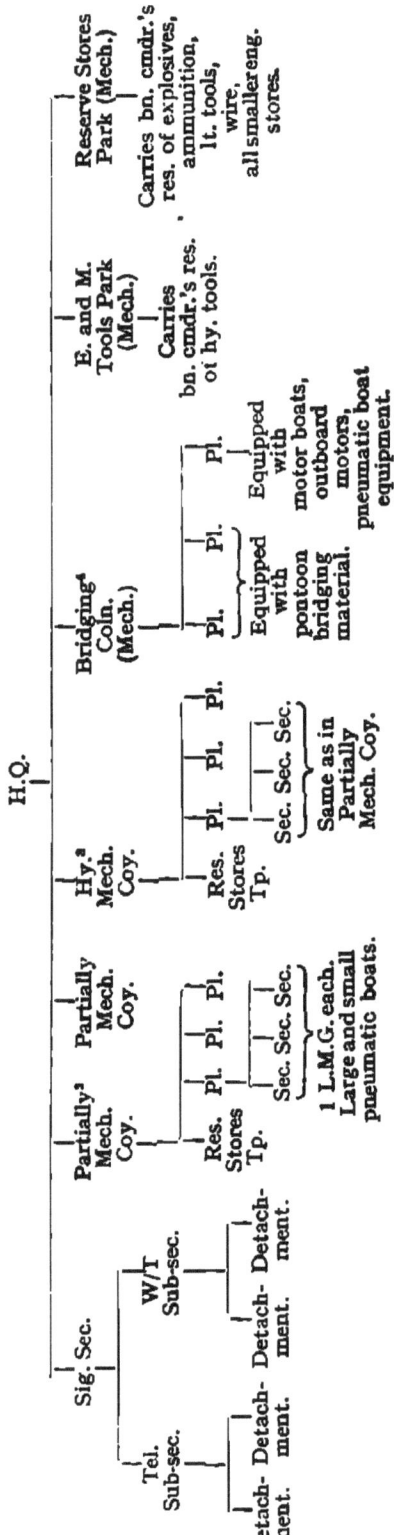

[1] The engineer battalion of a motorized infantry division has three heavy mechanized companies and no partially mechanized companies. In every other respect its organization is identical with that of an infantry divisional engineer battalion.
[2] In this unit the men march, and equipment is carried in H.T. and M.T. vehicles.
[3] Men and equipment carried in M.T. vehicles.
[4] Withdrawn in most cases to the G.H.Q. pool.

APPENDIX XXVII

COMPOSITION OF A G.H.Q. ENGINEER BATTALION

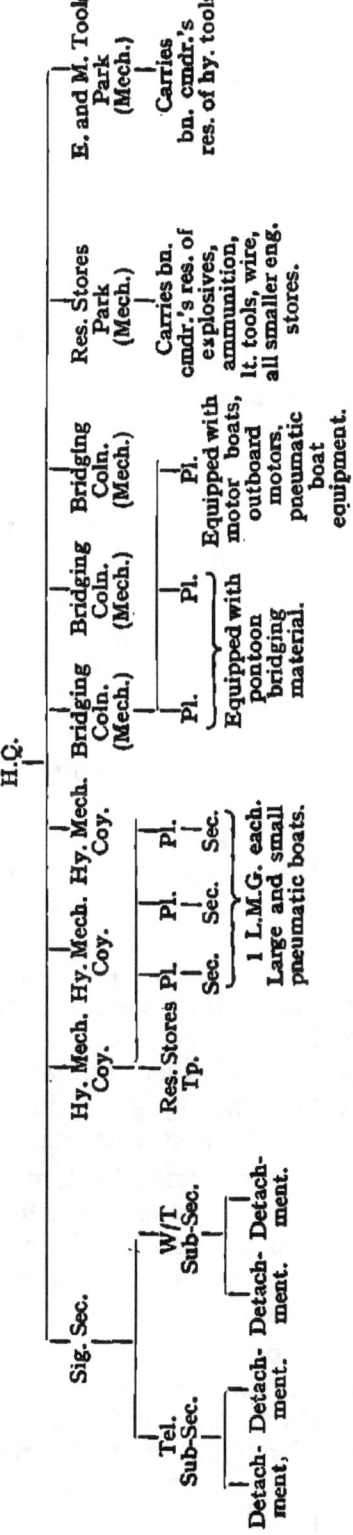

CHAPTER IX

SIGNAL SERVICE

1. General note on signal communications

The Germans attach the greatest importance to communications and their signal units are lavishly equipped. The following are some notes, which, though they contain little new, may give an indication of the general doctrine :—

(a) Technical means of communication are of the greatest importance to the commander. He must, however, never permit himself to be entirely dependent on them, for the lessons of the last war show that the most primitive form of transmitting messages, *i.e.*, the human being, is still most reliable.

(b) The higher unit is responsible for the establishment and maintenance of communication with the next lower unit. Line communication with neighbouring units is always established with the unit on the right. This rule does not, however, release commanders of responsibility to maintain contact with units on their left.

If an artillery unit is under command of an infantry unit, then the latter is responsible for establishing communications. If the artillery is supporting an infantry unit, but not under its command, then the artillery is responsible for the connection. If, however, the artillery, through some special circumstances, is unable to establish the connection, then the infantry must undertake it. Connection with heavy infantry weapons (mortars, infantry guns) is the responsibility of the infantry commander concerned.

(c) The commander normally issues orders for the employment of his signal units after receiving the recommendations of the signal officer. It is essential that the signal officer be given a complete picture of the situation, intentions, etc.

(d) In the advance the divisional signal battalion builds and maintains a main signal cable artery along the route on which the divisional headquarters is advancing. In friendly territory maximum use is made of the existing communications. In enemy territory, heavy poled field cable is normally used.

(e) When contact with the enemy has been established by the division, line communication, originally established by corps, must be maintained at all costs with the corps and also supplemented by W/T and other means.

(f) Within the division all headquarters will be connected according to their relative importance. The divisional signal battalion will establish lines to the infantry regiment, from artillery commander to the artillery units operating under the artillery commander and lateral connection to adjoining divisions. When there is a deficiency of means the establishment of the artillery connections has priority.

(g) In the defence an extensive communications net is established. Every means of communication is used, and buried cables are put down. Alarm circuits for gas and air attacks are arranged.

It is noteworthy that the Germans rely on wireless communications only when cable is not feasible. Stress is laid on the importance of keeping messages sent by wireless as short as possible on account of technical limitations. Messages of more than 180 letters must be sent in two parts, which means delay. The importance of using cipher is also stressed.

2. General organization

The Inspector of Signals (*Inspekteur der Nachrichtentruppen*) in the War Ministry supervises the training and technical development of army signals. The same officer holds the post of Inspector of Defence Communications (*Inspekteur der Wehrmachtverbindungen*), and as such directs that section of the Combined Staff of the Defence Forces. This section is responsible for inter-service communications and for the location of national trunk lines constructed by the Post Office, etc.

Signal units in formations and in independent brigades are composed exclusively of signals personnel; unit signallers are provided from regimental personnel.

The policy in the German army is to use W/T—

(i) To duplicate telephone communications;

(ii) To communicate with highly mobile troops when on the move.

The use of R/T, except in forward areas, is reduced to a minimum as it is considered vulnerable to interception.

3. Organization and strength of a signals unit in an infantry division

Divisional signals are responsible for communication from divisional headquarters to the headquarters of the infantry regiments, artillery regiment, engineer battalion and anti-tank battalion of the division, and to the headquarters of the formation on the right.

For the organization in detail, *see* Appendix XXXI.

4. Organization and strength of a signals unit in a motorized infantry division

It is probable that this unit is organized and equipped in the same way as the equivalent unit in an infantry division (*see* para. 3). It is, however, fully mechanized.

No details regarding its strength are known.

5. Organization and strength of a signals unit in an armoured division

See Appendix XXXII.

6. Organization and strength of a signals unit in a corps.

Corps signals are responsible for communications to the divisions within the corps and to corps troops. They also provide divisions with additional communications, as and when required.

For detailed organization, *see* Appendix XXIX.

7. Organization and strength of a signals unit in an armoured corps

See Appendix XXX.

8. Organization and strength of a signals regiment in an army

Army signals are responsible for communications to army troops and to the corps within the army. They also provide additional communication for subordinate formations, as and when required. Army signals are wholly mechanized and their organization in detail is shown in Appendix XXVIII.

9. Organization and strength of a signals unit in a mountain division

It is probable that the organization and strength of the mountain divisional signals correspond to those of the equivalent unit in an infantry division. Its transport consists largely of pack animals and horsed vehicles.

10. Organization and strength of the signals unit in the cavalry division

A signalling company, organized as follows, formed part of the cavalry brigade :—

(a) Four sections, able to provide :—

Ten telephone sub-sections (8 mech., 2 horsed).
Sixteen wireless sub-sections (10 mech., 6 horsed).
One cipher sub-section.

(b) A. and B. echelon transport for :—

Accumulator charging.
Petrol, stores, rations.
Field kitchens.

(c) In addition it had the following equipment :—

3 wireless receivers Fu. I.T.E.
17 Enigma cipher machines.

Its strength was :—

5 officers.	28 motor cars.
36 N.C.Os.	8 lorries.
165 O.Rs.	1 trailer.
22 draught horses.	11 M.Cs.
40 riding horses.	3 side cars.
6 pack horses.	

On the expansion of the cavalry brigade to form a division at the outbreak of war, it is probable that this company was also expanded.

11. Organization and strength of a signals section in a tank brigade

A signal section, organized as under, forms part of a tank brigade :—

Two lt. telephone sub-sections (mot.).
One Fu 5 S.E. 10 U transmitter in tank (Pz. Kw. II).
Three Fu 2 E.U. receivers and three Fu 6 S.E. 20 U transmitters in three armoured command vehicles (Sd. Kfz. 265).
Two Fu 6 S.E. 20 U and 2 Fu 8 S.E. 30 transmitters in two armoured command vehicles (Sd. Kfz. 267).

One spare transmitter Fu 6 S.E. 20 U.
Spare crews of 4 N.C.Os. and 12 O.Rs.

In addition No. 3 section W/T company of the armoured divisional signalling battalion may be attached to the headquarters tank brigade.

12. Signals experimental and research establishments

So far as is known all signals research and experimental work is carried out at the Army Signal School at Halle, where a training and experimental battalion exists for the purpose.

13. Cipher personnel

Cipher personnel is included in the establishments of all formation signals. Details as to their strength are shown in Appendices XXVIII-XXXII.

14. Messenger dogs

Messenger dogs are not now included in the establishment of formation signals. They are still employed with infantry regimental and battalions signal sections, but this method of communication is being gradually replaced by the infra-red ray telephone.

15. Carrier pigeons

Carrier pigeons are still employed by formation signals and are carried in mobile pigeon lofts which are constructed to hold 100-200 pigeons each. This method of communication is gradually being superseded by other means.

16. Despatch riders

Despatch riders are provided for formation signals on a very limited scale. It appears that they are used mainly in cases of emergency.

17. Armament of signal personnel

Signal personnel are armed with a rifle and bayonet, or revolver. No light or heavy machine guns are carried.

18. Equipment

(a) *Line telegraph—*

(i) *General.*—Sounder or buzzer telegraph instruments are seldom used. The teleprinter is now being introduced for line communication in rear of divisional headquarters.

(ii) *Exchanges.*—The types of exchanges in general use are :—

A 2-line exchange with visual indicator consisting of a small wooden box approximately 2 in. by 6 in. by 6 in., with four terminals, two of which are used for line connection and two for coupling an additional 2-line exchange.

A light 10-line exchange with shutter indicators. Connection is made by the use of plugs and cords. The push button discs are mounted on the scale of one for each subscriber. The method of calling a subscriber is to press the required red button and ring on exchange operator's telephone. No magneto for ringing is embodied in this exchange.

A light 10-line exchange with plugs and cords. The magneto calling device is embodied in the exchange microphone and ear-pieces are plugged into the exchange. On this exchange the first three jacks are normally used for trunk circuits and the exchange has a special ringing off indicator. A special battery is normally used for the microphone circuit, but the standard pattern can be used if required. The method of calling a subscriber is the same as above.

The F.K. 16 or heavy exchange is used where two 10-line exchanges coupled together are not sufficient. This is a magneto exchange made up of one or more 30-line components. Each 30-line component consists of 3 tiers of 10-line jacks and indicators—the indicators are of the drop-shutter pattern. Cross-connections are made by the use of plugs and cords.

The F.K. 16 exchange may be adopted for use on a central battery system by the use of an additional component. A breast set and separate head receiver are also provided with this type of exchange.

The light 10-line and the F.K. 16 exchanges may also be used on post office lines of various systems by the use of an instrument (different in each case) called the "Amtszusatz," which is connected direct to the exchange. The method of calling a subscriber is then similar to automatic dialling on G.P.O. systems.

(b) *Line telephones*.—The following types of field telephones are used :—

(i) *The telephone No. 26*.—This telephone has buzzer and magneto generator. The hand-set is supported on a bracket on the side of the instrument and an additional ear receiver is provided. The buzzer can be easily removed from the instrument, as it is plugged in by means of a 5-pin plug. Current is supplied by two cells. The total weight of the instrument is about 14½ lb.

(ii) *The telephone No. 33*.—This is a more modern edition of the telephone No. 26, the casing and handset being made of bakelite. A hand generator and bell are provided, but the buzzer has been omitted. Current is supplied by one cell. The total weight of the instrument is approximately 12½ lb.

The telephone No. 33 may be used on post office lines by the use of an adaptor (*Amtsanschliesser* 33). On automatic systems the use of an additional component (*Nummernscheibenkästchen*) containing the automatic dial is necessary. This can be connected to the telephone by plug and cord.

The labelling of terminals on the telephone 26 and 33 is as follows :—

La	Line terminal.
Lb/E	Line or earth terminal.
LB/ZB	Condenser terminal only on the telephone 26.

(iii) *Table telephone O.B.05*.—A Post Office pattern instrument for use indoors. The peculiarity of this instrument is the presence of magneto handles on each end of the case.

(c) *Teleprinters*.—Teleprinters have largely superseded morse instruments in higher formations. The Siemens and the Helle teleprinters have been adopted in the German army.

(d) *Interception Sets, W/T direction finders and ground listening sets*.—It is known that certain interception sets between them can cover all frequencies between 200,000 and 65 kc/s. but information regarding their sensitivity is not available. A few details are known about one portable W/T direction finder, but this model is believed to be obsolescent. An ingenious ground listening device is known to be in use. It consists of a cylindrical aluminium container, at one end of which are two terminals connected to the end of an internal winding. The other end can pivot around an axis perpendicular to the axis of the cylinder, forming a jaw firmly retained upon its seating by a strong spring. The side of the cylinder carries two openings diametrically opposite, which allows a telephone line to be held therein by the jaw. The inside face of this jaw carries a moving armature of a transformer core made of soft laminated iron. The spring forces the moving armature against the fixed part of the transformer, thus closing the magnetic circuit. The external terminals are connected by a pair of wires to a low frequency amplifier. The telephone line, when inserted, acts as the primary of the transformer. The apparatus can be easily put in place, and no indication is given of its presence while it is in place or after it has been removed.

(e) *W/T jamming devices.*—Details of W/T jamming sets employed are not available, but it is known that this type of wireless interference is practised and that the type of signal emitted is plain C.W.

(f) *W/T and R/T instruments.*—Details of these are given in Appendices XXXIII and XXXIV at the end of this chapter. Appendix XXXV shows the positions in the spectrum occupied by British and German army wireless sets so that the possibilities of mutual interference may be estimated.

(g) *Cipher equipment.*—The " Enigma " cipher machine is part of the equipment of W/T stations in formation signals. Its distribution is shown in Appendices XXVIII-XXXII.

(h) *Visual equipment*—

   (i) *Signalling lamps.*—Two types of lamps are used :—

   The medium lamp has a range by day of 3 miles and by night of 10 miles. It can be attached to a tripod or to a tree or pole by a knife blade protruding from the bottom of the lamp. Power supply is either by battery (two 4·5 v. batteries connected in series) or by hand generator. An optical indicator, consisting of five small metal tongues is incorporated in the generator box, the oscillations of which show whether the dynamo is being turned at the correct speed to produce the requisite current and voltage. The lamp also has a shutter attachment, which can be varied to six different apertures according to the intensity of light required.

The small lamp, similar to (i) above, has a range of 2 miles by day and $3\frac{1}{2}$ miles by night.

(ii) *Infra-red ray telephone.*—This instrument is now being introduced for use in forward areas for communication between infantry regimental headquarters and battalions. It is not used, so far as is known, in formation signals.

(iii) *Disc signalling equipment.*—Two discs, coloured red and white, approx. 4 in. in diameter and mounted on handles, are used for signalling in regimental, battalion and company signal sections, in accordance with a recognized code.

(*i*) *Visual equipment for air co-operation.*—Large red and white ground strips are used for communication from ground to air.

(*j*) *Light signals*—

(i) *Verey pistol lights*—

These are of 4 or more different colours, burn for 6 seconds to a height of approx. 250 ft., and can be seen from a radius of about 1 mile.

(ii) *Signal grenades*—

These can be fired to a height of 750 ft., burn for 8 seconds, and can be seen from a radius of $1\frac{1}{2}$ to 3 miles by day and 10 miles by night.

(iii) *Flares for communication with aircraft*—

These burn for 45 seconds.

(*k*) *Message throwers and projectors.*—These are no longer in use.

(*l*) *Line construction*—

(i) *Air line.*—The building of open wire routes of light air line is not considered satisfactory and is gradually being replaced by a heavy quad cable: see below. When used, however, the wire is of 2-mm. bronze or 3-mm. iron and built on light posts.

Rate of construction of 2 pairs, $4\frac{1}{2}$ miles per day by one section and 10 miles per day by a company.

(ii) *Types of cable.*—The following main types of cable are in general use :—

A light insulated cable for use in forward areas—single conductor.

A heavy cable similar to the British D VIII pattern single conductor.

A heavy quad cable similar to that in use in the British army.

The distance at which speech is considered good under favourable circumstances with light and heavy cables is as under :—

Light cable, earth return.
    On poles   8 miles.
    On the ground $2\frac{1}{2}$ miles.

Light cable, metallic return.
    On poles   15 miles.

Heavy cable, earth return.
    On poles   30 miles.
    On ground   8 miles.

Heavy cable, metallic return.
    On poles   45 miles.

(iii) *Methods of laying.*—*Light cable.*—The cable is wound on drums in lengths of about 550 yards and is laid out by hand from a carrier supported either on the chest of a man or carried in the hand. A thumb brake is provided to prevent the drum over-riding. A separate carrier is used for reeling-in.

Collapsible back harness is also provided for the laying of light cable. This consists of a knapsack containing 3 drums of cable, each of 550 yard lengths, a crookstick, spindles for reeling out and in, and various accessories.

Heavy field cable.—Heavy field cable is wound on drums each containing about 1,100 yards of cable. The drum is placed on a spindle supported by an iron frame, which can be strapped to the body of a man or laid on the floor of a vehicle. To reel in, the drum is revolved by means of a chain attached to a separate reeling-in spindle. As the reeling-in spindle is rotated, a guide, through which the cable is passed, traverses backwards and forwards, thus enabling the cable to be wound evenly on the drum.

Heavy quad cable.—Heavy quad cable is wound on drums. Connection is made by a plug and socket, about 5 in. diameter. A loading coil can be inserted into the connector. Normal superimposing is carried out on this cable.

(*m*) *Vehicles*—

(i) *Horse transport.*—Heavy cable is carried either on a light telephone limbered wagon or on a signal limber.

The light telephone limbered wagon is drawn by two, four or six horses. The rear half-limber contains the cable and line construction accessories and five miles of heavy and two-and-a-half miles of light cable, whilst the front half-limber contains telephones, exchanges, men's kits and two collapsible knapsack pattern cable-laying apparatus. For laying, three drums of heavy cable are mounted on separate spindles in the rear half-limber, and the cable is drawn off by hand. The poles are carried in iron brackets below the rear half-limber.

The infantry signal limber is similar to the light telephone wagon above, but carries equipment for four signal cable parties and two miles of heavy field cable. A collapsible trailer (normally carried on the front half-limber when not in use) can be attached to the rear half-limber when laying the heavy field cable.

(ii) *Motor transport.*—The rapid mechanisation of signalling formations has led to the introduction of many types of lorries. In addition to the General Service pattern there are fourteen types of special lorries for use by signals units. Of these, five are for use in telephone and telephone operating sub-sections, and nine in wireless sub-sections. In the majority of cases, these special types consist of a standard chassis, with a special body.

Chapter IX

Chapter IX

APPENDIX XXVIII

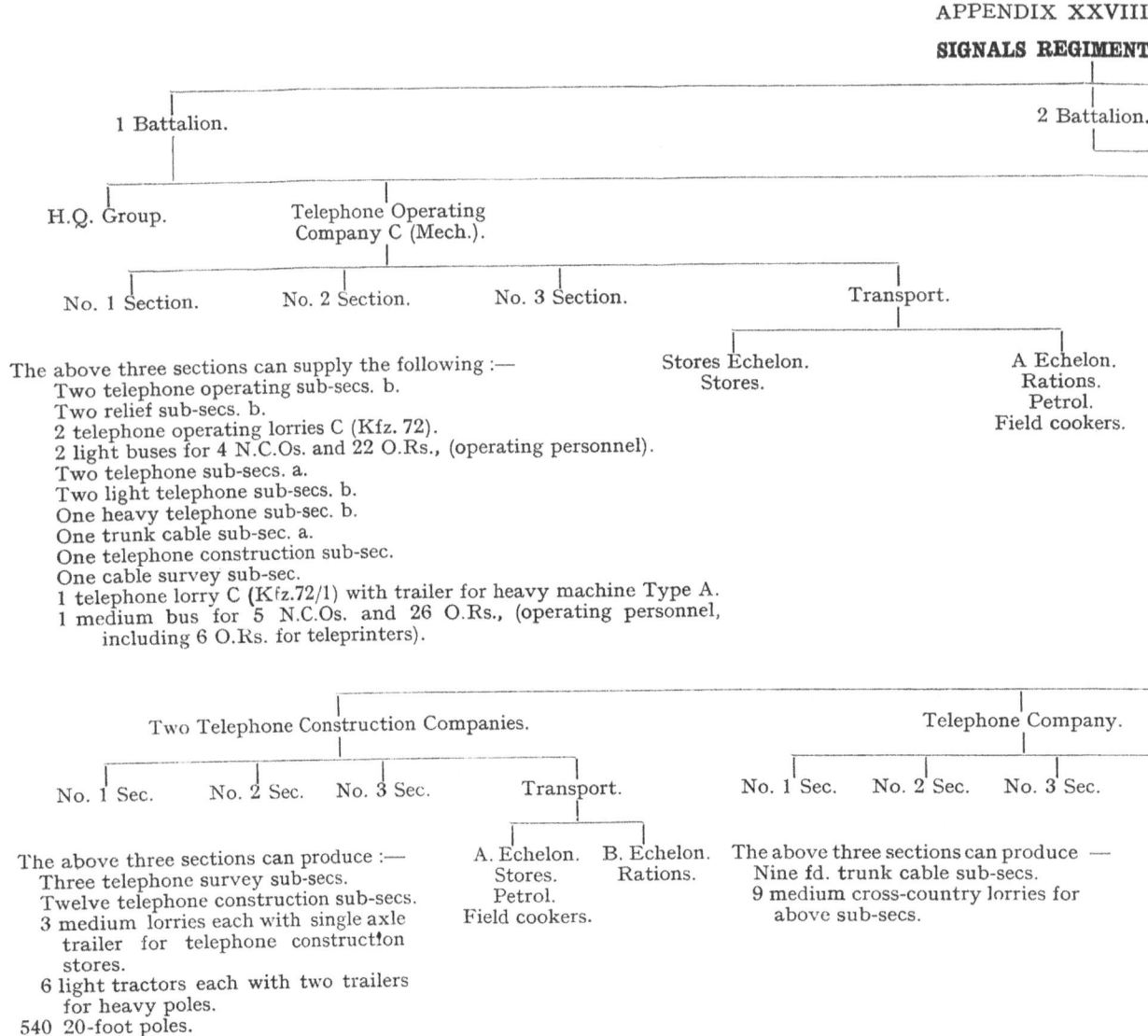

SIGNALS REGIMENT

— 1 Battalion.
— 2 Battalion.

1 Battalion:
- H.Q. Group.
- Telephone Operating Company C (Mech.).
  - No. 1 Section.
  - No. 2 Section.
  - No. 3 Section.
  - Transport.
    - Stores Echelon. Stores.
    - A Echelon. Rations. Petrol. Field cookers.

The above three sections can supply the following :—
- Two telephone operating sub-secs. b.
- Two relief sub-secs. b.
- 2 telephone operating lorries C (Kfz. 72).
- 2 light buses for 4 N.C.Os. and 22 O.Rs., (operating personnel).
- Two telephone sub-secs. a.
- Two light telephone sub-secs. b.
- One heavy telephone sub-sec. b.
- One trunk cable sub-sec. a.
- One telephone construction sub-sec.
- One cable survey sub-sec.
- 1 telephone lorry C (Kfz.72/1) with trailer for heavy machine Type A.
- 1 medium bus for 5 N.C.Os. and 26 O.Rs., (operating personnel, including 6 O.Rs. for teleprinters).

Two Telephone Construction Companies.
- No. 1 Sec. No. 2 Sec. No. 3 Sec.
- Transport.
  - A. Echelon. Stores. Petrol. Field cookers.
  - B. Echelon. Rations.

The above three sections can produce :—
- Three telephone survey sub-secs.
- Twelve telephone construction sub-secs.
- 3 medium lorries each with single axle trailer for telephone construction stores.
- 6 light tractors each with two trailers for heavy poles.
- 540 20-foot poles.
- 180 26-foot poles.

Telephone Company.
- No. 1 Sec. No. 2 Sec. No. 3 Sec.

The above three sections can produce —
- Nine fd. trunk cable sub-secs.
- 9 medium cross-country lorries for above sub-secs.

ARMY SIGNALS REGIMENT (Motorised)

Summary by Ranks

Unit.	Officers.	Officials.	N.C.Os.	O.Rs.	Field Cookers.	M.T.				
						Lorries.	Buses.	Tractors	Trailers.	M.Cs.
H.Q. Group, Signal Regiment	5	3	4	16	—	3	1	—	—	2
H.Q. Group	3(a)	2	4	15	—	3	2	—	—	2
Telephone Operating Company C.	4	—	33	158	2	12	22	—	1	12 (1)
W/T Company C.	4	—	33	125	2	19	16	—	3	11 (1)
Light Signalling Column	1	1	3	31	—	1	10	1	3	1 (1)
Total 1 Battalion	12	3	73	329	4	35	50	1	7	26 (3)
H.Q. Group	3(a)	2	4	15	—	3	2	—	—	2
Telephone Operating Company	4	—	26	116	1	22	15	—	—	11 (1)
Telephone Company	4	—	18	164	2	14	38	—	—	11 (1)
Telephone Construction Company	4	—	24	200	2	20	20	9	21	11 (1)
" " "	4	—	24	200	2	20	20	9	21	11 (1)
Light Signalling Column	1	1	3	45	—	1	13	5	11	1 (1)
Total 2 Battalion	20(a)	3	99	740	7	80	108	23	53	47 (5)
Total 3 Battalion	20(a)	3	99	740	7	80	108	23	53	47 (5)
Total Regiment	57(b)	12	275	1,825	18	198	267	47	113	122 (13)

Note.—(a) Includes one Medical Officer. Figures in brackets indicate numbers of M.C. combinations.
(b) Includes three Medical Officers.

IN AN ARMY

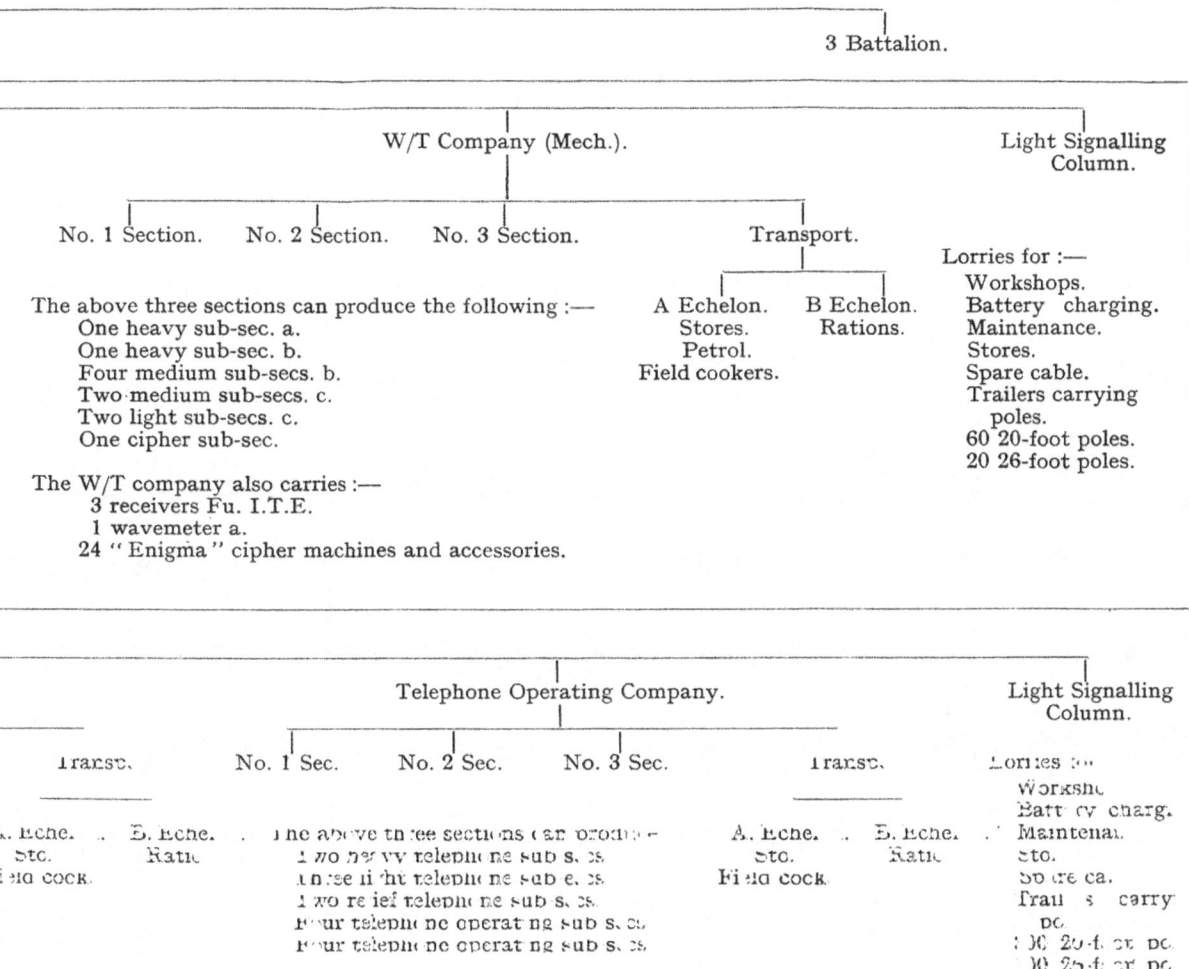

```
                                                    │
                                              3 Battalion.
┌─────────────────────────────────────────────────────────────────────┐
│                                                                     │
W/T Company (Mech.).                                          Light Signalling
                                                                  Column.
┌──────────┬──────────┬──────────┬──────────┐
No. 1 Section.  No. 2 Section.  No. 3 Section.  Transport.
                                                    │
The above three sections can produce the following:—   ┌────────┬────────┐      Lorries for:—
    One heavy sub-sec. a.                        A Echelon.  B Echelon.       Workshops.
    One heavy sub-sec. b.                        Stores.     Rations.         Battery charging.
    Four medium sub-secs. b.                     Petrol.                      Maintenance.
    Two medium sub-secs. c.                      Field cookers.               Stores.
    Two light sub-secs. c.                                                    Spare cable.
    One cipher sub-sec.                                                       Trailers carrying
                                                                                poles.
The W/T company also carries:—                                                60 20-foot poles.
    3 receivers Fu. I.T.E.                                                    20 26-foot poles.
    1 wavemeter a.
    24 "Enigma" cipher machines and accessories.
```

```
                        Telephone Operating Company.                    Light Signalling
                                                                            Column.
Transpt.   No. 1 Sec.  No. 2 Sec.  No. 3 Sec.          Transpt.         Lorries for
                                                                          Workshops.
A. Eche.   B. Eche.   The above three sections can produce—   A. Eche.  B. Eche.   Battery charg.
Sto.       Ratio.         Two heavy telephone sub-secs.       Sto.      Ratio.     Maintenan.
Field cook.               Three light telephone sub-secs.     Field cook.          etc.
                          Two relief telephone sub-secs.                           Spare ca.
                          Four telephone operating sub-secs.                       Trailers carry
                          Four telephone operating sub-secs.                         po.
                                                                                   60 20-ft. or po.
                                                                                   30 25-ft. or po.
```

Chapter IX

APPENDIX XXIX

SIGNALS UNIT

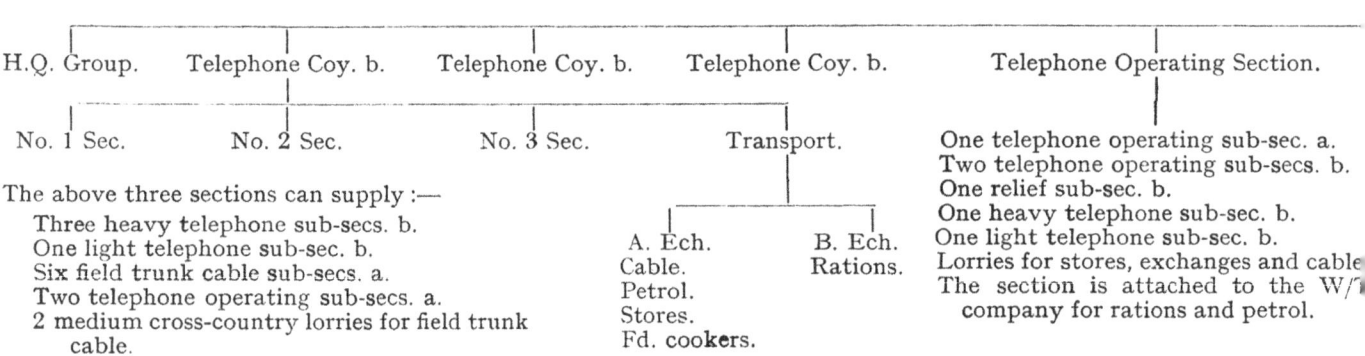

```
H.Q. Group.    Telephone Coy. b.    Telephone Coy. b.    Telephone Coy. b.                Telephone Operating Section.

No. 1 Sec.     No. 2 Sec.           No. 3 Sec.           Transport.                      One telephone operating sub-sec. a.
                                                                                          Two telephone operating sub-secs. b.
The above three sections can supply :—                                                    One relief sub-sec. b.
    Three heavy telephone sub-secs. b.                   A. Ech.        B. Ech.           One heavy telephone sub-sec. b.
    One light telephone sub-sec. b.                      Cable.         Rations.          One light telephone sub-sec. b.
    Six field trunk cable sub-secs. a.                   Petrol.                          Lorries for stores, exchanges and cable
    Two telephone operating sub-secs. a.                 Stores.                          The section is attached to the W/T
    2 medium cross-country lorries for field trunk       Fd. cookers.                        company for rations and petrol.
        cable.
```

Unit.	Officers.	Officials.	N.C.Os.	O.Rs.	Field Cookers.	M.T		
						Motor Cars.	Lorries.	Tractor
H.Q. Corps Signalling Bn.	3[ii]	2	2	15	—	3	2	—
Telephone Coy. b	4	—	21	150	2	19	25	—
,, ,,	4	—	21	150	2	19	25	—
,, ,,	4	—	21	150	2	19	25	—
,, Operating Section	1	—	8	43	—	7	7	—
L/T Company b	4	—	32	102	2	27	9	—
Light Signalling Company b	1	1	3	39	—	1	14	1
TOTALS	21[ii]	3	108	649	8	95	107	1

Notes.—(i) Figures in brackets indicate number of M.C. combinations.
(ii) Includes one M.O.

Mech.) **IN A CORPS**

```
                    |
        _____
        |                                                      |
   W/T Company b.                                      Light Signalling
        |                                                  Column.
   _____                             |
   |         |        |        |                        _____
No. 1 Sec. No. 2 Sec. No. 3 Sec. Transport.
```

The above three sections can provide :—
    Four light sub-secs. a.
    Four medium sub-secs. b.
    One medium sub-sec. c.
    One cipher sub-sec.
    3 receivers Fu. I.T.E.
    1 transmitter Fu. 12 S.E. 120 u.
    1 wavemeter.
    22 " Enigma " cipher machines with accessories and spares.

Lorries for workshops.
Battery charging.
Maintenance.
Petrol.
Stores.
Cable.
Tractor with 2 trailers for poles.
Sixty 20-ft. poles.
Twenty 26-ft. poles.

Trailers.	M.Cs.
—	2
—	11(1) [i]
—	11(1)
—	11(1)
—	2
1	9(1)
3	1(1)
4	47(5)

Chapter IX

APPENDIX XXX

SIGNALS UNIT IN AI

(*Nachrichte*

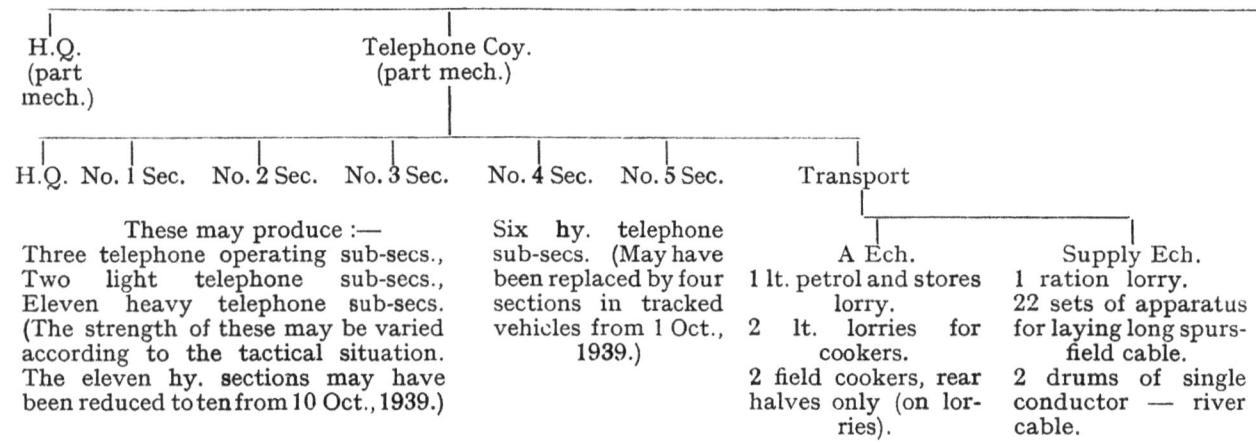

```
        |                    |
      H.Q.              Telephone Coy.
      (part             (part mech.)
      mech.)                 |
        |                    |
H.Q. No. 1 Sec. No. 2 Sec. No. 3 Sec.   No. 4 Sec. No. 5 Sec.   Transport
                                                                   |
                                                                   |
                                                          A Ech.        Supply Ech.
```

	These may produce:—	Six hy. telephone	A Ech.	Supply Ech.
	Three telephone operating sub-secs., Two light telephone sub-secs., Eleven heavy telephone sub-secs. (The strength of these may be varied according to the tactical situation. The eleven hy. sections may have been reduced to ten from 10 Oct., 1939.)	sub-secs. (May have been replaced by four sections in tracked vehicles from 1 Oct., 1939.)	1 lt. petrol and stores lorry. 2 lt. lorries for cookers. 2 field cookers, rear halves only (on lorries).	1 ration lorry. 22 sets of apparatus for laying long spurs-field cable. 2 drums of single conductor — river cable.

	Personnel.					M.T. Vehicles.				Horses.		H.T. Vehicles.	
	Officers.	Officials.	N.C.Os.	Other Ranks.	Field Cookers.	Personnel Lorries.	Equipment Lorries.	Single-axle Trailers.	M.Cs. (Combinations).	Draught.	Riding.	6-Horse Wagons.	4-Horse Wagons.
H.Q. Group	3 (ii)	2	2	17	—	3	2	—	2	—	4	—	—
Telephone Company	6	—	36	211	2	27	16	—	14(1) (i)	40	12	6	1
W/T Company	5	—	40	116	2	36	6	1	11(1)	—	—	—	—
Light Signalling Column	1	1	3	31	—	1	11	1	1(1)	—	—	—	—
TOTALS	15 (ii)	3	81	375	4	67	35	2	28(3) (i)	40	16	6	1

Notes.—(i) Figures in brackets indicate numbers of M.C. combinations.
(ii) Includes medical officers.

INFANTRY DIVISION
(*Abteilung*)

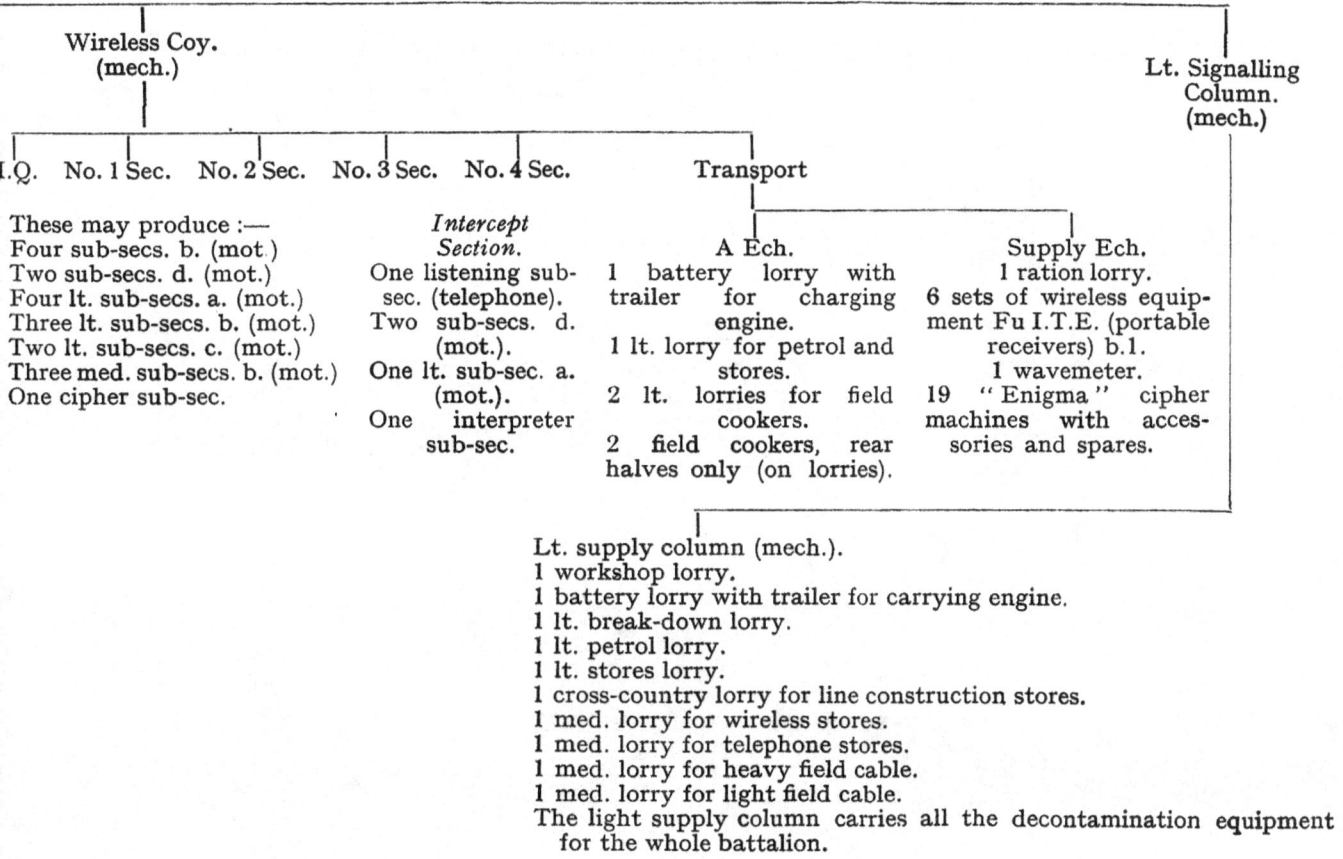

```
            Wireless Coy.                                                           Lt. Signalling
              (mech.)                                                                  Column.
                                                                                        (mech.)

H.Q.   No. 1 Sec.   No. 2 Sec.   No. 3 Sec.   No. 4 Sec.      Transport
```

These may produce :—
Four sub-secs. b. (mot.)
Two sub-secs. d. (mot.)
Four lt. sub-secs. a. (mot.)
Three lt. sub-secs. b. (mot.)
Two lt. sub-secs. c. (mot.)
Three med. sub-secs. b. (mot.)
One cipher sub-sec.

Intercept Section.
One listening sub-sec. (telephone).
Two sub-secs. d. (mot.).
One lt. sub-sec. a. (mot.).
One interpreter sub-sec.

A Ech.
1 battery lorry with trailer for charging engine.
1 lt. lorry for petrol and stores.
2 lt. lorries for field cookers.
2 field cookers, rear halves only (on lorries).

Supply Ech.
1 ration lorry.
6 sets of wireless equipment Fu I.T.E. (portable receivers) b.1.
1 wavemeter.
19 "Enigma" cipher machines with accessories and spares.

Lt. supply column (mech.).
1 workshop lorry.
1 battery lorry with trailer for carrying engine.
1 lt. break-down lorry.
1 lt. petrol lorry.
1 lt. stores lorry.
1 cross-country lorry for line construction stores.
1 med. lorry for wireless stores.
1 med. lorry for telephone stores.
1 med. lorry for heavy field cable.
1 med. lorry for light field cable.
The light supply column carries all the decontamination equipment for the whole battalion.

Chapter IX

APPENDIX XXX

SIGNALS UNIT IN A

```
         H.Q. Group.        Armoured W/T Coy. a.
                                   |
              ┌────────────┬───────────────┬──────────────┐
           No. 1 Sec.   No. 2 Sec.    No. 3 Sec.(iii)   Transport.
                                                            |
                                                     ┌──────┴──────┐
                                                   A. Ech.      B. Ech.
```

No. 1 Sec.:
One lt. armoured sub-sec. c.
Six lt. armoured sub-sec. d.
3 Armoured command vehicles Kfz. 267.
1 armoured command vehicle Kfz. 268.

No. 2 Sec.:
Six medium armoured sub-secs. b.

No. 3 Sec.:
One light armoured sub-sec. c.
2 armoured command vehicles Kfz. 267.
1 armoured command vehicle Kfz. 268.

Transport:
A. Ech. — Petrol and stores. Ammunition. Field cookers. Battery charging.
B. Ech. — Rations.

Relief detachment for above three sections :—
  8 N.C.Os. .. .. 1 W/T Lorry Kfz. 2.
  30 O.Rs. .. .. 3 light cross-country vehicles for personnel.

In addition the following equipment is carried :—
  3 receivers .. .. Fu. I.T.E.   1 wavemeter.
  2 ,, ... Fu. 2 E.U.   12 " Enigma " cipher machines with accessories and spares.
  5 transmitters .. .. Fu. 6 S.E. 20 u.   26 reciphering tables.
  2 ,, ... Fu. 7 S.E. 20 u.
  7 ,, ... Fu. 8 S.E. 30.

Unit.	Officers.	Officials.	N.C.Os.	O.Rs.	Motor Cars.	Lorries.	Armoured Command Vehicles
H.Q. Group	3[ii]	2	2	15	3	2	—
Armoured W/T Coy. a.	5	—	45	138	12	11	21
Armoured Signalling Coy.	4	—	33	145	24	14	6
Light Armoured Signalling Coy.	1	1	3	25	1	8	—
TOTALS	13[ii]	3	83	323	40	35	27

Notes.—
(i) Figures in brackets indicate number of M.C. combinations.
(ii) Includes one M.O.
(iii) No. 3 section of the W/T Coy. may be attached to the tank brigade. If this is done two light telephone sub-secs. b. are also included from the armoured signalling company.
(iv) No. 3 section of the armoured signalling company may be attached to the lorried infantry regiment If this is done, a light armoured W/T sub-section is added from the W/T company.

ARMOURED DIVISION

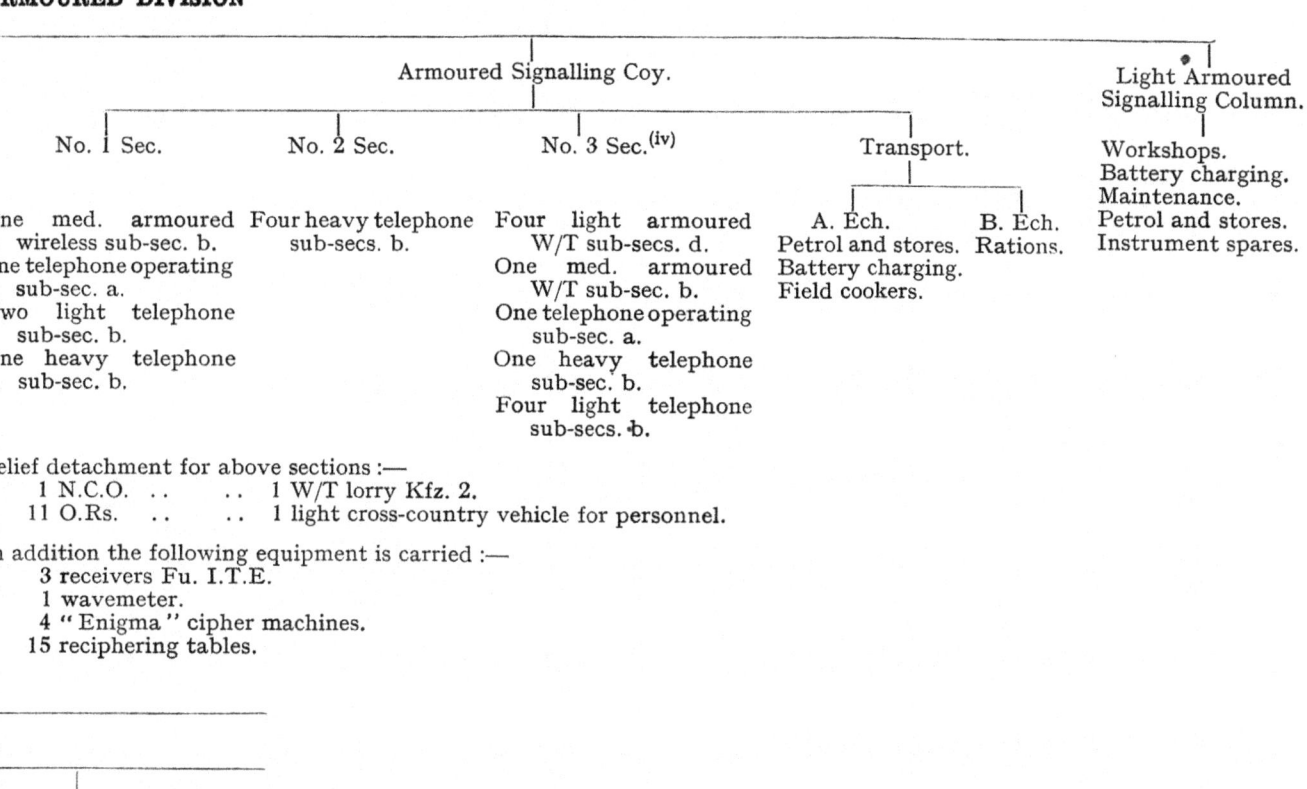

Armoured Signalling Coy.

- No. 1 Sec.
- No. 2 Sec.
- No. 3 Sec.(iv)
- Transport.

Light Armoured Signalling Column.

No. 1 Sec.: One med. armoured wireless sub-sec. b. One telephone operating sub-sec. a. Two light telephone sub-sec. b. One heavy telephone sub-sec. b.

No. 2 Sec.: Four heavy telephone sub-secs. b.

No. 3 Sec.: Four light armoured W/T sub-secs. d. One med. armoured W/T sub-sec. b. One telephone operating sub-sec. a. One heavy telephone sub-sec. b. Four light telephone sub-secs. b.

Transport:
- A. Ech. Petrol and stores. Battery charging. Field cookers.
- B. Ech. Rations.

Light Armoured Signalling Column: Workshops. Battery charging. Maintenance. Petrol and stores. Instrument spares.

Relief detachment for above sections :—
  1 N.C.O. .. .. 1 W/T lorry Kfz. 2.
  11 O.Rs. .. .. 1 light cross-country vehicle for personnel.

In addition the following equipment is carried :—
  3 receivers Fu. I.T.E.
  1 wavemeter.
  4 " Enigma " cipher machines.
  15 reciphering tables.

Trailers.	M.Cs. (Combinations).
—	2
1	12(1) (i)
1	12(1)
—	1(1)
2	27(3) (i)

APPENDIX XXXIII.—GERMAN WIRELESS TRANSMITTERS

Serial No.	Apparatus.	Transmitters and Valves.	Power in Aerial.	Wave Band. m.	Wave Band. Kc/s.	Aerial.	Working Methods.	Range (miles). CW.	Range (miles). ICW.	Range (miles). R/T.	Source of Energy.	Remarks.
a.	b.	c.	d.	e.	f.	g.	h.	i.	j.	k.	l.	m.
1	Heavy wireless set Type A.	1·5 kw. transmitter. 2 RE.084K. 7 RS.282. 2 RS.329. 3 RGN.2004.	1,500 watts.	500 to 3,000.	100 to 600.	80 foot mast with 6 or 12 spoke umbrella.	Local or remote keying, hand speed or high speed CW. or ICW. teleprinter picture transmission.	725	725	180–370.	Type A machine connected to convertor Type U 1500.	Circuit:— (a) R.F. master oscillator (RS.282), amplifier (two RS.282 in parallel), output (two RS.329 in parallel); (b) L.F. amplifier (two RS.282, two RE. 084); (c) Keying, two RG. 282, three rectifiers RGN.2004. Use.—Army H.Q.
2	Heavy wireless set Type B.	1 kw. transmitter. 2 RE.084K. 7 RS.282. 2 R.329. 3 RGN.2004.	1,000	45–275	1,090–6,700	80 foot masts with single wire aerial 83 feet long for medium waves or 33 feet long for short waves.	As for Serial 1	725	725	300	As above	—
3	Medium wireless set Type A.	—	80	100–268	1,120–3,000	—	CW. Local keying and speech. Picture transmission.	—	—	—	—	—

170   Chapter IX

4	Medium b. Medium armoured b. Fu. 11 S.E. 100.	100 watt transmitter. 2 RS.237. 1 RS.241.	100 watt can be switched to provide 1/10th output.	250–1,500	200–1,200	33 ft. mast with 4 spoke umbrella, 20 ft. sectional mast with 3 spoke umbrella. Roof masts according to type of lorry in which carried.	CW. Local and remote keying. Local speech. Picture transmission (television).	125	—	45	Type C. machine connected to convertor Type U. 100a or U. 100 with 12 volt accumulator.	*Circuit.* Master oscillator, power amplifier, modulation in the grid circuit of the power amplifier by means of valve control. Arrangements for "break in" operation. *Weight.* 75 lbs. *Use.* Army, Corps and Divisional Signalling Bus.
								100	—	30		
								25 to 50	—	6 to 12½		
5	Medium c. Fu. 12 S.E. 120 U.	120 watt transmitter.	120	5·5–7·1	42,100–54,000.	70 ft. mast, with vertical stub aerial on top.	CW. and ICW. local and remote keying and speech. Hand speed and high speed keying. Teleprinter. Picture telegraphy.	—	—	—	—	For use at Army H.Q. Corps H.Q.
6	Light a. Light b. Light Mtn. b. Fu. 9 S.E.5.	5 watt transmitter with 2 RS.241.	5	96–316	950–3,150.	21 foot sectional mast high with aerial 1/1 or 2/2. 5 foot mast, aerial with low aerial 1/1, two 7 foot ground aerials. Roof aerial (Kfz. 17).	CW. Local keying and speech.	45	—	12½	Convertors U. 5a. or U. 5a. 1, connected to a 12 volt accumulator.	Used with Pack Receiver a. (*see* Appx. XXXVI for types of receivers). Both transmitter and receiver in 3 boxes, each 24 in. by 18 in. by 15 in. Total weight 200 lbs. Can be operated on the move when carried in a vehicle. *Use.*—Div. H.Q.
								30	—	10		
								10 15	— —	1 5		

APPENDIX XXXIII.—GERMAN WIRELESS TRANSMITTERS—contd.

Serial No.	Apparatus.	Transmitters and Valves.	Power in Aerial.	Wave Band. m.	Wave Band. Kc/s.	Aerial.	Working Methods.	Range (miles). CW.	Range (miles). ICW.	Range (miles). R/T.	Source of Energy.	Remarks.
a.	b.	c.	d.	e.	f.	g.	h.	i.	j.	k.	l.	m.
7	Light c. Light armoured c. Light Mtn. c. Fu. 7 SE 20 U.	20 watt transmitter with 5 RL 12 T 15.	20	6·3–7·1	42,100 to 47,800.	16 foot mast with 5 foot stub aerial on top and four counterpoises.	ICW. Local keying and speech.	—	30	30	As for serial 6.	For use at Army H.Q.
8	Light d. Light armoured d. Fu. 8 SE 30. Fu. 10 SE 30 (TE).	30 watt transmitter with 5 RS 241 or 30 watt transmitter a.	30 30	180–316 100–268	950 to 1,670. 1,120 to 3,000.	21 foot sectional mast with aerial 3/3. 5 foot mast with low aerial 3/3. Roof aerials on lorries.	ICW. Local keying and speech.	— — —	75 55 25–35	25 16 6–12	As for serial 6.	Use.—Div. H.Q.
9	Pack a.	Pack transmitter a. with— 3 RE 084k. 2 RE 134. 1 H 406D or 1 RES 094.	2	45–100	3,000– 6,670.	Low Dipole aerial. Ground aerial	ICW. Local keying. Local or remote speech.	— —	15 5	5 1½	Two 90 volt anode batteries, one accumulator type NC10.	Used with Pack Receiver b. (see Appx. XXXVI for types of receivers). Both together form two loads, transmitter, receiver, aerial in one, batteries, accessories, spares, in other. Total weight of each load about 22 lbs.

172 Chapter IX

10	Pack a.2	Pack transmitter a.2 with—2 RE 084K. 2 RES 164. 1 H 406 D or 1 RES 094.	1	45–100	3,000–6,670.	Single wire aerial with 8 rods. Single wire aerial with 3 rods.	I.C.W. Local keying. Local or remote speech.	—	18	4–7	As for serial 9.	See serial 9.
								—	13	4		
11	Pack b.1	Pack transmitter b.1 with—7 RV 2 P 800. 1 RL 2 P3.	·65	60–100	3,000–5,000.	7½ foot mast single wire aerial with 8 rods. Single wire aerial with 3 rods. Lorry aerial, Kfz. 2 or 15.	ICW. Local keying. Local or remote speech.	—	15	7½	Two 90-volt anode batteries, one accumulator Type 2 B.38.	Used with Pack Receiver b. (see Appx. XXXVI for types of wireless receivers). Transmitter and receiver housed in one box, batteries and accessories in second box. Total weight 120 lbs. Automatic switching to send/receive carried out by key or pressel switch. Use.—In forward areas.
								—	15	7½		
								—	10	4		
								—	10	4		
12	Pack d.1	Pack transmitter d.1 with—8 RV 2 P 800. 1 RL 2 T 2.	1	7·9–8·8	33,800 to 38,000.	7-foot mast, 6-foot roof aerial on lorries, Kfz. 2 or 15.	ICW. Local keying. Local or remote speech.	—	10	4	As for serial 11.	Can be carried together with its receiver by one man. Consists of two half knapsacks which can be clamped together to form one load. Crystal control on two fixed frequencies. Weight 40 lbs.
								—	7½	2		

APPENDIX XXXIII.—GERMAN WIRELESS TRANSMITTERS—contd.

Serial No.	Apparatus.	Transmitters and Valves.	Power in Aerial.	Wave Band. m.	Wave Band. Kc/s.	Aerial.	Working Methods.	Range (miles). CW.	Range (miles). ICW.	Range (miles). R/T.	Source of Energy.	Remarks.
a.	b.	c.	d.	e.	f.	g.	h.	i.	j.	k.	l.	m.
13	Pack d.2	As for d.1	1	7·9–8·8	33,800 to 38,000.	7-foot mast, 6-foot roof aerial on lorries, Kfz. 2 or 15.	ICW. Local keying. Local or remote speech.	—	10	4	As for Serial 11.	As for Serial 12.
14	Pack f. Fu. 19 TF.	Pack transmitter f. with— 7 RV 2 P 800. 1 RL 2 P 3.	·65	45–67	4,500– 6,670.	As for Serial 11	ICW. Local keying. Local or remote speech.	—	7½	2	As for Serial 11.	Use.—Batteries of Field Artillery.
15	Fu. 5 SE 10 U.	10-watt transmitter a., b., or c. with— 1 RV 12 P 4,000. 2 RL 12 P 35	10	a. 10–11 b. 9–10 c. 9–11	27,200 to 30,400. 30,200– 33,400. 27,200– 33,400.	7-foot mast aerial on Armd. Kfz. 121. Armd. Kfz. 141 or Kfz. 622.	CW. Local keying and speech.	—	15	7½	Convertor U 10 with 12-volt accumulator.	Use.—Armoured fighting vehicles.
								4	15	7½		
									10	4		
										2½		
16	Fu. 6 SE 20 U.	20-watt transmitter c. with 5 RL 12 T 15.	20	9–11	27,200– 33,400.	7-foot mast aerial on armd. lorries Kfz. 265, 266, 267.	CW. Local keying and speech.	6	—	5	Convertor U 20 a. 2 with 12-volt accumulator.	Is believed to have been replaced by Serial 20 below.
17	Fu. 15 SE dm.	—	—	·53–·57	526,310 to 566,000	—	—	—	—	—	—	—

No.	Name	Description	Power (watts)		Wavelength	Aerial	Modulation				Power supply	Remarks
18	Wireless telephone "Fildfunk Sprecher."	—			—	—	—				—	No details are available.
19	Wireless set for sound ranging position.	20-watt transmitter with 5 RL 12 T 15.	20		11–12	25,000 to 27,200.	—	Local speech for transmitting survey results.	—	—	—	Convertor U 20 a.S with 12-volt accumulator.	—
20	Transmitter for use in tanks.	20-watt transmitter.	20		9·6–11	27,200 to 31,200.	7-foot rod with counterpoise.	Local keying and speech.	?	?	?	12-volt accumulator and rotary transformer.	*Circuit.*—Crystal oscillator, heterodyne oscillator, mixer, power stage. Aerial is semi-flexible, with "Set" at any random angle, if hit. Can be straightened by hand. *Weight.*—18 lbs.
21	A.K.S.25	25-watt transmitter.	25		25–100	3,000–12,000.	33-foot aerial on one 33-foot mast. Counterpoise four 33 feet wires.	Local keying and speech.	?	?	?	—	*Circuit.*—3 H.F. stages:— (i) Masteroscillator. (ii) Neutralized buffer amplifier. (iii) Neutralized push-pull pan amplifier. Modulation in grid of power amplifier valve. Keying in grid circuit of all stages. *Uses.*—Divisions, Infantry and Artillery Regiments.

APPENDIX XXXIII.—GERMAN WIRELESS TRANSMITTERS—contd.

Serial No.	Apparatus.	Transmitters and Valves.	Power in Aerial.	Wave Band. m.	Wave Band. Kc/s.	Aerial.	Working Methods.	Range (miles). CW.	Range (miles). ICW.	Range (miles). R/T.	Source of Energy.	Remarks.
a.	b.	c.	d.	e.	f.	g.	h.	i.	j.	k.	l.	m.
22	—	8-watt transmitter.	8 switch provided to reduce power by ¼.	100–300	1,000–3,000.	—	Local keying and speech. Send/receive operated by presser switch in R/T.	—	?	?	90-volt battery and 2·4-volt Edison cell.	*Circuit.*—Two stages, Master oscillator and power amplifier. Grid modulation in latter. Used with Receiver (Serial 14, Appx. XXXVI). To be standard portable set for forward and mobile troops. *Transmitter.*—Weight about 25 lbs. Size 24 in. by 18 in. by 15 in. *Receiver.*— Weight about 28 lbs. Size as for transmitter.
23	—	V.H.F. transmitter with 2 Acorn D.S. 202/2. 2 R.L.	40–60 m.w.	·59 to ·66	454,000 to 508,000.	Saw tooth aerial (double diamond with reflector). Highly directional.	Local or remote keying and speech ICW.	—	Quasi-optical path. 125?	125?	2 volt lead accumulator. Two 90-volt anode batteries.	Used with receiver (Serial 15, Appx. XXXVI), in 3 boxes. (i) Transmitter and receiver. (ii) Accessories. (iii) Stand, etc. *Circuit.*—Series tuned Hartley. Anode modulation through 1 : 1 transformer. M.C.W. by keying modulator valve, which acts as A.F. oscillator.

APPENDIX XXXIV.—GERMAN WIRELESS RECEIVERS

Serial No.	Type.	Wave Range.		Valves.	Source of Energy.	Working Time hrs.	Allocation to transmitters.	Remarks
		metres.	kcs.					
(a)	(b)	(c)	(d)	(e)	(f)	(g)	(h)	(j)
1	Pack Receiver (445 Bs).	45 to 3,000	100 to 6,670	4 RE 074 N	1 Accumulator, Type 4·8 NC10 1 90-volt anode battery.	50 40	Serial 1 and 2 can be used with any of the following transmitters:— Heavy a and b. Medium b.	
2	Pack Receiver B	43 to 3,000	100 to 6,670	4 RV 2 P 800	1 Accumulator, Type 2 B 38 1 90-volt anode battery or 1 convertor.	42 40	Medium Armoured b. Light and Pack a, b and d. Light Armd. d. Light Mtn. d. Fu. 1 TE. Fu. 9 SE 5. Fu. 10 SE 30. (TE). Fu. 11 SE 100. Intercept a and b.	
3	Long Wave Receiver a.	197 to 4,000	75 to 1,525	8 RV 2 P 800	1 Accumulator, Type 2 B 38 1 90-volt anode battery.	20 8	Heavy a and b.	
4	Medium Wave Receiver b.	150 to 517	580 to 2,000	6 RV 12 P 4,000	1 convertor, Type EU a.		Fu. 8 SE 30. Fu. 4 E.	
5	Medium Wave Receiver c.	100 to 360	835 to 3,000	—	1 convertor, Type EU a.		Fu. 8 SE 30. Fu. 4 E.	

178 Chapter IX

6	Short Wave Receiver a.	80 to 3,000	1,000 to 10,000	11 RV 2 P 800	1 Accumulator, Type 2 B 38 1 90-volt anode battery.	13 / 10	Heavy a and b.
7	Ultra Short Wave Receiver b.1.	11 to 12	25,000 to 27,200	9 RV 12 P 4,000	1 convertor, Type EU a 8.		Serial 19 of transmitters. For sound ranging position.
8	Ultra Short Wave Receiver c.1.	9 to 11	27,200 to 33,300	8 RV.12 P 4,000	1 convertor, Type EU a.		Fu. 2 EU. FU 6 SE 20.
9	Ultra Short Wave Receiver d.	6.3 to 7.1	42,100 to 47,800	8 RV 12 P 4,000	Two 90-volt anode Batteries or 1 convertor Type EU a.		Light c. Light Armd. c. Light Mtn. c. Fu. 3 EU. Fu. 7 SE 20 U..
10	Ultra Short Wave Receiver e.	9 to 11	27,200 to 33,300	7 RV 12 P 4,000	1 convertor Type EU a.		FU. 2 EU. Fu 5 SE 10 U. Fu 6 SE 20 U.
11	Ultra Short Wave Receiver f.	5.5 to 7.1 (?)	42,100 to 54,000				Medium c. Fu. 12 SE 120 U.
12	Ultra Short Wave Receiver.	7.9 to 8.8	33,800 to 38,000				Pack d 1. Pack d 2.
13	Receiver for Armoured vehicles.	9 to 12	25,000 to 33,300	9 RE 084 K 1 H. 406 D	Rotary transformer Input 12 v, 12.5 amps. output 350 volts, 170 ma.		Serial 20,Appx.XXXV for transmitters. *Circuit.* Straight H.F. Detector. Regenerative. Two L.F. *Weight*—24 lbs. *Size.*— Height 8 in. Breadth 16 in. Depth 10 in.

APPENDIX XXXIV.—GERMAN WIRELESS RECEIVERS—contd.

Serial No.	Type.	Wave Range.		Valves.	Source of Energy.	Working Time hrs.	Allocation to transmitters.	Remarks.
		metres.	kcs.					
(a)	(b)	(c)	(d)	(e)	(f)	(g)	(h)	(j)
14	Receiver for 8-watt set.	30 to 3,000 (in 8 switched ranges).	1,000 to 10,000	RV 2 P.700	2·4-volt Edison cell 90-volt anode battery.		Serial 22, Appx. XXXV for transmitters.	*Circuit.* 2 H.F. detector, 1 L.F. Note filter incorporated in final stage. *Weight.*—55 lbs. *Size.*—Height 18 in. Breadth 14 in. Depth 10 in.
15	Receiver for V.H.F. transmitter.	59 to 69	454,000 to 508,000	RL 2 T RV 2 P.800	2-volt lead accumulator. 2 90-volt anode batteries.		Serial 23, Appx. XXXV for transmitters.	*Circuit.* Super regenerative detector 1 L.F. Stage. *Alarm Unit.* Anode band detector. Relay causes lamp to light and bell to ring.

Chapter IX

APPENDIX XXXV

Comparative positions in the Spectrum of German & British Army Wireless sets.

Wave Length	German	British Army	Frequency
		Mc/s	
·5–·6	V.H.F. Transmitters		508·000 / 457·000
5·5	a Fu ger c Fu 12 SE 120u 120w 5·5–7·1m		54·5
5·8–6·0	Kl. Fu ger C Fu 7 SE 20u		51·5–50·
7·1			42·2
7·9	Tora Fuger d 1w 7·9–8·8m		37·9
9	Fu 5 SE 10v. Fu 6 SE 20v. 10w 9·11m 20w 9–11m.	No 77 set	33·3
11			27·2
		Kc/s.	
25	A.K.5 25 25w. 25–100m.		
33	gr. Fu. ge. b 1000w 45·275m	No 8 set	9070
40	Torn. Eu. ge. f 0·65w. 75–67m.		7500
45			6650
50			6000
60			5000

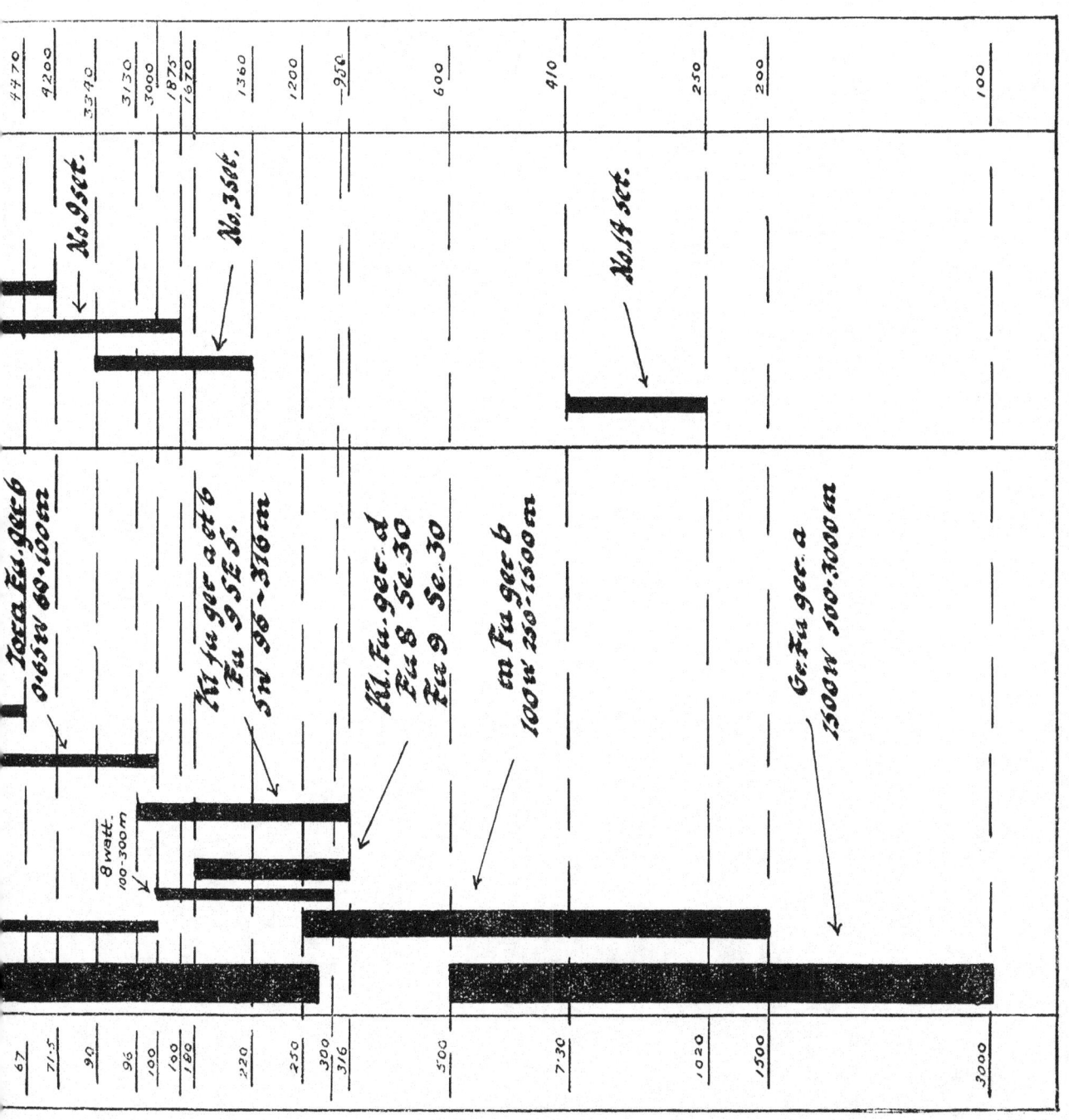

Chapter IX

CHAPTER X

CHEMICAL WARFARE AND SMOKE

1. General policy

Though the German Government has ratified the International Convention prohibiting the use of gas as a weapon of war, it should be borne in mind that the Germans were instrumental in introducing the gas weapon into warfare and, despite the stress of active war, independently discovered and tried out during the last war many of the most effective war gases known, at the same time developing an effective, if sometimes faulty, chemical warfare technique. Since the last war, German research on chemical warfare methods has been pursued unremittingly. Moreover, the German chemical industry is very highly developed. It must be assumed, therefore, that Germany is in a high state of preparedness, both offensively and defensively, for gas warfare, and if the Germans deem it expedient to introduce gas warfare, it will be pursued with their characteristic vigour, ingenuity and ruthlessness.

The introduction of the gas weapon in the form of cloud attacks from cylinders on the Western Front in the last war was, to some extent, a tactical error on the part of Germany, for the prevailing wind was unfavourable to such operations on over 60 per cent. of occasions. Modern chemical warfare methods are much less dependent on wind conditions. Consequently, it is improbable that this factor will deter them from the use of gas and, in the light of all information available, the indications are that the Germans are in a position to bring the gas weapon into effect as soon as they see fit to do so.

2. General organization, administration and policy

An Inspectorate of Smoke Troops and Gas Defence (*Inspektion der Nebeltruppen und für Gasabwehr*) in the War Ministry not only deals with smoke and gas defence, but is also believed to concern itself with the possible offensive use of gas.

The technical side of chemical warfare is controlled by the Anti-Gas Section in the Testing Department of the Army Ordnance Branch. Despite the name it is probable that research regarding offensive gases is also the concern of this section.

3. Defence

(a) Organization, administration and strength.—Anti-gas training in the army is on a sound and efficient basis; large-scale field exercises or "gas war games" have been reported on a number of occasions.

Army anti-gas schools are located in Berlin, Celle and Breloh, and the schools attached to the firms of Auer and Draeger are also extensively used for training instructors for the army.

It is believed that there is, in each battalion or equivalent unit, an anti-gas officer, assisted by a non-commissioned officer, and in each company an anti-gas N.C.O. These specialists instruct their units in anti-gas measures and carry out periodical inspections of all anti-gas equipment.

It is probable that about six men in each company or equivalent unit are trained as gas sentries (*Gasspürer*) and issued with such equipment as gas detectors and alarms.

It is stated that in addition to these specialists, decontamination, or anti-gas detachments exist in all formations.

(b) Equipment. (i) *Respirators. S-Mask Model 30/31.*—Since 1934 the respirator issued to the German armed forces has been of the type known as the "S-Mask" Model 30/31, essentially a somewhat rigid facepiece with directly attached (screw-in) drum container, the whole carried in a cylindrical sheet metal carrier.

Spare gelatine-coated anti-dimming discs are carried in a compartment on the inside of the lid.

A carrier of grey canvas with an aluminium "zip" fastener to open at the side is also in use, but is probably intended only for parachute or air-landing troops. The spare anti-dimming discs are carried in a pocket on the side of the carrier.

Special spectacle frames with flat side-pieces and anti-dimming compound for the lenses are provided.

The facepiece is composed of canvas, rubber and cotton fabric, with a fitting band of suede leather and adjustable head harness of cotton webbing and coiled steel springs. The eyepieces are of cellulose acetate in screwed brass rims, the anti-dimming discs being held in position by an annular spring. A rubber disc inlet valve and a spring-loaded mica disc outlet valve together with a protective grid are housed in the container attachment piece, which is screwed to take the neck of the container.

The containers are made by the firm of Auer (Degea) and Draeger and in general appearance are similar, being grey-painted tinned plate drums.

The German navy is stated to have an extension piece providing protection against carbon monoxide, and there are indications that a limited quantity of carbon monoxide masks and also oxygen respirators is available for land forces.

It is understood that a spare container may be carried by troops on active service. As the container is merely screwed into the facepiece it can be rapidly changed, if necessary even in a gas cloud. It is improbable therefore that penetration would be achieved except by delivering a massive concentration on the target, and the element of surprise would be essential for attack by any but persistent gas.

(ii) *Protective clothing.*—Reports indicate that the German anti-gas suits are of two kinds, one consisting of separate trousers and jacket with fixed hood and the other of one piece, overall type, also with a fixed hood. There are also two types of material, one which is rubberized on both sides and will keep out liquid mustard gas for about seven hours and the other rubberized on one side only in which the protective period is reduced to two and a half hours. Protective boots and gloves are also issued.

The Germans realize that this anti-gas clothing is cumbersome and can only be worn for limited periods, but they lay much stress on training to accustom men to wear it.

Reports now suggest that troops are issued with equipment to protect them from vesicants and for use as an anti-gas pathway in crossing contaminated ground. The earlier types of this equipment, known as "gas-plane," were believed to take the form of a sheet of rubberized fabric about 5 ft. square with a hole in the centre for the head, and reaching down to the knees.

More recent information indicates that the "gas-plane" in general issue takes the form of a sheet of waxed paper with no hole for the head. The sheet is carried folded in a pouch on the chest, and to gain protection the man crouches or kneels and throws the sheet over his head so that it covers him.

There is no evidence of eye-shields having been issued.

(iii) *Mobile laundries.*—It appears that some form of mobile decontamination plant may be available in units for the decontamination of clothing and equipment. These may take the form of motor lorries mounting a water tube boiler for the rapid generation of steam, a steam chamber and a drying chamber.

(iv) *Decontamination materials.*—Bleaching powder is the usual substance for ordinary decontamination work.

(v) *Anti-gas ointment.*—All German troops are equipped with two small bakelite boxes containing tablets of Losantin, a high quality stabilized bleaching powder. The method of use is to mix one of the tablets with water or saliva and apply to the affected skin the paste so formed.

(vi) *Gas detectors.*—Little is known of gas detectors but they are said to exist in the form of sheets of test paper which change colour when applied to the contamination.

(vii) *Collective protection.*—Anti-gas curtains will probably be available with the German army, and it is stated that the artillery make a practice of gas-proofing their gun positions. Gas-proofing of tanks and armoured cars has also been mentioned. It is believed that many of the fixed fortifications in Germany are equipped with filtered ventilation.

4. Offence

(a) *Organization, administration and strength.*—Germany is apparently convinced of the utility of specialist troops for conducting large scale gas operations. For several years the Germans have been experimenting secretly with different forms of offensive gas units and special smoke units, but no accurate information as to the final form of this organization is available.

(i) *Special gas units.*—It is believed that it is intended eventually to include a gas battalion in each army corps; these battalions are reported to consist of two to four mechanised companies, equipped variously with bulk contamination vehicles, portable contamination apparatus, such as sprayers and chemical mines, projectors or mortars, smoke generating apparatus and flame throwers. There are also believed to be a number of independent offensive gas companies (each about 250 strong). It is at present uncertain whether these companies will be formed into the corps gas battalions mentioned above, or whether they will be retained as additional gas troops.

(ii) *Gas in smoke units.*—There is good reason to believe that the special smoke units (*Nebelwerfer-Abteilungen*) (*see* Section 5(*a*)) are to be used for chemical warfare purposes when required, and there may well be some connection between them and the units mentioned above.

(iii) *Gas in tank units.*—It appears certain that a proportion of the tanks in a tank regiment are fitted with apparatus for the emission of gas.

(iv) *Gas in engineer battalions.*—There have been reports of mechanised engineer battalions equipped with offensive gas weapons, including flame throwers and gas sprayers driven by motor pumps. Such units are reported to be fully trained for offensive and defensive gas warfare; they are also reported to carry smoke apparatus for screening bridging operations.

(b) *Contemplated gases for offensive use.*

(i) *General—All types.*—Blister, choking, tear and nose gases.

In the following tables the main gases likely to be met are given. Experimental work on a wide variety of other gases has been reported from time to time, but it is not thought that any important new war gas has been discovered.

Recent information suggests that the Germans are familiar with the potentialities of arseniuretted hydrogen and it has been shown that their respirator containers afford protection against this gas.

TABLE I

(ii) *Blister gases.* German classification—" Yellow Cross."

Common names	German names
1. Mustard H.S.	Lost Senfgas ; Gelbkreuz.
2. Lewisite I	Possibly Gelbkreuz II.

Notes.—(1) Mixtures of mustard gas and lewisite may be used in cold weather to reduce the freezing point.

(2) It is not thought that Germany regards lewisite alone very favourably, but reserve stocks are reported to exist.

(3) The mustard gas is likely to be an improvement on the 1914-18 German mustard, more persistent, and possibly more vesicant and more difficult to decontaminate.

(4) It should be noted that the fumes from some German explosives set up respiratory and skin effects which might easily be mistaken for the effects of exposure to blister gases.

TABLE II

(iii) *Choking gases.* German classification—"Green Cross."

Common names	German names
1. Phosgene : C.G.	D. Stoff : Grünkreuz.
2. Diphosgene	K. Stoff : Perstoff Grünkreuz I and II.
3. Chloropicrin : P.S.	Klop.

Note.—There have been frequent references to mixtures of these choking gases.

TABLE III

(iv) *Nose gases (toxic smokes).* German classification—"Blue Cross."

Common names	German names
1. D.A.	Clark I : Blaukreuz.
2. D.C.	Clark II : Cyan Clark.
3. D.M.	D.M. Adamsite.

Note.—Germany shows a preference for D.A. and D.C.

TABLE IV

(v) *Tear gases.* German classification—T.-Stoff or "White Cross."

Common names	German names
1. C.A.P.	
2. B.B.C.	

Note.—Neither of these gases was used by the Germans during the last war. They relied on a number of bromine compounds which are less powerful than the two substances mentioned above.

It is thought that Germany attaches little importance to tear gases by themselves, but the possible use of other gases camouflaged by tear gas should not be overlooked.

(c) *Offensive weapons and equipment.*

(i) *General.*—As has already been stated, research in chemical warfare methods has been almost continuous in Germany since the last war. The marked attention given to aerial and ground methods of contamination may be taken as an indication that the Germans regard these as being more efficient and economical than artillery shell for the dispersion of gas. The possible development of some ingenious new gas weapon cannot be ignored.

(ii) *Aerial Spray.*—Considerable research has been carried out on aerial spray. The Germans undoubtedly regard low altitude spray (below 1,000 feet) as an effective weapon both against personnel and for ground contamination, and a number of trials have been carried out in which as many as six aircraft have been employed together or in relays. Information as to designs of spray apparatus is meagre and of little value, as so many factors have a material influence on results. The charging will probably be mustard gas, but lewisite and mixtures of mustard gas and lewisite have also been mentioned.

(iii) *Chemical aircraft bombs.*—Marked attention has been given by Germany to aircraft gas bombs. Types of bombs which have been mentioned are :—

10 kg. (22 lbs.) bombs with H.E. or toxic smoke effect.

50 kg. (110 lbs.) mustard gas bombs with highly sensitive impact fuse; small burster for ground contamination or larger burster for anti-personnel effect, giving an area of contamination about 22 yards radius from point of burst.

250 kg. (550 lbs.) mustard gas bombs with time fuse, to function at about 330 ft. above the ground and contaminate an area of about 6,000 square yards.

Plain glass bombs and glass capsules, charged with mustard gas.

(iv) *Projectors.*—No reference has been made to any efforts to increase the range or improve the mobility of these weapons which may form part of the equipment of the special gas units.

(v) *Artillery shell.*—The limitations of gas shell for artillery are clearly realized. Nevertheless, reports suggest that Germany has for some time been building up extensive stocks of gas-charged shell. The evidence is rather against any development of a base-ejection design of shell, but this point is by no means certain.

The Germans mainly favour the 10·5-cm. (4·14-in.) and 15-cm. (5·91-in.) calibres with chargings of choking gas (using small bursters), and blister gas, using a larger burster to scatter the liquid over a considerable area. The area of contamination is given as about 60 square yards for the 10·5-cm. and 120 square yards for the larger calibre. A highly sensitive percussion fuze will be used to minimize crater formation and consequent loss of the charging in the soil.

Another type which the Germans used during the last war and which they still regard as highly effective is their " Blue Cross " shell, in which a fragile container (glass) filled with D.A. or D.C. is embedded in a H.E. charging. The shells have considerable H.E. effect, the detonation dispersing the D.A. as an effective toxic smoke cloud.

(vi) *Mortars.*—Mortars for the dispersion of gas and smoke are included in the equipment of the chemical troops.

The 8·1-cm. (3·16-in.) mortar could, if necessary, fire a projectile containing gas, but no details are available of special designs of mortar gas projectiles.

(vii) *Gas grenades.*—Experiments have been carried out with these weapons, but no details are available.

Gas grenades having twice the capacity of the last war designs are stated to be available in Germany.

(viii) *Gas cylinders.*—Although little is said about these, Germany is certainly familiar with this method of attack.

(ix) *Gas mines.*—The Germans used a variety of designs of large calibre mortar bombs during the last war. These could be adapted to gas chargings and might be used as contamination mines.

Reference has also been made to large gas containers sunk at the sides of roads, actuated by a time mechanism, by the passage of vehicles or fired electrically. Gas mines in frontier fortifications and on tidal beaches to harass landing parties are also mentioned.

(x) *Bulk contamination.*—Tanks, armoured cars and lorries are stated to be equipped with apparatus for spraying gas and smokes. Chemical lorries are included in the equipment for the special gas units.

Portable sprayers are also envisaged.

(xi) *Toxic generators.*—No evidence has been obtained that the Germans possess an official design of thermal toxic generator, but generators made by a private firm, Stoltzenberg, containing D.A., D.C. and diphenylarsenic acid, have been found to be very effective, though their storage properties were not good.

The French had a large number of arsenical smoke generators which are now presumed to be in German hands. They are large in size, contain D.M. and function for about eight minutes. They are intended to be used in groups of four arranged to function one after the other, to give a total period of emission of about 30 minutes.

5. Smoke

(a) *Smoke units (Nebelwerfer-Abteilungen).*

(i) *General.*—The Germans attach great importance to the use of smoke units, formerly a part of the artillery but now constituted as a separate arm of the Service. These units are fully mechanized. Seven have been identified.

It is possible that each corps will eventually include a smoke unit. They could, if necessary, be used as gas troops, as the weapon with which they are equipped could be employed to fire a gas projectile.

(ii) *Organization.*—Each smoke unit consists of :—

Headquarters.
Signal section.
Three smoke companies each of two sections, each provided with four mortars. One company is equipped with material for decontaminating gassed areas.

(iii) *Strength.*—Little information is available. It is believed that the strength of a smoke company is about 120 all ranks, and that it has approximately twenty-four vehicles (four cars for commanders, twelve lorries for personnel and eight lorries for weapons and equipment).

(iv) *Armament.*—Each smoke unit has twenty-four and each company eight 8·1-cm. (3·16-in.) mortars. It is possible that a 10 cm. (3·93-in.) mortar may be introduced.

(b) *Equipment.*—Information is lacking as to actual smoke materials used, but it is reasonably certain that' they possess :—

(i) *Generators or " smoke candles."*—These are probably filled with Berger type mixtures. These are small and readily portable, and give an effective emission of smoke for periods of five to ten minutes.

(ii) *Pressure-type smoke apparatus.*—This is probably filled with chlorsulphonic acid (C.S.A.) or oleum. It consists of large drums or containers to hold the acid and a cylinder of compressed air to force the liquid out of a jet under pressure.

This type of apparatus can be readily transported in lorries and is suitable for large scale smoke screens.

(c) *Smoke units and apparatus in other arms of the service.*

(i) *Artillery.*—It is believed that the Germans consider the dispersion of smoke by artillery weapons uneconomical, as the latter are thereby prevented from carrying out their primary function. Smoke shell is, however, still carried in artillery units.

(ii) *Tank units.*—It is believed that a proportion of the tanks in a tank regiment (and possibly other A.F.Vs.) are provided with smoke-producing apparatus.

(iii) *Engineer units.*—It is probable that engineer units are or will be equipped with smoke-producing apparatus to cover working parties engaged in bridging and similar operations and will use it for screening special sites such as railheads.

(iv) *Aircraft.*—It is reasonably certain that the Germans possess smoke curtain apparatus for aircraft, using titanium tetrachloride. German aircraft also lay smoke screens (as distinct from vertical curtains) in conjunction with land forces.

(d) *Other special smoke units (Einnebelungs-Abteilungen).*—Other special smoke units exist, but their organization is not known. It is probable that they come under the Air Ministry and form part of the air defence organization of the country. They are, it is believed, responsible for protection, by means of smoke screens, of stations, bridges, industrial areas, etc., against air attack. They are said to be equipped with small generators and large smoke spray apparatus.

6. Effect of weather conditions on the production of smoke or gas

German teaching on the effect of weather conditions on the production of smoke or gas may be summarized as follows :—

(a) *Good conditions.*—Steady wind from rear or flank, preferably from 4 to 18 miles per hour, sky overcast and high relative humidity. When own troops are to be screened the direction of the wind is less important, but front line screening must not be attempted with a contrary wind. In general, early morning or the cool of the evening are likely times for good conditions, and cool weather is preferred. Slight rain or snow are aids to production, a heavy downpour is considered harmful. In the case of gas or smoke from artillery shells or mortar or projector bombs, and from aircraft, the direction of the wind is of little importance since the gas or smoke source is within, or above, the enemy's area, and winds of under four miles per hour, down to calm, are good conditions.

(b) *Unfavourable conditions.*—Mainly the reverse of the above. Wind of unfavourable direction; of velocity less than one mile per hour or more than 20 miles per hour, or unduly gusty. Hot sunny weather, or great cold, unfavourable.

7. Bacteria

Methods of bacteriological warfare have been thoroughly investigated by scientific experts and courses on this subject were held from time to time in Berlin. The students at these courses which, it is believed lasted for six weeks, were advanced gas specialists.

Experiments on the spraying of " foot and mouth " disease, dispersal of anthrax spore, pollution of water supplies and destruction of crops by means of germs dropped from the air, have been specifically mentioned.

Chapter X

CHAPTER XI

THE ADMINISTRATIVE SERVICES

1. General

The Services of the German Army in the field include the following:—

Supply and Administrative Services (*Nachschubdienst* and *Verwaltungsdienst*).

Medical Service (*Sanitätsdienst*).

Veterinary Service (*Veterinärdienst*).

Provost Service (*Ordnungsdienst*).

Postal Service (*Feldpostdienst*).

2. Supply and Administrative Services (*Nachschubdienst* and *Verwaltungsdienst*)

(a) *General.*—The supply service is responsible not only for the provision of ammunition, food, equipment and motor fuel, but also provides mobile workshops for the repair of motor vehicles and arms, and equipment of all types. In addition, it includes the personnel necessary for the loading and unloading of the vehicles of its various columns and for the establishment of refilling points, dumps, parks, etc.

The supply organization is kept very fluid. As far as can be ascertained, the establishment of the supply service in a formation is not at any time fixed. Columns are of standardized carrying capacity and are transferred from one formation to another, according to the requirements of the situation.

In addition to the supply columns described in sub-paras. (b), (c) and (d) below, G.H.Q. has a reserve of mechanical transport columns, each with a carrying capacity of 60 tons. These can be used to augment the divisional, corps or army columns.

The system as regards food supply is that one day's rations are carried on the unit field kitchens, two days' in the unit supply transport, and one day's in the divisional supply columns. Each man carries one day's iron rations and a similar reserve is kept on the unit field kitchens. With regard to forage, the day's ration is carried on the animal or on its vehicle, two days' forage are carried by the unit supply transport, and a further day's forage in the divisional supply column. An iron ration of forage is carried on the animal or on its vehicle.

The delivery of rations to sub-units is organized as a general rule, as follows :—

At the divisional delivery point (*Verpflegungsausgabestelle*), the second echelon (mechanized) of the regimental supply transport receives the supplies on a battalion, etc., basis. These are then handed over from the second echelon to the first (in the case of an infantry battalion, composed of horsed vehicles). In exceptional cases the second echelon delivers direct. In this case the first (horsed) echelon follows its sub-unit loaded. Motorized units have lorries which carry two days' supply and consequently only draw every other day from the divisional delivery point. (*See* Appendix XXXVI.)

The system as regards ammunition supply is similar to that of the British army, *i.e.*, systematic replacement from rear to front. (*See* Appendix XXXVIII.)

Petrol, oil and grease are replaced systematically from rear to front. M.T. vehicles of non-motorized units fill up from the divisional M.T. column for petrol and oil. Motorized units have special motor fuel and stores lorries which act as a link between unit vehicles and the divisional M.T. column (or army M.T. column) for petrol and oil. In calculating the quantities of petrol, etc., needed, the Germans classify motor vehicles according to their nature and petrol consumption, the unit of consumption being that quantity of petrol, etc., which the vehicle requires for a 60-mile (100 km.) run. (*See* Appendix XXXVII.)

(b) *Supply Service in a division.*—The supply service of a division is under the command of an officer known as the " Nachschubführer der Division," who corresponds to the C.R.A.S.C. He has under his control a number of units of the types given below, the actual number being dependent on the situation :—

(i) *Supply Columns* (*Nachschubkolonnen*)

These may be horsed (*bespannte Fahrkolonnen*) or mechanized (*Kraftwagenkolonnen*). The mechanized column consists of 1 officer and 60 other ranks, with 27 motor vehicles and 1 motor cycle. There are probably eight of these supply columns in a normal infantry or motorized infantry division*, and seven in an armoured division*. In certain terrain it is necessary to

---

* Supply columns of motorized infantry divisions and armoured divisions will invariably be mechanized.

employ mountain horsed columns (*Gebirgsfahrkolonnen*) and pack transport columns (*Tragtierkolonnen*). Each of the former has a carrying capacity of 15 tons only, while a pack transport column under the most favourable conditions cannot transport more than 5 tons ; each pack load is between 100 and 180 lbs.

These columns provide the fighting troops with ammunition, food, clothing, arms and equipment of all kinds and evacuate damaged weapons and equipment, captured material, used cartridge cases, etc., as well as, in case of necessity, wounded men and animals.

These columns normally form the link between the army supply columns (*see* sub-para. (*d*) (i) below) and the divisional refilling points, but may, however, in certain cases operate from railhead to the divisional refilling points. At the latter, ammunition is handed over to the light infantry, cavalry, artillery, engineer or signal columns, and rations to the mechanized portion of units' supply transport. When action is imminent an artillery ammunition echelon is formed from the mechanized columns carrying ammunition ; this echelon is placed under orders of the C.R.A. division and transports ammunition to the unit ammunition echelons or to the gun positions.

(ii) *M.T. Columns for Petrol and Oil* (*Kraftwagenkolonnen für Betriebsstoff*)

In the case of an infantry division this divisional unit is believed to consist of 1 officer and 30 other ranks, with 24 motor vehicles. It establishes petrol delivery points for motor vehicles of the staff and of non-motorized units and also for the motorized units. The divisional M.T. column for petrol and oil procures its supplies of motor fuel, oil and lubricant, etc., direct from petrol railhead or from the army M.T. column for petrol and oil.

(iii) *Workshop Company*

There is believed to be one unit of this type in a normal infantry division, consisting of 3 officers and 190 other ranks, with 100 motor vehicles, 12 trailers and 8 motor cycles. The personnel carry out repairs to arms, equipment, vehicles and M.T. which are beyond the capacity of armourers and tradesmen on unit establishments.

(iv) *Supply Companies (Nachschubkompanien)*

These companies, which are divided into ammunition, ration, technical and collecting sections, are responsible for loading and unloading vehicles at divisional refilling points.

The " Nachschubführer der Division " has under him an officer in charge of supplies, who controls the divisional supply refilling point and the divisional field bakery and butchery.

(c) *Supply Service in a Corps.*—The commander of the supply service of a corps is known as the " Nachschubführer des Korps " and acts as the C.R.A.S.C. of the corps. He has under his control a number of units of the same type as those in the supply service of a division. These units are used to reinforce the supply columns of divisions when necessary and also to supply troops attached to corps.

(d) *Supply Service in an Army.*—The commander of the supply service of an army is known as the " Nachschubführer der Armee," an appointment which corresponds approximately to the A.D.S. and T. of a corps in the British army. He has under his control a number of units of the types given below, the actual number being dependent on the situation :—

(i) *Supply Columns (Nachschubkolonnen)*

These are mechanized columns which have a carrying capacity of either 30 or 60 tons (10 or 20 3-ton lorries). They normally form the link between the ammunition and supply railheads of the army and the army ammunition and supply depôts, where their loads are partly taken over by the divisional supply columns and partly retained in the depôts.

(ii) *M.T. Columns for petrol and oil (Kraftwagenkolonnen für Betriebsstoff)*

These columns have a tank capacity of either 25 or 50 cubic metres (5,500 or 11,000 gallons) of motor fuel. They work on the " endless band " system, direct from supply railhead to the units in divisions, or to the divisional M.T. column for petrol and oil.

(iii) *Field workshops (Feldwerkstätten)*

These units carry out repairs to weapons and vehicles which are beyond the capacity of divisional workshop companies.

(iv) *Supply Battalions (Nachschub-Bataillone)*

These units are divided into ammunition, ration, technical and collecting companies which are stationed at the various army parks. They are responsible for the loading and unloading of vehicles of the divisional and army supply columns, and for other duties in connection with the parks themselves.

The ration supply system is shown in Appendix XXXVI.

(v) *Parks (Parke) and Depôts (Lager)*

The following types of parks and depôts exist in an army :—

Depôts :—
  Ammunition.
  Supply.

Parks :—
  Infantry.
  Artillery.
  Engineer.
  Signals.
  Mechanical transport.
  Equipment.
  Anti-gas equipment.

In addition, the "Nachschubführer der Armee" has under him an officer in charge of supplies who controls the army supply depôt and the army field bakeries and butcheries.

3. Medical Service (*Sanitätsdienst*)[*]

G.H.Q. of the armies in the field has at its disposal ambulance units (*Krankentransport-Abteilungen*), field hospital units (*Kriegslazarett-Abteilungen*) and army medical units (*Heeressanitäts-Abteilungen*). There are in addition hospital ships and hospital trains with the necessary medical personnel. Each army disposes of a number of ambulance units, one field hospital unit and one medical unit as well as hospital trains. The field hospital unit establishes separate hospitals for serious and for light cases, the latter for casualties who are likely to return to their units after three or four weeks' treatment. The army medical unit contains medical companies (*Sanitätskompanien*), detachments to establish field hospitals (*Feldlazarette*) together with M.T. ambulance sections (*Krankenkraftwagenzüge*). The army medical companies and field hospital detachments reinforce or relieve the divisional medical companies and field hospital detachment; the army M.T. ambulance sections are generally employed in rear of the divisional areas.

---

[*] For ranks in the medical service, with their British equivalents, see "The German Forces in the Field," 1(g).

No medical units are allotted to a German army corps.

Each infantry division has one, or on occasion two, medical companies. A company consists of 6 officers and 278 other ranks, and 84 of its personnel are armed with pistols. This unit is partially mechanized and is reported to contain 14 motor vehicles and 6 motor cycles, as well as 50 horses. There is also in each division a field hospital* (*Feldlazarett*) which, it is believed, consists of 7 officers and 85 other ranks, with 30 motor vehicles and 5 motor cycles. There are also 2 ambulance sections, each of 1 officer, 50 other ranks with 21 motor vehicles and 3 motor cycles. There may also be a H.D. ambulance section.

Wounded are in the first place collected and tended at regimental aid posts (*Truppenverbandplätze*) by unit medical personnel. They are then taken to one of the car posts (*Wagenhalteplätze*) where they are taken over by divisional M.T. ambulance sections or H.D. ambulance sections and transported to the advanced dressing station (*Hauptverbandplatz*). Adjacent to the advanced dressing station are the walking wounded collecting posts (*Leichtverwundetensammelplätze*) to which walking wounded proceed on foot. Thereafter casualties are evacuated either to the divisional field hospital* or to the casualty clearing stations and army hospitals.

It is not known how many dressing stations, etc., can be formed by a divisional medical company, but it is probable that the latter has sufficient personnel and equipment for the provision of one main and two or three advanced dressing stations.

Divisional medical services are responsible for the care and evacuation of wounded from the car posts or walking wounded collecting posts to divisional field hospitals or, until evacuated, to the casualty clearing stations or army hospitals.

4. Veterinary Service (*Veterinärdienst*)†

G.H.Q. of the armies in the field has at its disposal veterinary hospitals (*Pferdelazarette*), mobile animal blood-testing units (*bewegliche Tierblutuntersuchstellen*) and horse transport columns (*Pferdetransportkolonnen*). There are in addition hospital trains and ships for the evacuation of sick and wounded animals, which may be sub-allotted to army commands.

---

* This is thought to correspond to a main dressing station in the British army.

† For ranks in the veterinary service, with their British equivalents, *see* " The German Forces in the Field," 1(*g*).

Armies have veterinary hospitals (*Armeepferdelazarette*) which receive animal casualties evacuated by the divisions, and also horses which have become available by purchase or capture. Horses which have recovered from wounds or sickness are accommodated in veterinary depôts (*Armeepferdeparke*).

Should the distance between army veterinary hospitals and the divisional veterinary companies (*Veterinärkompanien*) be too great, veterinary evacuating stations (*Pferdesammelplätze*) are established by order of G.H.Q. from resources provided by the army hospitals. Army horse transport columns evacuate animal casualties from the divisional veterinary hospitals.

No veterinary units are allotted to a German army corps.

The infantry divisional veterinary company consists of 6 officers and 228 other ranks and 188 horses. It comprises a collecting (*Sammelstaffel*), a hospital (*Lazarettstaffel*) and a stores (*Vorratsstaffel*) section. In action, the veterinary company establishes one or more horse collecting stations which are also distributing centres for remounts and for veterinary stores.

It is believed that the evacuation of sick and wounded animals is approximately the same as in the British army.

5. Provost Service (*Ordnungsdienst*)

The provost service contains the following :—

(a) Military Police (*Feldgendarmerie*)*

Units of military police are employed with divisions and higher formations. The divisional military police unit consists of 2 officers and 18 other ranks. In home territory their duties include military police and security services and the custody of prisoners of war, in close co-operation with the civil police. In enemy territory they are also responsible for traffic control, collection of stragglers, prisoner of war cages, burial of the dead, establishment of information bureaux, control of civilians (including the organization of civilian labour), control of animals and fire fighting and A.R.P. services. The military police work in close co-operation with the field security police (*Geheime Feldpolizei*) and with district commanders and town majors.

The system of evacuation of prisoners is shown in Appendix XXXIX.

---

* *See also* " The German Forces in the Field," 5(*k*).

(b) **L. of C. Guard battalions** (*Wachbataillone*)

These units police the depôts, L. of C. installations, etc. They are included in each army, and are believed to be of the "Landsturm" category, *i.e.*, composed chiefly of men over 40 years of age.

(c) **Field security police** (*Geheime Feldpolizei*)*

It is believed that the duties of this organization are the same as those of the field security police in the British army, *e.g.*—

    (i) To prevent and discover espionage and other offences against the security of the army, and to control identification cards, permits and passes, and the movements of all civilians;

    (ii) To prevent civilians living in the area occupied by the army, and capable of bearing arms, from joining the enemy forces;

    (iii) To supervise war correspondents, press photographers, etc.;

    (iv) To recruit suitable persons to act as agents for the intelligence service.

It is probable that the secret state police (*Gestapo*) have furnished some of the personnel of the field security police.

District commanders and town majors with their detachments (*Feldkommandanturen* and *Ortskommandanturen I and II*) are established as required in the back areas. They are responsible for provost duties in their areas in addition to their other administrative duties. For this purpose military police are included in their detachments, and additional police units are placed under their command where necessary by the G.O.C. Lines of Communication. In enemy territory civil authorities are subordinate to the district commanders and town majors.†

6. Postal Service (*Feldpostdienst*)

This service, which only exists in war, is, it is believed, organized in the same way as the equivalent service in the British army. The divisional field post unit consists of 2 officers and 37 other ranks.

In order to disguise the locations of formations and units, a system of field post numbers (*Feldpostnummer*) came into force at the outbreak of war.

---

* *See also* "The German Forces in the Field," 5(*l*).
† *See also* "The German Forces in the Field," 6(*b*).

Field post numbers are allotted to the field army and to certain units and offices of the home forces.

These are five-figure numbers assigned to formations, units and sub-units; L or M prefixed indicates an air force (*Luftwaffe*) or naval (*Marine*) unit; the letters A-E, when added to a military number, indicate headquarters (A) and the four companies (B-E) of a battalion. Numbers are assigned to units with a studied absence of system, army, air force, naval and police numbers occurring at random in the same series. In addressing letters, or other communications, the field post number alone is used, no mention of the unit being permitted; and it seems likely that, for security reasons, the field post number will replace the name of the unit on identity discs and in pay-books.

Chapter XI

Chapter XI 204

APPENDIX XXXVI
Supply of Rations.

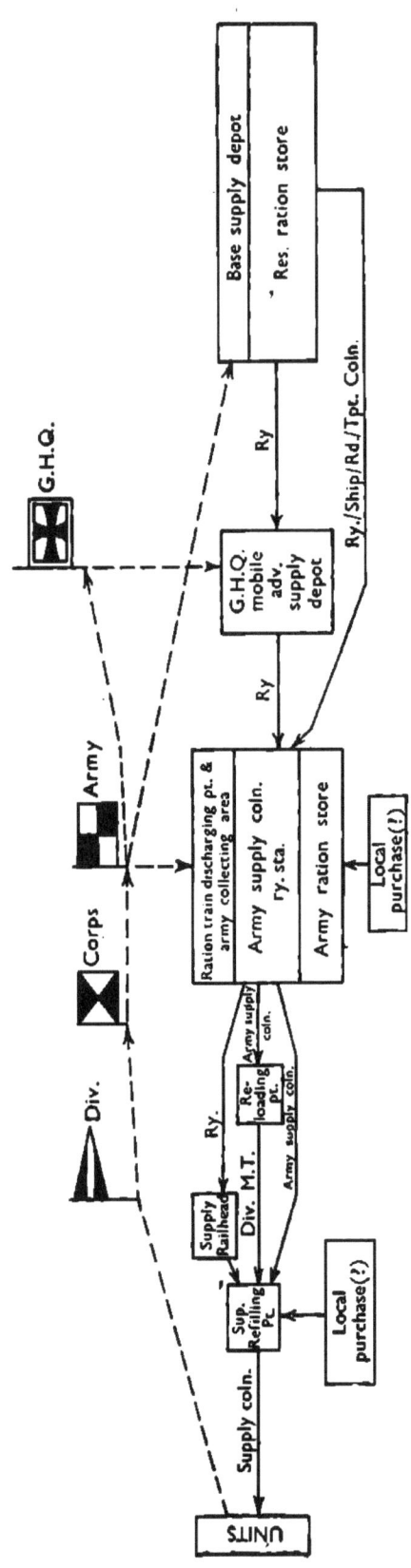

APPENDIX XXXXVI—contd.
Supply of Rations—contd.

Channel of demand and of instruction (dotted line).

In so far as rations cannot be obtained in the area of operations demand is made as follows:—

By units on Divisional Senior Supply Officer (for iron rations only: other rations are supplied to units at refilling points without demand having to be made.)

By Divisional S.S.O. or Corps S.S.O., the latter on Army S.S.O.

By Army S.S.O. on base supply depôt.

Channel of Supply (uninterrupted line).

The base supply depôt draws from reserve ration store and despatches by means of ration, flour, oats and meat trains.

Army H.Q. either stores the rations in the Army ration store or, in case of need, allocates ration trains or army supplycolns. as a mobile ration depôt.

Divisional H.Q. receives rations by rail to supply railhead or by army supply coln. to the reloading point or fetches them by Divisional M.T. from the army ration store.

Units receive from supply refilling points by means of a supply coln.

Chapter XI

APPENDIX XXXXVII
Supply of Fuel for Motor Vehicles.

Chapter XI

APPENDIX XXXVII—contd.

Supply of Fuel for Motor Vehicles—contd.

Channel of indenting and of instruction (dotted line).

Individual vehicles belonging to the Staff or to non-motorised troops draw from pet. points for individual vehicles on the authority of Divisional H.Q., only in special cases.

Indents are made as follows :—

By mot. troops on Divisional H.Q., which controls the mot. petrol supply coln.

By Divisional H.Q. on Corps H.Q., the latter in turn on Army H.Q., which controls the railway petrol tank points, the fuel dumps and the mot. petrol supply coln.

By Army H.Q. on Q.M.G., G.H.Q., who gives instruction for the required supply to be provided either out of the mobile fuel reserve or from the Army supply tank depôt.

Channel of Supply (uninterrupted line).

From Army supply tank depôt and/or the G.H.Q. mobile fuel reserve to Army railhead for the supply at the disposal of the Army command, which in its turn forms fuel units and railway petrol tank points and/or erects fuel dumps.

Railway petrol tank points are moved forward by rail and distribute M.T. fuel to the mot. petrol supply coln.

Fuel dumps (for units holding depôts) will be set up forward of railhead.

The mot. supply colns. fill mot. troops heavy fuel and equipment lorries at fuel issuing points and allocate individual lorries to serve as fuel tanks for individual vehicles belonging to the Staff and to non-motorised troops.

Chapter XI 208

APPENDIX XXXXVIII

Supply of Ammunition

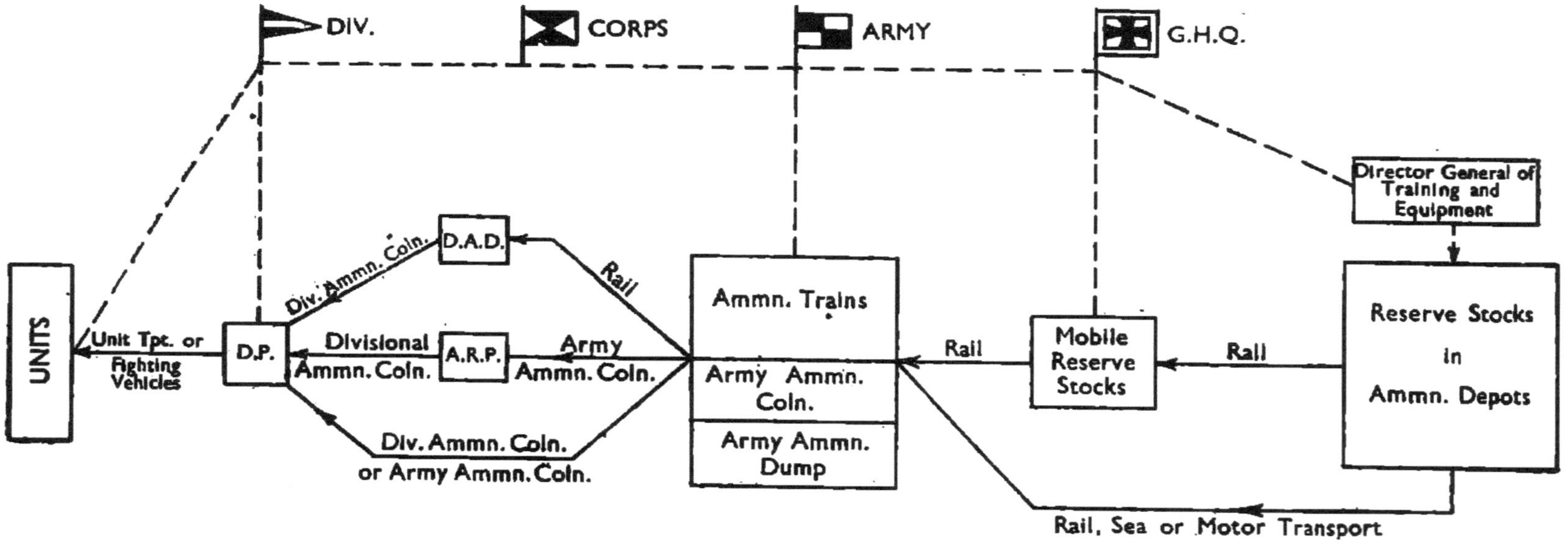

D.A.D.   Divisional ammunition dump.
D.P.   Delivery point.
A.R.P.   Ammunition refilling point.

APPENDIX XXXVIII—contd.
Supply of Ammunition—contd.

Channel for indenting and forwarding (dotted line) :—

The following send in daily returns of ammunition on hand :—

    Units (number of rounds of each calibre) to div.

    Divs. (consolidated return according to calibres) to corps H.Q.

Indents are sent :—

    By corps H.Q. (according to calibres) to army H.Q.

    By army H.Q. to G.H.Q. (Q.M.G.).

Channel of Supply (uninterrupted line) :—

G.H.Q. (Q.M.G.) either supply ammunition indented for by armies from G.H.Q. mobile reserve stocks, or instruct the Director General of Training and Equipment to supply from reserve stocks in G.H.Q. ammunitions depots. Transport usually by rail.

Army H.Q. store ammunition, when received, in army ammunition dumps, or hold it as a mobile reserve in the army ammunition column, or deliver it to the ammunition trains in the army supply collection area.

Div. receives ammunition sent by rail at supply railhead, ammunition sent by army ammunition column at the refilling point, or in exceptional cases at the delivery point, or collects it by div. supply column from army ammunition dumps.

Units collect from delivery points with light columns or "A" echelon transport. Artillery ammunition is delivered by the artillery echelon.

Chapter XI 210

APPENDIX XXXIX
Evacuation of Prisoners.

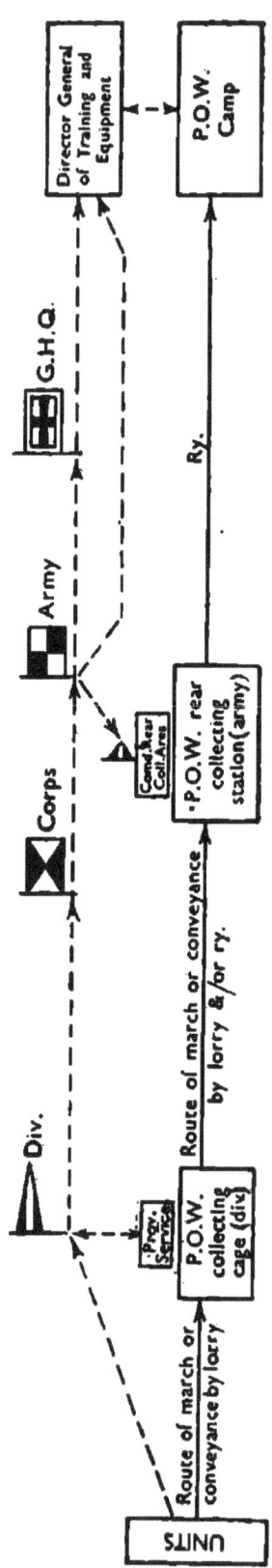

APPENDIX XXXIX—*contd.*

Evacuation of Prisoners—*contd.*

Channel of reporting and instruction (dotted line).	Evacuation (uninterrupted line).
Reports are dispatched as follows:—	Units send P.O.W. to Divisional P.O.W. collecting cage. Escort is provided either by provost or unit personnel.
By units to Divisional H.Q., which erects the P.O.W. collecting cage through the provost service.	
By Divisional H.Q. to Corps H.Q., the latter to Army H.Q., which erects the rear P.O.W. collecting station through the commandant of the rear collecting area.	Divisional H.Q. send P.O.W. to the Army collecting station or Army H.Q. fetch them, escort being provided by provost or by unit personnel or by L. of C. guard battalions.
By Army H.Q. to Q.M.G., G.H.Q., who advises the Director-General of Training and Equipment of the number of P.O.W., according to ranks.	Army H.Q. send P.O.W. to P.O.W. camps, escort being provided by L. of C. guard battalions or by home defence troops.
The Director-General of Training and Equipment erects P.O.W. camps through home defence units and issues instructions to Army H.Q. for the dispatch of P.O.W.	

CHAPTER XII

POLICE, GENDARMERIE, SEMI-MILITARY FORCES AND LABOUR SERVICE

1. General organization of the police

All police now come under the control of Department III of the combined Reich and Prussian Home Office. The present head of the police is also head of the "Schutz-Staffeln" (SS) (*see* para. 4 (*a*)) and has the title of "Reichsführer S.S. und Chef der Deutschen Polizei."

The police proper are divided into :—

   (*a*) Constabulary (*Ordnungspolizei*).

      (i) Town constabulary (*Schutzpolizei*).

      (ii) Rural constabulary (*Gendarmerie*).

   (*b*) Security police (*Sicherheitspolizei*).

      (i) Secret state police (*Geheime Staatspolizei* or *Gestapo*).

      (ii) Criminal police (*Kriminalpolizei*).

The command of all constabulary is vested in a general of police; the security police come under a senior officer of the "Schutz-Staffeln" (SS).

2. The various branches of police

(*a*) *Town constabulary* (*Schutzpolizei*).—The constabulary performs the ordinary patrol and traffic control duties and is generally responsible for public order.

The organization of the constabulary is not definitely known, but it is probable that its "Bereitschaften," which correspond to companies, are grouped into higher formations known as "Kommandos" and "Inspektionen."

Candidates for entry to the constabulary must be between the ages of 20 and 25. Normally recruits are accepted only if they have done their two years' service with the colours or with the permanently embodied S.S. units (*see* para. 4 (*a*)). Recently, however, candidates were admitted from classes which had not performed their military service.

(b) *Barrack police.*—The constabulary also provides personnel for the barrack police which are being extensively employed in the occupied territories, thereby releasing troops for service elsewhere. The operational unit is the battalion composed of four companies, the fourth being the heavy M.G. company. For administration, battalions are sometimes grouped in regiments. Most battalions are partially motorized and include armoured car, signal, medical and repair shop units.

A division formed from the barrack police (*S.S. Polizei-Division*) also exists. It is organized as an ordinary infantry division.

(c) *Rural constabulary (Gendarmerie).*—The duties of the rural constabulary correspond to those of the county police in Great Britain.

The motorized branch of this force is organized into 42 " Bereitschaften " (companies), which are widely distributed over the whole country and are responsible for the supervision of traffic on the new motor roads (*Reichsautobahnen*), and other main roads.

(d) *Auxiliary police (Hilfspolizei).*—This additional body of police was employed in Poland, where it helped the barrack police (*see* (b) above) to clean up back areas. It is still employed in this connection and may also be encountered in other occupied countries.

(e) *Secret state police (Geheime Staatspolizei* or *Gestapo).*—This is the supreme organization responsible for countering any movement directed against the State. Among its far-reaching activities, which permeate the whole life of the nation, is the censoring of all correspondence and literature to and from other countries which might in any way prove inimical to the interests of the state. Its regular personnel is mainly drawn from the " Schutz-Staffeln " (*see* para. 4), but it will employ any man, woman or child who can usefully be cajoled or menaced into serving its ends.

(f) *Criminal police (Kriminalpolizei).*—The criminal police are solely concerned with the prevention and detection of crime. They do not wear uniform.

(g) *Technical Emergency Corps (Technische Nothilfe,* or *Teno).*—This is an auxiliary police force subordinated to the Ministry of the Interior. It provides essential services during emergencies, its personnel being specially trained in fire fighting, decontamination, etc. P.A.D. units are distributed throughout cities, the industrial centres, and traffic junctions. " Teno " men are also employed in army rear areas and occupied territory to rebuild damaged bridges, canal locks, power houses and buildings generally, thus freeing army engineers and personnel for other tasks.

3. Special Bodyguard troops

Leibstandarte Adolf Hitler.—This unit, the nearest equivalent of which is a regiment, belongs to the permanently embodied " Schutz-Staffeln " (*see* para. 4 (*a*)). It was originally formed in 1933 to act as the Führer's bodyguard ; it also finds guards for important government buildings, and for Hitler's residences. Since the war it has also been engaged on purely military service in Poland and in the West.

Its strength and organization are believed to be similar to those of an infantry regiment. In addition it has its own artillery and armoured car sections, as well as machine-gun and motor cyclist rifle companies. The regiment is wholly mechanized with its own service transport.

4. Semi-Military and Political Organizations

(*a*) *Schutz-Staffeln* (*SS*).—The " Schutz-Staffeln " are composed of good National Socialists, picked for their mental and physical qualities, and its primary function is to ensure internal security.

It is composed of the following :—

Ordinary S.S. units.—These are organized in 14 regional groups known as " Oberabschnitte," which correspond to the " Wehrkreise." These groups are subdivided into "Abschnitte " and " Reiterabschnitte " (both large formations), " Standarten " (regiments), " Sturmbanne " (battalions), " Stürme " (companies), etc. These formations are not permanently embodied, but receive part-time training. They consequently provide a useful reserve of manpower for the regular forces and for the " Waffen S.S." (*see* below). Certain " Standarten " are named after a locality or a " martyr " (*e.g.*, No. 11 Standarte bears the name " Planetta ").

Permanently embodied and militarized S.S. Units (*Waffen S.S.*).

These are composed of :—

" Verfügungstruppen." In addition to the " Leibstandarte Adolph Hitler," described in para. 3, these troops consist of three regiments. These are—

    The S.S. Standarte No. 1 Deutschland.
    The S.S. Standarte No. 2 Germania.
    The S.S. Standarte No. 3 Der Führer.

Each regiment consists of three battalions, and is organized, armed, and equipped in exactly the same way as a motorized infantry regiment of the normal type. These regiments form a separate motorized infantry division—the " S.S. Verfügungsdivision " with its own artillery, reconnaissance, anti-tank, pioneer and other ancillary units.

The " S.S. Verfügungsdivision " is in every way the equivalent of a regular motorized infantry division, and it was employed with conspicuous success in the West.

Concentration Camp Guards (Totenkopfverbände).—The " S.S. Totenkopfverbände " originated as concentration camp guards and a proportion of them is still employed in this capacity, the men being armed as infantry and living in barracks.

A " Totenkopf " division has been created since the war, composed of three infantry regiments, an artillery regiment, etc. Like the " Verfügungsdivision," described above, it was in action in France and is the equivalent of a regular motorised infantry division. Non-divisional " Totenkopf Standarten " also exist.

(b) *Storm detachments (Sturm-Abteilungen) (S.A.).*—The Storm Detachments consist of :—

Active S.A. (men from 18 to 35).
S.A. Reserve I (men from 35 to 45).
S.A. Reserve II (men over 45).

They are divided into 21 groups, which are sub-divided into " Brigaden," " Standarten," etc. Since the outbreak of war the majority have been absorbed into the army.

The S.A. is responsible for the pre- and post-military training of German manpower in co-operation with the heads of the fighting services. To this end " Wehrmannschaften " (lit. " defence detachments ") have been created in which the men are trained in shooting, scouting, map drawing, compass reading, wireless, hand grenade throwing, bayonet practice and ordinary drill. This training lasts in the ordinary way three months and takes a good deal of work off army instructors' hands.

(c) *National Socialist Motor Corps (Nationalsozialistisches Kraftfahrerkorps) (N.S.K.K.).* From the army's point of view a most important part of the National Socialist organization is the National Socialist Motor Corps. The latter is designed to :—

    (i) Train as drivers and mechanics men who are destined to join the mechanized units of the army.

    (ii) Provide the personnel required for the rearward services of the army in war.

    (iii) Co-operate with the military authorities in carrying out trials of mechanical transport so as to influence manufacturers in putting on the market standard types suited for army use.

    (iv) Organize cross-country driving competitions in which army personnel, driving army vehicles, are amongst the competitors.

    (v) Make the German nation mechanically minded.

Germany is divided into five "Obergruppen" (North, South, East, West, and Middle) ; each of these large units is sub-divided into a varying number of motor " Gruppen," the latter consisting of a number of "Standarten" (regiments), "Staffeln" (battalions) and "Stürme" (companies). In addition the N.S.K.K. run special schools (Motorsportschulen) where courses are held varying in length from five weeks to three months. A large number of men have passed through these schools, and, as well as those about to perform their military service, *i.e.*, men aged 18 onwards, the N.S.K.K. accepts members of the motorized section of the Hitler Youth at the age of 16. The N.S.K.K. consequently plays a very important part in the M.T. training of Germany's future soldiers. All those passing through the schools are in fact well fitted to enter the motorized units of the army.

The purely military activities of the N.S.K.K. are undertaken by its defence units (*Wehrstaffeln*) which are run in co-operation with the S.A. (*see* para. 4 (*b*)).

In addition to the foregoing activities the N.S.K.K. is responsible for traffic arrangements in Germany, and a Traffic Training Service (*Verkehrserziehungsdienst*) has been created. As its name implies it trains personnel specially to deal with traffic problems, and in a general way to encourage the development of road sense in the German citizen.

(*d*) *National Socialist Mounted Corps* (*Nationalsozialistisches Reiterkorps* (*N.S.R.K.*).—The National Socialist Mounted Corps has two functions :—

    (i) To train young men to the standard of cavalry recruits of six months' service before they join the army. A man who wishes to join a mounted arm of the Service has now to be in possession of a certificate from this organization before he is accepted.

(ii) To enable ex-soldiers of mounted units to practise their riding after leaving the Colours.

(e) *National Socialist Flying Corps (Nationalsozialistisches Fliegerkorps) (N.S.F.K.)*.—Its functions are :—

(i) To organize the pre-military training of personnel destined for the Air Force, in particular the members of the flying section of the Hitler Youth. At the technical schools of the N.S.F.K. courses are held which include theoretical and practical instruction in the construction of gliders, as well as in W/T, R/T, etc.

(ii) To promote air-mindedness amongst the civilian population.

5. Hitler Youth

Membership of the Hitler Youth (*Hitler-Jugend*) is compulsory for all boys—except those whose blood is not pure Aryan. The pre-military training of the " Hitler-Jugend " between the ages of 16 and 18 has been taken over by the army.

6. Railway, post and factory guards

(a) *Railway guards and railway police (Bahnschutz and Bahnschutzpolizei)*.—This organization, the personnel of which is drawn from railway employees, is responsible for the protection of the railways in time of war and civil disorder. There is a railway guard group in each of the areas into which the German railway system is divided. Units are armed with rifles and light and heavy machine-guns.

(b) *Post guards (Postschutz)*.—This organization, the personnel of which is found from post office employees, is responsible for the protection of postal communications.

(c) *Factory guards (Werkschutz)*.—This organization, the personnel of which is drawn from factory workers, is responsible for the protection of industrial concerns.

7. National Labour Service

Every young man is obliged to serve a period of six months in the " Reichsarbeitsdienst " (R.A.D.) before joining the army.

The men live in camps and are trained in drill, marching and digging, but are not armed. They are engaged chiefly on drainage and irrigation work in connection with land improvement schemes, land reclamation and afforestation projects. Since the war they have been called upon to level roads and aerodromes, clear away rubble, collect captured war material, and generally perform manual labour in the occupied territories.

8. Ex-soldiers' organization

The only ex-soldiers' association in Germany is the "N.S. Deutscher Reichskriegerbund Kyffhäuser." One of its objects is to keep the ex-soldier's military knowledge fresh by means of weapon training, field training, demonstrations and lectures.

9. Voluntary police corps

This corps consists of German nationals in ex-Polish territory. Officially called "Selbstschutz" (lit. self-protection), *i.e.*, it is a Home Guard which helps the regular police and S.S. formations to maintain law and order and encourage the diffusion of German culture.

10. Military farmers

One of the possibilities open to ex-members of the "Waffen S.S." (*see* para. 4 (*a*)) is to settle on the land in the Eastern Marches and acquire special status as "Wehrbauer" (lit. "defence peasant").

11. Czech police corps

The formation of this "Schutzkorps" was authorised in March, 1939. Its function is to preserve law and order in the Protectorate. The personnel of this corps is, so far, limited to senior N.C.O.s of the former Czech army. Regulations regarding strength, organization and equipment remain in the hands of the Reich.

Chapter XII

CHAPTER XIII

Uniform

1. General notes on field service uniform (*see* Plates 71 to 73)

The present type of uniform has been evolved from that worn during the last war, the chief consideration being that it should be light, comfortable, weatherproof and inconspicuous.

(*a*) *Officers*.—In field service order officers wear a steel helmet or forage cap. The helmet* is made of seamless sheet steel and is painted inside and out with rust resisting grey matt paint. Lugs are drilled on either side of the helmet so that a face shield can be worn. The forage cap is made of greenish-grey cloth with a peak of black leather and a band of dark grey-green cloth. It has no chin strap.

The jacket is made of greenish-grey cloth with a collar of a darker shade fastened up to the neck. Trousers of grey cloth are worn by dismounted officers and riding breeches of the same colour with leather strappings and riding boots by mounted officers. The greatcoat, which is also of grey cloth, is double-breasted and has a dark green collar. Changes, it is reported, are being made to the quality of officers' uniforms, owing to the high percentage of losses among officers during the Polish campaign of September, 1939, and according to a recent decree officers' uniforms must henceforth be of the same cloth and quality as those of the rank and file. This order likewise extends to officers' belts, in place of which the ordinary soldier's belt must be worn.

In addition to a pack (replaced by a haversack in the case of mounted officers) officers carry a bivouac sheet with cords, a waterbottle, a map case and message book, a whistle, field glasses, respirator and gas cape, an automatic pistol and an entrenching tool. (For badges of rank *see* Plate 77.).

(*b*) *Other ranks*.—In field service dress other ranks wear either a steel helmet or a forage cap. The former is of the same type as that worn by officers; the latter is made of greenish-grey cloth without peak or chin strap and can be worn under the steel helmet.

---

* Parachute troops are issued with a modified type of brimless helmet with chin and neck straps. (*See* para. 10.)

The jacket is made of greenish-grey cloth with a darker collar which may be folded back and left open at the neck. Personnel of dismounted arms wear trousers made of grey cloth, which are tucked into half-jack boots. In mounted arms riding breeches and boots of the same type as those worn by officers are issued. In all arms the greatcoat is the same as that worn by officers.

Other ranks wear a black soft leather belt with a dull white metal buckle to which cartridge pouches are attached. Their equipment includes a pack (replaced by a haversack in the case of mounted personnel), a bivouac sheet with cords, a water bottle, a respirator and gas cape, an entrenching tool and sidearms. For badges of rank *see* Plate 77. Particoloured bayonet and sword knots are not worn on active service, so that this means of identification no longer exists.

(c) *Special types of uniform* :—

(i) *Armoured fighting troops (see Plates 74 and 75).—*Armoured fighting units wear a loose-fitting black uniform with a black beret.

(ii) *Mountain troops and rifle (Jäger) battalions.*—The units named above wear a mountain cap (similar to the forage cap worn by other ranks, but with the addition of a peak of the same material), the ordinary type of service jacket, grey cloth trousers, fastened round the ankles by puttees and ankle boots with a form of snow shoe attached when operating in snow. They carry a rucksack instead of a pack and a large size water-bottle. Officers and N.C.Os. are sometimes equipped with skis instead of snow shoes.

During the heavy falls of snow in the winter of 1939–40 mountain troops on the Western Front were also equipped with long, white, short-sleeved overalls with hoods.

(iii) *Raiding (Stoss-) and reconnaissance parties (Spähtrupps)* are also equipped with white overalls similar to those described under para. (c) (ii) above in snowy weather.

(iv) *Smoke units.*—Smoke units (*Nebelwerfer-Abteilungen*) are, it would appear, now equipped with leather suits consisting of jacket, breeches and mask with goggles.

2. Distinguishing marks and badges of rank

(a) *Distinguishing marks.*

Apart from badges of rank and special badges (described in para. 7), the only distinguishing mark that has apparently been retained on active service is the colour of the arm of the service. (*See* Plate 76.) The various arms, certain classes of officers, and various non-combatant services each have a distinguishing colour. In field service order this colour appears in the piping of the shoulder strap and in the centre of the collar patch. Distinguishing marks on shoulder straps are concealed in the case of officers by means of a sleeve fitting on the shoulder strap (on the greatcoat the shoulder straps are detachable) and in the case of other ranks by removing the shoulder straps altogether or rolling them up in such a way that the distinguishing marks are not visible.

Recent reports indicate that when the above practice is not followed, a flash of coloured material may be worn in place of the numeral on the shoulder strap to distinguish the regiment. Officers and men when on leave or when in back areas are still believed to display all their distinguishing marks and rank badges as illustrated in Plate 77.

(b) *Badges of rank.*

These are illustrated in Plate 77. Numerals on shoulder straps indicating the unit are removed on active service, the shoulder strap button (indicating the company or equivalent unit) alone being retained.

3. National crests and badges. (*See* Plate 78).

The regimental crests and badges of the type worn by the British army are replaced by the national badge, the national rosette and the national colours.

(a) *National badge.*—This is worn in field service order :—

(i) On the forage cap, the mountain cap and the black beret. In aluminium thread on a field grey ground (except in the case of the black beret when it is on a black ground).

(ii) Above the right breast pocket of the service dress jacket. In the case of generals in gold, and in the case of other officers, non-commissioned officers and men in aluminium.

(iii) On the black jacket worn by certain armoured fighting troops. In aluminium on a black ground.

(iv) On steel helmet. In aluminium on a black shield. In this case the national badge is of a different design.

(b) *National rosette.*—This is a small circular badge in red, white and black worn below the national badge in all headdresses except the steel helmet. It is usually made of metal but in the mountain cap it is woven. On all peaked caps except the mountain cap, and on the black beret, it is flanked by oak leaves.

(c) *National colours.*—The national colours, black, white and red, are worn in the form of a shield painted on the right side of the steel helmet.

4. Para-military formations

(a) *Schutz-Staffeln.*—The principal distinguishing mark is a skull and cross-bones badge on the headdress. The uniform is entirely black except that the shirt worn is brown. Militarized S.S. (*Verfügungstruppe*) have, however, in addition, a field grey uniform identical with the field service uniform of the army. It can always be distinguished from the latter as the national badge is worn on the left sleeve instead of on the right breast. The S.S. helmet is similar to the standard type, except that the shield on the right hand side bears the device ᛋᛋ in place of the national colours.

(b) *Storm detachments.*—S.A. normally wear a brown uniform with a red armlet, having a black swastika on a circular white ground, on the left arm. S.A. when employed in the war zone now wear a field grey uniform with olive green tabs bearing badges of rank, shoulder straps and a grey peaked cap.

(c) *National Socialist Motor Corps.*—The N.S.K.K. wear the same uniform as the storm detachments but with special badges on caps and forearm (motor wheel) and collar patch.

5. Identity discs and means of identification

Identity discs were issued on mobilization and are worn at all times by all ranks.

The identity discs of German soldiers and airmen bear the letters A, B or O indicating their blood groups. This step has been adopted since the Polish campaign of September, 1939, to facilitate urgent blood transfusions.

The " Soldbuch " (pay book) carried by every German soldier (except when employed in raiding parties) gives particulars of the soldiers' regiment and company, etc.

Chapter XIII

6. Orders, decorations and medals

Appendix XL contains a note on the more common German orders, decorations and medals.

7. Special badges

Appendix XLI contains a description of the infantry assault badge, the A.F.V. badge, the assault badge for other arms of the service, and the wound badge.

Specialist badges are worn by unit signallers, farriers, artificers, W.T. operators, etc. Marksman and gun-layer badges are also awarded.

8. Personal equipment

In field service the following personal equipment is carried :—

> (a) *On the man.*—Bivouac sheet with cords, forage cap, water bottle, mess tin, drinking mug, knife, fork and spoon, iron ration. These are carried in a special pack for the march (*Marschgepäck*).

> (b) *In the first line transport.*—In or attached to the pack (*Tornister*)—greatcoat, shoes, shirt, towel, socks, housewife, shaving and cleaning kit, iron ration.

> In a clothing bag—canvas clothing, drawers, socks, neck-cloth.

9. Air Force uniform

The uniform of the German Air Force is of a shade of blue-grey similar to that of the Royal Air Force. The distinguishing colours worn by the different arms of the service are illustrated in Plate 79, the national badge (which differs from that worn by the Army) and specialist badges in Plate 80 and badges of rank in Plate 81.

10. Uniform worn by parachute troops (*see* Plates 82, 83 and 84)

Parachute troops wear the following uniform :—

> (i) Steel helmet—round in shape, with narrow brim and no neck shield, fitting closely on the head and thickly padded with rubber.

> (ii) Tunic—short and loose, with turned-down collar. Slatish-grey colour, open at the neck, with yellow distinguishing badges (officers wear collar and tie), no buttons showing.

(iii) Badge—ring, encircling a diving eagle, worn on the left hand side, immediately above the belt, by men who have made a minimum of six jumps.

(iv) Belt—leather, with flat rectangular buckle.

(v) Trousers—very loose, tucked into the top of the boot.

(vi) Boots—non-lacing, special type, with thick rubber soles.

When jumping, the parachutist wears a loose grey-green gabardine overall, closing at the neck with a " zip " fastener, the trousers being very short, wide trunk-drawers. This garment is worn over uniform and equipment. On landing, the " zip " fastener is opened, equipment taken off and put on again over the overall. It seems that this overall is nearly always used to cover the uniform when fighting.

APPENDIX XL

ORDERS, DECORATIONS AND MEDALS

1. The Iron Cross

This is an award for conspicuous bravery in face of the enemy or for outstanding services in leadership. There are four classes of the Iron Cross, and they rank in the following order :—

Grand Cross of the Iron Cross.
Knight's Cross of the Iron Cross.
Iron Cross, Class I.
Iron Cross, Class II.

The Grand Cross of the Iron Cross is awarded only for conspicuous services which have a decisive bearing upon battle engagements. The only difference between the present design of the Iron Cross, Classes I and II, and that of the last war, is that the face of the medal now bears, in the centre of the cross, a swastika, in place of the Kaiser's "W" surmounted by a crown. The year of the award is shown beneath the swastika. The medal is in dull silver. The ribbon of the Iron Cross, Classes I and II, is black-white-red. Whilst the Iron Cross, Class I, is worn without a ribbon on the left breast tunic pocket, the Class II with ribbon may be worn there or in the second button-hole of the tunic. The Knight's Cross of the Iron Cross is slightly bigger than the Iron Cross I and II and is worn about the neck, suspended from a black-white-red ribbon. The bar to the Knight's Cross consists of three silver oak leaves on the medal ribbon. The Grand Cross is approximately double the size of the Iron Cross I and II, is in gold instead of in dull silver, and is worn about the neck with a broader ribbon than that of the Knight's Cross.

The bar, which may be awarded in this war to men who gained the Iron Cross in the last war, is silver and bears the date of the new award and the national emblem of eagle and swastika.

2. The War Service Cross or Star

This was inaugurated in October, 1939, for special services which are not performed in face of the enemy. It may be awarded to personnel in rearward services and garrisons, as well as to male civilians. The decoration is in two classes and consists of an eight-pointed star, bearing the swastika in its centre, the whole surrounded by a wreath of oak-leaves. The lower or Class II star is in bronze and the First Class in silver. The Class II star is worn with a ribbon on a clasp or from the second button-hole of the tunic, while the Class I Star is worn without ribbon on the left breast of the tunic.

3. The Narvik Decoration

After the operations in Norway, Hitler inaugurated a Narvik decoration to "commemorate the heroic and victorious joint operations by mountain regiments, and units of the Navy and Air Force at Narvik."

The decoration is in the form of a shield showing the "edelweiss" of the mountain regiments, an anchor and an aeroplane propeller, and the device "Narvik, 1940," the whole surmounted by the German eagle on a wreath surrounding a swastika.

The decoration, in silver for the Army and Air Force and gold for the Navy, is to be worn, when in uniform, on the left upper arm. All members of the armed forces, who participated honourably in the landing at Narvik, or in the operations of the Narvik Force are eligible for the decoration.

4. Meritorious Service Cross

A Meritorious Service Cross has been instituted in three classes :—

> Knight's Cross of the Meritorious Service Cross.
> Meritorious Service Cross, Class I.
> Meritorious Service Cross, Class II.

The cross may be awarded in each of these classes with or without swords.

There is also a Meritorious Service Medal.

The Meritorious Service Cross is a Maltese cross with a swastika in the centre, embossed on a plain surface edged with oak leaves. The reverse bears the year of the award. Class II is in bronze, Class I in silver. The Knight's Cross is also silver, but it is larger than that of Class II. The medal is bronze, with the device "Für Kriegsverdienst" and the year of the award on the reverse. Class II and the medal are worn with a ribbon on the left breast pocket, or in the second button-hole of the tunic. Class I is worn on the left breast pocket without a ribbon. The Knight's Cross is worn about the neck on a broader ribbon.

The ribbon for the three classes is black, edged with white and red. That of the medal has in addition a thin red line down the middle.

5. The Service Medal

This is awarded to all soldiers who have served in the army for four years or more. There are four classes :—

> Class I (gold)—24 years' service.
> Class II (silver)—18 years' service.
> Class III (bronze)—12 years' service.
> Class IV (silver)—4 years' service.

Chapter XIII

The figures 4, 12, 18 and 24, surrounded by a wreath of oak leaves, appear on the reverse of the medal. A bar consisting of three oak leaves is awarded to the holder of Class I medal in recognition of 40 years' service.

The medal for Class I is rather bigger than the others and is in the shape of a Maltese cross with a polished surface bearing in its centre the German eagle and swastika.

The medal for Class II is similar in design but is unpolished, and has bevelled edges.

For Classes III and IV the medal is round and bears on its face the German eagle and swastika. The reverse bears either the figure 12 or 4 (as the case may be) surrounded by a wreath of oak leaves.

The ribbon in all cases is of cornflower blue.

6. Social Welfare Badge

This badge now embraces four classes and is awarded for services rendered in the field of social welfare, Red-Cross work, life saving, efforts on behalf of the Winter Help Fund, etc. It may be awarded to soldiers as well as civilians, but not to soldiers whose normal duties lie in one or the other of the fields named. It takes the form of a gilt-edged white enamelled cross with the swastika in its centre.

>Class I is worn with a ribbon from the neck.

>Class II is worn without ribbon on the left breast pocket of the tunic.

>Class III is worn with a narrow ribbon on the left breast pocket of the tunic.

>Class IV is worn with a narrow ribbon on the left breast pocket of the tunic and is in silver instead of white.

The ribbon for all four classes is red, edged with white.

7. The National-Socialist " Blutorden " (Order of Blood)

This medal was originally struck at Hitler's command, in 1933, and was awarded to all those who took part with him in the abortive " Putsch " in Munich, in 1923. It was later given a wider distribution, and was awarded to many Nazi Party members who had taken part in the street fighting of the pre-1933 years. The order is regarded with the highest respect in the Party. The medal is circular, and the ribbon is red. It is worn on the right breast of Nazi Party uniforms. When worn on military tunics, the ribbon is placed above the left breast pocket in line with any other decorations that may have been awarded.

8. Miscellaneous

Among other military medals likely to be met with are the following :—

(a) "*Erinnerungs*" *Medaille*, which marks the "Anschluss" with Austria. The ribbon is dark red with a black and white edging. The reverse of the medal bears the inscription, " Ein Volk, Ein Reich, Ein Führer," with the date " 13 März, 1938."

(b) *Sudeten Medal*, which commemorates the cession to Germany of the Sudetenland. The reverse of the medal bears the inscription, " Ein Volk, Ein Reich, Ein Führer," with the date " 1 Oktober, 1938." The ribbon is black-red-black.

(c) *Memel Medal*, which marks the return to Germany of the Memelland. The reverse of the medal bears the inscription " Medaille zur Erinnerung an die Heimkehr des Memellandes, 22 März, 1939." The ribbon is green-white-red.

All three medals are in bronze ; the face shows two naked warriors bearing the German flag with, as their stepping stone, the German emblem.

APPENDIX XLI

ASSAULT AND WOUND BADGES

1. Infantry Assault Badge (Infanterie-Sturmabzeichen)

This badge may be awarded to officers, N.C.Os., and other ranks of rifle companies in infantry regiments and mountain rifle companies who have—

(i) taken part in three assault operations on three different days,

(ii) been in the foremost line,

(iii) penetrated the enemy line, weapon in hand.

Successful armed reconnaissance as well as counter attacks may count as assault operations provided they led to close fighting.

The badge, in bronze, consists of a rifle with fixed bayonet, surrounded by an oval wreath of oak leaves, surmounted by the German eagle and swastika. It is worn on the left breast pocket of the tunic immediately beneath the Iron Cross or any other decoration worn.

2. The Tank Badge (Panzerkampfwagen-Abzeichen)

This badge may be awarded to officers, N.C.Os. and other ranks of A.F.V. units who have served as tank commanders, gunners, drivers or W/T operators in at least three engagements on three different days.

The badge, in bronze, consists of an oval wreath of oak leaves surrounding a tank, the whole surmounted by the German eagle and swastika. It is worn on the left breast pocket of the tunic immediately beneath the Iron Cross or any other decoration.

The award of this badge, also in bronze, has now been extended to personnel of lorried infantry regiments and motor-cyclist battalions in armoured divisions, and armoured car units.

3. Assault Badge for all other arms of the service

This badge may be awarded to officers, N.C.Os. and other ranks of all other arms of the service which co-operate closely with the infantry or tanks, e.g., close support artillery, or to individual members of other arms who fulfil the conditions upon which the infantry assault badge would be awarded to infantrymen. The badge, in silver, is a stick grenade crossed with a bayonet and surmounted by the swastika and German eagle, the whole surrounded by an oval wreath of oak leaves. Like the infantry and tank badge it is worn on the left breast pocket of the tunic.

4. Wound Badge

This badge is similar to the wound badge worn in the last war and consists of two crossed bayonets beneath a steel helmet, the whole encircled by a round wreath of oak-leaves. The only innovation is the swastika which replaces the former " W " and crown on the helmet. It is in three classes and of three colours—

> Class I, in gold, for those wounded more than four times.
> Class II, in silver, for those wounded three or four times.
> Class III, in black, for those wounded once or twice.

All these are worn on the left breast pocket of the tunic.

CHAPTER XIV

AIR FORCE

1. General organization, distribution and strength

(a) *General outline.*—The German Air Force, like the Army and the Navy, is constituted as a separate arm of the defence services.

The air force includes all ground air defence units with the exception of the motorized A.A. M.G. battalions, which are retained by the Army as G.H.Q. troops. (It is believed, however, that 2-cm. (·79-in.) A.A. M.Gs. have been issued to army units, and there are also a few A.A. guns mounted in coastal forts, which are manned by the Navy. It is also an axiom in the German Army that all units armed with M.Gs. and rifles are responsible for their own defence against low-flying aircraft.)

All air requirements for the army and navy are met by the Air Ministry.

The German Air Force is divided into—
>   Flying branch.
>   Anti-aircraft artillery.
>   Signal corps.
>   Engineer corps.
>   Parachute troops.
>   General Goering Regiment.
>   Observer corps.
>   Air police.

In addition, the German Air Ministry controls every aspect of civil and commercial aviation to a degree which can only be achieved under a dictatorship. It is also responsible for all measures of passive air defence.

The German Air Force is organized on a territorial basis. There are five commands, called air fleets (*Luftflotten*) and one major frontier air defence command known as the "Luftverteidigungskommando West."* Within the air fleet commands, the majority of operational units, with the exception of home defence fighters, army co-operation

---

* It is not certain whether since the capitulation of France it has been considered necessary to maintain this as an independent command

and coastal reconnaissance units, are grouped into air corps (*Fliegerkorps*) and divisions (*Flieger-Divisionen*). These air corps are mobile formations and constitute Germany's striking force. The area within each air fleet is divided into smaller areas called "Luftgaue" (*see* sub-para. (*e*) below).

(*b*) *The air fleets* (*Luftflotten*).—There are five air fleet commands—

> Luftflotte No. 1 and East Command H.Q., Berlin.
> Luftflotte No. 2 and North Command H.Q., Brussels.
> Luftflotte No. 3 and West Command H.Q., St.Cloud.
> Luftflotte No. 4 and South East Command H.Q., Vienna.
> Luftflotte No. 5 and North West Command H.Q., Kristiansand. (This "Luftflotte" embraces units in Denmark and Norway.)

The "Luftflotten" move as required by the High Command. They appear to correspond to the army groups of ground forces, while the "Luftgaue" correspond to "Wehrkreise."

(*c*) *The Air Corps* (*Fliegerkorps*).—The air corps are composite operational formations, consisting of a headquarters and bomber, dive bomber, fighter, coastal and reconnaissance formations. Organization is not rigid, and frequent instances are known in which a bomber "Gruppe" (*see* sub-para. (*f*) below) has been placed temporarily under the command of another corps.

The following air corps have been identified :—

> I, II, IV, V, VIII, IX, X, XI.

(*d*) *The air divisions* (*Flieger-Divisionen*).—In peace-time, air divisions were mobile operational formations consisting of a headquarters and a varying number of bomber, fighter, coastal and reconnaissance "Geschwader" or "Gruppen" (*see* sub-para. (*f*) below). Most of them have expanded and become air corps retaining, however, the same organization.

One air division has been identified as still operating; "Flieger-Division" 7 (air transport).

(*e*) *Territorial areas* (*Luftgaue*).—"Luftgau" commanders are responsible for the administration and maintenance of all units situated within their area, although as a rule only the fighter units come under them for operational purposes.

They have under their command all training and ancillary units and anti-aircraft artillery not allotted to the field army or for other special tasks. They are also responsible for training (other than unit training), recruitment, mobilization and training of the Air Force Reserve.

" Luftgau " commanders are responsible for all forms of active and passive air defence of their areas and for this purpose within " Luftgaue " large cities or vital industrial areas have been formed into air defence commands called " Luftverteidigungskommandos," which have ground air defence units and, according to their importance and vulnerability, fighter units.

The following " Luftgaue " are known to exist :—

"Luftgau" No. or Name.	Headquarters.	"Luftflotte."
I	Königsberg	1
II	Posen	1
III	Berlin	1
IV	Dresden	4
VI	Münster	2
VII	Munich	3
VIII	Breslau	4
XI	Hanover	2
XII	Wiesbaden	3
XIII	Nuremberg	3
XVII	Vienna	4
XVIII	Brünn	4
Norway	Oslo	5
Belgium-Northern France	Brussels	2
Holland	Amsterdam	2
West France	Etampes	3

Extensions of " Luftgaue " during war period :—

" Luftgau " II to include Warsaw, Deblin and Radom areas.
" Luftgau " IV to include the Prague area.
" Luftgau " VII to include Württemberg, Baden and Alsace.
" Luftgau " VIII to include Southern Poland.
" Luftgau " XI to include Denmark.
" Luftgau " XII to include Luxemburg.

Existence of " Luftgaue " Paris and Hamburg is possible, within the framework of " Luftgaue " West France and XI, respectively.

(f) *Formations and flying units—General.*—German operational formations and flying units are grouped as follows :—

Geschwader*	a formation of 2–4 *Gruppen*.
Gruppe*	a unit of 3–5 *Staffeln*.
Staffel*	a unit of 12–18 aircraft.

(i) *Geschwader.*—A " Geschwader " is a mobile formation. It has its own headquarters flight of three aircraft of the same type of aircraft with which its units are equipped. " Geschwader " are homogeneous formations, but may have other units attached to them. Their size may vary as follows :—

Bomber *Geschwader*	2 to 4 *Gruppen*.
Fighter *Geschwader*	2 or 3 *Gruppen*.

A bomber " Geschwader " has, normally, one long-reconnaissance " Staffel " attached to it, but this has been reduced to 5 or 6 aircraft since the outbreak of war.

(ii) *Gruppen.*—A " Gruppe," like a " Geschwader," is mobile, and has its own headquarters flight. " Gruppen " contain a varying number of " Staffeln " (a formation between a British squadron and flight), and, with the exception of reconnaissance or coastal units, are homogeneous.

A " Gruppe " may consist of :—

Bomber *Gruppe*	3 *Staffeln* and one *Stabstaffel* for reconnaissance purposes.
Fighter *Gruppe*	3 *Staffeln*.
Reconnaissance *Gruppe*	3 to 5 long- or short-reconnaissance *Staffeln*.
Coastal *Gruppe*	3 *Staffeln* of different types.

(iii) *Staffeln.*—A " Staffel " is a mobile operational unit. For tactical purposes only it may be divided into two or three " Schwärme " (generally 5 to 6 aircraft) or " Ketten " (generally 3 aircraft) or " Rotten " (generally 2 aircraft).

---

* The German names have no exact English equivalent.

The peace strengths of "Staffeln" (excluding reserve aircraft) are :—

Bombers ..	12 aircraft.
Fighters ..	12–18 aircraft.
Reconnaissance ..	12 aircraft.
Coastal	12 aircraft.

Bomber and fighter "Staffeln" have one or two transport aircraft.

(g) *Types of aircraft in first line units :—*

Long-range bombers	Heinkel 111. Dornier 17. Junker 88.
Short-range (dive) bombers.	Junker 87.
Fighters	Messerschmitt 109 (short-range). Messerschmitt 110 (long-range). } These may also be used as bombers.
Ground attack	Focke Wulf 189.
Reconnaissance	Dornier 17, Junker 88, Messerschmitt 110 (long-distance reconnaissance) Henschel 126 (army co-operation).
Troop transport	Junker 52. Junker 86, FW 200, Junker 90.
Coastal aircraft	Heinkel 114. Heinkel 115. Heinkel 59. Heinkel 60. Dornier 18. Dornier 26. Hamburger 139. Arado 196. Arado 95.
Inter-communication aircraft.	Fieseler-Storch.

(h) *Armament and bombs.*—German aircraft are armed with machine-guns and 2-cm. (·79-in.) cannon guns.

Bombs are :—

    10-Kg. (22 lbs.) anti-personnel.
    50-Kg. (110 lbs.) H.E. general purpose.
    100-Kg. (220 lbs.) H.E. general purpose.
    250-Kg. (550 lbs.) H.E. general purpose.
    500-Kg. (1,100 lbs.) H.E. general purpose.
    1,000-Kg. (2,200 lbs.) H.E. general purpose.
    1,400-Kg. (3,080 lbs.) H.E. general purpose.
    1,800-Kg. (3,960 lbs.) H.E. general purpose.
    ·9-Kg. (1·98 lbs.) Incendiary.
    2-Kg. (4·4 lbs.) Incendiary.
    30-Kg. (66 lbs.) Incendiary.
    10-Kg. (22 lbs.) Gas.
    Oil bombs.
    "Molotov breadbaskets."

Parachute mines may also be used against land targets.

Nothing definite is known of gas spraying apparatus, but it should be assumed to be in existence.

2. Aircraft markings

For national marking on German aircraft, *see* plate 85.

First line type aircraft are camouflaged in dark green on upper and keel surfaces. The underneath surface is painted light blue.

3. The role of the German Air Force in co-operation with the Army

(a) *General.*—The theory that there is such a thing as a separate air strategy is rejected by the German General Staff, as the following quotation shows :—" The Air Force, as an independent arm, is not called upon to conduct an independent war apart from the Army and Navy. Just as in a nation only the united march of all towards one goal leads to success, so only one man's will can conduct a total war The Air Force, Army, and Navy form a single unit within the framework of the conduct of a total war."

Air support for the army may be indirect or direct.

(b) *Indirect support.*—This term, rather difficult to define, may be said to include distant reconnaissance of enemy territories and seas, the bombing of enemy bases, sea and land communications, telegraph and telephone systems, dumps, aerodromes and industrial centres, and war industries. German air policy also aims at breaking the enemy's will to resist by bombing the civil population.

(c) *Direct support.*—This includes close reconnaissance and army co-operation work (*see* para. 4 (*d*) below), bombing and machine-gunning of enemy ground forces and especially their artillery and anti-tank positions, attacks on reserves, headquarters, rear services, road and rail communications ; the occupation of points of tactical importance by parachute and air-landing troops (*see* Chapter XV) ; and the prevention by fighter aircraft and anti-aircraft defences of enemy reconnaissance and army co-operation.

In particular, the employment of aircraft in direct support of swift-moving armoured formations should be noted. Aircraft are also used to supply air force operational units and army mobile formations, such as armoured or motorized divisions, with petrol, ammunition and supplies.

(*d*) *Liaison between army and air force.*—In order to facilitate the closest co-operation between the two services, small air force staffs are attached to army formations on the following scale :—

> One lieutenant-general and staff per group of armies.
>
> One major-general or colonel and staff per army.
>
> These officers are known as " Koluft " (*Kommandeur der Luftwaffe*) officers.

It is possible that small staffs or liaison officers are also attached to lower formations as circumstances demand.

The final decision as to whether bomber and fighter formations or parachutists are to be employed with ground forces in any particular operation rests with the air force commanders.

4. Tactics

(*a*) *Indirect support.*—The German methods are in general similar to those of our own air force.

(*b*) *Direct support.*—The tasks, other than reconnaissance and protective duties, are carried out mainly by medium and dive-bomber aircraft. The latter are used as a form of mobile artillery. Air intelligence liaison units, provided with the necessary signal equipment, accompany the forward elements of attacking troops, and keep the air force constantly informed of the exact position of their own front lines. For list of ground signs used by troops for communication with aircraft, *see* Appendix XLIX.

(c) *Roles of different types of aircraft:* —

(i) *Bombers.*—They may bomb from high altitude or low, when they will fly as close to the ground as possible for purposes of surprise and security. They may also make shallow dive attacks, which are gliding descents upon objectives from a height to carry out a low bombing attack.

(ii) *Dive bombers.*—They attack targets by diving upon them at an angle between 60 to 70 degrees below the horizontal, employing bombs or machine-gun fire.

(iii) *Fighters.*—They are used for home defence, and general defensive tasks; for direct or indirect escort of bombing forces; for attack on enemy fighters, balloon barrages, anti-aircraft defences and aerodromes; for attack against troops and dive-bombing.

(iv) *Ground attack.*—Their role is to attack ground forces using guns and bombs.

(*N.B.*—It is possible that units equipped with this type of aircraft will be permanently allotted for army use.)

(v) *Reconnaissance (including army co-operation).*— They are employed in co-operation with bomber forces, for strategical or close reconnaissance, and to extend the air raid reporting service.

(d) *Army co-operation.*—Air reconnaissance for the army is provided by the air force.

An air force officer of general rank is attached to the commander-in-chief of the army for liaison.

Observation is carried out by the observer, who is an officer. The pilot is generally a non-commissioned officer.

Army co-operation aircraft normally fly singly but if strong opposition is anticipated they may be given an escort of fighters, if it can be spared.

The allotment of units, which are all mobile, is believed to be :—

> One long-reconnaissance *Staffel* (12 aircraft) per army or higher formation;
>
> One short-reconnaissance *Staffel* (12 aircraft) per corps;
>
> One short-reconnaissance *Staffel* (12 aircraft) per armoured division.

Short reconnaissance *Staffeln* are allotted to divisions, other than armoured divisions, only in special circumstances.

CHAPTER XV

PARACHUTE AND AIR-LANDING TROOPS

1. General

The German military leaders decided some years ago that parachutists and air-landing troops should become an integral part of the German armed forces. Parachutists are highly trained specialist troops and are organized in parachute rifle regiments (*Fallschirmjäger-Regimenter*) under the " Inspectorate of Air-landing and Parachute troops " at the Air Ministry.

Air-landing troops, which are now part of the army, are troops of all arms and services who are organized and equipped for transport by air and who have received training in emplaning and deplaning. In an emergency, any troops with suitable arms and equipment can be (and have been in the past), transported by air. Air-landing troops may be carried either in transport aircraft or in gliders.

2. Parachute troops

(a) *General*.—It is believed that there were at least 5,000 trained parachutists in the German forces before the outbreak of war. The extreme youth and inexperience and the inferior character of prisoners taken in the Low Countries, indicated that the original 5,000 had been supplemented by young "roughs," whose fate was a matter of indifference to themselves. Although some of these latter were obviously not sufficiently trained, the training of parachutists is, in fact, continuing steadily, and it is estimated that there may now be as many as 50,000 trained parachutists.

The training received by parachutists is primarily designed to bring out the qualities of independence, and to ensure that they use initiative, particularly when they find themselves cut off from their comrades. The idea is that they are independent fighters who continue being " offensive " under all and any conditions. Their basic training is that of infantry, and each man can use a rifle, automatic pistol, light and heavy machine gun and mortar. A typical training course lasts four weeks, and includes six practice jumps, the first at 800 ft., the last at 250 ; lectures and practice in packing parachutes ; instruction in foreign languages ; map-reading, cross-country running and pack marches. This is followed by strenuous infantry training for some months. Parachutists are probably trained to work in close co-operation with air-landing troops.

(b) *Organization and equipment.*—Parachute regiments consist of three battalions and a staff; each battalion is probably about 500 men strong and contains both heavy and light companies.

Each battalion is equipped with one 7·5-cm. (2·95-in.) mountain gun, one 8·1-cm. (3·16-in.) mortar, 12 heavy machine guns and 54 machine pistols; most men carry rifles.

This organization is not necessarily standard and parachute troops may be organized, armed and equipped according to their task. For example, on one occasion in Central Norway it is reported that each platoon had three groups of 13 to 15 men. The groups were subdivided into sections of five men each. Each section had its own armament and equipment, which was dropped separately in a container.

These containers are cylindrical or hexagonal, made of wood or metal, with coloured markings to denote the section to which they belong. They are released from the tail of the aircraft by a lever after every third parachutist has jumped. They hold all except the personal equipment of the men, and are fitted with wheels, on which they can be hauled by the detachment.

Bicycles and wireless and signalling sets also form part of their equipment, and anti-aircraft gunners who were landed by parachute in Holland declared that their guns (presumably 2-cm. (·79-in.)) were to be dropped to them later.

Appendices XLII and XLIII give what is believed to be the organization of a parachute rifle regiment of three battalions, and the equipment of parachutists, though this last may vary according to task.

Appendix XLIV gives an indication of the amount of damage which a party equipped as in Appendix XLIII might be able to inflict.

(c) *Maintenance.*—The men carry rations consisting of biscuits, sausage, chocolate and cigarettes, as well as " Vitamin C " tablets. In Central Norway the Germans intended to maintain parachute troops with ammunition and supplies by air. Owing to bad weather, however, only one aircraft succeeded in dropping food and warm clothing, and in consequence the parachutists surrendered.

Chapter XV

In Holland considerable quantities of small arms, ammunition, grenades, etc., were dropped, as well as many sorts of supplies in containers. Parachute troops probably have orders to live on the country as soon as their food supplies are exhausted.

3. Air-landing troops

(a) *Organization and armament.*—Units of most arms and services can be armed and equipped for air transport, and can speedily be trained to emplane and deplane. The German High Command moved many ordinary infantry units and some artillery, viz. 5-cm. (2-in.) and 8·1-cm. (3·16-in.) mortars, 7·5-cm. (2·95-in.) infantry guns and possibly some 10·5-cm. (4·14-in.) gun-howitzers by air during the campaigns in Norway and the Low Countries. A special divisional organization (*see* Appendix XLV) has, however, been evolved, and was employed in Holland. The approximate strength and armament of this division are also shown.

The organization, strength and armament could be easily modified to suit the operation intended and the number of aircraft available.

Attention is drawn to the main differences between this air-borne division and the normal German infantry division, which are as follows :—

(i) The strength is only approximately 40 per cent. of the normal infantry division.

(ii) Two instead of three infantry regiments.

(iii) A higher percentage of riflemen and a smaller percentage of supporting weapons.

(iv) No artillery of a greater calibre than the 7·5-cm. (2·95-in.) mountain gun.

(v) Skeleton supply services.

(vi) A higher proportion of officers and non-commissioned officers.

(vii) No transport vehicles.

Normally a number of parachute rifle companies will be placed " under command " of an air-borne division for a specific operation.

(b) *Maintenance.*—Air-borne troops are able to carry with them only a limited amount of ammunition and supplies. Supplies must therefore be augmented from local resources in enemy country. It should be possible to carry a good supply of small arms ammunition, but ammunition for heavier weapons must be strictly limited.

4. Gliders

The Germans are known to have been experimenting with towed gliders in order to increase the effective load of transport aircraft. There is no technical objection to light tanks being transported by this means. Several types of German aircraft are capable of towing gliders, but that probably used is the Ju.52. The only glider on which information is available is one of a span of 55 ft. and probably capable of carrying 15 men. The gliding angle would probably be about 1 in 15, which would give a gliding range in still air of about 28 miles from 10,000 ft. The standard German Ju.52 troop carrying aircraft can tow three such gliders at a speed of 120 m.p.h., its radius of action being about 300 to 350 miles. The limiting factor would be the take-off. Gliders can land where aircraft cannot, and have the added advantage of silent approach. Gliders, however, are difficult to handle when towed in cloud or in conditions of poor visibility. It is probable, therefore, that towing or landing at night would be a difficult operation unless visibility was fairly good.

Gliders were, in fact, used in the attack on Fort Eben Emael in Belgium, though their exact rôle in this operation has not been determined.

5. Uniforms

A description of the uniform worn by parachutists is given in Chapter XIII, para. 10, and there are photographs of parachutists on Plates 82–84.

There is no positive proof that parachute troops or airborne troops have ever landed in disguise or in uniforms other than their own in spite of countless reports to this effect.

6. Landing grounds

It is reported that in Norway, owing to high wind, low cloud and the difficulty of judging height accurately in hilly country, men were dropped from heights of between 100 and 150 feet. In consequence many were killed or badly injured, and morale was such that a number of uninjured parachutists surrendered. In Belgium parachutists were often successfully dropped in scrub and heathland and even in forests, the object being to conceal their landing and reorganization. On the other hand, airborne troops need open, flat ground for successful landings; it was previously estimated that an area 600 yards by 600 yards was sufficient,

Chapter XV 244

but these figures must now be substantially modified as in Holland the Germans landed aircraft on arterial roads and beaches as well as on airports, car parks, etc. In Holland landing places were most frequently indicated by signals from Fifth Columnists, and it is the opinion of at least one German pilot that landings are impossible without such signals. Troop-carrying aircraft will hardly ever attempt a landing until the ground is securely held by parachutists, Fifth Columnists or land forces, unless the positions are known to be undefended. At Rotterdam troops were landed by seaplane on the river.

7. Method of landing

(a) *Parachutists*.—It was previously considered that an essential preliminary of employment was a careful reconnaissance of the area chosen for landing, reports of agents, air photographs, etc., being used to gain knowledge of the area. However, the extensive and successful dropping of parachutists in Holland, Belgium and France may indicate that this is no longer considered so necessary.

As regards protection, fighter aircraft will be used to establish whether the particular area chosen is defended, and to escort the transport aircraft. Their task will be to attack the defence and nullify its efforts. While the troops are landing the area is protected by these aircraft. The troop-carrying aircraft fly in flight formation with 500 yards distance between each flight. The speed of the aircraft during the jumping period is in the neighbourhood of 80 miles an hour. Men spring from heights of 200–800 ft., and the times of the descents have been as brief as $4\frac{1}{2}$ seconds, according to reliable reports, while a normal time was about ten seconds. Sometimes dummy figures (often containing bombs) are dropped by parachute in order to deceive the defenders as to the point of attack. The men jump, following each other as quickly as possible, usually springing from the aircraft in detachments of 12–14 men. The time taken for landing troops depends on how quickly the men jump out. The ideal aimed at is to land a company on a space of 170 yards by 400 yards. It is reckoned, as an average, that after the first man jumps, a company can be assembled complete with its weapons in 12–15 minutes. Presumably for security reasons, the commander of a parachute sub-unit is often the only person who has been given maps or orders regarding the task to be carried out. On landing he rallies his detachment by means of a special signal, not likely to attract general attention, *e.g.*, a bird or animal call, or a motor horn. One of the first objects of parachute troops on arrival is likely to be, to indicate their presence to German aircraft, and also to report when required, if the terrain is suitable for the landing of troop-carrying aircraft.

The following details of the jump have been obtained :—

> On reaching the position for the jump a klaxon is sounded, and the men place the spring hook of the pull-out cord on a wire which runs along the aircraft. They then walk towards the port-side door, sliding the hook along the wire, and fling themselves out. The ideal height for jumping is 300 ft., and 12 men should be able to jump out of one door of an aeroplane in 10 seconds. When about 60 ft. from the ground, the men spread-eagle their limbs to stop any rotation or pendulum movement. They are taught to land with their feet together, make a " ju-jitsu roll fall," either forwards or backwards, returning to their feet by pulling on the parachute cords. If in difficulties in strong wind, they cut themselves adrift with a knife.

(b) *Air landing troops and troops transported in aircraft.*—The methods which have been employed by the Germans in landing troops from aircraft are as follows :—

> In the occupation of Austria the aerodrome was first secured by parachutists while patrols of fighter aircraft flew overhead ; this operation was immediately followed by the landing of 37 transport aircraft carrying the equivalent of a battalion. These troops completed the occupation of the aerodrome and surrounding area. Finally large transport planes arrived with artillery, ammunition and equipment.

This procedure seems to have been modified in Norway, where perhaps less opposition was expected. The occupation of the civil aerodrome at Oslo on 9th April, 1940, was effected as follows :—

> While fighter aircraft circled overhead to crush any possible resistance, up to 5 transport aircraft landed every 30 seconds. Machine guns were pointing through the windows ; within one hour it is reported that no less than 3,000 troops were landed ; 10 aircraft crashed but these and their occupants were cleared to one side with the least possible delay. Air landing operations in Holland seem to have been a repetition of those in Norway. Aircraft were used to carry whatever was required most urgently in each particular case.

8. Objectives of parachute troops

The main objectives of parachutists are as follows :—

(a) The capture of landing grounds for troop-carrying aircraft ;

(b) Contact with agents, Fifth Columnists, etc., in order to arm them or give them instructions ;

(c) The destruction of bridges ;

(d) Cutting and tapping of telephone wires ;

(e) Incendiarism and the destruction of public utility enterprises ;

(f) Firing on troops, supply columns and refugees to create confusion and panic ;

(g) Indication of bombing targets by pre-arranged signal, e.g., ground strips, lamps, clearing areas of long grass or crops in special shapes such as rings or crosses ;

(h) Spreading of false news.

9. Objectives of air-landing troops

Where opposition is to be expected, air-landing troops are unlikely to be landed until landing grounds have been secured by parachute troops. The main objectives of these troops are as follows :—

(a) *To block the approaches of reserves to the main battlefield.*—This will involve landing in the neighbourhood of an obstacle and the seizing and holding of the crossings over it, or the seizing of certain nodal points on road or rail communications if no obstacle is available.

(b) *To attack defences from the rear.*—This would involve a landing probably not more than 3 to 5 miles behind the defences, simultaneously with the main attack from the " front."

(c) *To seize and clear a harbouring area for an armoured formation.*—Armoured formations cannot continue even with the assistance of supporting infantry to fight by day and guard themselves by night indefinitely. Now that rear areas are organized for tank defence and tank hunting, the strain on an armoured division will increase rapidly, and at the end of two, three or more days, it will probably need the shelter of a secure harbour. Such a harbour could be supplied by an air-borne force landed ahead of the armoured formation to clear and hold an area into which the latter could move in safety for maintenance and rest.

(*d*) *As a feint to draw off reserves or to create disorganization.*—This would entail landing at some distance from other ground troops, and probably out of reach of their support. It would be contrary to German tactics to date, but cannot be dismissed for that reason alone.

(*e*) *To seize a nerve centre* (*i.e.*, a seat of government, a communication centre, a broadcasting station, etc.).— In this country nerve centres are largely duplicated, and in most cases defended ; they are therefore unattractive targets and would have the additional drawback of (*d*) above, of being remote from possible reinforcement.

(*f*) To seize and hold an undefended obstacle or area in advance of ground troops.

Air-landing troops would probably be employed in areas where they could shortly be reinforced by ground troops, as problems of maintenance and transport would arise if they were left unsupported for any length of time.

APPENDIX XLII

The organization of a parachute rifle regiment of the German Air Force is believed to be as follows:—

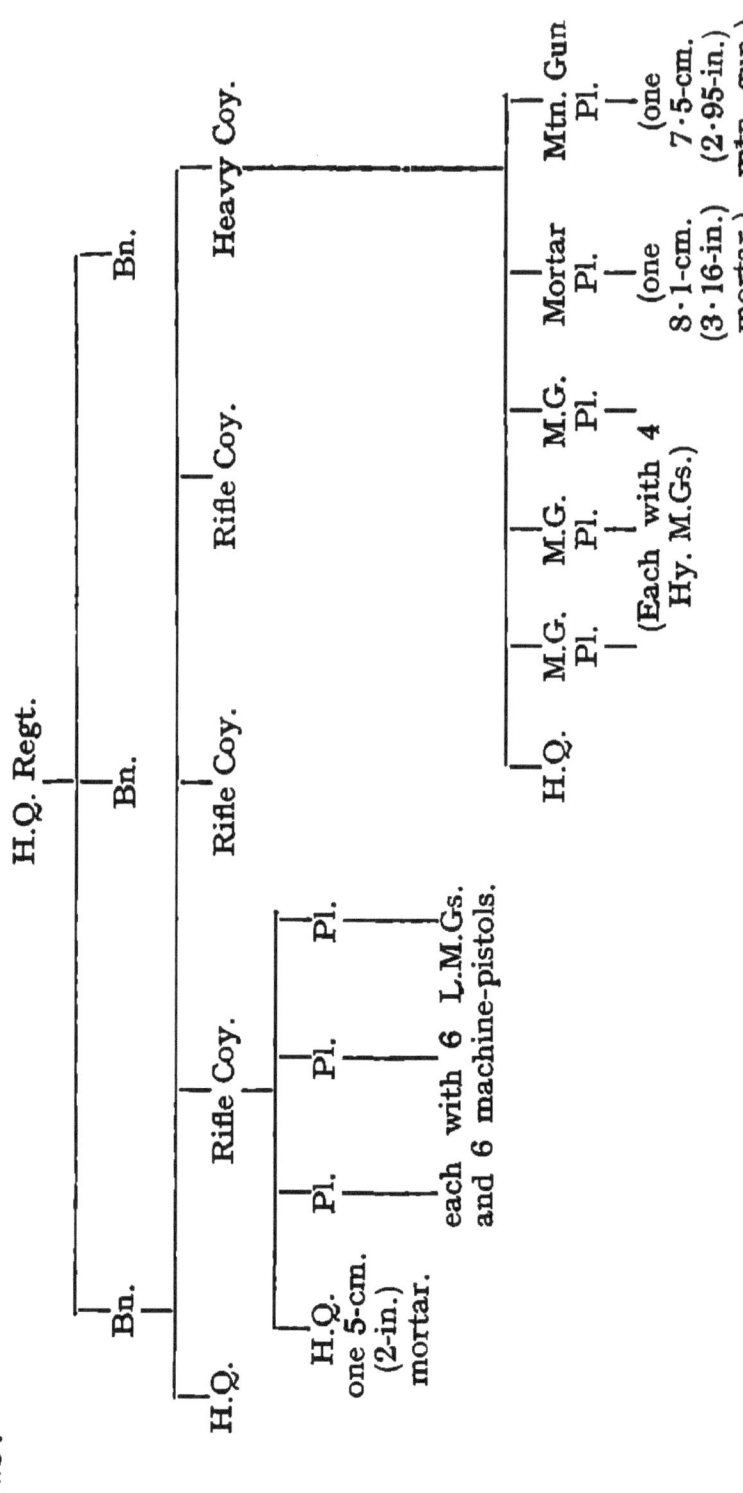

APPENDIX XLIII

EXAMPLE OF EQUIPMENT WHICH MAY BE DROPPED FOR A GROUP OF 13 PARACHUTISTS

	Rifles	Ammunition belts	Field glasses	Field compasses	Pocket lamps	Hand grenades	Smoke grenades	Hand grenade pouches	Packs	M.G. magazine boxes	Detonators	Time fuze	Crowbars	Spades	M.G. Model 34	Tool cases	Barrel cradles and tripods	M.G. slings	Smoke candles	Wire cutters	Boxes of explosives	Made-up charges	Detonating fuzes	Pull igniters	120 metres wire	Machine-pistols	Bangalore torpedoes	Borehole charges	Machine-pistol holsters	
Group leader	1	1	1	1	1	4	2	1	1	1	15	10	1	—	—	—	—	—	—	—	—	—	—	—	—	—	—	—	—	
Rifleman—																														
No. 1	—	—	—	—	—	1	—	—	—	—	—	—	—	1	1	1	1	1	—	—	—	—	—	—	—	—	—	—	—	⎫ Protective duties.
No. 2	—	—	—	—	—	1	—	—	1	3	—	—	—	1	1	—	—	1	1	—	—	—	—	—	—	—	—	—	—	⎬ No. 1 ═
No. 3	1	1	—	—	1	3	—	1	—	2	—	—	—	1	1	—	—	1	1	—	—	—	—	—	—	—	—	—	—	⎭ No. 2 ═ No. 3 ═ Smoke duties.
Equipment Container No. 1	2	2	1	2	2	7	2	2	2	6	15	*10	1	3	1	1	1	2	1	—	—	—	—	—	—	—	—	—	—	
Deputy Group Leader Rifleman—	1	1	1	1	1	6	2	1	1	1	—	—	—	—	—	—	—	—	—	1	—	—	—	—	—	—	—	—	—	Deputy group leader = wire cutting duties.
No. 1	—	—	—	—	—	1	—	—	—	—	—	—	—	1	1	1	1	1	—	—	—	—	—	—	—	—	—	—	—	⎫ Protective duties.
No. 2	—	—	—	—	—	1	—	—	1	3	—	—	—	1	1	—	—	1	1	—	—	—	—	—	—	—	—	—	—	⎬ No. 1 ═
No. 3	—	—	—	—	—	3	—	1	—	2	—	—	—	1	1	—	—	1	1	—	—	—	—	—	—	—	—	—	—	⎭ No. 2 ═ No. 3 ═ Smoke duties.
Equipment Container No. 2	2	2	1	2	2	9	2	2	2	6	—	—	—	3	1	1	1	2	1	—	—	—	—	—	—	—	—	—	—	
Automatic pistolman Rifleman—	—	—	—	—	—	2	—	1	—	—	—	—	—	—	—	—	—	—	—	1	—	1	4	—	—	1	4	4	—	⎫ Demolition duties.
No. 1	1	1	—	—	—	4	2	1	1	—	15	—	—	1	—	—	—	—	—	—	2	1	3	10	—	—	—	—	—	⎬
No. 2	1	1	—	—	—	6	1	1	1	—	—	—	—	1	—	—	—	—	—	—	2	2	3	—	1	—	—	—	—	⎬
No. 3	1	1	—	—	—	6	1	1	1	—	—	—	—	1	—	—	—	—	—	—	1	2	3	—	1	—	—	—	—	⎬
No. 4	1	1	—	—	—	—	—	1	1	—	—	—	—	1	—	—	—	—	—	—	1	2	3	—	—	—	—	—	2	⎭
Equipment Container No. 3	4	4	—	—	—	18	2	4	4	—	15	—	—	4	—	—	—	—	—	1	4	6	*16	10	2	1	4	44	2	

* It is not known whether these figures denote "metres" or "prepared lengths" of fuze.

Chapter XV

APPENDIX XLIV

It is estimated that the demolition stores in the table in Appendix XLIII could be utilised by such a party to infl damage approximately as follows :—

(a) Blow gaps in barbed wire entanglements up to a total length of about 15 yards.

(b) Set 10 booby traps and/or trip wires to a total length of 250 yards with warning explosive charges attached.

(c) Cut railway lines, light girder sections, suspension bridge cables, etc., at not more than six points.

(d) Make not more than four small craters.

(e) Fell up to six trees, telegraph poles, etc., using a necklet of borehole charges.

N.B.—Many variations of the above programme are, of course, possible, but a definite limit is set by the number of detonators and the probable weight of explosive carried. It is considered that little damage could be inflicted on stone, reinforced concrete, or brick tunnels and bridges. Damage to girder bridges, etc., would probably amount to weakening rather than complete destruction.

APPENDIX XLV

Organization of an infantry division for air-landing operations

Divisional H.Q.
  One M.C.D.R. sec.
H.Q. Mot. A.A. M.G. Bn.
  Four mot. A.A. M.G. coys.
H.Q. Div. Sigs.
  One W/T coy.
  One tel. sec.
H.Q. Div. Recce. Unit.
  Two cyclist sqns.
  One cavalry gun troop.
  One hy. M.G. troop.
  One pioneer troop.
H.Q. Div. A.Tk. Bn.
  Two A.Tk. coys.
H.Q. Div. Engineer Bn.
  One engineer coy.
H.Q. Inf. Regt.
  One sig. sec.
  One M.C.D.R. sec.
  Three bns. each of three rifle coys., and one M.G. coy.
  One infantry gun coy.
  One A.Tk. coy.
  One lt. inf. column (without vehicles).
Inf. regt. organized as above.
H.Q. Div. Arty. Regt.
  One sig. sec.
  Three btys. (two btys. of three tps., one of two).
One coy. and one pl. Div. Medical Unit.
Three pls. Div. Supply Coy. (without vehicles).

Strength (approximate) :—

          270 officers.
      7,130 other ranks.

Total   7,400 all ranks.

Armament (approximate)—

  5,000 carbines.
    400 machine-pistols.
    110 A.Tk. rifles.
     60 5-cm. (2-in.) light mortars.
     36 8·1-cm. (3·16-in.) heavy mortars.
      8 7·5-cm. (2·95-in.) infantry guns.
      2 7·5-cm. (2·95-in.) cavalry guns.
     30 2-cm. (·79-in.) A.A. and A.Tk. M.Gs.
   200 L.M.Gs.
     60 Hy.M.Gs.
     30 3·7-cm. (1·45-in.) A.Tk. guns.
     32 7·5-cm. (2·95-in. mountain guns.

CHAPTER XVI

TACTICS

1. General

German tactical teaching insists on the importance of speed and surprise in battle ; on the need for concentration of all available means, moral, physical and material, at the decisive place and time, and finally on the ruthless exploitation of success. With a view to obtaining speed and surprise, the Germans make the most careful preparations beforehand.

Good leadership depends in the first place upon boldness and decision. The German teaches that if two equally reasonable alternatives exist, the bolder course must be adopted.

The following slogans are, therefore, impressed on all leaders :—

> Strive to maintain the initiative.
>
> Keep your main objects always in mind.
>
> Simplicity of plan ensures speed in execution.
>
> Put as much power in the " main effort " and as little power in the subsidiary effort as possible.
>
> Your constant aim must be to preserve and renew the fighting power of your troops.
>
> Be quick to recognize a favourable situation or turn of events and do everything to utilize it to your own advantage.
>
> Pay due regard to the tactical doctrine and methods of your opponents.

The Germans firmly believe that their army, by virtue of its size and excellence, is invincible. They consider that their soldiers are superior in training, equipment and morale, to those of any other nation. Considerable attention is paid to instilling into the individual soldier the offensive spirit in all circumstances. Nevertheless, the Great War, 1914–18, and recent fighting, have demonstrated that man for man, the British soldier is superior.

2. The attack

(a) *General.*—In the conduct of the attack, certain principles are observed whether operations are carried out by armoured and motorized formations or by infantry divisions :—

(i) The plan is simple but flexible. Orders give subordinate commanders considerable latitude. Below divisions, they are normally issued verbally and in the shortest and simplest form.

(ii) A point is selected at which the " main effort " is to be made. Superiority in numbers and weapons is provided at this point.

(iii) Where possible, centres of resistance and defended obstacles are first neutralised by infiltration methods ; once surrounded they can be reduced systematically.

(iv) Formations and units do not stop when they have lost touch with flanking troops.

(v) Mobile reserves are held available to reinforce success.

(vi) Should success be achieved in an unexpected quarter, troops and fire are concentrated to take advantage of the new situation.

(b) *Forms of attack.*—Although envelopment should be aimed at *wherever possible*, it is realised that the attacker will often be faced with the task of having to break through a well prepared position, strengthened by every possible means and organized in depth. Only after he has defeated the defending troops and has reached the open country can he achieve victory by mobile operations. A successful break-through is the necessary preliminary for the strategical development of the situation.

The Germans envisage the following types of attack, all of which should, whenever possible, be accompanied by threats of attack or by feints in other quarters.

(i) *Frontal attack* is considered the most frequent form of attack, though the introduction of armoured and motorized forces is thought likely to make it less common. Requires great superiority in strength and produces decisive results only when hostile front has been penetrated.

(ii) *Envelopment* is considered the most effective form of attack and, if successful, may result in annihilation of enemy. Presumes marked superiority in means. Most effective when launched in a wide movement against flanks. The enemy must not be given time to take counter measures.

(iii) *Penetration* should be attempted at a selected weak spot in the enemy front and over suitable ground. Surprise is essential. Penetration must be on a wide front and permit manœuvre. Troops carrying it out must be organized in depth in order to deal with enemy reserves and to check hostile counter-attacks. Once achieved, it must be followed by continuous pressure until disintegration and panic have been ensured, and the penetration is converted into a break-through.

(c) *General conduct of the attack.*—Successful attack is based on the following principles :—

(i) Co-ordination and control prevent disintegration into separate actions.

(ii) "Main effort" requires narrow battle sectors, co-ordination and concentration of fire of all weapons.

(iii) Choice of locality for "main effort" dictated by ground, facilities for artillery, and suitability for use of armoured forces and reserves. If the sector for decisive action cannot be determined beforehand, the resources for the "main effort" must, notwithstanding, be built up, in readiness for employment as and when the situation demands.

(iv) A crisis will develop in every battle. Victory will go to the commander who can turn this crisis to his own favour.

(v) If it is intended to persevere in an attack that has come to a standstill, it can only be done by—
>Regrouping of forces.
>Throwing in of fresh forces.
>Reorganization of fire.

(vi) Important to launch an attack on the correct frontage, which depends on the probable strength of the enemy's resistance. German regulations give the following approximate frontages :—
>Battalion (encadre)—400–1,000 yards.
>Infantry division in favourable circumstances as regards ground, artillery support, etc.—4,000–5,000 yards.
>Infantry division, as above, carrying out the main attack against enemy in strong position—3,000 yards.

Throughout an attack, ground troops will be given direct support by air forces. This includes reconnaissance, the bombing of communications, reserves, etc., and close support against forward troops. The German dive-bombing aircraft have, in fact, become a form of highly mobile close support artillery. Close support will almost invariably be available at short notice in the sector of the " main effort." By continuous raids and the use of loudspeakers before the attack, and by the noise of whistling bombs, loud explosions and the lavish employment of grenades during it, the German hopes to destroy the morale of his opponents, particularly of those in the forward defences.

3. The defence

(a) *Organization of position.*—The defensive position is organized in great depth so as to attain the maximum power of resistance ; the beaten zone in front of the defences is carefully planned, continuous and deep, and all weapons are allotted tasks in the defensive fire plan. The bulk of the fire is employed to defend that part of the front which the commander decides must be held at all costs. (*Schwerpunkt.*)

German teaching divides a defensive position into three main zones :—

    (i) Advanced position.

    (ii) Battle outposts.

    (iii) The main line of resistance (organized in depth).

(b) *Advanced position.*—Troops in the advanced position are intended to delay the enemy in his attempt to gain possession of localities which would assist him to launch an attack against the main line of resistance.

Although these troops are provided with their own artillery, A.Tk. guns and machine-guns, it is laid down that at least a portion of the artillery covering the main position should be sited so as to support them by its fire.

Consequently the advanced position must usually be some 5,000–7,000 yards in front of the main line of resistance.

The advanced troops are usually placed under the commander of the zone immediately in rear. The advanced position is sometimes held by motorized machine-gun battalions.

(c) *Battle outposts.*—The task of battle outposts is to gain time for the troops responsible for the defence of the main line of resistance and to deceive the enemy as to its exact location.

Battle outposts are usually some 2,000 yards in front of the main line of resistance, *i.e.*, within effective support of the artillery of the main defensive position.

These outposts may be ordered to remain in position until a certain time or to retire when the enemy reaches a particular line or appears to be developing a major attack.

(d) *The main line of resistance.*—The defence of the main position necessitates the distribution of the available troops in depth; distribution in depth should not, however, be so great that the majority of the infantry weapons cannot bring down fire in front of the main position. As regards frontages, an encadre division is normally allotted 6,000–7,000 yards. Defence is based on mutually supporting centres of resistance organized in depth and capable of all-round defence. Obstacles are constructed to supplement the natural defensive characteristics of the ground, and full use is made of concealment and camouflage.

Priority of defensive preparations is governed by the rule " Effectiveness before cover." Thus clearing of fields of fire, taking of ranges and camouflage take precedence over digging of cover and provision of dug-outs.

Unless a unit receives definite orders to withdraw, defence must be to the last man and to the last round.

4. Protection at rest

In general the method of organization and employment of outposts and patrols does not differ from that adopted in the British army.

Outposts protect their positions with wire and show their ingenuity by installing trip-wires and booby traps covering the approaches; land mines are also used. The Germans maintain the offensive spirit by continuous patrolling activity. Small patrols consisting of three to seven men attempt to penetrate deep into enemy lines with the object of locating dispositions and possible avenues for infiltration. On occasions patrols have succeeded in tapping telephone wires far inside the enemy lines and have thus obtained valuable information.

In the conduct of raids the Germans skilfully vary their methods. Before attempting a raid they study in great detail the dispositions and habits of enemy posts, the most favourable approaches and how to make the best use of supporting weapons.

5. Protection on the move

German formations are protected on the move by a screen of mechanized or semi-mechanized reconnaissance units (*see* para. 6), according to whether they are armoured, motorized infantry or infantry divisions.

These units work in close co-operation with reconnaissance aircraft. The mechanized reconnaissance units have a wide radius of action (155 miles) and are used for strategical as well as tactical ground reconnaissance. The semi-mechanized units, having considerably lower mobility and radius of action, are only employed for the tactical ground reconnaissance on the divisional front.

For protective duties on the move the Germans also make considerable use of motorized machine-gun battalions and motorized anti-aircraft machine-gun battalions. The former are equipped with A.Tk. guns while the A.A. battalions are armed with dual purpose A.A. and A.Tk. machine-guns.

6. Mechanized reconnaissance units

These units include armoured cars and motor-cyclist riflemen, together with heavy companies (also mechanized and armed with close-support weapons, light guns, mortars, machine-guns and A.Tk. guns) and mechanized engineer detachments.

Their tasks are as follows :—

(*a*) To push rapidly ahead of slower moving formations to discover the strength and dispositions of enemy forces.

(*b*) While avoiding combat with large forces or strongly defended localities, to overrun small centres of resistance which would impede the advance of the main forces.

(*c*) To prevent the carrying out of demolitions and to disrupt communications, *e.g.*, telephone exchanges, wireless stations, etc.

(*d*) By rapid movement and indiscriminate firing to give the impression of the presence of large forces, with the object of creating panic and confusion.

(e) To seize and hold covering positions or bridgeheads; to protect demolitions prepared by engineer troops; to hold an exposed flank.

(f) To establish contact with air-borne troops already landed.

The mobility of these units and their large radius of action enable them to reconnoitre rapidly, and they can, if necessary, fight for information. Fighting is primarily the duty of the motor-cyclist squadrons (these include motor-cycle combinations, carrying three men and a machine-gun) supported by the guns and mortars of the heavy companies; their object is to clear the way for the armoured cars. All vehicles have a considerable cross-country performance, and they can deploy rapidly off roads when road blocks or other opposition are encountered. They usually operate in small patrols consisting of armoured cars, motor-cyclists and possibly a few light tanks.

Mechanized reconnaissance units possess limited offensive power; but their mobility and cross-country performance enable them by infiltration methods to penetrate into enemy territory. On such occasions no attempt is made to keep touch with flanking reconnaissance units.

7. A.F.Vs.

The main principles for the employment of A.F.Vs. are :—

(a) Surprise.
(b) Selection of suitable ground.
(c) Employment in large numbers and in depth.
(d) Speed.

Where possible, armoured units avoid attacking fortified positions and instead, endeavour to turn the flank of opposition. Where, however, an organized or semi-organized opposition cannot be avoided, the ground and strength of enemy defences are the deciding factors as to whether tanks will attack ahead of, or simultaneously with infantry, or whether they will be launched after the infantry have attacked.

In the case of strongly organized defences, it is considered necessary to "loosen up" the enemy defensive system, especially the A.Tk. organization, befoe tanks can operate successfully. A.F.Vs. will therefore not be launched against suspected or known minefields or formidable A.Tk. obstacles and defences until artillery fire, dive-bombing attacks and specially trained and equipped infantry and engineer assault detachments (*Stosstrupps*) have prepared the way by clearing minefields and obstacles, and reducing defensive works. In certain circumstances, tanks may provide covering fire to the assault detachments during the preliminary operations before advancing through the gaps made.

In river crossings, bridgeheads are secured by infantry and engineers before tanks cross by pontoon rafts or rubber boats.

On the other hand, where defences are relatively weak or hastily organized (as was the case in Poland and in the later stages of the Battle of France), tanks attack well ahead of infantry relying on such air and artillery support as is immediately available.

A tank attack against organized or semi-organized opposition normally takes the following form:—

(*a*) Attack in two or three waves on a relatively narrow frontage and in grèat depth.

(*b*) The leading wave deals with the enemy anti-tank guns and artillery; this wave is allotted the furthest objectives, *i.e.*, enemy artillery reserves and enemy headquarters.

(*c*) The subsequent wave (or waves) attacks enemy infantry and strong points, and may precede or accompany the leading infantry.

(*d*) Close support by the other arms is provided during the attack. The task of the artillery is to neutralise or destroy enemy artillery and anti-tank resources, or to engage counter-attacking enemy tanks; that of the infantry and engineers is to follow up closely and consolidate.

Armoured formations were the decisive factor in German successes in Poland, in Flanders and in France. Once having "broken through the crust," they aimed at deep penetration into the enemy's country regardless of flanks and communication, relying mainly on air co-operation chiefly in the form of dive-bombing and reconnaissance to help them on. By spreading out across the enemy's communications they attempted to disrupt his whole rearward organization. Centres of resistance were not allowed to hold up the advance, but were either avoided and later attacked from the rear, or were dealt with by motorized troops following up close behind. Close co-operation between armoured units and the reconnaissance, artillery, anti-tank and engineer units, and also the lorried infantry and motor-cyclists was an important feature at all stages of the advance.

8. Infantry

In view of the predominant rôle played by German armoured forces since the outbreak of the present war, German infantry both motorized and non-motorized (with the exception of the specially trained and equipped assault detachments) has been chiefly employed in following up, exploiting and consolidating the ground gained by armoured formations.

Infantry tactics in the attack are chiefly remarkable for :—

(a) Boldness and skill in infiltration ; small detachments penetrate between enemy posts which they engage from the flanks and rear. They often attempt to create the impression of large numbers by a liberal expenditure of ammunition (*e.g.*, from machine-pistols).*

(b) Reliance on prompt and efficient fire support of considerable volume from their heavier weapons which are handled with great skill and dash, and are brought into action well forward. Units are lavishly supported by infantry guns as well as A.Tk. guns, mortars and machine-guns, and the co-operation between these weapons and infantry is excellent. Where necessary, support is given by dive-bomber aircraft.

The infantry of the active divisions and of the majority of reserve divisions reaches a high standard of physical fitness. Their training aims at developing initiative and the offensive spirit.

Assault detachments (*Stosstrupps*) are small bodies of troops composed of infantry and engineers which are employed for special tasks, such as reducing pill-boxes and over-running centres of resistance, etc. They are picked men, trained for specific operations and equipped with automatic weapons, flame-throwers, Bangalore torpedoes, pole charges and small smoke generators, according to the requirements of each task. Further details are given in Chapter III, para. 12 (a), and Chapter VIII, para. 16.

9. Artillery

All types of German divisions are weaker in artillery than their British equivalents. On the other hand, German infantry are stronger in close support weapons, which include 7·5-cm. (2·95-in.) and 15-cm. (5·91-in.) infantry guns. In consequence, German artillery is rarely placed " under command " of infantry units, though batteries may be detailed " in support." The Germans consider the

---

Note.—Nine automatic weapons may mean the presence of only one platoon.

enemy artillery the most important objective and attach the greatest importance to keeping down enemy artillery fire whilst maintaining their own.

The importance of getting their artillery into action before the enemy can do so is constantly impressed upon the German gunners, who are taught to shoot first and correct afterwards. Ranging methods are varied as much as possible in order to achieve surprise fire for effect. Much use is made of " roving " guns and also of guns firing from alternate positions.

The efficiency of artillery observation and communications and also of artillery observation aircraft are important factors in the success of German artillery support.

Artillery support in the attack varies somewhat from the British. Barrage fire is avoided whenever possible and support is given by means of concentrations. By rapidity of deployment and the sudden opening of intense fire on selected points, the Germans aim at reducing the defender to a state when he will be unable to use his weapons.

Once the enemy's position is over-run, F.O.Os. and guns are pushed forward with great determination. At this stage close co-operation between artillery and infantry is assured by artillery liaison detachments. Light signals are freely used as a means of communication between leading troops and artillery observers.

A.A. artillery is employed well forward in the attack, guns following close behind the leading troops. A.A. guns are frequently used against land targets, *e.g.*, pill-boxes and A.F.Vs.

In defence, German artillery is trained to make the fullest use of the range of its weapons, and a proportion of the artillery is sited well forward. The enemy is subjected to an ever increasing artillery bombardment as he closes with the defenders. German manuals state that the artillery must have done a great part of its work before the enemy's attack is finally brought to a standstill in front of the main line of resistance.

10: Engineers

German engineers are highly trained and efficient fighting troops, lavishly equipped with engineering stores of all kinds

In the attack they are employed in removing obstacles such as wire, A.Tk. mines, etc., and in bridging water obstacles.

For this latter purpose assault boats and large and small pneumatic boats are used in large numbers and on a wide front and, although heavy casualties may be sustained, a portion are expected to gain a footing on the opposite bank.

Supporting troops and light equipment, including anti-tank guns, are ferried across in large rubber boats and on rafts made up from rubber boats.

Light and heavy pontoon bridges are constructed and heavy loads (exceeding 18 tons) are ferried across on special heavy rafts.

In addition, engineers are trained in the use of explosive charges, flame-throwers and smoke generators, and are employed as assault troops with infantry, co-operating in the reduction of pill boxes and centres of resistance.

In defensive operations, engineers are employed in constructing pill boxes and obstacles, laying minefields, and preparing and carrying out demolitions and setting booby traps. They may also act in close support of infantry and may be used to defend the obstacles and demolitions they have established.

11. Smoke

The Germans have not yet made extensive use of smoke, but their manuals draw attention to its great possibilities.

Although the German teaching does not differ greatly from our own, it appears that they have developed the use of smoke rather further in certain respects. For example, German smoke equipment includes, in addition to the normal smoke projectiles and smoke candles, smoke sprays and generators designed to function up to 30–40 minutes and to reproduce the conditions of fog. The laying of smoke screens from the air is also advocated.

Smoke is much used in attacks by assault detachments on strongly defended positions.

The landing of troops in a combined operation is likely to be covered by smoke screens if the weather conditions are favourable. Limited use of smoke may be made to cover the crossing and bridging of water obstacles and to conceal the direction of a main attack or the advance of tanks.

12. Gas

The Germans are known to have studied fully the use of gas and are also believed to have made every preparation to use gas if it should suit their purpose.

Available information indicates that the methods most likely to be adopted by the Germans are :—

(a) Low altitude spray with mustard (possibly mixed with lewisite).

(b) Air-bursting bombs charged with mustard.

(c) Percussion bombs charged with a mixture of H.E. and arsenical toxic smoke.

(d) Percussion bombs charged with phosgene.

Gas emitted from special craft may be used in conjunction with smoke in combined operations.

13. Irregular methods of warfare

The Germans do not admit that there are any " rules " in warfare, and any form of trickery or cunning which would assist them in attaining their object must be expected.

The following are some of the methods believed to have been employed by the Germans :—

(a) A small party allows itself to be captured; then produces concealed weapons, kills its captors and holds an important point until reinforcements arrive.

(b) A telephone call to a demolition party in perfect English saying that the bridge should not be blown until a party of British troops have crossed. The party arrives in British uniforms, is allowed to pass and then turns on the demolition party and annihilates it.

(c) Tanks flying British or Allied flags arrive at a bridge. The defenders lead the tanks through a minefield covering the position. Once through, the tanks turn and attack the position from the rear.

(d) Spreading false rumours among the civilian population concerning the approach of German troops, thereby blocking the roads in rear of the enemy with refugees.

(e) Bombing and machine-gunning columns of refugees to cause blocking of roads in rear of the enemy.

(f) Concealing A.Tk. guns in farm carts driven by civilians or troops in civilian clothes.

(g) Employment of agents to guide troops and aircraft; to increase panic among civilians; to interfere with defensive measures; for sabotage; to spread defeatism among enemy troops, and even to fire on them.

APPENDIX XLVI

LIST OF ABBREVIATIONS

Abbreviation.	Signification.	Translation.
A.A.2 (mot.)	Aufklärungs-Abteilung 2 (Mot.).	2nd Mechanized Reconnaissance Unit.
A.B.	Armee-Befehl	Army order.
a.B.	auf Befehl	By command of, by order, signed for ......
Abl.	Ablage ..	Dump; depot.
Abt.	Abteilung	Unit, artillery bty., etc.
a.D.	ausser Dienst	Retired.
Adj.	{ Adjutant / Adjutantur	Adjutant. / " A " branch of the staff.
A.H.A.	Allgemeines Heeresamt	General Army Branch (in the War Ministry).
A.H.Q.	Armee-Hauptquartier ..	Army H.Q.
A.K.	{ Artillerie-Kommandeur / Artilleriekolonne	C.R.A. / Gun column.
A.K. III	Armeekorps III	III Corps.
ält.	ältester	Senior.
A.M.Tr.	Artilleriemesstrupp	Artillery survey troop.
A.N.R.	Armee-Nachrichten-Regiment.	Army signals regiment.
-anw.	-anwärter	Candidate.
A.O.K. 6	Armee-Oberkommando 6	6th Army H.Q.
A.R. 12	Artillerie-Regiment 12..	12th Artillery Regiment.
II/A.R. 43	II Abteilung Artillerie-Regiment 43.	2nd Battery of the 43rd Artillery Regiment.
4/A.R. 5	4 Batterie Artillerie-Regiment 5.	4th Troop of the 5th Artillery Regiment.
Art.	Artillerie	Artillery.
Art.Kdr.	Artillerie-Kommandeur	Artillery commander.
Art.Sch.	Artillerieschule ..	Artillery school.
Aufkl.	Aufklärung	Reconnaissance.
Ausb.	Ausbildung	Training.
Ausr.	Ausrüstung	Arms and equipment.
A.W.	Aussenwache	Outlying piquet.
B.	{ Bach .. / Beobachtung	Brook. / Observation.
Bäck.	Bäckerei	Bakery.
Battr.	Batterie	Troop.
B.Btl.	Baubataillon ..	Construction battalion.
B. d.E.	Befehlshaber des Ersatzheeres.	Director General of Training.
Bekl.	Bekleidung	Clothing.
B(eob).Abt.3	Beobachtungs-Abteilung 3	3rd Artillery Survey Unit.

Abbreviation.	Signification.	Translation.
Beob.Lehr. Abt.	Beobachtungs-Lehr-Abteilung.	Artillery survey training unit.
ber.	beritten	Mounted.
Bez.	Bezirk	District.
Bf.	Bahnhof	Railway station.
Blst.	Blockstation	Signal box.
Br.	Brücke	Bridge.
	Brunnen	Well.
Bruko.	Brückenkolonne	Bridging column.
B.St.	Beobachtungsstelle	O.P.
Btl., Btln...	Bataillon	Battalion.
Btl.G.St.	Bataillonsgefechtsstand	Battalion battle H.Q.
Bttr.	Batterie	Troop.
ch.	characterisiert	Brevet.
D.A.A.	Divisions-Aufklärungs-Abteilung.	Divisional recce. unit.
d. B.	des Beurlaubtenstandes	Retired.
1 Div.	1. Division	1st Division.
D.L.	Doppellafette	Twin mounting.
Drh.L.	Drehlafette	Revolving mounting.
E.B.	Ersatz-Bataillon	Training battalion.
Eisb.	Eisenbahn	Railway.
E.M.	Entfernungsmesser	Rangefinder.
Ers.	Ersatz	"Ersatz," training.
F.	Fähre	Ferry.
	Fahr	H.T.
Fbr.	Fabrik	Factory.
Fda.	Feldartillerie	Field artillery.
Fl.	Fluss	River.
Fla.	Flugabwehr	A.A.
Flak.	Flugabwehrkanone	A.A. gun.
Flw.	Flammenwerfer	Flame thrower.
Fnd.	Feind	Enemy.
Ft.	Furt	Ford.
Fw.	Feldwebel	Sergeant.
	Flammenwerfer	Flame thrower.
G.	Geheim	Secret.
Geb. Jäg. R. 99.	Gebirgsjäger-Regiment 99.	99th Mountain Rifle Regiment.
Geb.Pi. 54	Gebirgs-Pionier-Bataillon 54.	54th Mountain Engineer Battalion.
Gefr.	Gefreiter	Lance-corporal.
Gef.St.	Gefechtsstand	Battle headquarters.
-geh.	-gehilfe	Assistant.
Gel.	Gelbkreuz	Yellow cross (i.e., vesicant) gas.
Gen.	General	General.
Gen.Kdo. III A.K.	Generalkommando III Armeekorps.	III Corps H.Q.
Genst. d. H.	Generalstab des Heeres	Army general staff.
Gestapo	Geheime Staatspolizei	Secret State Police.
Gew.	Gewehr	Rifle.
gez.	gezeichnet	"Signed."

Abbreviation.	Signification.	Translation.
gl.	*geländegängig*	Cross-country (as applied to vehicles).
Gr...	{ *Granate* { *Gruppe*	Shell. Section (esp. of Inf.); Force; Army-Group.
Grz.Kdo.	*Grenzkommando*	Frontier Division.
H...	*Heeres-* ..	Army, G.H.Q.
Hbf.	*Hauptbahnhof*	Main station.
H.Dv.	*Heeres-Dienstvorschrift*	Army Manual.
Höh. Kav. Offz.	*Höherer Kavallerieoffizier.*	Senior Cavalry Officer at Army H.Q.
Höh. Nachr. Offz.	*Höherer Nachrichtenoffizier.*	Chief Signals Officer at Army H.Q.
Höh. Offz. Art. Beob. Tr.	*Höherer Offizier der Artillerie-Beobachtungstruppen.*	Senior Artillery Survey Officer at Army H.Q.
Höh. Pi. Offz.	*Höherer Pionieroffizier.*	Chief Engineer at Army H.Q.
Höh. Pz. Abw. Offz.	*Höherer Panzerabwehroffizier.*	Senior Anti-tank Officer at Army H.Q.
Horn.	*Hornist* ..	Bugler.
Hp.	*Haltepunkt*	Stopping place.
Hptm.	*Hauptmann*	Captain (except in cavalry and horse artillery.
Hs.	*Haus*	House.
H.V.Bl.	*Heeres-Verordnungsblatt*	Army orders.
i.A.	*im Auftrage*	Signed " for."
I.A.W.	*Inspekteur des Ausbildungswesens.*	Inspector of Training.
I.D.	*Infanterie-Division*	Infantry division.
I.G.	*Infanteriegeschütz* ..	Infantry gun.
13./(I.G.)/ I.R.11.	*13. (Infanteriegeschütz) Kompanie Infanterie--Regiment 11.*	13th (Infantry Gun) Company of the 11th Infantry Regiment.
Inf. Kdr. 4.	*Infanteriekommandeur 4.*	Infantry Commander of the 4th Division.
Inf. Sch. ..	*Infanterieschule*	Infantry school.
Insp.	{ *Inspekteur* { *Inspektion*	Inspector. Inspectorate.
Intdt.	*Intendant*	Official on " Q " Branch of the Staff.
Intdtr.	*Intendantur*	" Q " Branch of the Staff.
I.R.6.	*Infanterie-Regiment 6.*	6th Infantry Regiment.
II./I.R.24.	*II. Bataillon Infanterie-Regiment 24.*	2nd Battalion of the 24th Infantry Regiment.
6./I.R.20.	*6. Kompanie Infanterie-Regiment 20.*	6th Company of the 20th Infantry Regiment.
i.V.	*in Vertretung*	Signed " for."
Jäg. Jg.	} *Jäger*	Rifleman or rifle (unit).
K...	*Kirche*	Church.
Kan.	{ *Kanal* .. { *Kanonier*	Canal. Gunner.

Abbreviation.	Signification.	Translation.
Kap.	*Kapelle*	Chapel.
Kas.	*Kaserne*	Barracks.
Kav.	*Kavallerie*	Cavalry.
Kav. R.11.	*Kavallerie-Regiment 11.*	11th Cavalry Regiment.
5./Kav.R.10.	*5. Schwadron Kavallerie-Regiment 10.*	5th Squadron of the 10th Cavalry Regiment.
Kav. Sch.	*Kavallerieschule*	Cavalry school.
K.D.	*Kavallerie-Division*	Cavalry Division.
Kdo.	*Kommando*	Headquarters.
Kdr.	*Kommandeur*	Commander.
Kdt.	*Kommandiert*	Detached, detailed.
	Kommandant	Commandant.
Kdtr.	*Kommandantur*	Commandant's office.
Kf.	*Kraftfahr-*	M.T.
Kf. Lehrst.	*Kraftfahrlehrstab*	M.T. training staff.
Kfw.	*Kampfwagen*	Tank.
Kfz.	*Kraftfahrzeug*	M.T. vehicle.
K.G.	*Kavalleriegeschütz*	Cavalry gun.
Kkw.	*Krankenkraftwagen*	Motor ambulance.
kl.	*klein*	Small.
Kol.	*Kolonne*	Column.
Kp.	*Kompanie*	Company.
Kr.	*Krug*	Public house, inn.
	Kranken-	Sick (etc).
Krad.	*Kraftrad*	Motor-cycle.
Krad. mit Beiwg. Krad.mitB.	*Kraftrad mit Beiwagen*	Motor cycle combination.
Kradf.	*Kraftradfahrer*	Motor-cyclist.
Kradsch. Btl. 3.	*Kradschützen-Bataillon 3.*	3rd Motor Cyclist Battalion.
2./Kradsch. Btl. 3.	*2. Kompanie Kradschützen-Bataillon 3.*	2nd Company of the 3rd Motor Cyclist Battalion.
Kraftf.	*Kraftfahrer*	Lorry or car driver.
Krkw.	*Krankenkraftwagen*	Motor ambulance.
Krw.G.	*Kraftwagengeschütz*	Tractor-drawn gun.
Kst.	*Küste*	Coast.
Kw.	*Kraftwagen*	Lorry.
Kw.Ah.	*Kraftwagenanhänger*	Trailer for lorry.
Kw.Flak	*Kraftwagenflak*	Mechanized A.A. artillery tractor-drawn A.A. gun.
Kw.K.	*Kraftwagenkanone*	Tractor-drawn gun.
kz.	*kurz*	Short.
L.	*Luft-*	Air.
l.	*leicht*	Light.
Laf.	*Lafette*	Gun-carriage.
l. Art.	*leichte Artillerie*	Light artillery.

Abbreviation.	Signification.	Translation.
Ldst.	Landsturm	"Landsturm."
Lehrg.	Lehrgang	Course of instruction.
l. F.H.	leichte Feldhaubitze	Light field howitzer.
lg.	lang	Long.
l. Gr.W.	leichter Granatwerfer	Light mortar.
l. J.	laufenden Jahres	Of the current year.
Lkw.	Lastkraftwagen	Lorry.
L.L.T.	Luftlandungstruppen	Air landing troops.
L.M.Tr.	Lichtmesstrupp	Flash spotting troop.
Lst.	Ladestelle	Loading platform.
Lt., Ltn.	Leutnant	Second Lieutenant.
lt.	laut	In accordance with.
Lw.	Landwehr	"Landwehr" (i.e., men aged 35–45).
M.	Mühle	Mill.
m.	mittler	Medium.
Mag.	Magazin	Magazine, store, depot.
Maj.	Major	Major.
M.E.Z.	mitteleuropäische Zeit	Central European time.
M.G.	Maschinengewehr	Machine-gun.
M.G.Btl. 6 (mot.).	Maschinengewehr-Bataillon 6 (mot.).	6th Machine-gun Battalion (mot.).
4/(M.G.)I.R. 10.	4 (Maschinengewehr) Kompanie Infanterie-Regiment 10.	4th (Machine-gun) Company of the 10th Infantry Regiment.
Mil.	Militär	Military.
Min.	Ministerium	Ministry.
M.K.	Munitionskolonne	Ammunition column.
Mk.	Marschkolonne	March column.
Mldg.	Meldung	Message.
mot.	motorisiert	Motorized, mechanized.
M.P.	Maschinenpistole	Machine-pistol.
M.P.L.	Mittelpivotlafette	Central pivot mounting.
M.S.W.	Militärsanitätswesen	Army medical service.
Mun.	Munition	Ammunition.
Mun. Anst.	Munitionsanstalt	Ammunition depot.
m.V.	mit Verzögerung	With delayed action.
N.Abt.	Nachrichten-Abteilung	Signals unit.
N.Abt. 1	Nachrichten-Abteilung 1	1st Signals.
2/N.Abt.2	2 Kompanie Nachrichten-Abteilung 2.	2nd Company of the 2nd Signals.
Nachh.	Nachhut	Rearguard.
Nachr.	Nachrichten	Signals or Intelligence.
Nachr.Abt. 1	Nachrichten-Abteilung 1	1st Signals.
Nachr.Z. I/I.R. 8.	Nachrichtenzug I-Bataillon Infanterie-Regiment 8.	Signal Section of the 1st Battalion of the 8th Infantry Regiment.
Nachsch.	Nachschub	Reinforcement, supply.
Nebelw.-Abt. 1.	Nebelwerfer-Abteilung 1	1st Smoke Unit.
3/Nebel-werfer-Abt. 4.	3 Kompanie Nebelwerfer-Abteilung 4.	3rd Company of the 4th Smoke Unit.
N.G.	Nahkampfgeschütz	Close-support gun.

Abbreviation.	Signification.	Translation.
N.O.	Nachrichtenoffizier	Signal officer.
N.S.D.A.P.	Nationalsozialistische Deutsche Arbeiterpartei	German National Socialist Labour Party.
N.S.F.K.	Nationalsozialistisches Fliegerkorps	National Socialist Flying Corps.
N.S.K.K.	Nationalsozialistisches Kraftfahrerkorps.	National Socialist Motor Corps.
N.S.K.O.V.	Nationalsozialistische Kriegsopferversorgung.	National Socialist War Victims Welfare Association.
N.S.R.K.	Nationalsozialistisches Reiterkorps.	National Socialist Mounted Corps.
N.Z., N.Zg.	Nachrichtenzug	Signals Section.
O.A.	Offiziersanwärter	Candidate for commissioned rank.
Ob.d.H.	Oberbefehlshaber des Heeres.	Commander-in-Chief of the Army.
Ob.d.L.	Oberbefehlshaber der Luftwaffe.	Commander-in-Chief of the Air Force.
Ob.d.M.	Oberbefehlshaber der Marine.	Commander-in-Chief of the Navy.
Oblt(n)	Oberleutnant	Lieutenant.
Obst.	Oberst	Colonel.
Obstlt(n)	Oberstleutnant	Lieutenant-colonel.
Offz.	Offizier	Officer.
O.K.H.	Oberkommando des Heeres.	High Command of the Army.
Ordz.	Ordonnanz	Orderly.
o.V.	ohne Verzögerung	Instantaneous, without delay.
O.V.L.	Oberste Verkehrsleitung	Road Traffic Control Sec. at G.H.Q.
PA.	Heerespersonalamt	Army Personnel Branch (War Ministry).
P.A.A.	Panzerabwehr-Abteilung	Anti-tank unit.
Pak.	Panzerabwehrkanone	Anti-tank gun.
14./(Pz. Jg.) I.R.17.	14. (Panzerjäger) Kompanie Infanterie-Regiment 17.	14th (Anti-tank) Company of the 17th Infantry Regiment.
Patr.	Patrone	Cartridge.
Pers.	Personal	Personnel.
Pi. or Pion.	Pioniere	Engineers.
Pi.4.	Pionier-Bataillon 4	4th Engineer Battalion.
2./Pi.30	2. Kompanie Pionier-Bataillon 30.	2nd Company of the 30th Engineer Battalion.
Pi. Lehr- und Vers. Btl. 2.	Pionier Lehr- und Versuchs-Bataillon 2.	2nd Engineer Training and Experimental Battalion.
Pi.Sch. II.	Pionierschule II.	2nd Engineer School.
Pi.Üb.Pl.	Pionierübungsplatz	Engineer training area or ground.
P.K.	Propaganda-Kompanie	Propaganda company.
Pkw.	Personenkraftwagen	Motor car.
P.S.	Pferdestärke	Horse power.

Chapter XVI

Abbreviation.	Signification.	Translation.
Pz.Abw. Abt. 4.	Panzerabwehr-Abteilung 4.	4th Anti-tank Battalion.
2./Pz. Abw. Abt. 7.	2. Kompanie Panzerabwehr-Abteilung 7.	2nd Company of the 7th Anti-tank Battalion.
Pz. B.	Panzerbüchse	Anti-tank rifle.
Pz.B.Tr.	Panzerbüchsentrupp	Anti-tank rifle section.
II. Pz. Brig.	II. Panzer-Brigade	2nd Tank Brigade.
2. Pz. D.	2. Panzerdivision	2nd Armoured Division.
Pz. Jg. Abt.	Panzerjäger-Abteilung*	Anti-tank battalion.
Pz. Kpf.Wg.	Panzerkampfwagen	Tank.
Pz. Kw.	Panzerkraftwagen	Armoured fighting vehicle.
Pz. Rgt. 1.	Panzer-Regiment 1	1st Tank Regiment.
II./Pz.Rgt.4.	II. Abteilung Panzer-Regiment 4.	2nd Battalion of the 4th Tank Regiment.
1./Pz.Rgt.5.	1. Kompanie Panzer-Regiment 5.	1st Company of the 5th Tank Regiment.
Pz.Sp.Wg.	Panzerspähwagen	Armoured car.
Qu.	{ Quartier / Quelle	Quarters. / Spring.
R.	{ Regiment / Ruine	Regiment. / Ruin.
I(r) A.Abt.	I (reitende) Artillerie-Abteilung.	1st Horse Artillery Battery.
R.A.D.	Reichsarbeitsdienst	National Labour Service Corps.
Radf.	Radfahrer	Cyclist.
Rem.	Remonte	Remount.
Res.	Reserve	Reserve.
R.G.St.	Regimentsgefechtsstand	Regimental battle H.Q.
Rgt.	Regiment	Regiment.
Rittm.	Rittmeister	Captain (cavalry and horse artillery).
R.K.M.	Reichskriegsministerium	War Ministry.
R.K.O.	Regiments-Kommando-Ordnung.	Regimental order.
R.L.B.	Reichsluftschutzbund	National Air Defence League.
R.O.A.	Reserveoffiziersanwärter	Candidate for a commission in the Reserve.
R.R.2	Reiter-Regiment 2.	2nd (horsed) Cavalry Regiment.
R.St.	Regimentsstab	Regimental staff.
S.	{ See / Sanitäts-	Lake. / Medical.
s.	schwer	Heavy (medium in the case of artillery weapons).
S.A.	Sturmabteilung	Storm detachment (National Socialist Party).

* Interchangeable with *Panzerabwehr-Abteilung*.

Abbreviation.	Signification.	Translation.
San.	*Sanitäts*	Medical.
S.B.	*Soldbuch*	Pay-book.
Sch.	*Schütze* ..	Rifleman, Private.
Schiesspl. ...	*Schiessplatz*	Range.
III.Sch. Brig.	*III. Schützen-Brigade*	3rd Lorried Infantry Brigade.
Sch. Rgt. 2.	*Schützen-Regiment 2.*	2nd Lorried Infantry Regiment.
I./Sch. Rgt. 2.	*I. Bataillon Schützen-Regiment 2.*	1st Battalion of the 2nd Lorried Infantry Regiment.
s.F.H.	*schwere Feldhaubitze* ..	Heavy field howitzer.
s.I.G.	*schweres Infanteriegeschütz.*	Heavy infantry gun.
S.K.	*Schnellfeuerkanone*	Q.F. Gun.
S.Kp.	*Sanitätskompanie*	Medical company.
S.Kol.	*Sanitätskolonne*	Medical column.
S.M.Tr.	*Schallmesstrupp*	Sound ranging section.
Sp...	*Spitze* ..	Point (of advanced guard).
Spielm. ..	*Spielmann*	Bandsman.
S.S. or ⚡⚡ ..	*Schutz-Staffeln* ..	Nazi party troops.
St.III/A.R.7	*Stab III Abteilung Artillerie-Regiment 7.*	Headquarters, 3rd Battery of the 7th Artillery Regiment.
stãnd.	*ständig* ..	Permanent.
St.B.	*Steinbruch*	Quarry.
Stell. ..	*Stellung*	Position.
St./I.R. 12	*Stab Infanterie-Regiment 12.*	Headquarters, 12th Infantry Regiment.
St.K.	*Strassenkommandantur*	Area road traffic control H.Q.
St.O. ..	*Standort*	Location, garrison.
Sto. (Art., Mag., Nach.,etc.)	*Stabsoffizier (der Artillerie, Maschinengewehrtruppen, für Nachrichtenverbindungen, etc.).*	Staff officer (for artillery, M.G. troops, communications, etc.).
St. Pi. 12 ..	*Stab Pionier-Bataillon 12*	Headquarters, 12th Engineer Battalion.
St. R.R. 1	*Stab Reiter-Regiment 1*	Headquarters, 1st (horsed) Cavalry Regiment.
stv.	*stellvertretend*	Deputy.
S.W. ..	*Scheinwerfer*	Searchlight.
T. ..	{ *Teich* .. { *Turm* ..	Pond. Tower.
Tamb. ..	*Tambour* ..	Drummer.
Teno T.N.	} *Technische* .. } *Nothilfe*	} Technical Emergency } Corps.
Tr.	*Trupp* ..	Squad, party, section.
Tromp.	*Trompeter* ..	Trumpeter.
Tr.Üb.Pl. ..	*Truppenübungsplatz*	Training area.

Abbreviation.	Signification.	Translation.
T.V.	*Totenkopfverband*	Concentration camp guard unit.
T.V.P	*Truppenverbandplatz*	R.A.P.
V. Abt.	*Vermessungs-Abteilung*	Survey (mapping) section.
V.A.	*Heeres-Verwaltungsamt*	Army Administration Branch (War Ministry).
Vb.G.	*Verbindungsgraben*	Communication trench.
verst. Rgt.	*verstärktes Regiment*	Infantry regiment with attached troops of other arms.
Vert.	*Verteidigung*	Defence.
Verw.	*Verwaltung*	Administration.
viersp.	*vierspännig*	Four-horsed.
Vorh.	*Vorhut*	Advanced guard.
V.T.	*Verfügungstruppe*	Permanently embodied S.S. troops.
WaA.	*Heereswaffenamt*	Army Ordnance Branch.
Wffm.	*Waffenmeister*	Armourer.
Wkr.	*Wehrkreis*	Administrative area.
W.L.	*Wiederstandslinie*	Line of resistance.
Zahlm.	*Zahlmeister*	Paymaster.
z.b.V.	*zur besonderen Verwendung.*	For special employment.
Z., Zg.	*Zug*	Platoon or equivalent unit.
Zgf.	*Zugführer*	Platoon commander.
z. V.	*zur Verfügung*	Retired.
Zweisp.	*zweispännig*	Two-horsed.

APPENDIX XLVII

GERMAN COINAGE, WEIGHTS AND MEASURES

Note.—The metric system is employed in Germany.

1. Coinage

The basic unit is the mark.

At par 20·43 marks = 1 pound sterling.
100 pfennigs = 1 mark = 1s. at par.

At present the exchange is approximately 12·25 marks to the pound sterling. This is, however, a purely nominal rate.

2. Weights

(a) *Solid*

1 gramme	= ·035 oz.	1 oz.	=	28·34 grammes.
1 kg.	= 2·204 lb.	1 lb.	=	453·58 grammes.
1 metric		1 cwt.	=	50·802 kgs.
ton	= ·984 ton.	1 ton	=	1,016·04 kgs.

(b) *Liquid*

1 litre	= 1·76 pts. or	1 gal.	=	4·54 litres.
	·22 gals.	1 pint	=	·567 litres.

3. Measures

(a) *Lineal*

·1 cm.	= ·0393 in.	·303 in.	=	·77 cm.
·792 cm.	= ·311 in.	·38 in.	=	·96 cm.
1 cm.	= ·393 in.	·5 in.	=	1·27 cm.
1·32 cm.	= ·518 in.	1 in.	=	2·54 cm.
2 cm.	= ·79 in.	1·57 in.	=	4 cm.
3·7 cm.	= 1·45 in.	3 in.	=	7·62 cm.
4·7 cm.	= 1·85 in.	3·3 in.	=	8·38 cm.
7·5 cm.	= 2·95 in.	3·45 in.	=	8·76 cm.
7·7 cm.	= 3·03 in.	3·7 in.	=	9·39 cm.
8·1 cm.	= 3·16 in.	4·5 in.	=	11·43 cm.
8·8 cm.	= 3·46 in.	5 in.	=	12·7 cm.
10·5 cm.	= 4·14 in.	5·16 in.	=	13·1 cm.
15 cm.	= 5·91 in.	6 in.	=	15·24 cm.
17 cm.	= 6·69 in.	7·85 in.	=	19·93 cm.
21 cm.	= 8·26 in.	8 in.	=	20·32 cm.
28 cm.	= 11·02 in.	9·2 in.	=	23·37 cm.
30·5 cm.	= 11·99 in.	1 ft.	=	30·48 cm.
35 cm.	= 13·75 in.	1 yd.	=	·914 metres.
38 cm.	= 14·93 in.	1 mile	=	1·609 km.
42 cm.	= 16·50 in.			
1 metre	= 1·09 yds.			
1 km.	= 1,093·6 yds.			

(b) *Area*

1 hectare	= 2·47 acres.	1 sq. mile	= 2·58 sq. km. or
1 sq. km.	= ·386 sq. mile or 100 hectares.		258 hectares.

4. Convenient approximate conversions

(a) *Centimetres to Inches.*—Multiply by 4 and divide product by 10.

(b) *Metres to Yards.*—Add 10 per cent. to the number of metres.

(c) *Kilometres to Miles.*—Divide the number of kilometres by 8 and multiply the result by 5.

(d) *Litres to Pints.*—Add 75 per cent. to the number of litres.

(e) *Kilogrammes to Pounds.*—Double and add 1/10 of the figure arrived at.

(f) *Kilogrammes to Cwts.*—Divide by 50.

APPENDIX XLVIII

CONVENTIONAL SIGNS FOR MILITARY FORMATIONS, UNITS, ETC.

1. Formation Headquarters and units attached

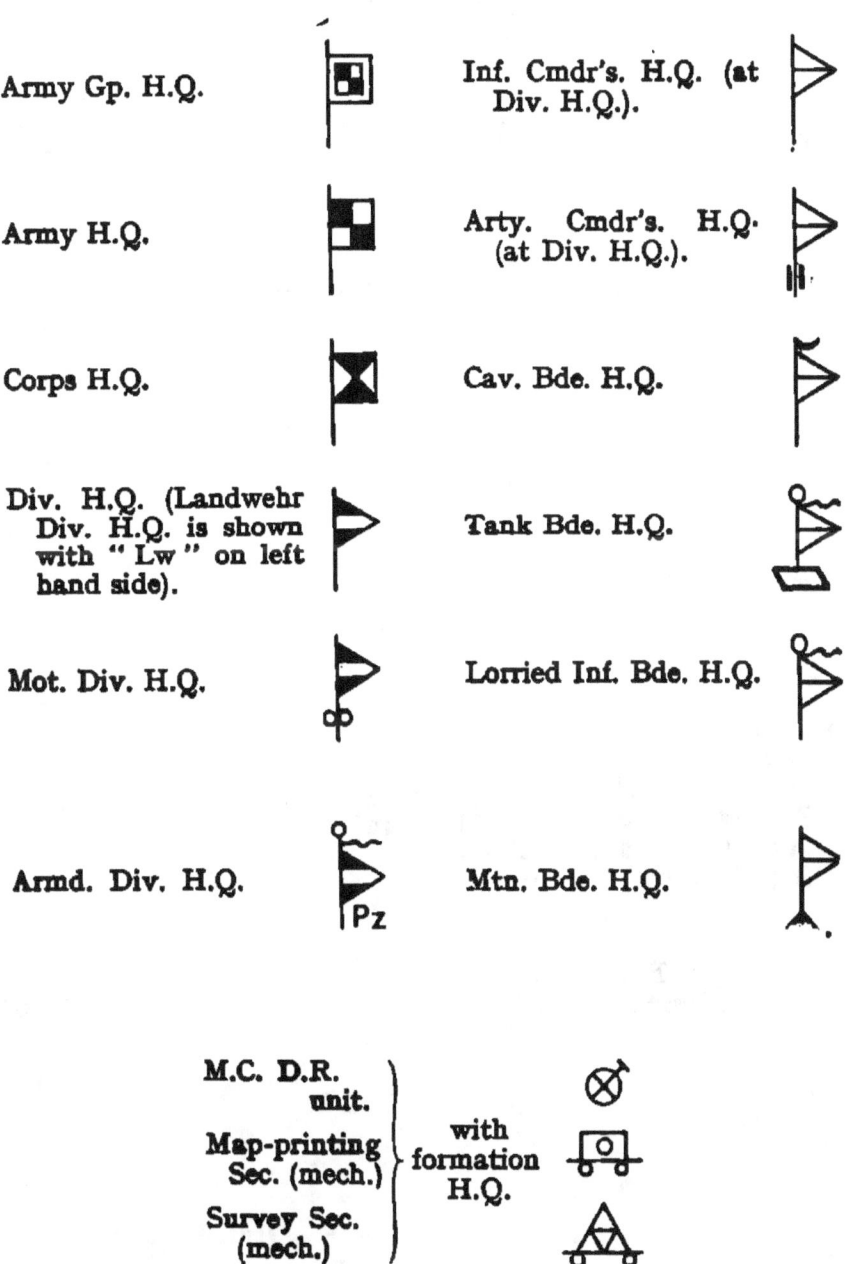

2. Infantry

Regt. H.Q.	🚩	Mtn. Rifle Coy.	▲
Mtn. Rifle Regt. H.Q.		Cyclist Coy.	⊗
Bn. H.Q.		M.C. Coy.	
Mtn. Rifle Bn. H.Q.		M.G. Coy.	
Mot. M.G. Bn. H.Q.		M.G. Coy. of a Mtn. Rifle Bn.	
Cyclist Bn. H.Q.		M.C. M.G. Coy.	
Inf. Bn. (showing composition and number of L.M.Gs. and Hy.M.Gs. and Signal Section).	12 12 12 12	Inf. Gun Coy.	
Inf. Bn. (1st Bn. of 21st Regt.).	I/21	A.Tk. Coy.	
Coy. H.Q.		M.I. Pl.	
Rifle Coy.		Sig. Sec. (Inf. Regt. or Bn.).	

2. Infantry—*continued*.

Sig. Sec. (Mtn. Rifle Regt. or Bn.).		Med. mortar.	
Lt. Inf. Coln. (H.D.).		A.Tk. gun.	
Lt. Inf. Coln. (mech.).		A.Tk. gun in position.	
L.M.G.		Company Commander.	
L.M.G. in position.		Individual rifleman.	
Hy. M.G.		Patrol.	
Hy. M.G. in position.		Piquet.	F.W
Inf. gun.		O.P.	B.
Lt. mortar.		Rifle sec. in position.	
Hy. mortar.		Extended riflemen.	
A. Tk. rifle			
		Inf. on the march (showing unit numbers).	1/1 13/1

Chapter XVI   278

3. Cavalry

Horsed or mech. Cav. Regt. H.Q.		Eng. Troop (mech.)	
Horsed or mech. Cav. Regt.		Sig. Troop.	
Inf. Div. Recce. Unit H.Q.		Lt. Cav. Coln.	
Inf. Div. Recce. Unit.		Individual cavalryman.	
Sqn. H.Q.		Cavalry patrol.	
Sabre Sqn.		Cav. piquet.	
M.G. Sqn.		Cyclist patrol.	
Cyclist Sqn.		Movement of cav.))))))))→	
Cav. gun Tp.		Cav. on the march.	

4. Artillery

Fd. or Med. Regt. H.Q. (horsed).		Mtn. Troop.	
Fd. or Med. Regt. H.Q. (mech.).		Fd. How. Troop.	
Fd. or Med. Bty. H.Q. (horsed).		Fd. How. Troop in position.	
Fd. Bty. (1st Bty. of 1st Regt.).		Horse Arty. Troop.	
Fd. or Med. Bty. H.Q. (mech.).		Med. Gun Troop.	
Horse Bty. H.Q.		Med. How. Troop.	
Horse Bty. in position.		Lt. Arty. Coln.	
Survey Unit H.Q. (mech.).		Lt. Arty. Coln. (mech.).	
Mtn. Bty. H.Q.		Map-printing Sec. (mech.).	
Fd. Gun Troop.		Arty. Survey Troop.	

Chapter XVI 280

4. Artillery—*continued.*

Met. Sec. (mech.).

Mtn. Bty. Sig. Sec.

Regt. or Bty. Sig. Sec.

O.P.

Arty. on the march.

5. Armoured Fighting Troops

Tank Regt. H.Q.

Tank Bn. H.Q.

Recce. Unit H.Q. (mech.).

Tank Bn.

Recce. Unit (mech.).

Lorried Inf. Bn. H.Q.

A.Tk. Bn. H.Q.

M.C. Bn. H.Q.

A.Tk. Bn.

Sqn. or Coy. H.Q. (armoured fighting troops).

5. Armoured Fighting Troops—*continued.*

M.C. Sqn.   Armd. C. Sqn.

Rifle Coy.   Tank Sqn.

M.G. Coy.   Sig. Sec.

Hy. Coy.    Tank Troop.

A. Tk. Coy.   Mech. Coln. on the move.

6. Engineers

Eng. Bn. H.Q. (part mech. Bn.).    Mtn. Eng. Bn. H.Q.

Eng. Bn. H.Q. (mech. Bn.).    Eng. Bn.

Chapter XVI

6. Engineers—continued.

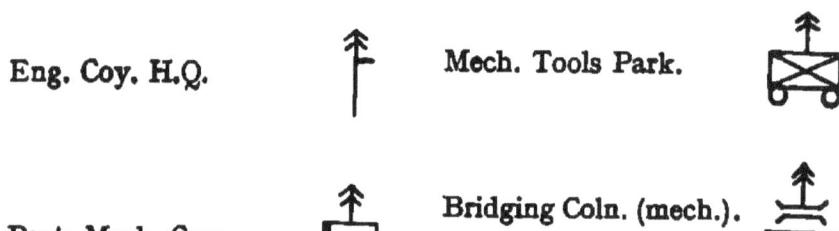

7. Signals

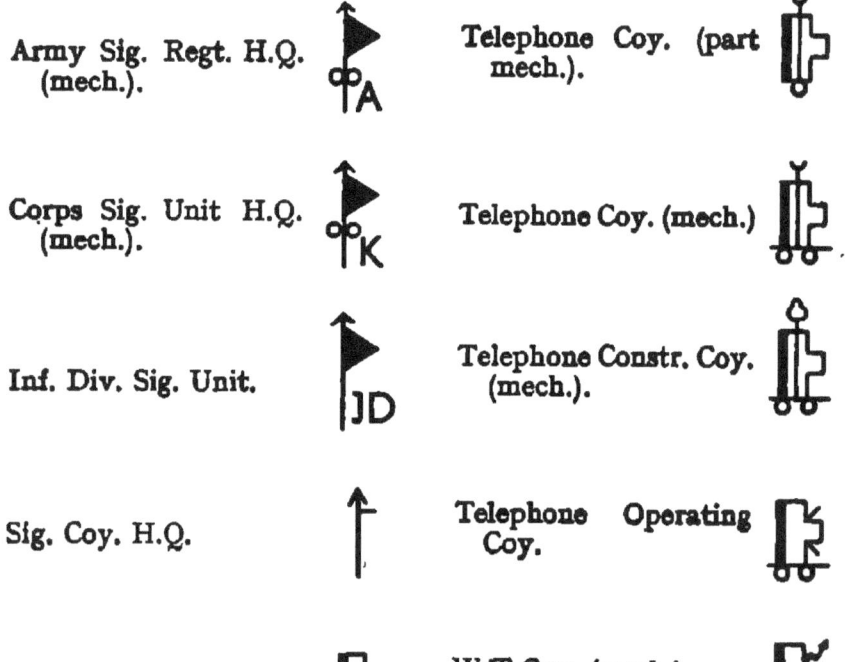

7. Signals—*continued*.

Lt. Sig. Coln. (mech.).		Carrier pigeon Sub-sec.	
Hy. Telephone Sub-sec.		Signal Office.	●
Lt. Telephone Sub-sec.		Telephone Exchange.	○
Telephone Operating Sub-sec.		Lamp Signal Station.	⚭
Hy. W/T Sub-sec. (mech.).		Lamp terminals.	⚭-⚭
Lt. W/T Sub-sec. (mech.).		Communication by messenger dog.	∿∿
Low-power Field W/T Sub-sec. (mech.).		Telephone earth return.	○—○
Pack W/T Sub-sec.		Telephone metallic cct.	○╫○
Lamp Sig. Sub-sec.	⚭	W/T terminals.	
Messenger dog Sub-sec.		Report Centre.	M.S.St.

Chapter XVI   284

8. Transport

  (a) *M.T. and H.T. Units*

M.T. Coy.   H.T. Coy.

M.T. Coy. H.A.

  (b) *Tpt. of Fighting Tps.*

1st line Tpt.
- Supply Tpt. (H.D.).   Vpfl.
- Supply Tpt. (mech.).   Vpfl.
- Baggage Tpt. (H.D.).   Gep.
- Baggage Tpt. (mech.). Gep.
- Battle Tpt.   Gef Stff.

9. Supply Service

H.Q. of a supply unit.   H.Q. of an H.D. Sup. Coln.   Kol

H.Q. of a supply unit with a mtn. div.   Bg   Sup. Coy.

9. Supply Service—*continued.*

Sup. Coy. for Mtn. Tps	⬒	Army Amn. Depôt (at base).	[H.Ma]
Lt. M.T. Coln.	🛒	Amn. Depôt (in forward area).	[Mun.]
Lt. M.T. Coln. for petrol and oil.	🛒🛒	Ordnance Depôt.	[H.Za]
Hy. M.T. Coln. for petrol and oil.	🛒🛒🛒	Salvage Dump (equipment).	[S St. Gerät]
Hy. M.T. Coln.	═	Salvage Dump (amn.).	[S.St. Mun.]
H.T. Coln.	═	Inf. Pk.	[J]
H.T. Coln. for Cav. units.	⊥	Arty. Pk.	[A]
H.T. Coln. for Mtn. units.	▲	Eng. Pk.	[Pi]
Wkshp. Coy. (mobile)	Kw. ⊡	Sig. Pk.	[N]
Petrol filling station.	🛒	M.T. Pk.	[Kf]

10. Administrative Service

Army Supply Depôt.	A.Vpfl.A	Fd. Butchery (semi-permanent).	
Div. Supply Depôt.	Vpfl.A	Sup. Depôt.	
Fd. Bakery (open).		Supply Refilling Point.	
Fd. Butchery (open).		Cattle Park.	Vieh
Fd. Bakery (semi-permanent).			

11. Medical Service

Army Med. Unit H.Q.		Medical Coy. (mech.).	
Base Hospital.		Half medical Coy. (mech.).	
Field Hospital.		Hospital Train (empty).	
Hospital ship.		Train for walking wounded (full).	
Hospital in home country.		Amb. Sec. (mech.).	

Chapter XVI

11. Medical Service—*continued*.

Medical Pk.	⊞		Regt. Aid Post.	●̇
Branch Medical Pk.	⊞ Zweig		A.D.S.	⊡̇
In billets or barracks. { M.I. Room.	⊙̇	In the field. { Car Post.	⊕̇
Reception Station.	⌒̇		M.D.S.	△̇
Hospital.	⊡̇		W.W.C.P.	○

12. Veterinary Service

Vet. Hosp.	(ʂ)	Sick lines for horses.	⊙̇
Horse Pk.	⊡	Vet. Aid Post.	⊡̇
Vet. Stores Pk.	⊡	Collecting Point for sick and wounded horses.	○̇
Horse Amb. Sec. (mech.).	Pf.Kr. 🛒	Remount Depôt.	⊡ Heim

13. Provost Service

Military Police Unit.	⊘	Town Major's Office.	O Kdtr

Chapter XVI 288

13. Provost Service—*continued*.

L. of C. Guard Coy.   Prisoners' collecting point.

Information office.

14. Postal Service

Fd. P.O.   Fd. P.O. (mech.).

15. Railway

M.C.O.   Petrol Train (empty).

R.T.O.   Personnel Train (stationary).

Embarkation officer.   Personnel Train (on the move).

Entraining Sta. (Spandau).   Empty train (stationary).

Detraining Sta. (Bremen).   Empty train (on the move).

Amn. Train.    7. Inf. Div. moving by rail to Ulm (24 trains per day).

Sup. Train.   Area containing 72 loaded trains.

Chapter XVI

15. Railway—*continued*.

Forwarding office. [Wl.St.] Drinking or watering place. [glass symbol]

16. Obstacles

Wire fence. ×××××× Felled trees.

Wire entanglement. ××××× Buildings razed to the ground.

Wire-netting obstacle. ·×·×·× Flooded area (coloured blue).

Tripwire. –o–o–o– Dam.

Tree blocks.

17. Boundaries

Army. ——— Bn. (or equivalent unit). –··–··–

Corps. ⊢·⊢·⊢ Coy. (or equivalent unit). – – –

Div. ⊢⊢⊢

Objective. ·····⋘

Regt. –··–··– • Limit of Recce. –+–+–

Chapter XVI

18. Air Force

(a) *Parachute Units*

Parachute Bn   Parachute Rifle Coy.

(b) *Anti-aircraft Units*

= A.A. Regt. H.Q.

= Light A.A. Battery H.Q.

= Heavy A.A. Battery H.Q.

= A.A. Searchlight Battery H.Q.

= A.A. battery of twelve 2-cm. (·79-in.) guns.

= A.A. battery of nine 3·7-cm. (1·45-in.) guns.

= A.A. battery of four 8·8-cm. (3·46-in.) guns.

= A.A. searchlight section of four (60-cm.) searchlights.

= A.A. searchlight battery of nine (150-cm.) searchlights.

= A.A. column (22 metric tons).

= A.A. column (48 metric tons).

= A.A. battery signals.

= Reserve A.A. batteries.

Chapter XVI

APPENDIX XLIX

Ground signs used by troops for communication with aircraft

Sign	Meaning
✚	Position for dropping messages.
Y	Do not understand.
V	Understood (can also mean " Yes ").
⊐	Enemy preparing attack.
A	Enemy is attacking.
I I I	Enemy has penetrated our position.
⌐ ⁻	Enemy has penetrated on our left.
⁻ ⌐	Enemy has penetrated on our right.
V̱	Front line.
▽ ▽	No.
⊓ ⊔	We are surrounded.
⊔	Reinforcement necessary.
⊢─o	Centre of enemy resistance.
‖⊢─o	Enemy batteries.
N	Enemy attack repulsed.
_ _ _	We are holding the line.
⫾⫾⫾	We require ammunition.
H⊢	Food supplies required.
⋀	We advance (are ready to attack).

APPENDIX L

ROAD SPACES

1. The following table shows the approximate length of the marching column of units with horsed vehicles and horsed first line transport :—

H.Q. Inf. Div.	55 yards.
Rifle company	165
Machine-gun company of an infantry battalion	350
Infantry gun company	495
Infantry battalion	1,045
Infantry regiment	4,620
Sabre squadron (cavalry)	310
Machine-gun squadron (cavalry)	420
Cyclist squadron	300
Cavalry regiment, horsed	2,150
Field artillery troop	420
Field artillery battery	1,485
Engineer company (part mech.)	200
Signal company (part mech.)	155

2. The following tables show the road spaces required by units of motorized and armoured divisions at rest :—

(a) Motorized infantry division

Div. H.Q.	330 yards.
Reconnaissance unit	2,310
Infantry regiment	3,270
Artillery regiment	10,780
Anti-tank battalion	1,815
Engineer battalion	2,200
Signal unit	1,210

(b) Armoured division

Div. H.Q.	385 yards.
Reconnaissance unit	2,310
Tank brigade (H.Q. and two tank regiments)	13,490
Lorried infantry brigade (H.Q., lorried infantry regiment and motor cyclist battalion)	12,320
Artillery regiment	6,160
Anti-tank battalion	1,815
Engineer battalion	2,200
Signal unit	1,210

3. On the march the road spaces required by motorized and armoured formations vary with their speed. The interval between each pair of vehicles in yards will generally be approximately eight-fifths of the speed in miles, but a greater interval may be ordered, *e.g.* on roads open to observation from the air.

Chapter XVI

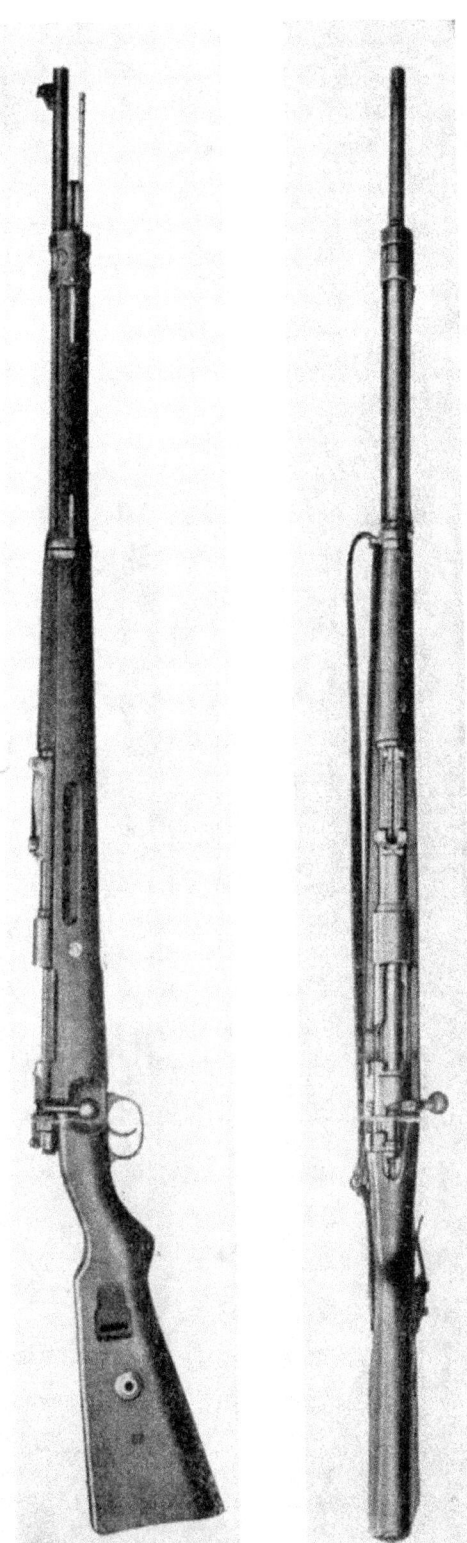

PLATE 1.—Carbine (Karabiner 98b).

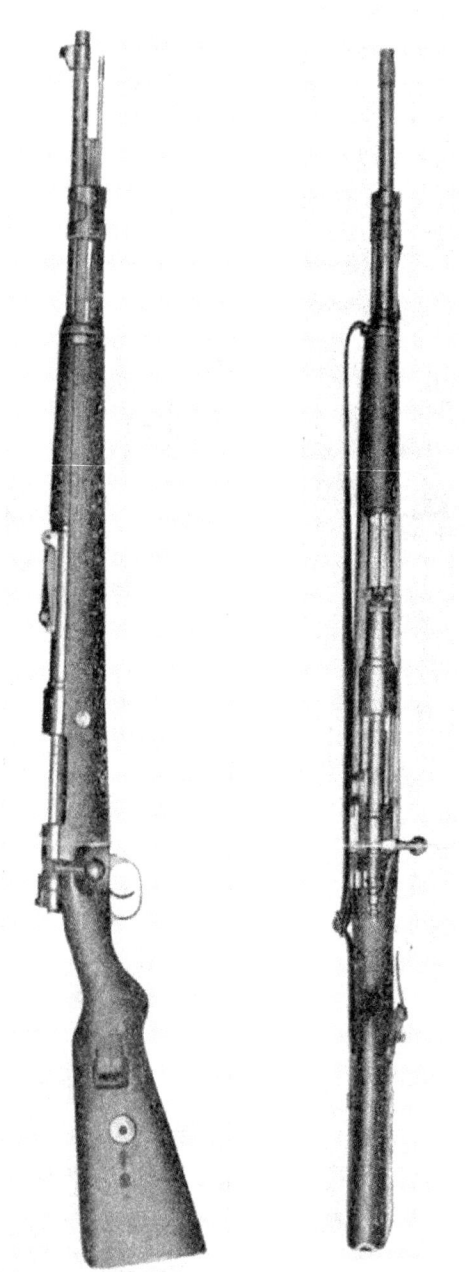

PLATE 2.—Carbine (Karabiner 98k).

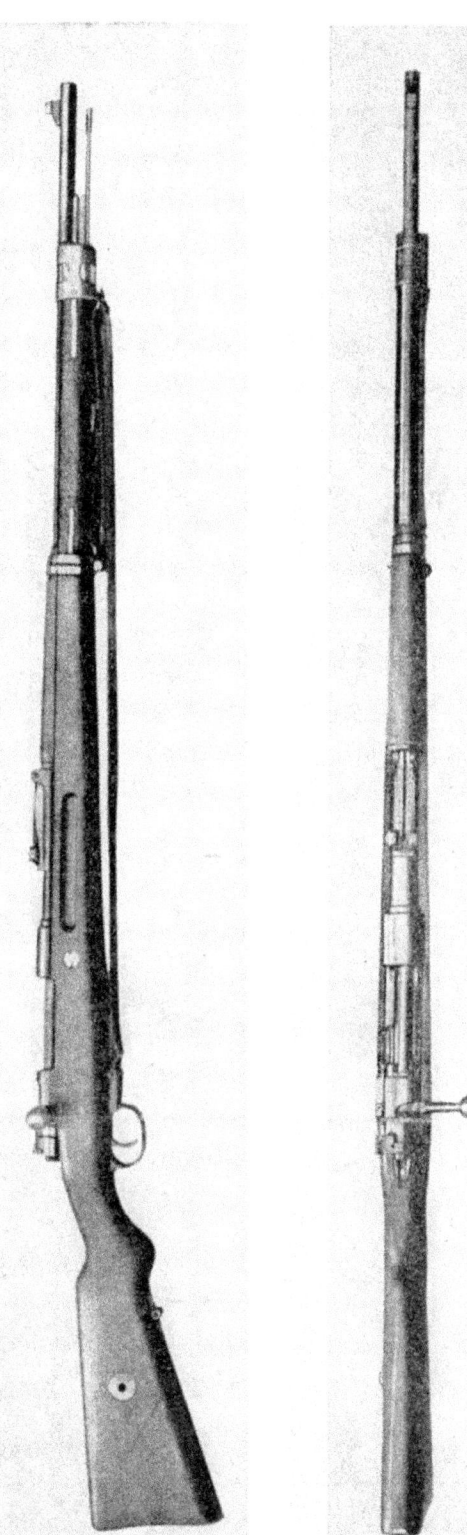

PLATE 3.—Rifle (Gewehr 98).

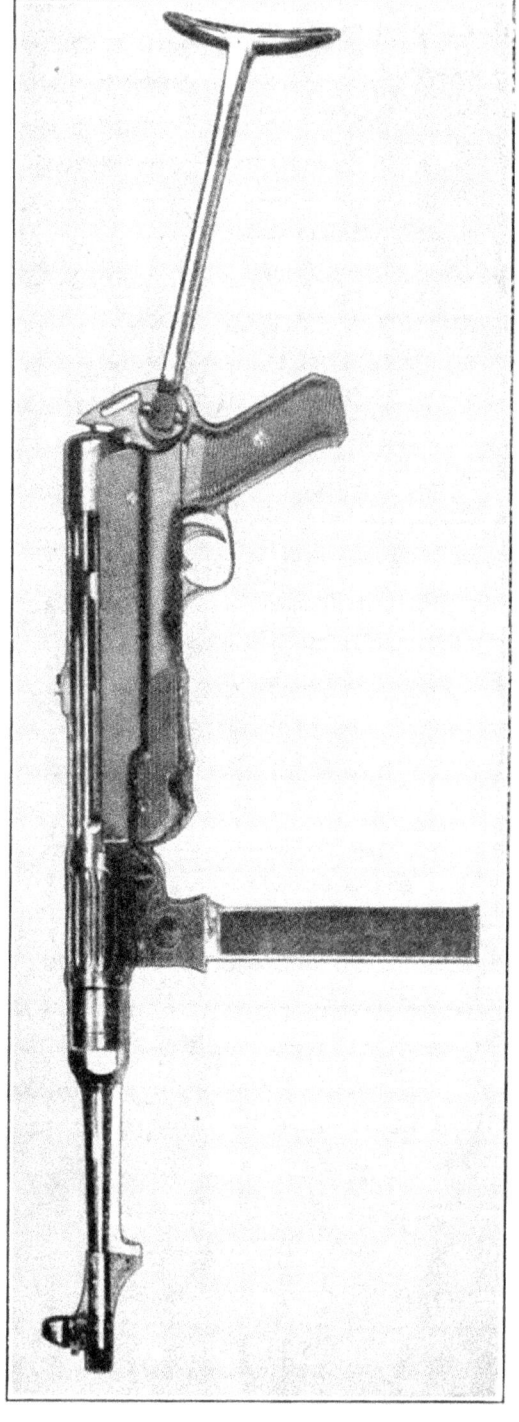

PLATE 4.—Schmeisser Machine Pistol M.P.38.

Calibre, ·9-cm. (·36-in.). Weight (without magazine) 9 lb. 4 oz. (with full magazine, 32 rounds) 10 lb. 9 oz. Range—Very inaccurate over 200 yds.

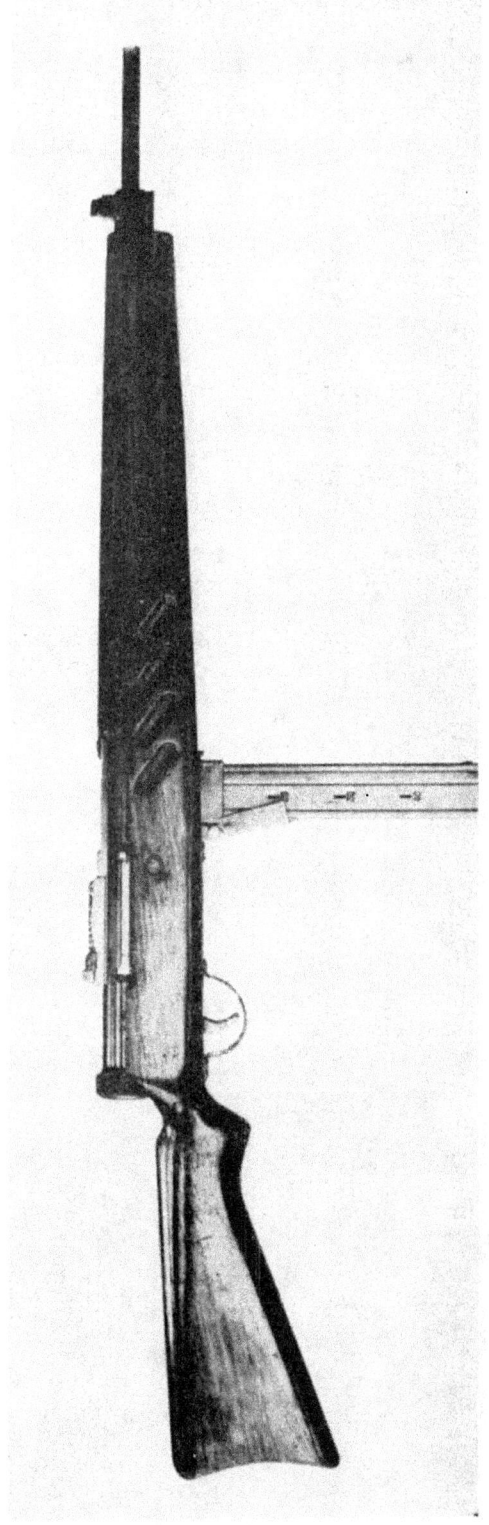

PLATE 5.—Neuhausen Machine Pistol (short model).

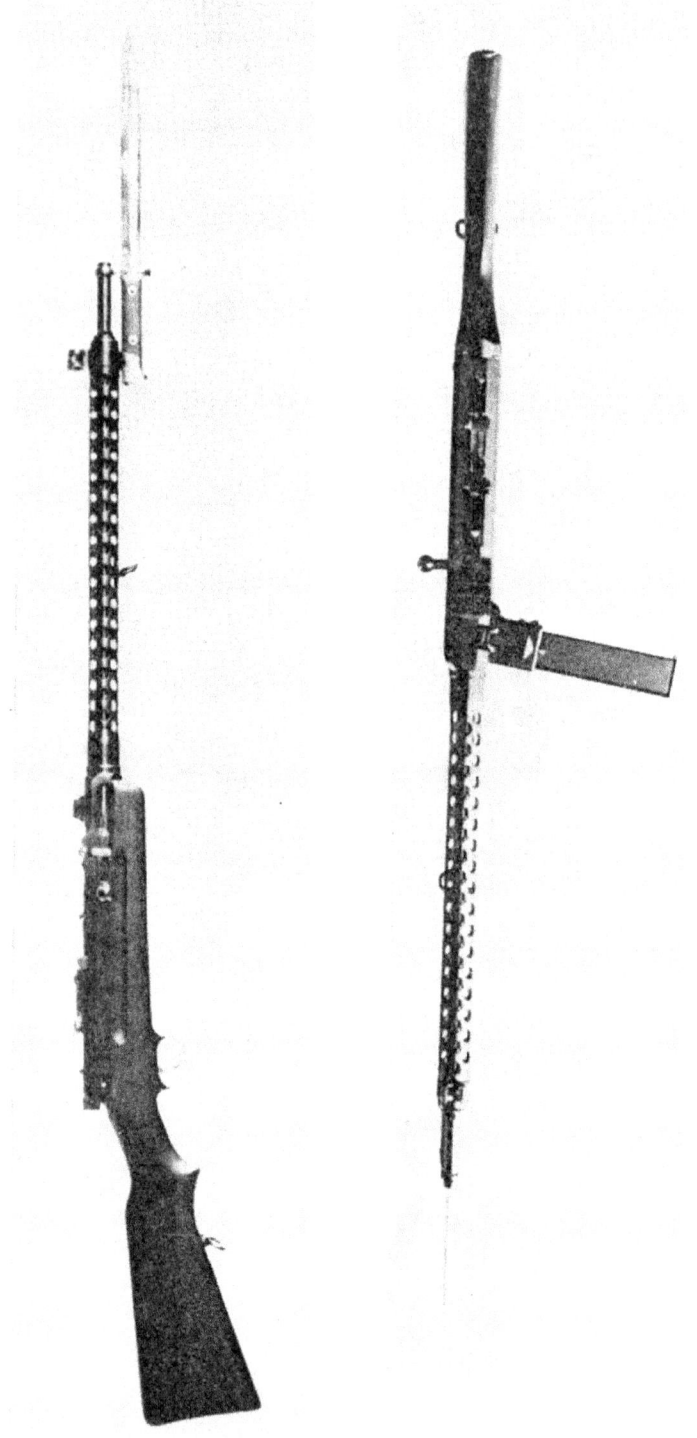

PLATE 6.—Steyr-Solothurn Machine Pistol S.1-100 (long model).

PLATE 7.—Steyr-Solothurn Machine Pistol S.1-100 (short model).

PLATE 8.—Dreyse L.M.G.13.

PLATE 9.—M.G. 34 on Heavy Mounting.
Note the dial sight with which this weapon is equipped.

PLATE 10.—M.G. 34 on an A.A. Mounting.

305

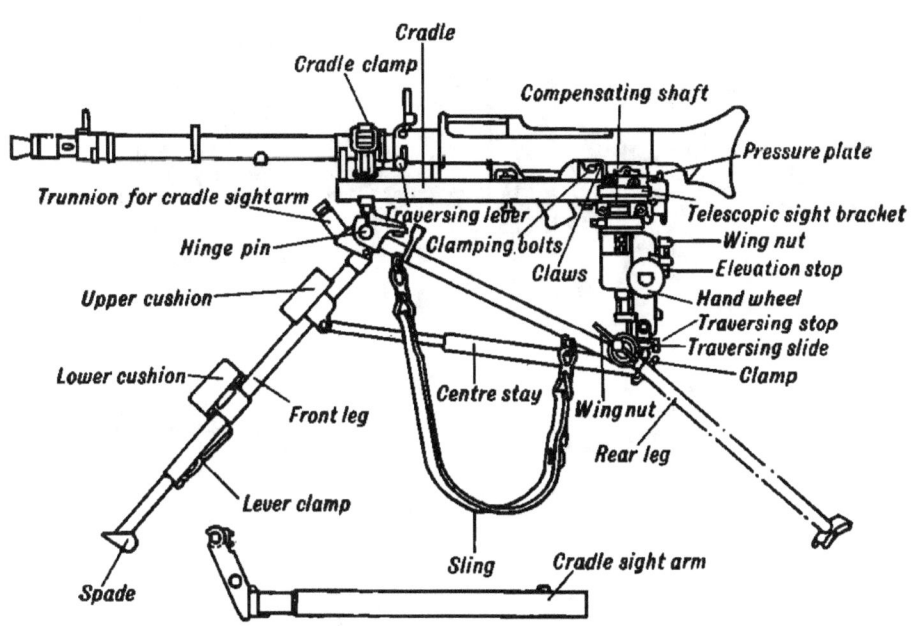

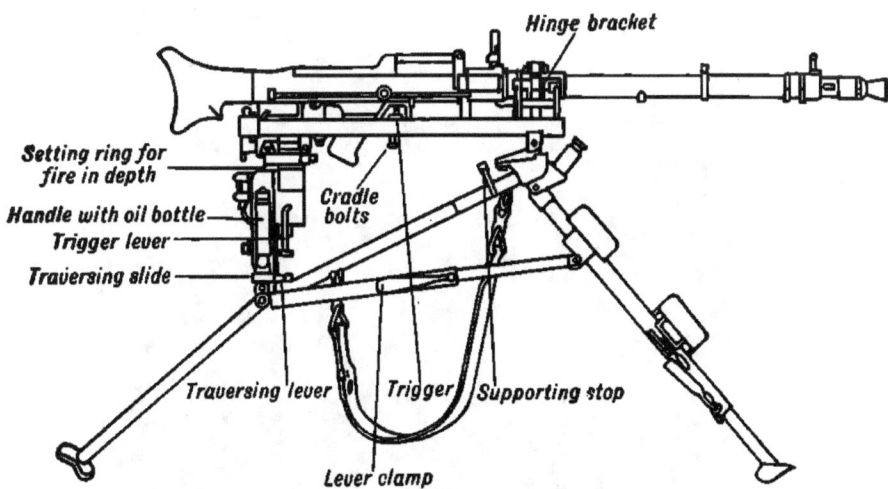

PLATE 11.—Diagram of M.G. 34 on Tripod.

PLATE 12.—08 Hy. M.G. on Tripod Mounting.
Calibre ·31-in. Water-cooled belt fed. (Obsolescent.)

PLATE 13.—08 Hy. M.G. on Sledge Mounting.
Calibre .31-in. Water-cooled belt fed. (Obsolescent.)

PLATE 14.—5-cm. (2-in.) Mortar.

PLATE 15.—8·1-cm. (3·16-in.) Mortar.

PLATE 16.—10-cm. (3·94-in.) Mortar (10-cm. Nebelwerfer).
Used in smoke units.

PLATE 17.—17-cm. (6·69-in.) Medium Mortar.

PLATE 18.—7·5-cm. (2·95-in.) Light Infantry Gun L.M.W.18.

PLATE 19.—7·5-cm. (2·95-in.) Light Infantry Gun with Split Trail (L.13).

PLATE 20.—15-cm. (5·91-in.) Heavy Infantry Gun.

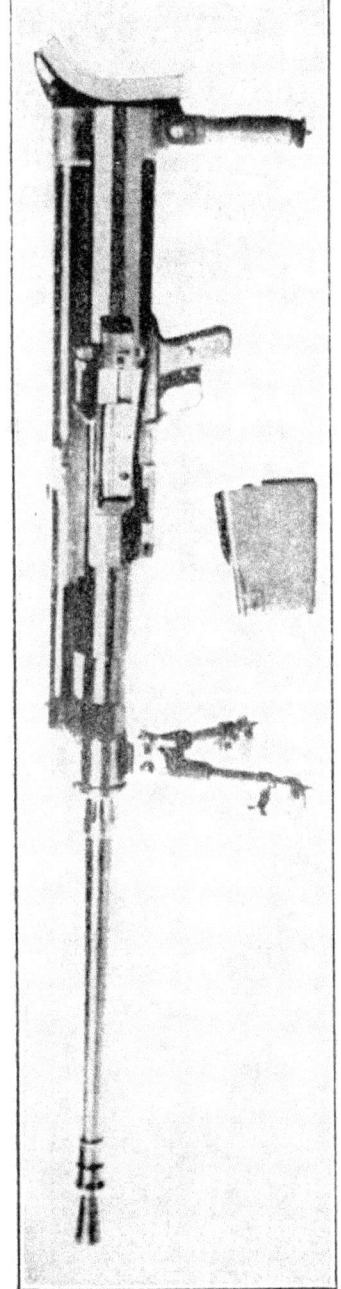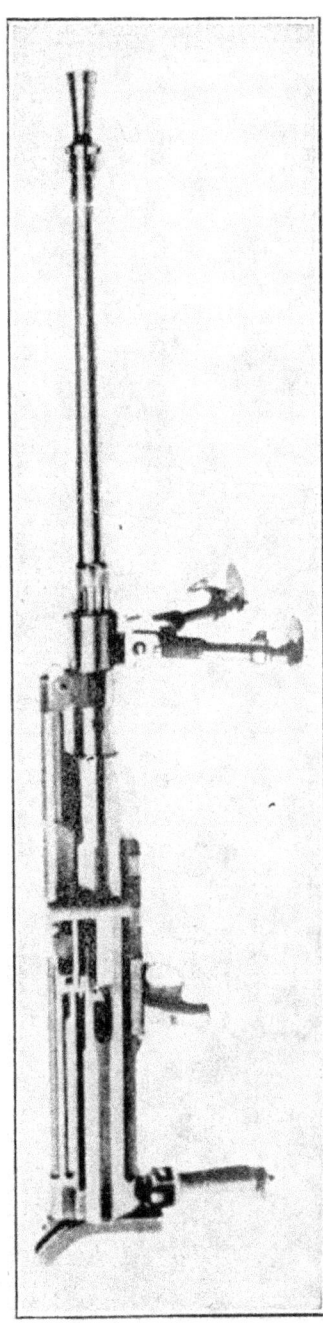

PLATE 21.—2-cm. (·79-in.) Anti-Tank Rifle.

PLATE 22.—3·7-cm. (1·45-in.) Anti-Tank Gun.

PLATE 28.—3·7-cm. (1·45-in.) Anti-Tank Gun.

PLATE 24.—10-cm. (3·93-in.) Mountain Howitzer.

PLATE 25.—10·5-cm. (4·14-in.) Gun-Howitzer L.F.H.18.

PLATE 26.—10·5-cm. (4·14-in.) Field Gun K.18.

PLATE 27.—15-cm. (5·91-in.) Howitzer S.F.H.18.

PLATE 28.—15-cm. (5·91-in.) Howitzer S.F.H.18.

PLATE 29.—15-cm. (5·91-in.) Field Gun K.16.

PLATE 30.—21-cm. (8·27-in.) Howitzer.

PLATE 31.—Railway Guns.

In foreground: Two 21-cm. (8·27-in.) railway guns.
In background: Two 24-cm. (9·45-in.) railway guns.

PLATE 32.—Railway Gun.

Believed to be the "Theodor Kanone." Calibre about 38-cm. (14·93-in.).

PLATE 33.—Long Range Gun on Fixed Mounting. Calibre believed to be about 38-cm. (14·93-in.).

PLATE 34.—2-cm. (·79-in.) Anti-Aircraft and Anti-Tank Gun.

PLATE 35.—2-cm. (·79-in.) Anti-Aircraft and Anti-Tank Gun.

PLATE 36.—8·8-cm. (3·46-in.) Anti-Aircraft Gun.

PLATE 37.—8·8-cm. (3·46-in.) Anti-Aircraft Gun towed by Half-Tracked Armoured Troop-Carrying Vehicle.

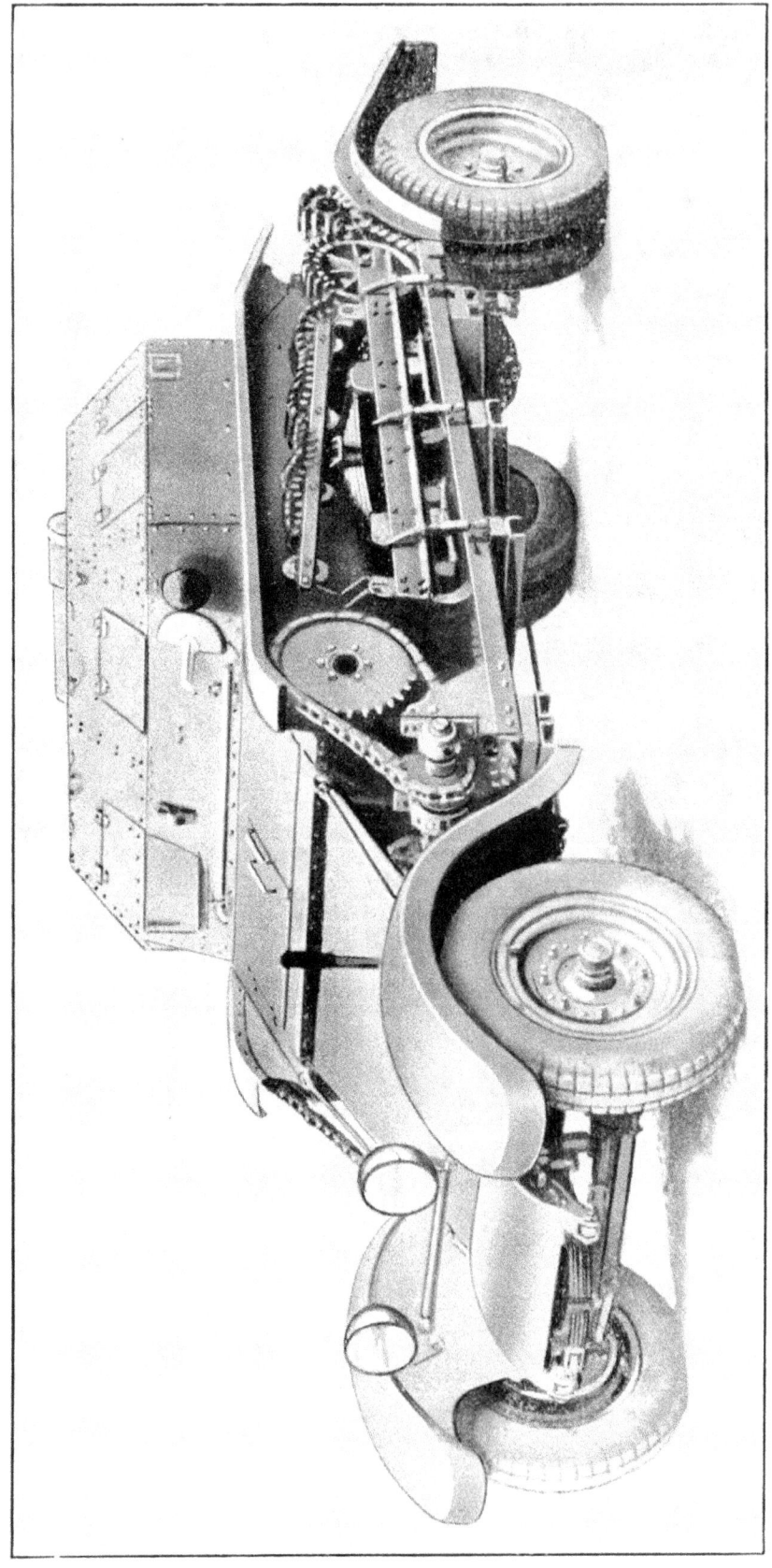

PLATE 38.—T.K.S. Light Tank (Polish) (2·5 tons) mounted on chassis.

PLATE 39.—T.K.S. Light Tank (Polish) (2·5 tons) hauling engineless chassis.

PLATE 40.—Pz.Kw.I two-man Light Tank (5·7 tons).

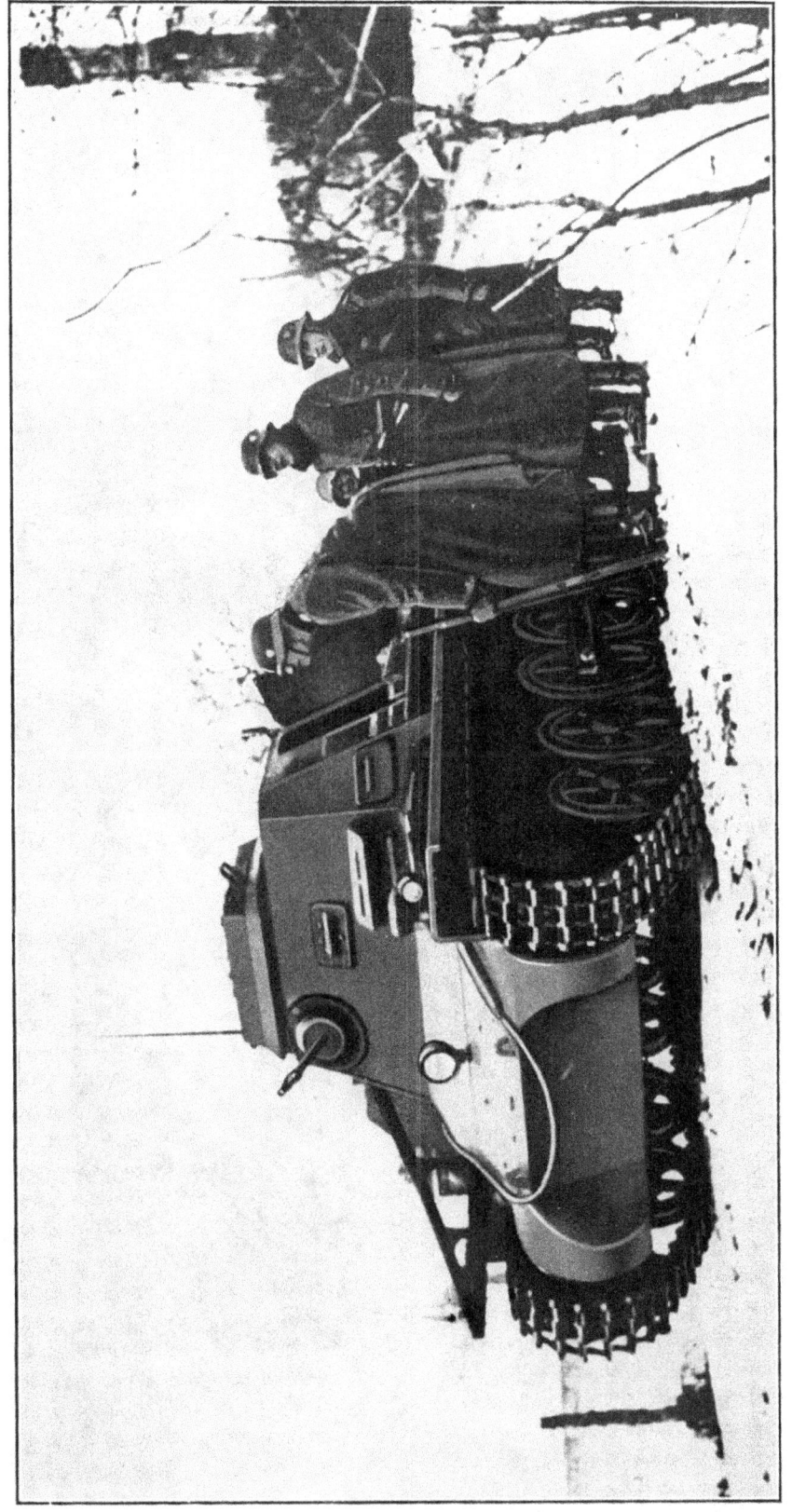

PLATE 41.—Light Commander's Tank (Pz.Kw.I).

PLATE 42.—Pz.Kw.I Converted to Tractor or Carrier.

PLATE 43.—F.IV.H.E. Light Amphibian Tank (Czech) (6·2 tons).

PLATE 44.—F.IV.H.E. Light Amphibian Tank (Czech) (6·2 tons).

PLATE 45.—T.N.H.P. Light Tank (Czech) (10 tons).

PLATE 46.—Pz.Kw.II Three-man Light Tank (9 tons).

PLATE 47.—Pz.Kw.II Three-man Light Tank (9 tons).

PLATE 48.—Pz.Kw.II Mounting Recovery Vehicle.

PLATE 49.—Pz.Kw.II Mounted on Recovery Vehicle.

PLATE 50.—Pz.Kw.II Mounted on Tank Carrier.

PLATE 51.—7.T.P. Light Medium Tank (Polish) (9·5 tons).

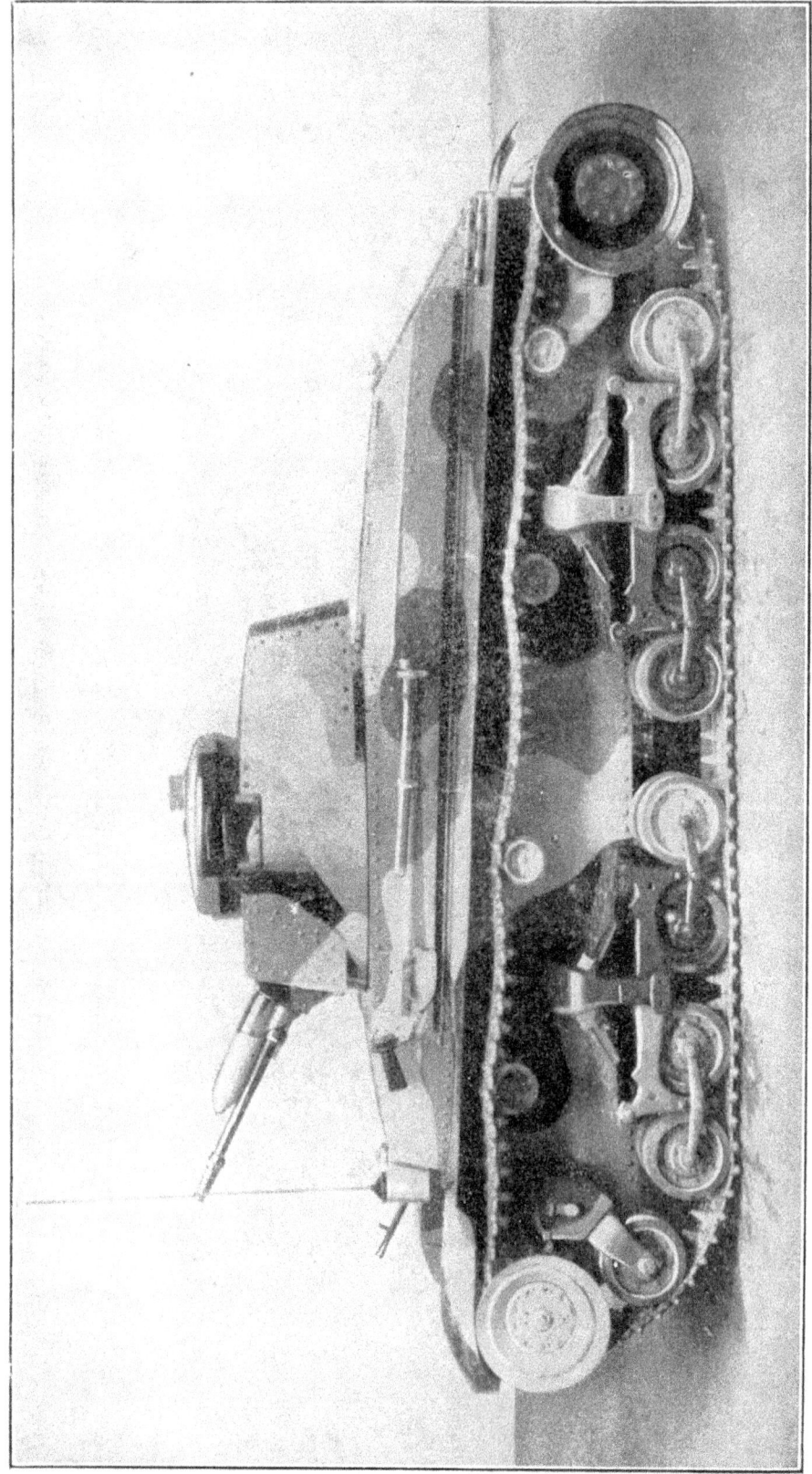

PLATE 52.—L.T. 35 Light Medium Tank (Czech) (11·5 tons).

PLATE 58.—C.K.D. V.8.H. Light Medium Tank (Czech) (16·5 tons).

PLATE 54.—Pz.Kw.III Light Medium Tank (18-20 tons).
(Showing original 8-wheel suspension.)

PLATE 55.—Pz.Kw.III Light Medium Tank (18-20 tons).
(Showing later 5-wheel Christie suspension.)

PLATE 56.—Pz.Kw.III Light Medium Tank (18–20 tons).
(Showing latest type of suspension.)

PLATE 57.—Pz.Kw.IV Medium Tank (22 tons).

PLATE 58.—Pz.Kw.V Heavy Tank (32/35 tons).

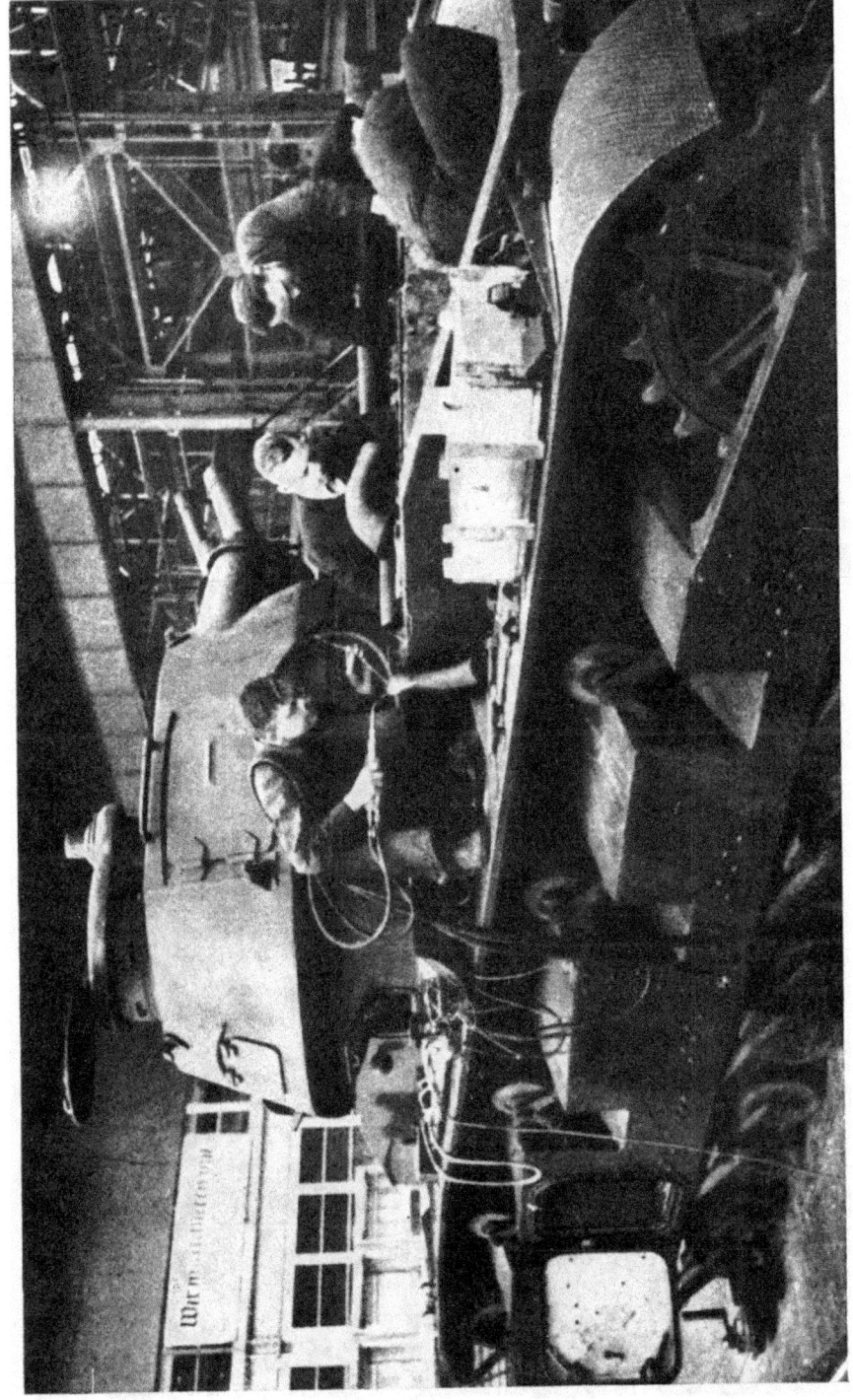

PLATE 59.—Pz.Kw.VI Heavy Tank (35 tons).
(Note 3·7-cm. and 10·5-cm. guns in turret mounted co-axially vertically.)

PLATE 60.—Light Reconnaissance Car.

PLATE 61.—Sd.Kfz.223 Light Armoured Car.

PLATE 62.—A.S.P.6 Medium Armoured Car.

PLATE 63.—Heavy 8-wheeled Armoured Car.

PLATE 64.—A.D.G.Z. Heavy 8-wheeled Armoured Car (ex-Austrian).

PLATE 65.—Armoured Troop-carrier.

PLATE 66.—9/18-ton Pontoon Equipment made up as 18-ton Bridge.

PLATE 67.—Pneumatic Boat Raft.

The 21 ft. × 2 ft. strips of superstructure from the 3½/5-ton pontoon equipment used as decking for the raft.

PLATE 68.—Assault Boats.

Three boats are carried, nested, on each trailer.

PLATE 69.—Assault Boat, showing Outboard Motor.
These boats each carry 15/20 men with full equipment.

PLATE 70.—Assault Boat, showing Outboard Motor Oar.

PLATE 71

FIELD SERVICE UNIFORM.

Colour shows arm
White is infantry

Number shows unit
(6th Inf. Regt.)

Button on shoulder
strap gives company
number
(3rd Coy. 6th Inf. Regt.)
Badge on arm shows rank
(L/Cpl)

(F55). Wt. 22066— 15360. 9/40. Gp. 961. FOSH & CROSS LTD.

PLATE 72.—German Soldiers in Field Service Uniform.

PLATE 78.—German Soldiers in Field Service Uniform.

PLATE 74.—Uniform Worn by Armoured Fighting Troops.

UNIFORM WORN BY ARMOURED FIGHTING TROOPS.

(Private shown.)

(F55). F. & C. LTD.

PLATE 75

ARMY.
DISTINGUISHING COLOURS WORN BY THE VARIOUS ARMS OF THE SERVICE.

Infantry:
    Infantry regiments (normal type)

Now known as "Schnelle Truppen" (Mobile Troops)
- Lorried infantry regiments (Schutzenregimenter) and motor cyclists (Kradschützen) in armoured divisions as for tank corps but with the addition of the letter S or K;
- Cavalry:
      Horsed cavalry regiments, partly horsed cavalry regiments.
- Armoured troops:
      Tank Corps
- Reconnaissance units as for tank corps or cavalry but with the addition of the letter S or K.

Rifle ("*Jäger*") battalions.

Smoke troops

Engineers.

Artillery (also worn by Generals).

M.T. and H.T.

Signals.

Officials (main colour).

Medical.

General Staff Officers, Officers of the Ministry of Defence. Veterinary Officers.

Temporarily re-employed ("*Ergänzungs*") officers and recruiting personnel.

PLATE 77

ARMY.
RANKS AND BADGES OF RANK.

(1) REGULAR OFFICERS.

German rank.	British equivalent.	Badge.
Leutnant (1st Smoke Unit shown).	Second Lieutenant.	
	Lieutenant.	As for Second Lieutenant but with one star.
Rittmeister (Cavalry and Horse Artillery only). Hauptmann (all arms except Cavalry and Horse Artillery).	Captain.	As for Second Lieutenant but with two stars.
Major (14th Cavalry Regiment shown).	Major.	
Oberstleutnant.	Lieutenant-Colonel.	As for Major but with one star.
	Colonel.	As for Major but with two stars.
Generalmajor.	Major-General.	As for General-oberst but without any stars.
Generalleutnant.	Lieutenant-General.	As for General-oberst but with only one star.
General der Infanterie. ,, ,, Kavallerie. ,, ,, Artillerie. ,, ,, Pioniere. ,, ,, Panzer-truppen. ,, ,, Nachrichten-truppen.	General.	As for General-oberst but with only two stars.
		/Generaloberst.

All numerals are removed or covered when units are in the line.

(F55).   Wt. 22066—15360.   9/40.   Gp. 961.   FOSH & CROSS LTD.

PLATE 77
(CONT)

Generaloberst.	None.	
Generalfeldmarschall.	Field Marshal.	

(ii) "ERGÄNZUNGS" (TEMPORARILY RE-EMPLOYED RESERVE AND "LANDWEHR" OFFICERS.

Major (E) (Corps of Fortress Engineers shown).	Temporarily re-employed officer. (note brick-coloured border)	
Hauptmann der Reserve (4th Signal Unit shown).	Reserve Officer (Note the grey border)	
Hauptmann der Landwehr (1st Army Corps Area shown).	"Landwehr" Officer. (Note the aluminium Roman numerals as well as the grey border)	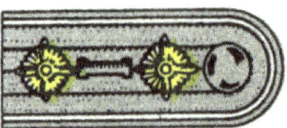

(iii) DIRECTORS OF MUSIC.

Musikmeister.	Junior Bandmaster.	As for Bandmaster but with no star.
Obermusikmeister. (19th Infantry Regiment shown).	Bandmaster.	
Stabsmusikmeister.	Senior Bandmaster.	As for Bandmaster but with two stars.

/N.C.Os.

PLATE 77
(CONT.)

(iv) N.C.Os.

Oberschütze. Oberkanonier.	Senior private.) Senior gunner.)	⊙
Gefreiter.	Junior Lance-Corporal.	As for Obergefreiter with less than six years' service but with only one stripe.
Obergefreiter.	Senior Lance-Corporal with less than six years' service.	
Hauptgefreiter.	Senior Lance-Corporal with more than six years' service.	
Stabsgefreiter.	Senior Lance-Corporal.	As for Senior Lance-Corporal with more than six years' service but with two stripes.

Unteroffizier (Headquarters Staff shown).	Corporal.	
Unterfeldwebel. (6th Medical Unit shown).	Lance Sergeant. (note cloth numeral)	
Fähnrich (2nd Tank Regiment shown).	Junior Officer Candidate. (Note aluminium numeral)	
Feldwebel (3rd Engineer Battalion shown).	Sergeant.	
Oberfeldwebel.	Company Sergeant-major.	
Oberwachtmeister. (17th Cavalry Regiment shown).	Squadron Sergeant-major.	
Oberfähnrich	Senior Officer Candidate.	

ARMY.

NATIONAL BADGE.

As worn on forage cap.

As worn on Service dress jacket of N.C.Os. & Men.

As worn on left side of steel helmet.

NATIONAL ROSETTE.

As worn on all peaked caps and on the black beret flanked by oak leaves.

NATIONAL COLOURS.

Worn on right side of steel helmet.

PLATE 79

AIR FORCE.
DISTINGUISHING COLOURS WORN BY THE VARIOUS ARMS OF THE SERVICE, ETC.

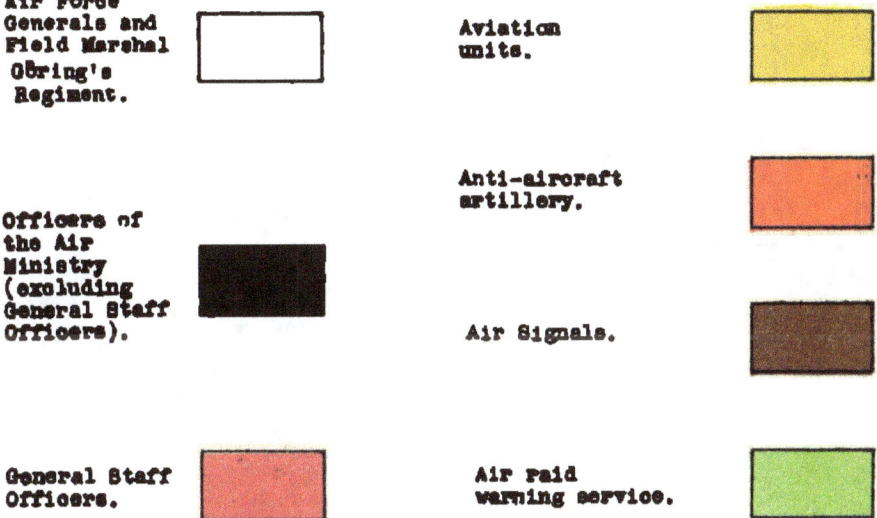

NOTE:- The colours worn by medical personnel and by officials are the same as those worn by their equivalents in the army.

(F55). F. & C. LTD.

PLATE 81

AIR FORCE.
RANKS AND BADGES OF RANK.

(1) OFFICERS.

Rank.	Nearest British equivalent.	Collar Patch.	Shoulder-strap.
Leutnant (Aerodrome Supervisory Service unit shown).	Pilot Officer.		
Oberleutnant (air signals unit shown).	Flying Officer.		
Hauptmann (aviation unit shown).	Flight-Lieutenant.		
Major (Air Ministry shown).	Squadron-Leader.		
Oberstleutnant (anti-aircraft artillery unit shown).	Wing Commander.		
Oberst (aviation unit shown).	Air Commodore or Group Captain.		
Generalmajor.	Air Vice-Marshal.	As for Generalleutnant but with one wing.	As for Generalleutnant but with no star.

/Generalleutnant

PLATE 81
(CONT.)

Rank.	Nearest British equivalent.	Collar Patch.	Shoulder-strap.
Generalleutnant.	Air Marshal.	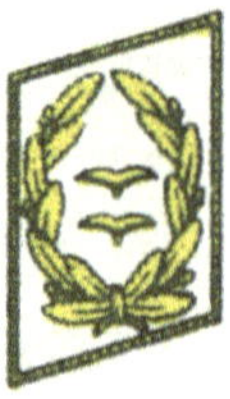	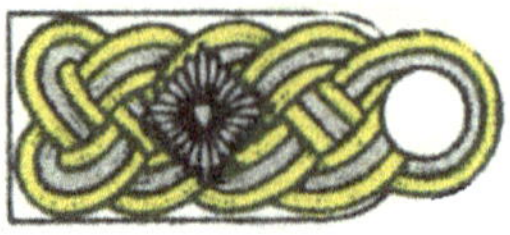
General der Flieger.	Air Chief Marshal.	As for Generalleutnant but with three wings.	As for Generalleutnant but with two stars.
Generaloberst.	Marshal of the Royal Air Force.	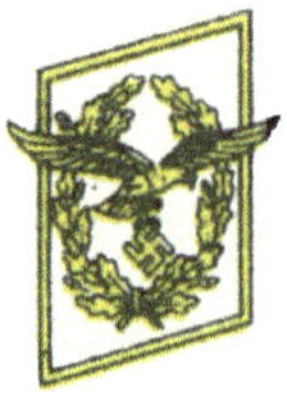	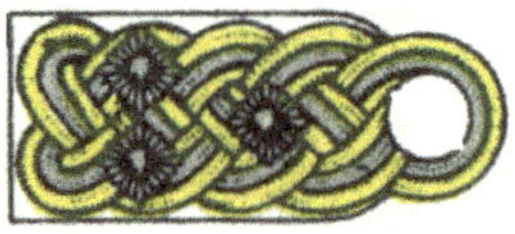
(ii) **N.C.O.s**			
Flieger. Kanonier. Funker. (aviation unit shown*).	Aircraftman II.	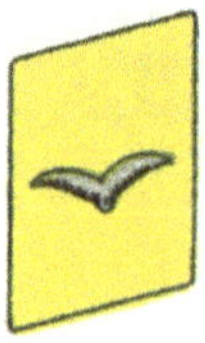	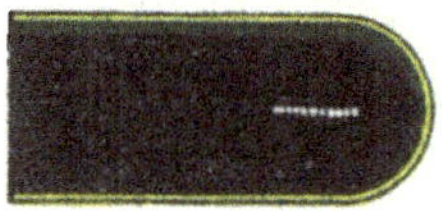
Gefreiter. (Reserve shown*).	Aircraftman I.	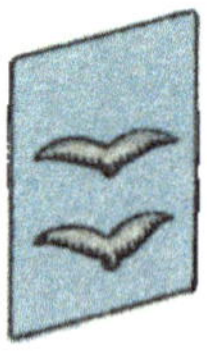	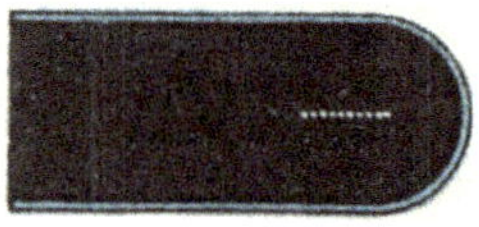
Obergefreiter. (Air Ministry shown*).	Leading Aircraftman.		

* Equivalent ranks in aviation, anti-aircraft artillery, air signals, air reserve, etc, units all wear the same badge but with different coloured background.

Rank.	Nearest British equivalent.	Collar Patch.	Shoulder-strap.
Hauptgefreiter. (aviation unit shown*).	Leading Aircraftsman.		
Unteroffizier. (Aerodrome Supervisory Service unit shown*).	Corporal.		
Unterfeldwebel. (air signals unit shown*).	Lance-Sergeant.		
Feldwebel. (anti-aircraft artillery unit shown*).	Sergeant.		
Oberfeldwebel. (aviation unit shown*).	Flight-Sergeant.		

*Equivalent ranks in aviation, anti-aircraft artillery, air signals, air reserve, etc. Units all wear the same badge but with different coloured background.

PLATE 82.—A Group of Parachute Troops.

PLATE 83.—German Parachutist.

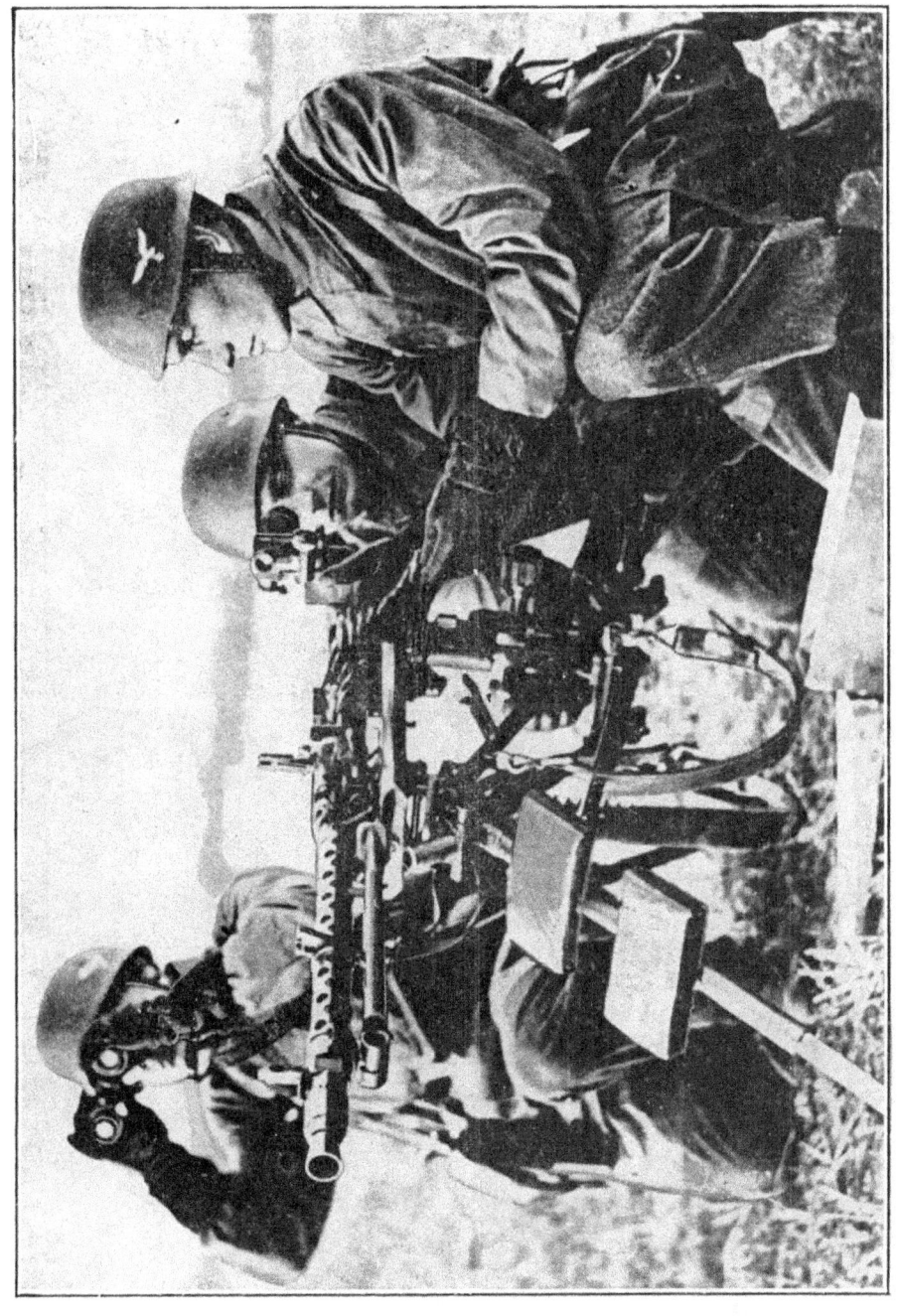

PLATE 84.—German Parachute Troops with M.G.

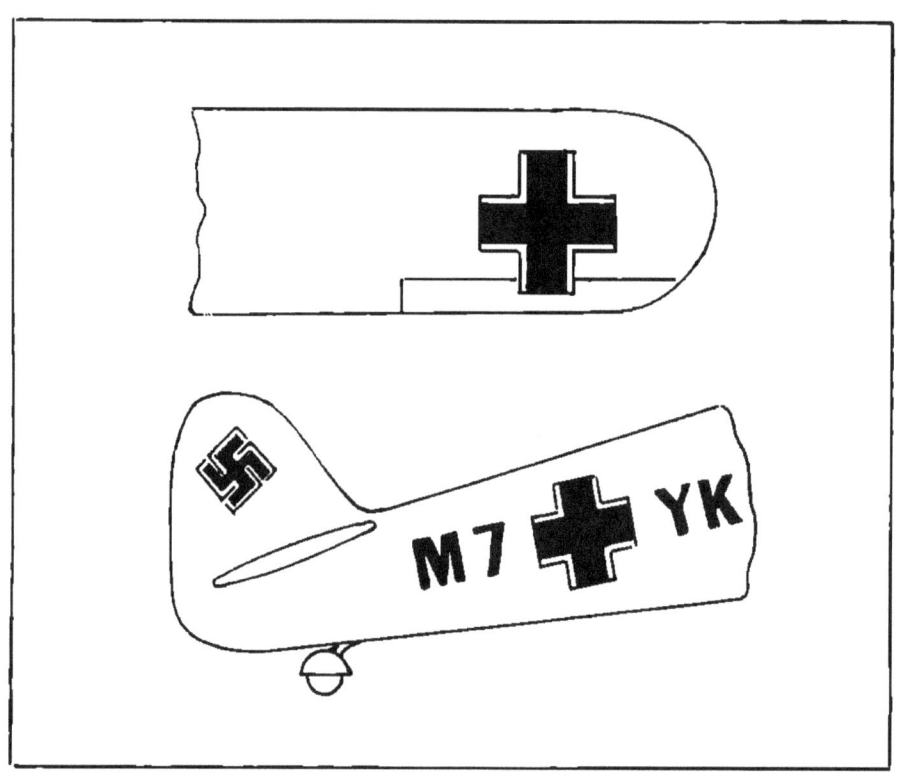

PLATE 85.—National Marking on German Aircraft.

INDEX

A

	Page
Abbreviations, list of	264
Administration, commands and staff	10
Administrative areas	11
services, *see* Services, supply and administrative.	
A.F.V. badge	224
A.F.Vs., special types of (*see also* Armoured cars and tanks)	98
tactics	258
Air-borne troops, *see* Air-landing troops and Parachute troops.	
Air defence troops, organisation and strength of (*see also* Artillery, anti-aircraft)	7
Air defences, chain of command for	14
Air Force :—	
aircraft, armament	237
types of	236
roles	239
air corps	233
defence commands	232, 234
divisions	233
fleets	233
air liaison officers (*see also* " Koluft " officers)	13
allotment of units to army formations	2, 239
anti-aircraft units, *see* Artillery, anti-aircraft.	
army co-operation	239
bombs, types of	237
civil aviation, control of	232
formations	235
" Geschwader," organisation of	235
" Gruppe," organisation of	235
" Koluft " officers	238
liaison between army and air force	238
markings on aircraft	237, Plate 85
organisation, distribution and strength	232
parachute troops, *see* Parachute troops.	
" Staffel," organisation of	235
support of army	237, 255, 259, 260
tactics	238
territorial areas	233
uniform	224, Plates 79–81
units, flying	235
Air-landing troops (*see also* Parachute troops) :—	
armament	242
gliders	243
infantry division, organised as	242, 251
Inspectorate of Air-landing and Parachute Troops	240
landing grounds	243
landing, method of	245
maintenance	242
objectives	246

	Page
Air-landing troops—*contd.*	
organisation, general	240
strength of infantry division, organised as	242
tactics, *see* objectives.	
transport, lack of	242
uniforms	243
Air liaison officers (*see also* "Koluft" officers)	13
Ammunition :—	
artillery, types of	81
small arms, types of	54
supply :—	
anti-tank battalions	104
artillery	80
cavalry	46
infantry	30
system of	196, 208
Anti-aircraft artillery, *see* Artillery, anti-aircraft.	
Anti-aircraft machine-gun battalion, motorised, organisation, strength and armament	28
tactics	257
Anti-tank guns :—	
2-cm. (·79-in.) A.A. & A.Tk.	95, Plates 34–35
3·7-cm. (1·45-in.)	57, Plates 22–23
4·7-cm. (1·85-in.)	58
mines	135, 140
obstacles	140
rifles	57, Plate 21
Anti-tank units :—	
ammunition supply	104
anti-aircraft company in	104
armament	103
battalion, divisional, organisation, strength and armament	103
G.H.Q., *see* heavy.	
heavy, organisation, strength and armament	98
company (infantry regiment)	16
(motorised M.G. battalion)	26
equipment :—	
road blocks	105
signal	105
tools	105
maintenance	105
mechanics	104
Mobile Troops, Inspectorate of	97
Motorised A.A.M.G. battalions, secondary role as	28
organisation, general	97
signallers	104
specialists	104
strength	98
terminology	97
Anti-tank weapons, captured (*see also* anti-tank guns, rifles)	63

	Page
Armoured cars, distinguishing features	122, Plates 60–64
particulars of	120
Armoured division, composition, strength and fire-power	4
summary of A.F.Vs. and weapons	114
Armoured fighting troops :—	
A.F.V. badge	224
A.F.Vs., special types (*see also* armoured cars, and tanks)	98
tactics	258
armoured cars, distinguishing features	122, Plates 60–64
particulars of	120
commanders' cars	98
division, composition, strength and fire-power	4
summary of A.F.Vs. and weapons	114
troop-carrying vehicles	98, Plate 65
flame-throwing tanks	98
independent tank regiments	102
infantry tanks, *see* tanks, super-heavy.	
liaison sections	99
light aid sections	102
tank columns	99
maintenance	102
mechanics	102
mixed tank regiment, organisation, strength and armament	99
Mobile Troops, Inspectorate of	97
organisation, general	97
signal equipment	103
signallers	102
specialists :—	
mechanics	102
signallers	102
strength	97
tactics	258
tank brigade organisation, strength and armament	5
regiment, mixed, organisation, strength and armament	99
tanks, distinguishing features	117, Plates 38–59
particulars of	115
tanks, super-heavy	98
terminology	97
transport	102
unarmoured units, *see* Anti-tank battalions.	
workshop companies	103
Arms of the Service	1
Army, composition and strength of	2
Army group, composition and strength of	2
Artillery :—	
ammunition :—	
system of supply	80
types of	81

Artillery—*contd*.   *Page*
    anti-aircraft artillery :—
        allotment to field army 75
        anti-tank weapons, employment as 75
        armament 76, 93
        balloon barrage units 75
        battery, *see* light or mixed battery.
        coast defence units 77
        control of units operating with army 75
        equipment, *see* Artillery equipment.
        fortress, A.A. artillery 76
        guns, particulars of 95
        land targets employment against 75
        light battery, organisation, strength and armament 74, 93
        mixed battery, organisation, strength and armament 74, 93
        mobile units, organisation, strength and armament 74
        organisation, general 73
        regiment, organisation, strength and armament.. 74, 93
        searchlight units 74, 75
        searchlights, particulars of 80
        semi-mobile units, organisation, strength and armament 74
        static defences 75
        tactics 260
        transport 75, 93
        vulnerable points, defence of 76
    anti-gas specialists 72
    armament, general note (*see also* guns, particulars of) 66
    artificers 72
    calibres 65
    coastal defence artillery, organisation and strength .. 76
    commander, corps 13, 66
        divisional 13, 66
    corps artillery, *see* medium, heavy and super-heavy artillery.
    divisional artillery :—
        armoured division 70
        cavalry division 67
        infantry division 68
        "Landwehr" division 69
        motorised infantry division 70
        mountain division 68
        weakness of 66
    equipment :—
        command instruments 79
        guns and howitzers—general note 77
        observation instruments 79
        predictors 79
        searchlights 80

Artillery—*contd.*   *Page*

	Page
equipment—*contd.*	
signal	78
sound locators	80
survey instruments..	79
farriers	72
field artillery in an armoured division	70
infantry division	68
" Landwehr " division	69
motorised infantry division	70
flash-spotting troops	73
fortress artillery	77
fuzes, types of	81
guns, particulars of types of captured	92
German..	85
German A.A.	95
heavy artillery, organisation, strength and armament	71
horse artillery, organisation, strength and armament	67
Inspector of	65
liaison detachments	261
light artillery columns	196
map-printing sections	70, 73
mechanics	72
medium artillery in infantry division	68
G.H.Q. pool	71
motorised infantry division	70
meteorological sections ..	70, 73
mountain artillery, organisation, strength and armament	68
observation balloon troops	73
organisation, general	65
signallers	72
sound-ranging troops	73
specialists :—	
anti-gas	72
artificers	72
farriers	72
mechanics	72
signallers	72
survey	72
staffs :—	
army	12, 66
corps	13, 66
division	13, 66
regiment	66
battery	66
super-heavy artillery, organisation, strength and armament	71
survey specialists	72
units	68, 72
tactics	260
troop, four-gun organisation	65

Artillery—*contd.*   *Page*

- units, equivalent British and German 65
- vehicles 77

Assault badges 224
    battalions, engineer 124
    boats .. .. 136, 139, Plates 68–70
    detachments 29, 124, 259, 260
    equipment 124, 142
    guns 16, 55, 66
Attack, *see* Tactics.

B.

Bacteriological warfare 192
Badges, *see* Uniform.
Bakeries 3, 198
Balloon barrage units 75
Bangalore torpedoes 142
Bayonet 51
Bivouac sheets 33, 48, 220, 221
Bodyguard troops, special 214
Booby traps 136
Bridge construction battalions 2
Bridges (*see also* Bridging equipment) :—
    girder 140
    improvised 140
    small box girder 140
Bridging columns 2, 125, 126, 128, 129
    equipment .. .. 136, Plate 66
Brigade, lorried infantry, composition and strength .. 5
    tank, composition and strength 5
Butcher units 3, 198

C.

Camouflage 256
Capes, gas 184
Captured artillery weapons 92
    small arms, close-support and anti-tank weapons .. 63
Carbines 51
Carrier pigeons 150
Cavalry :—
    ammunition, system of supply 46
    cyclist battalion, organisation, strength and armament 44
    division, composition and strength 5
    equipment :—
        anti-A.F.V. 48
        bivouacs 48
        engineer 48
        saddlery 47
        signal 47
        tools 47

	Page
Cavalry—*contd.*	
gun	55
horsed cavalry regiment, organisation, strength and armament	40
infantry divisional reconnaissance unit, organisation, strength and armament	43
light cavalry column	196
mechanics	46
mechanised reconnaissance unit, organisation, strength and armament..	41
numbering of units	46
signallers	46
specialists	46
tactics	257
transport ..	46
Chain of command of air defence troops	14
coastal defence troops	14
in the field	11
Chemical warfare :—	
aerial spray	188
aircraft, bombs, chemical	188
smoke apparatus	191
anti-gas ointment	185
personnel	183
artillery shell (gas)	188
(smoke)	191
bacteriological warfare ..	192
blister gases	186
capes, gas	184
choking gases	187
clothing, protective	184
contamination, bulk	189
cylinders, gas	189
decontamination detachments ..	183
materials for	185
defence against gas, organisation, administration and strength	183
detectors, gas	185
engineer units, gas in	186
smoke in	191
gas capes	184
detectors	185
equipment	187
tactics	262
weapons	187
units, organisation, strength and equipment	185
gases, types of	186
generators, toxic	189
grenades, gas	189
Inspectorate of Smoke Troops and Gas Defence	182
meteorological conditions, effect of, on smoke and gas	191
mines, gas	189
mobile laundries	184

	Page
Chemical warfare—*contd.*	
mortars, gas	189
N.C.Os., anti-gas	183
nose gases	187
officers, anti-gas	183
ointment, anti-gas	185
policy, general	182
projectors	188
protection, collective	185
respirators	183
schools, anti-gas	183
sentries, gas	183
smoke apparatus in other arms	191
tactics	262
units organisation, strength and equipment	190
gas in	185, 190
special smoke units	191
tank units, gas in	186
smoke in	191
tear gases	187
toxic generators	189
smokes	187
weather, effect of, on smoke and gas	191
Cipher personnel	150
Close support weapons :—	
assault gun	16, 55, 66
captured	63
cavalry gun	55
infantry guns :—	
light 7·5-cm. (2·95-in.) L.M.W. 18	55, Plate 18
light 7·5-cm. (2·95-in.) L.13	55, Plate 19
heavy 15-cm. (5·91-in.)	56, Plate 20
mortars :—	
5-cm. (2-in.)	54, Plate 14
8·1-cm. (3·16-in.) L.15	54, Plate 15
8·1-cm. (3·16-in.) S.Gr.W. 34	56
10-cm. (3·93-in.) (smoke)	56, Plate 16
17-cm. (6·96-in.)	56, Plate 17
Coast defence artillery, organisation and strength of	76
coast defence troops, organisation and strength of	7
Coast defences, chain of command	14
Coinage	273
Combined Staff of Defence Forces	10
Concentration camp guards	28, 215
Constabulary, rural	213
town	212
Construction battalions	129
bridge	2
mobile	129
road	129
training	130
Construction company, organisation and strength	130
construction units, fortress	130

	Page
Conventional signs	275
Corps, composition and strength	2
Cyclist battalion, organisation, strength and armament	44
Czech police corps	218

D.

Decontamination, *see* Chemical Warfare	
Decorations	224
Defence, *see* Tactics.	
Despatch rider sections, motor-cycle	16, 251
Despatch riders	150
Division, armoured, organisation, strength and armament	4, 107
cavalry, organisation, strength and armament	5
infantry, organisation, strength and armament	3, 34
organised as air-landing troops	242, 251
motorised, infantry, organisation, strength and armament	3
mountain, organisation, strength and armament	4
types of	1
Dogs, messenger	38 (Note 12), 150

E.

Engineers:—

armament	127, 128, 130, 132
assault battalions	124
boats	136, 139, Plates 68–70
detachments	29, 124, 259, 260
equipment	124, 142
Bangalore torpedoes	142
battalion in armoured division	128
G.H.Q. pool	129
infantry division	125
motorised infantry division	127
mountain division	128
booby traps	136
bridge construction battalions	2
bridges (*see also* bridging equipment):—	
girder	140
improvised	140
small box girder	140
bridging column	2, 125, 126, 128, 129
equipment	136, Plate 66
commander, corps	13
division	13
construction battalions	129
bridge	2
mobile	129
road	129
training	130

Engineers—*contd*.

	Page
construction company, organisation and strength	130
construction units, fortress	130
demolition equipment	134
equipment in company	134
electrical and mechanical tools park	134
reserve stores park	134
section	134
explosives	135
field engineers	124
flame-throwers	142
fortress construction units	130
engineers	125
Fortresses, Inspector of	125
Herbert pontoon bridge	138
Inspector of	124
labour battalions, *see* construction battalions	
"Landwehr" company, organisation and strength	132
light engineer column	196
mine exploding net	142
mines, anti-personnel	136
anti-tank	135, 140
motor boats	139
obstacles, anti-tank	140
outboard motors	140
pneumatic boats	137
pole charges	142
pontoons	136, 137
rafts	137, 262, Plate 67
heavy tank	139, 262
railway engineer units	132
searchlights	141
staffs :—	
army	12
corps	13
division	13
tactics	261
tools, *see* equipment.	
training and experimental battalions	129
unit in cavalry division	129
vehicles	143
Entrenching tools	32
Equipment, personal	224
Ex-soldiers' organisation	218

F.

Factory guards	217
Farriers	72
Field post numbers	201
Field security police	201
Fifth columnists	244, 246

	Page
Flame-throwers	142
Flame-throwing tanks	98
Forage, system of supply	194
Formations, distinguishing flags and signs	275
higher, organisation of	1
Fortress, artillery	77
, anti-aircraft	76
construction engineers	130
engineers	125
infantry	15
Fortresses, Inspectorate of	125
Frontages	254, 256
Frontier infantry	27

G.

Gas, *see* Chemical Warfare.	
General Staff in formations	11
in War Ministry	10
"Gestapo"	201, 213
G.H.Q. troops	1
specimen allotment to army and corps	8
Gliders, troop-carrying	243
Grenades	58
gas	189
"Grossdeutschland" Regiment	6
Guard battalions, L. of C.	201

H.

Herbert pontoon equipment	138
High Command, organisation in war	10
Higher formations, organisation of	1
Hitler, President of the War Cabinet	10
Supreme Commander of the Defence Forces	10
Hitler Youth	217

I.

Identity discs	223
Infantry :—	
ammunition supply	30
anti-tank company, regimental	16
arm of service	1
assault detachments	29, 124, 259, 260
guns	16, 55, 66
battalion, organisation, strength and armament	17
commander, divisional	13

Infantry—contd. *Page*
    division, organisation, strength and armament 3, 34, 36, 37
        organised as air-landing troops 242, 251
    divisional reconnaissance unit 43
    equipment :—
        anti-A.F.V. 33
        bivouacs 33
        engineer 33
        personal 31
        rangefinders 33
        signal 31
        tools 32
    fortress infantry 15
    frontier infantry 27
    gun company 16
    guns .. .. 55, 66, Plates 18–20
    light infantry column 30, 196
    lorried infantry brigade, organisation, strength and
        armament 5
        regiment, organisation, strength and armament .. 20
    machine-gun battalion, motorised, organisation,
        strength and armament 26
    mechanics 29
    motor-cyclist battalion, organisation, strength and
        armament 23
    motorised A.A.M.G. battalion, organisation, strength
        and armament 28
    motorised infantry regiment, organisation, strength
        and armament 5, 20
    motorised M.G. battalion, organisation, strength and
        armament 26
    mountain rifle regiments, organisation, strength and
        armament 23
    mounted infantry platoons 16
    numbering of units 30
    pioneer platoons 16, 29
    police division 213
    positional units 6
    protective regiments 6
    regiment, organisation, strength and armament .. 5, 16
    rifle battalions 16
    signallers 29
    specialists 29
    S.S. formations 27
    tactics 260
    tanks, *see* Armoured fighting troops, tanks, super-heavy
    transport 30
Inspectorates 11
    Air-landing and Parachute Troops 240
    Artillery 65
    Defence Communications 147
    Engineers 125

Inspectorates—*contd.*	Page
Fortresses	125
Infantry	15
Mobile Troops	97
Signals	147
Smoke Troops and Gas Defence	182
Instructional units, *see also* Training battalions, engineer	6
Iron Cross, *see* Orders, decorations and medals.	
Irregular methods of warfare	263

J.

Juvenile organisations, *see* Hitler Youth.

K.

"Koluft" officers, *see also* Air liaison officers	238

L.

Labour battalions, *see* Construction battalions.	
Service, National	217
Lance	59
"Landsturm"	201
"Landwehr"	6
"Leibstandarte Adolf Hitler"	214
Light aid sections, *see* Armoured fighting troops.	
Light machine guns, *see* Machine-guns.	
Local defence units	6
L. of C. guard battalions	201
Lorried infantry brigade, organisation, strength and armament	5
regiment, organisation, strength and armament	20

M.

Machine-gun battalion, motorised, organisation, strength and armament	26
tactics	255, 257
Machine-guns	
dual purpose (M.G. 34)	52, Plates 9–11
heavy (M.G. 08)	53, Plates 12–13
light (Dreyse L.M.G. 13)	51, Plate 8
(Knorr–Bremse)	52
(L.M.G. 08/15)	52
super-heavy	95, Plates 34–35
Machine-pistols	51, Plates 4–7
Main effort ("Schwerpunkt")	254, 255
Map-printing sections	70, 73
Measures	273

	Page
Mechanised reconnaissance unit, organisation, strength and armament	41
tactics	257
Medals	224
Medical service	198
Messenger dogs	150
Meteorological sections	2, 70, 73
Military farmers	218
police	200
Mine exploding net	142
Mines :—	
anti-personnel	136
anti-tank	135, 140
gas	189
Mobile laundries, *see* Chemical Warfare.	
troops	1, 97
Morale, destruction of enemy	255
Mortars, *see also* Chemical Warfare :—	
5-cm. (2-in.)	54, Plate 14
8·1-cm. (3·16-in.) L.15	55, Plate 15
8·1-cm. (3·16-in.) S.Gr.W.34	56
10-cm. (3·93-in.) (smoke)	56, Plate 16
17-cm. (6·69-in.)	56, Plate 17
Motor boats	139
Motor-cyclist battalion, organisation, strength and armament	23
Motorised A.A.M.G. battalion, organisation, strength and armament	28
tactics	257
Motorised infantry division, composition and strength	3
regiment, organisation, strength and armament	5, 20
Motorised machine-gun battalion, organisation, strength and armament	26
tactics	255, 257
Mountain artillery, organisation, strength and armament	68
Mountain division, composition and strength	4
rifle regiment, organisation, strength and armament	23
Mounted infantry platoons	16

N.

" Nachschubführer der Armee "	197
" des Korps "	197
" der Division "	195
National badge, *see* Uniform.	
National Labour Service	217
Socialist Flying Corps	217
Motor Corps	215
Mounted Corps	216
Non-commissioned officers—ranks	Plate 77 (iv)
Numbering of units :—	
cavalry units	46
infantry units	30

O.

	Page
Observation balloon units	2
Obstacles, anti-tank	140
Officers, ranks	Plate 77
Orders	253
Orders, decorations and medals	224
Outboard motors	140
Outposts	256

P.

Patrols 256, 258
Parachute troops (*see also* Air-landing troops) :—
    armament 241
    command 242
    damage, inflicted by 241
    disguises 243
    equipment 241
    Inspectorate of Air-landing and Parachute troops .. 240
    jumping, method of 245
    landing grounds 243
        method of 244
    maintenance 242
    objectives 246
    organisation, general 240
    regiment, organisation and equipment 241
    strength 240
    tactics, *see* objectives.
    training 240
    uniform .. .. 224, Plates 82–84
Para-military organisations (*see also* Police)
    bodyguard troops, special 214
    concentration camp guards (Totenkopfverbände) ..28, 215
    ex-soldiers' organisation 218
    factory guards 217
    Hitler Youth 217
    " Leibstandarte Adolf Hitler " 214
    military farmers 218
    National Labour Service 217
        Socialist Flying Corps 217
            Motor Corps 215
            Mounted Corps 216
    post guards 217
    railway guards 217
    S.A., *see* Storm detachments.
    " Schütz Staffeln " :—
        concentration camp guards (Totenkopfverbände) 215
        ordinary S.S. units 214
        permanently embodied and militarised S.S. units
            (" Waffen S.S.") 214
    S.S, *see* " Schütz Staffeln ".

Para-military organisations—*contd.*   *Page*
    Storm detachments 215
    " Totenkopfverbände," *see* concentration camp guards.
    " Verfügungstruppen " 27, 214
    " Waffen S.S." 214
Pay books 223
Petrol and oil, system of supply 195, 206
Pioneer platoons 16, 29
Pistols 51
Pneumatic boats .. .. 136, 262, Plate 67
Pole charges 124, 142
Police (*see also* Para-military organisations) :—
    auxiliary police 213
    barrack police 213
    constabulary, rural (Gendarmerie) 213
                  town 212
    criminal police 213
    Czech police corps 218
    field security police 201
    military police 200
    organisation, general 212
    railway police 217
    secret state police 213
    Technical Emergency Corps 213
    Voluntary police corps 218
Pontoons .. .. 136, 137, 138, Plate 66
Positional units 6
Post guards 217
Postal service 201
Predictors 79
Prisoners, system of evacuation 210
Propaganda companies 2
Protection at rest 256
    on the move 257
Protective regiments 6
Provost service :—
    field security police 201
    L. of C. guard battalions 201
    military police 200

R.

Rafts .. .. 137, 262, Plate 67
    heavy tank 139, 262
Raids 257
Railway engineer units 132
    guards 217
    police 217
Rangefinders 33, 79
Rations, system of supply 194, 195, 204

	Page
Reconnaissance, infantry divisional unit, organisation, strength and armament	43
mechanised unit, organisation, strength and armament	41
tactics	257
"Reichskriegerbund Kyffhäuser, N.S. Deutscher"	218
Respirators, anti-gas	183
Rifle battalions	16
regiments, mountain, organisation, strength and armament	23
Rifles	51, Plate 3
River crossings	259
Road spaces	292

S.

	Page
S.A., *see* Storm detachments	
Sabre	59
"Schütz Staffeln"	214
"Schwerpunkt," *see* Main effort.	
Searchlights in A.A. units	74, 75
engineer units	141
particulars of	80
Secret state police	213
Service dress, *see* Uniform.	
Services :—	
medical	198
postal	201
provost :—	
field security police	201
L. of C. guard battalions	201
military police	200
supply and administrative :—	
depôts	198
field workshops	197
M.T. columns for petrol and oil	196, 197
"Nachschubführer"	195, 197
organisation, general	194
parks	198
supply battalions	197
columns	194, 195, 197
companies	197
officer, senior, *see* "Nachschubführer."	
service in an army	197
corps	197
division	195
workshop companies	196
veterinary	199
Signal Service :—	
armament of signal personnel	150
army signals regiment, organisation and strength	148

	Page
Signal Service—*contd.*	
cable, methods of laying	155
types of	155
carrier pigeons	150
cipher personnel	150
communications, general note	146
corps signals unit, armoured corps, organisation and strength	148
infantry corps, organisation and strength	148
despatch riders	150
divisional signals units:—	
armoured division	148
cavalry division	149
infantry division	148
motorised infantry division	148
mountain division	149
equipment:—	
air co-operation, visual equipment for	154
cable, types of	155
cipher	153
disc signalling	154
exchanges	151
ground listening sets	152
infra-red ray telephone	154
interception sets	152
lamps	153
light signals	154
line construction	154
message throwers	154
projectors	154
R/T sets, types of	153
telegraph	151
telephone	152
teleprinter	152
visual	153
W/T direction finders	152
jamming devices	153
sets, types of	153
experimental and research establishments	150
Inspector of Defence Communications	147
Signals	147
light signals column	196
line construction	154
messenger dogs	150
organisation, general	147
projectors	154
spectrum, positions of British and German W/T sets in	153, 180
tank brigade, signals unit, organisation and strength	149
vehicles	156
Small arms:—	
ammunition, types of	54
captured	63

Small arms—*contd.*	*Page*
carbines	51, Plates 1–2
machine-guns :—
dual purpose (M.G. 34)	52, Plates 9–11
heavy (M.G. 08)	53, Plates 12–13
light :—
Dreyse, L.M.G. 13	51, Plate 8
Knorr–Bremse	52
L.M.G. 08/15	52
super-heavy	95, Plates 34–35
machine-pistols	51
pistols	51
rifles	51, Plate 3
Smoke, *see* Chemical Warfare.
Sound locators	80
S.S., *see* " Schütz Staffeln."
Specialists :—
anti-tank battalions	104
artillery	72
cavalry	46
infantry	29
tank units	102
Staff :—
anti-tank	12, 13
artillery	12, 13, 66
cavalry	12, 13
Chief of, in formations	11
Combined, of Defence Forces	10
engineer	12, 13
General :—
in formations	11
army	12
corps	13
division	13
supply group	13
tactical group	13
in War Ministry	10
signals	12, 13
uniform, distinguishing colour	Plate 76
Steel helmet, *see* Uniform.
Storm detachments	215
Supply officer, senior, *see* " Nachschubführer."
Supply service, *see* Services, supply and administrative.
Supreme Commander of the Defence Forces, Hitler as	10
Survey units, artillery	68, 72
(mapping)	2

T.

Tactics :— |
--- | ---
    A.F.Vs. | 258
    air support | 255, 259, 260
    artillery | 260
    assault detachments | 29, 124, 259, 260, 262

Tactics—*contd.*   *Page*

	Page
attack	253
conduct of, general	254
envelopment	254
frontal attack	253
general principles	253
penetration	254
camouflage	256
defence	255
advanced position	255
battle outposts	256
main line of resistance	256
organisation of position	255
frontages	254, 256
gas	262
general principles	252
infantry	260
irregular methods of warfare	263
"main effort" ("Schwerpunkt")	254, 255
mechanised reconnaissance units	257
morale, destruction of enemy	255
motorised A.A.M.G. battalions	257
motorised machine-gun battalions	255, 257
orders	253
outposts	256
patrols	256, 258
protection :—	
at rest	256
on the move	257
raids	257
river crossings	259
"Schwerpunkt," *see* "main effort."	
smoke	262
tanks, *see* A.F.Vs.	
Tank brigade, organisation, strength and armament	5
signals unit in	149
regiments, independent	102
Tanks, distinguishing features	117, Plates 38–59
particulars of	115
tactics	258
Technical Emergency Corps	213
Tools, entrenching	32
"Totenkopfverbände," *see* Concentration camp guards.	
Training battalions, engineer (*see also* Instructional units)	129
Trench mortars, *see* Mortars.	

U.

Uniform :—	
Air Force	224, Plates 79–81
Armoured fighting troops	221, Plates 74–75
badges :—	
A.F.V.	224

Uniform—*contd.*   *Page*

badges—*contd.*	
assault	224
rank	224
special	224
specialist	224
wound	224
colours, arms of the service, *see* distinguishing marks.	
decorations	224
distinguishing marks	221, Plate 76
concealment of	222
equipment, personal	224
field service dress	220
identification, means of	223
identity discs	223
medals	224
mountain troops	221
national badge	222
colours	223
rosette	223
National Socialist Motor Corps	223
orders	224
parachute troops	224, Plates 82–84
para-military organisations	223
pay books	223
raiding parties	221
reconnaissance parties	221
rifle battalions	221
S.A., *see* Storm detachments.	
" Schütz Staffel "	223
Smoke units	221
S.S., *see* " Shütz Staffel."	
steel helmet	220, 224
Storm detachments	223

V.

" Verfügungstruppen "	27, 214
Veterinary service	199
Voluntary police corps	218

W.

"Waffen S.S."	214
War Cabinet	10
Ministry	10
" Wehrkreise "	11
Weights	273
Workshop companies (*see also* Armoured fighting troops)	196
Wound badges	224
Wounded, system of evacuation	199

(B.40/330)   (C38685)   15,000   4/41

www.ingramcontent.com/pod-product-compliance
Lightning Source LLC
Chambersburg PA
CBHW082358010526
44113CB00040B/2367